STOCK TRADER'S ALMANAC 2O21

Jeffrey A. Hirsch & Christopher Mistal

WILEY

www.stocktradersalmanac.com

Published by John Wiley & Sons, Inc., Hoboken, New Jersey.

Editor in Chief	Jeffrey A. Hirsch
Editor Emeritus	Yale Hirsch
Director of Research	Christopher Mistal

For general information about our other products and services, please contact our Customer Care Department within the United States at 800-762-2974, outside the United States at 317-572-3993, or fax at 317-572-4002.

Wiley publishes in a variety of print and electronic formats and by print-on-demand. Some material included with standard print versions of this book may not be included in e-books or in print-on-demand. If this book refers to media such as a CD or DVD that is not included in the version you purchased, you may download this material at http://booksupport.wiley.com. For more information about Wiley products, visit our website at www.wiley.com.

ISBN: 978-1-119-77876-9 (paper)
ISBN: 978-1-119-77878-3 (ePDF)
ISBN: 978-1-119-77877-6 (ePub)

Printed in the United States of America.

SKY002151_122220

THE 2021 STOCK TRADER'S ALMANAC

CONTENTS

DIRECTORY OF TRADING PATTERNS & DATABANK

STRATEGY PLANNING AND RECORD SECTION

INTRODUCTION TO THE FIFTY-FOURTH EDITION

Once again, we have the honor of introducing the new edition of the *Stock Trader's Almanac*. The *Almanac* provides you with the necessary tools to invest successfully in the twenty-first century.

J.P. Morgan's classic retort "Stocks will fluctuate" is often quoted with a wink-of-the-eye implication that the only prediction one can make about the stock market is that it will go up, down, or sideways. Many investors agree that no one ever really knows which way the market will move. Nothing could be further from the truth.

We discovered that while stocks do indeed fluctuate, they do so in well-defined, often predictable patterns. These patterns recur too frequently to be the result of chance or coincidence. How else do we explain that since 1950 the Dow has gained 20,535.44 points during November through April compared to just 3,777.95 May through October? (See page 52.)

The *Almanac* is a practical investment tool. It alerts you to those little-known market patterns and tendencies on which shrewd professionals enhance profit potential. You will be able to forecast market trends with accuracy and confidence when you use the *Almanac* to help you understand:

■ How our Presidential Elections affect the economy and the stock market— just as the moon affects the tides. Many investors have made fortunes following the political cycle. You can be sure that money managers who control billions of dollars are also political cycle watchers. Astute people do not ignore a pattern that has been working effectively throughout most of our economic history.

■ How the passage of the Twentieth Amendment to the Constitution fathered the January Barometer. This barometer has an outstanding record for predicting the general course of the stock market each year, with only ten major errors since 1950, for an 85.7% accuracy ratio. (See page 16.)

■ Why there is a significant market bias at certain times of the day, week, month and year.

Even if you are an investor who pays scant attention to cycles, indicators and patterns, your investment survival could hinge on your interpretation of one of the recurring patterns found within these pages. One of the most intriguing and important patterns is the symbiotic relationship between Washington and Wall Street. Aside from the potential profitability in seasonal patterns, there's the pure joy of seeing the market very often do just what you expected.

The *Stock Trader's Almanac* is also an organizer. Its wealth of information is presented on a calendar basis. The *Almanac* puts investing in a business framework and makes investing easier because it:

■ Updates investment knowledge and informs you of new techniques and tools.

■ Is a monthly reminder and refresher course.

■ Alerts you to both seasonal opportunities and dangers.

■ Furnishes a historical viewpoint by providing pertinent statistics on past market performance.

■ Supplies forms necessary for portfolio planning, record keeping and tax preparation.

 The WITCH Icon signifies THIRD FRIDAY OF THE MONTH on calendar pages and alerts you to extraordinary volatility due to expiration of equity and index options and index futures contracts. Triple-witching days appear during March, June, September and December. Some readers have questioned why we do not use the term "quadruple witching," as some in the business do. As we point out on page 106 the market for single-stock and ETF futures remains small and their impact is virtually nonexistent. If and when single-stock futures trading volume expands and exerts influence on the market, we will reconsider. Until such time, we do not believe the term "quadruple witching" is applicable.

 The BULL Icon on calendar pages signifies favorable trading days based on the S&P 500 rising 60% or more of the time on a particular trading day during the 21-year period January 1999 to December 2019. The BEAR Icon on calendar pages signifies unfavorable trading days based on the S&P falling 60% or more of the time for the same 21-year period.

Also, to give you even greater perspective, we have listed next to the date every day that the market is open the Market Probability numbers for the same 21-year period for the Dow (D), S&P 500 (S) and NASDAQ (N). You will see a "D," "S" and "N" followed by a number signifying the actual Market Probability number for that trading day based on the recent 21-year period. On pages 121–128 you will find complete Market Probability Calendars, both long term and 21-year for the Dow, S&P and NASDAQ, as well as for the Russell 1000 and Russell 2000 indices.

Other seasonalities near the ends, beginnings and middles of months; options expirations, around holidays and other times are noted for *Almanac* investors' convenience on the weekly planner pages. All other important economic releases are provided in the Strategy Calendar every month in our e-newsletter, *Almanac Investor*, available at our website *www.stocktradersalmanac.com*.

One-year seasonal pattern charts for the Dow, S&P 500, NASDAQ, Russell 1000, and Russell 2000 appear on pages 40, 42 and 44. There are three charts each for the Dow and S&P 500 spanning our entire database starting in 1901 and one each for the younger indices. As 2021 is a post–presidential election year, each chart contains typical post–election year performance compared to all years.

We have included historical data on the Russell 1000 and Russell 2000 indices. The Russell 2000 is an excellent proxy for small- and mid-caps, and the Russell 1000 provides a broader view of large caps. Annual highs and lows for all five indices covered in the *Almanac* appear on pages 149–151. Top 10 best and worst days, weeks, months, quarters and years for all five indices are listed on pages 164–173.

We have converted many of the paper forms in our Record Keeping section into computer spreadsheets for our own internal use. As a service to our faithful readers, we are making these forms available at our website *www.stocktradersalmanac.com*.

Historically, post-election years have been the worst of the four-year cycle. But since 1985, post-election years have been the best of the four-year cycle. (See our 2021 Outlook on pages 8–9 for more.) You can find all the market charts of post-election years since the Great Depression on page 26, "Market Behavior Under New Presidents" on page 24, "Post–Election Year Performance By Party" on page 28, "Post-Election Years: Paying the Piper" on page 32, "Market Fares Better Under Democrats; Dollar Holds Up Better Under Republicans" on page 78 and "Republican Congress and Democratic President Is Best for the Market" on page 80.

Our 2021 Outlook on pages 8–9 lays out the different prospects for next year, depending on who is in the White House. "How to Trade Best Months Switching Strategies" appears on page 36. "Summer Market Volume Doldrums Drives Worst Six Months" is updated on page 48. Sector seasonalities, including several consistent shorting opportunities, appear on pages 92–96.

We are constantly searching for new insights and nuances about the stock market and welcome any suggestions from our readers.

Have a healthy and prosperous 2021!

2021 OUTLOOK

It's new world. No one could have imagined or predicted we would be smack-dab in the middle of a global pandemic the likes of which the world has not seen since the Spanish Flu of 1918. But this time around, central bankers and governments are better prepared and the modern economy has proven more resilient. After suffering the shortest bear market in history, which lasted only 40 days, the velocity and strength of the V-shaped rally off the March 23 low has been impressive. For the record, this rally became an official Ned Davis Research defined bull market on May 26 when DJIA was up 30% from the low and made a new recovery high after 50 calendar days (pages 131–132).

But climbing COVID cases and confusion about reopening the economy continue to threaten the market. A continued increase in national positive tests, hospitalizations and deaths will be hard for the market to ignore. The spread and uncertainty continue to make the market vulnerable to negative developments on the pandemic, economic and geopolitical fronts. Valuations are high. Technical chart resistance has become more prevalent and the incumbent president and party are on the ropes against the virus, civic unrest and deepening tensions with China.

Economic reopening efforts are getting rolled back as the virus surges. Weekly jobless claims remain elevated at well over a million a week. According to the Atlanta Fed's *GDPNow* model, 2020 Q2 GDP estimates have improved from a low of –53.8% in June 2020 to –34.7% at press time. Encouraging, yet still alarming. Despite these numbers, the worst is most likely over. That's the good news. The bad news is the economic recovery is not likely going to be as quick as the market's rebound. Covid-19 is still spreading and still impacting the economy.

NASDAQ is trading at new highs, but the Dow and S&P 500 continue to struggle. This divergence is indicative of the overall economy as big tech, IT, consumer discretionary and health care flourish, while other areas are still struggling. As the economy mends, the divide is likely to close, but until that time additional gains could be limited. We expect the major indexes to be range-bound and prone to correction ahead of the election.

However, the Fed continues to reaffirm its commitment to using its full range of monetary policy tools to support the U.S. economy and projects the Fed Funds rate to remain near zero through 2022. According to the IMF, as of July 15, 2020, global fiscal measures totaled about $11 trillion. Add in the $2 trillion in the new EU deal at press time and, collectively, governments around the world will have pumped nearly $13 trillion into their economies in the form of various fiscal stimulus packages with more likely to come. So while the pandemic still beleaguers the planet, and we contend with civic strife, geopolitical tension and a contentious U.S. presidential election, it is hard to be bearish with all that money flying around.

Post-election years have a long history of losses, bear markets, recessions and wars. It's what we call the "Post-Election Year Syndrome." But, over the last four decades post-election years have been the best year of the four-year presidential election stock market cycle, with pre-election running a close second. The S&P 500 is up eight of the last nine post-election years for an average gain of 17.1% since 1985. S&P is up seven of nine pre-election years for an average gain of 15.6%. Midterm years are up five of nine, average 4.6%, and election years are up six of eight with a 2.6% average gain.

The Dow's record is quite similar over the past 35 years. Average gain is also 17.1% for post-election years, up seven of the last nine. In pre-election years DJIA has an average gain of 15.4%, up eight down one. Midterm years average 5.4%, up six of nine and election years bring up the rear at 3.2%, up six of eight as well.

NASDAQ post-election years are even better, average gain 19.7%, up eight of nine. But pre-election years are still number one for NASDAQ, gaining a whopping 30.6% on average, up 7, down 2. This did not leave much left for midterm years, up five of nine with a 3.4% average and election years up only 0.7% though up also up six of eight. Huge losses in 2000 (–39.3%) and 2008 (–40.5%) crushed the average as the median election year gain was 12.9%.

Depending on state of pandemic, the economy and the market over the next three months, and how President Trump handles the Covid-19 situation as well as civic unrest and diplomatic machinations, the election could go either way. If things go south and the president is not reelected, the year-end rally will likely come from lower levels and be more robust.

However, as you can see in the chart below, since 1949, post-election years with a new party in power have underperformed, averaging a small gain of 2.3% for the S&P 500. In contrast, incumbent-party wins have been accompanied by outperforming post-election years with an average S&P 500 gain of 11.6% versus an average gain of 7.0% for all post-election years since 1949.

A change in party usually comes with a change in political ideology, agenda and policies. This is likely the cause of weaker markets in the year after the election, as the White House changes hands as the market recalibrates to the new order. We will also still be contending with the new socially distant world order that is already changing the economic landscape, especially for small businesses, bars and restaurants, the service industry, travel and retail.

We have had our bear market, which took all the major averages down over 30%, and though uncertainty remains, we are clearly on the road to recovery with the virus. We expect 2021 to be a good year, though gains could be muted by a change in administration. If President Trump is reelected, expect a slow start to the year as the market digests the situation, followed by a stronger second half. Our May 2010 Super Boom Forecast, made when the Dow was around 10,000 and predicting it to reach 38,820 by the year 2025, may still be ahead of schedule. (Check out the update of the Super Boom Forecast in the April 11, 2019, subscriber alert on our website.)
Jeffrey A. Hirsch, July 22, 2020

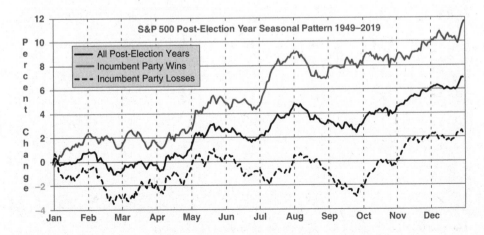

2021 STRATEGY CALENDAR

(Option expiration dates circled)

	MONDAY	TUESDAY	WEDNESDAY	THURSDAY	FRIDAY	SATURDAY	SUNDAY
JANUARY	28	29	30	31	1 JANUARY New Year's Day	2	3
	4	5	6	7	8	9	10
	11	12	13	14	(15)	16	17
	18 Martin Luther King Day	19	20	21	22	23	24
	25	26	27	28	29	30	31
FEBRUARY	1 FEBRUARY	2	3	4	5	6	7
	8	9	10	11	12	13	14 ♥
	15 Presidents' Day	16	17 Ash Wednesday	18	(19)	20	21
	22	23	24	25	26	27	28
MARCH	1 MARCH	2	3	4	5	6	7
	8	9	10	11	12	13	14 Daylight Saving Time Begins
	15	16	17 ♣ St. Patrick's Day	18	(19)	20	21
	22	23	24	25	26	27	28 Passover
	29	30	31	1 APRIL	2 Good Friday	3	4 Easter
APRIL	5	6	7	8	9	10	11
	12	13	14	15 Tax Deadline	(16)	17	18
	19	20	21	22	23	24	25
	26	27	28	29	30	1 MAY	2
MAY	3	4	5	6	7	8	9 Mother's Day
	10	11	12	13	14	15	16
	17	18	19	20	(21)	22	23
	24	25	26	27	28	29	30
JUNE	31 Memorial Day	1 JUNE	2	3	4	5	6
	7	8	9	10	11	12	13
	14	15	16	17	(18)	19	20 Father's Day
	21	22	23	24	25	26	27

Market closed on shaded weekdays; closes early when half-shaded.

2021 STRATEGY CALENDAR
(Option expiration dates circled)

MONDAY	TUESDAY	WEDNESDAY	THURSDAY	FRIDAY	SATURDAY	SUNDAY	
28	29	30	1 JULY	2	3	4 Independence Day	JULY
5	6	7	8	9	10	11	JULY
12	13	14	15	(16)	17	18	JULY
19	20	21	22	23	24	25	JULY
26	27	28	29	30	31	1 AUGUST	JULY
2	3	4	5	6	7	8	AUGUST
9	10	11	12	13	14	15	AUGUST
16	17	18	19	(20)	21	22	AUGUST
23	24	25	26	27	28	29	AUGUST
30	31	1 SEPTEMBER	2	3	4	5	SEPTEMBER
6 Labor Day	7 Rosh Hashanah	8	9	10	11	12	SEPTEMBER
13	14	15	16 Yom Kippur	(17)	18	19	SEPTEMBER
20	21	22	23	24	25	26	SEPTEMBER
27	28	29	30	1 OCTOBER	2	3	OCTOBER
4	5	6	7	8	9	10	OCTOBER
11 Columbus Day	12	13	14	(15)	16	17	OCTOBER
18	19	20	21	22	23	24	OCTOBER
25	26	27	28	29	30	31	OCTOBER
1 NOVEMBER	2 Election Day	3	4	5	6	7 Daylight Saving Time Ends	NOVEMBER
8	9	10	11 Veterans' Day	12	13	14	NOVEMBER
15	16	17	18	(19)	20	21	NOVEMBER
22	23	24	25 Thanksgiving Day	26	27	28	NOVEMBER
29 Chanukah	30	1 DECEMBER	2	3	4	5	DECEMBER
6	7	8	9	10	11	12	DECEMBER
13	14	15	16	(17)	18	19	DECEMBER
20	21	22	23	24	25 Christmas	26	DECEMBER
27	28	29	30	31	1 JANUARY New Year's Day	2	DECEMBER

JANUARY ALMANAC

JANUARY						
S	M	T	W	T	F	S
					1	2
3	4	5	6	7	8	9
10	11	12	13	14	15	16
17	18	19	20	21	22	23
24	25	26	27	28	29	30
31						

FEBRUARY

S	M	T	W	T	F	S
	1	2	3	4	5	6
7	8	9	10	11	12	13
14	15	16	17	18	19	20
21	22	23	24	25	26	27
28						

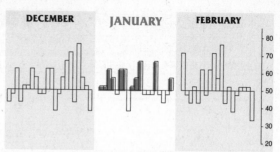

Market Probability Chart above is a graphic representation of the S&P 500 Recent Market Probability Calendar on page 124.

◆ January Barometer predicts year's course with .743 batting average (page 16) ◆ 14 of last 17 post–presidential election years followed January's direction ◆ Every down January on the S&P since 1950, *without exception*, preceded a new or extended bear market, a flat market, or a 10% correction (page 20) ◆ S&P gains January's first five days preceded full-year gains 82.2% of the time, 13 of last 17 post–presidential election years followed first five days' direction (page 14) ◆ November, December and January constitute the year's best three-month span, a 4.2% S&P gain (pages 50 & 147) ◆ January NASDAQ powerful 2.8% since 1971 (pages 58 & 148) ◆ "January Effect" now starts in mid-December and favors small-cap stocks (pages 110 & 112) ◆ 2009 has the dubious honor of the worst S&P 500 January on record ◆ Dow gained more than 1000 points in 2018 & 2019

January Vital Statistics

	DJIA		S&P 500		NASDAQ		Russell 1K		Russell 2K	
Rank	5		4		1		4		4	
Up	45		43		33		26		23	
Down	26		28		17		16		19	
Average % Change	1.0%		1.1%		2.8%		1.2%		1.5%	
Post-Election Year	0.6%		0.8%		2.3%		1.6%		1.8%	
Best & Worst January										
	% Change		% Change		% Change		% Change		% Change	
Best	1976	14.4	1987	13.2	1975	16.6	1987	12.7	1985	13.1
Worst	2009	−8.8	2009	−8.6	2008	−9.9	2009	−8.3	2009	−11.2
Best & Worst January Weeks										
Best	01/09/1976	6.1	01/02/2009	6.8	01/12/2001	9.1	01/02/2009	6.8	01/09/1987	7.0
Worst	01/08/2016	−6.2	01/08/2016	−6.0	01/28/2000	−8.2	01/08/2016	−6.0	01/08/2016	−7.9
Best & Worst January Days										
Best	01/17/1991	4.6	01/03/2001	5.0	01/03/2001	14.2	01/03/2001	5.3	01/21/2009	5.3
Worst	01/08/1988	−6.9	01/08/1988	−6.8	01/02/2001	−7.2	01/08/1988	−6.1	01/20/2009	−7.0
First Trading Day of Expiration Week: 1980–2020										
Record (#Up – #Down)	26–15		23–18		21–20		21–20		21–20	
Current streak	U1		U1		U1		U1		U1	
Avg % Change	0.08		0.06		0.06		0.03		0.01	
Options Expiration Day: 1980–2020										
Record (#Up – #Down)	24–17		24–17		24–17		24–17		24–17	
Current streak	U10		U6		U6		U6		D1	
Avg % Change	0.03		0.06		0.01		0.04		0.06	
Options Expiration Week: 1980–2020										
Record (#Up – #Down)	23–18		19–22		24–17		19–22		23–18	
Current streak	U3		U3		U3		U3		U3	
Avg % Change	−0.01		0.08		0.38		0.07		0.32	
Week After Options Expiration: 1980–2020										
Record (#Up – #Down)	23–18		25–16		24–17		25–16		28–13	
Current streak	D1		D1		D1		D2		D1	
Avg % Change	0.08		0.25		0.20		0.23		0.18	
First Trading Day Performance										
% of Time Up	60.6		50.7		58.0		47.6		47.6	
Avg % Change	0.26		0.17		0.24		0.18		0.07	
Last Trading Day Performance										
% of Time Up	54.9		60.6		64.0		57.1		71.4	
Avg % Change	0.18		0.23		0.28		0.28		0.22	

Dow & S&P 1950-June 19, 2020, NASDAQ 1971-June 19, 2020, Russell 1K & 2K 1979-January 19, 2020.

> *20th Amendment made "lame ducks" disappear.*
> *Now, "As January goes, so goes the year."*

DECEMBER 2020/JANUARY 2021

MONDAY
D 71.4
S 76.2
N 61.9
28

We are all born originals; why is it so many die copies?
— Edward Young (English poet, 1683–1765)

TUESDAY
D 52.4
S 57.1
N 52.4
29

In the twenty-two presidential elections from 1900 through 1984,
Americans chose the most optimistic-sounding candidate eighteen times.
— Martin E. Seligman, Ph.D (Professor of Psychology, University of Pennsylvania, *Learned Optimism*, 1990)

WEDNESDAY
D 42.9
S 52.4
N 42.9
30

No horse gets anywhere until he is harnessed. No steam or gas ever drives anything until it is confined.
No Niagara is ever turned into light and power until it is tunneled. No life ever grows great until it is
focused, dedicated, disciplined.
— Harry Emerson Fosdick (Protestant minister, author, 1878–1969)

Last Trading Day of the Year, NASDAQ Down 15 of Last 20
NASDAQ Was Up 29 Years in a Row 1971–1999

THURSDAY
D 42.9
S 38.1
N 28.6
31

The task of leadership is not to put greatness into humanity, but to elicit it, for the greatness is already there.
— Sir John Buchan (Scottish author, Governor General of Canada 1935–1940, 1875–1940)

New Year's Day *(Market Closed)*

FRIDAY
1

Get to the Point! Blurt it out! Tell me plainly what's in it for me!
— Roy H. Williams (The Wizard of Ads, A reader's mental response to a poorly constructed advertisement.
Quoted in *Your Company*, 12/98)

SATURDAY
2

January Almanac Investor Sector Seasonalities: See Pages 92, 94 and 96

SUNDAY
3

JANUARY'S FIRST FIVE DAYS: AN EARLY WARNING SYSTEM

The last 45 up First Five Days were followed by full-year gains 37 times for an 82.2% accuracy ratio and a 13.6% average gain in all 45 years. The eight exceptions include flat years 1994, 2011, 2015, four related to war, and 2018. Vietnam military spending delayed the start of the 1966 bear market. Ceasefire imminence early in 1973 raised stocks temporarily. Saddam Hussein turned 1990 into a bear. The war on terrorism, instability in the Mideast and corporate malfeasance shaped 2002 into one of the worst years on record. In 2018 a partially inverted yield curve and trade tensions triggered a fourth quarter sell-off. The 25 down First Five Days were followed by 14 up years and 11 down (44.0% accurate) and an average gain of 1.0%.

In post–presidential election years this indicator has a solid record. In the last 17 post–presidential election years, 13 full years followed the direction of the First Five Days.

THE FIRST-FIVE-DAYS-IN-JANUARY INDICATOR

Chronological Data

Year	Previous Year's Close	January 5th Day	5-Day Change	Year Change
1950	16.76	17.09	2.0%	21.8%
1951	20.41	20.88	2.3	16.5
1952	23.77	23.91	0.6	11.8
1953	26.57	26.33	−0.9	−6.6
1954	24.81	24.93	0.5	45.0
1955	35.98	35.33	−1.8	26.4
1956	45.48	44.51	−2.1	2.6
1957	46.67	46.25	−0.9	−14.3
1958	39.99	40.99	2.5	38.1
1959	55.21	55.40	0.3	8.5
1960	59.89	59.50	−0.7	−3.0
1961	58.11	58.81	1.2	23.1
1962	71.55	69.12	−3.4	−11.8
1963	63.10	64.74	2.6	18.9
1964	75.02	76.00	1.3	13.0
1965	84.75	85.37	0.7	9.1
1966	92.43	93.14	0.8	−13.1
1967	80.33	82.81	3.1	20.1
1968	96.47	96.62	0.2	7.7
1969	103.86	100.80	−2.9	−11.4
1970	92.06	92.68	0.7	0.1
1971	92.15	92.19	0.04	10.8
1972	102.09	103.47	1.4	15.6
1973	118.05	119.85	1.5	−17.4
1974	97.55	96.12	−1.5	−29.7
1975	68.56	70.04	2.2	31.5
1976	90.19	94.58	4.9	19.1
1977	107.46	105.01	−2.3	−11.5
1978	95.10	90.64	−4.7	1.1
1979	96.11	98.80	2.8	12.3
1980	107.94	108.95	0.9	25.8
1981	135.76	133.06	−2.0	−9.7
1982	122.55	119.55	−2.4	14.8
1983	140.64	145.23	3.3	17.3
1984	164.93	168.90	2.4	1.4
1985	167.24	163.99	−1.9	26.3
1986	211.28	207.97	−1.6	14.6
1987	242.17	257.28	6.2	2.0
1988	247.08	243.40	−1.5	12.4
1989	277.72	280.98	1.2	27.3
1990	353.40	353.79	0.1	−6.6
1991	330.22	314.90	−4.6	26.3
1992	417.09	418.10	0.2	4.5
1993	435.71	429.05	−1.5	7.1
1994	466.45	469.90	0.7	−1.5
1995	459.27	460.83	0.3	34.1
1996	615.93	618.46	0.4	20.3
1997	740.74	748.41	1.0	31.0
1998	970.43	956.04	−1.5	26.7
1999	1229.23	1275.09	3.7	19.5
2000	1469.25	1441.46	−1.9	−10.1
2001	1320.28	1295.86	−1.8	−13.0
2002	1148.08	1160.71	1.1	−23.4
2003	879.82	909.93	3.4	26.4
2004	1111.92	1131.91	1.8	9.0
2005	1211.92	1186.19	−2.1	3.0
2006	1248.29	1290.15	3.4	13.6
2007	1418.30	1412.11	−0.4	3.5
2008	1468.36	1390.19	−5.3	−38.5
2009	903.25	909.73	0.7	23.5
2010	1115.10	1144.98	2.7	12.8
2011	1257.64	1271.50	1.1	−0.003
2012	1257.60	1280.70	1.8	13.4
2013	1426.19	1457.15	2.2	29.6
2014	1848.36	1837.49	−0.6	11.4
2015	2058.90	2062.14	0.2	−0.7
2016	2043.94	1922.03	−6.0	9.5
2017	2238.83	2268.90	1.3	19.4
2018	2673.61	2747.71	2.8	−6.2
2019	2506.85	2574.41	2.7	28.9
2020	3230.78	3253.05	0.7	??

Ranked by Performance

Rank	Year	5-Day Change	Year Change
1	1987	6.2%	2.0%
2	1976	4.9	19.1
3	1999	3.7	19.5
4	2003	3.4	26.4
5	2006	3.4	13.6
6	1983	3.3	17.3
7	1967	3.1	20.1
8	1979	2.8	12.3
9	2018	2.8	−6.2
10	2019	2.7	28.9
11	2010	2.7	12.8
12	1963	2.6	18.9
13	1958	2.5	38.1
14	1984	2.4	1.4
15	1951	2.3	16.5
16	2013	2.2	29.6
17	1975	2.2	31.5
18	1950	2.0	21.8
19	2004	1.8	9.0
20	2012	1.8	13.4
21	1973	1.5	−17.4
22	1972	1.4	15.6
23	1964	1.3	13.0
24	2017	1.3	19.4
25	1961	1.2	23.1
26	1989	1.2	27.3
27	2011	1.1	−0.003
28	2002	1.1	−23.4
29	1997	1.0	31.0
30	1980	0.9	25.8
31	1966	0.8	−13.1
32	1994	0.7	−1.5
33	1965	0.7	9.1
34	2009	0.7	23.5
35	2020	0.7	??
36	1970	0.7	0.1
37	1952	0.6	11.8
38	1954	0.5	45.0
39	1996	0.4	20.3
40	1959	0.3	8.5
41	1995	0.3	34.1
42	1992	0.2	4.5
43	1968	0.2	7.7
44	2015	0.2	−0.7
45	1990	0.1	−6.6
46	1971	0.04	10.8
47	2007	−0.4	3.5
48	2014	−0.6	11.4
49	1960	−0.7	−3.0
50	1957	−0.9	−14.3
51	1953	−0.9	−6.6
52	1974	−1.5	−29.7
53	1998	−1.5	26.7
54	1988	−1.5	12.4
55	1993	−1.5	7.1
56	1986	−1.6	14.6
57	2001	−1.8	−13.0
58	1955	−1.8	26.4
59	2000	−1.9	−10.1
60	1985	−1.9	26.3
61	1981	−2.0	−9.7
62	1956	−2.1	2.6
63	2005	−2.1	3.0
64	1977	−2.3	−11.5
65	1982	−2.4	14.8
66	1969	−2.9	−11.4
67	1962	−3.4	−11.8
68	1991	−4.6	26.3
69	1978	−4.7	1.1
70	2008	−5.3	−38.5
71	2016	−6.0	9.5

Based on S&P 500

First Trading Day of the Year, NASDAQ Up 17 of Last 23

MONDAY

D 66.7
S 52.4
N 71.4

4

Liberals have practiced tax and tax, spend and spend, elect and elect but conservatives have perfected borrow and borrow, spend and spend, elect and elect.
— George Will (American political commentator and journalist, b. 1941)

Second Trading Day of the Year, Dow Up 21 of Last 29
Santa Claus Rally Ends (Page 116)

TUESDAY

D 61.9
S 52.4
N 47.6

5

Our philosophy here is identifying change, anticipating change. Change is what drives earnings growth, and if you identify the underlying change, you recognize the growth before the market, and the deceleration of that growth.
— Peter Vermilye (Baring America Asset Management, 1987)

WEDNESDAY

D 52.4
S 61.9
N 57.1

6

I do not rule Russia; ten thousand clerks do.
— Nicholas I (1795-1855)

THURSDAY

D 52.4
S 57.1
N 57.1

7

Obstacles don't have to stop you. If you run into a wall, don't turn around and give up. Figure out how to climb it, go through it, or work around it.
— Michael Jordan

January's First Five Days Act as an "Early Warning" (Page 14)

FRIDAY

D 38.1
S 47.6
N 66.7

8

Everyone blames the foreigners when the economy goes south. Always. It is human nature to blame others, and it is the same all over the world.
— Jim Rogers (Financier, *Adventure Capitalist*, b. 1942)

SATURDAY

9

SUNDAY

10

THE INCREDIBLE JANUARY BAROMETER (DEVISED 1972): ONLY TEN SIGNIFICANT ERRORS IN 70 YEARS

Devised by Yale Hirsch in 1972, our January Barometer states that as the S&P 500 goes in January, so goes the year. The indicator has registered **ten major errors since 1950, for an 85.7% accuracy ratio**. Vietnam affected 1966 and 1968; 1982 saw the start of a major bull market in August; two January rate cuts and 9/11 affected 2001; the anticipation of military action in Iraq held down the market in January 2003; 2009 was the beginning of a new bull market; the Fed saved 2010 with QE2; QE3 likely staved off declines in 2014; global growth fears sparked selling in January 2016; and a partially inverted yield curve and trade tensions fueled Q4 selling in 2018. (*Almanac Investor* newsletter subscribers receive full analysis of each reading as well as its potential implications for the full year.)

Including the eight flat-year errors (less than +/− 5%) yields a 74.3% accuracy ratio. A full comparison of all monthly barometers for the Dow, S&P and NASDAQ can be seen at *www.stocktradersalmanac.com* in the January 9, 2020, Alert. Bear markets began or continued when Januarys suffered a loss (*see page 20*). Full years followed January's direction in 14 of the last 17 post–presidential election years. *See page 18 for more.*

AS JANUARY GOES, SO GOES THE YEAR

	Market Performance in January					January Performance by Rank			
	Previous Year's Close	**January Close**	**January Change**	**Year Change**		**Rank**		**January Change**	**Year Change**
1950	16.76	17.05	1.7%	21.8%		1	1987	13.2%	2.0%	flat
1951	20.41	21.66	6.1	16.5		2	1975	12.3	31.5
1952	23.77	24.14	1.6	11.8		3	1976	11.8	19.1
1953	26.57	26.38	−0.7	−6.6		4	2019	7.9	28.9
1954	24.81	26.08	5.1	45.0		5	1967	7.8	20.1
1955	35.98	36.63	1.8	26.4		6	1985	7.4	26.3
1956	45.48	43.82	−3.6	2.6	flat	7	1989	7.1	27.3
1957	46.67	44.72	−4.2	−14.3		8	1961	6.3	23.1
1958	39.99	41.70	4.3	38.1		9	1997	6.1	31.0
1959	55.21	55.42	0.4	8.5		10	1951	6.1	16.5
1960	59.89	55.61	−7.1	−3.0	flat	11	1980	5.8	25.8
1961	58.11	61.78	6.3	23.1		12	2018	5.6	−6.2	X
1962	71.55	68.84	−3.8	−11.8		13	1954	5.1	45.0
1963	63.10	66.20	4.9	18.9		14	2013	5.0	29.6
1964	75.02	77.04	2.7	13.0		15	1963	4.9	18.9
1965	84.75	87.56	3.3	9.1		16	2012	4.4	13.4
1966	92.43	92.88	0.5	−13.1	X	17	1958	4.3	38.1
1967	80.33	86.61	7.8	20.1		18	1991	4.2	26.3
1968	96.47	92.24	−4.4	7.7	X	19	1999	4.1	19.5
1969	103.86	103.01	−0.8	−11.4		20	1971	4.0	10.8
1970	92.06	85.02	−7.6	0.1	flat	21	1988	4.0	12.4
1971	92.15	95.88	4.0	10.8		22	1979	4.0	12.3
1972	102.09	103.94	1.8	15.6		23	2001	3.5	−13.0	X
1973	118.05	116.03	−1.7	−17.4		24	1965	3.3	9.1
1974	97.55	96.57	−1.0	−29.7		25	1983	3.3	17.3
1975	68.56	76.98	12.3	31.5		26	1996	3.3	20.3
1976	90.19	100.86	11.8	19.1		27	1994	3.3	−1.5	flat
1977	107.46	102.03	−5.1	−11.5		28	1964	2.7	13.0
1978	95.10	89.25	−6.2	1.1	flat	29	2006	2.5	13.6
1979	96.11	99.93	4.0	12.3		30	1995	2.4	34.1
1980	107.94	114.16	5.8	25.8		31	2011	2.3	−0.003	flat
1981	135.76	129.55	−4.6	−9.7		32	1972	1.8	15.6
1982	122.55	120.40	−1.8	14.8	X	33	1955	1.8	26.4
1983	140.64	145.30	3.3	17.3		34	2017	1.8	19.4
1984	164.93	163.41	−0.9	1.4	flat	35	1950	1.7	21.8
1985	167.24	179.63	7.4	26.3		36	2004	1.7	9.0
1986	211.28	211.78	0.2	14.6		37	1952	1.6	11.8
1987	242.17	274.08	13.2	2.0	flat	38	2007	1.4	3.5	flat
1988	247.08	257.07	4.0	12.4		39	1998	1.0	26.7
1989	277.72	297.47	7.1	27.3		40	1993	0.7	7.1
1990	353.40	329.08	−6.9	−6.6		41	1966	0.5	−13.1	X
1991	330.22	343.93	4.2	26.3		42	1959	0.4	8.5
1992	417.09	408.79	−2.0	4.5	flat	43	1986	0.2	14.6
1993	435.71	438.78	0.7	7.1		44	2020	−0.2	??
1994	466.45	481.61	3.3	−1.5	flat	45	1953	−0.7	−6.6
1995	459.27	470.42	2.4	34.1		46	1969	−0.8	−11.4
1996	615.93	636.02	3.3	20.3		47	1984	−0.9	1.4	flat
1997	740.74	786.16	6.1	31.0		48	1974	−1.0	−29.7
1998	970.43	980.28	1.0	26.7		49	2002	−1.6	−23.4
1999	1229.23	1279.64	4.1	19.5		50	1973	−1.7	−17.4
2000	1469.25	1394.46	−5.1	−10.1		51	1982	−1.8	14.8	X
2001	1320.28	1366.01	3.5	−13.0	X	52	1992	−2.0	4.5	flat
2002	1148.08	1130.20	−1.6	−23.4		53	2005	−2.5	3.0	flat
2003	879.82	855.70	−2.7	26.4	X	54	2003	−2.7	26.4	X
2004	1111.92	1131.13	1.7	9.0		55	2015	−3.1	−0.7	flat
2005	1211.92	1181.27	−2.5	3.0	flat	56	2014	−3.6	11.4	X
2006	1248.29	1280.08	2.5	13.6		57	1956	−3.6	2.6	flat
2007	1418.30	1438.24	1.4	3.5	flat	58	2010	−3.7	12.8	X
2008	1468.36	1378.55	−6.1	−38.5		59	1962	−3.8	−11.8
2009	903.25	825.88	−8.6	23.5	X	60	1957	−4.2	−14.3
2010	1115.10	1073.87	−3.7	12.8	X	61	1968	−4.4	7.7	X
2011	1257.64	1286.12	2.3	−0.003	flat	62	1981	−4.6	−9.7
2012	1257.60	1312.41	4.4	13.4		63	1977	−5.1	−11.5
2013	1426.19	1498.11	5.0	29.6		64	2000	−5.1	−10.1
2014	1848.36	1782.59	−3.6	11.4	X	65	2016	−5.1	9.5	X
2015	2058.90	1994.99	−3.1	−0.7	flat	66	2008	−6.1	−38.5
2016	2043.94	1940.24	−5.1	9.5	X	67	1978	−6.2	1.1	flat
2017	2238.83	2278.87	1.8	19.4		68	1990	−6.9	−6.6
2018	2673.61	2823.81	5.6	−6.2	X	69	1960	−7.1	−3.0	flat
2019	2506.85	2704.10	7.9	28.9	??	70	1970	−7.6	0.1	flat
2020	3230.78	3225.52	−0.2	??		71	2009	−8.6	23.5	X

16

X = major error Based on S&P 500

First Trading Day of January Expiration Week, Dow Up 18 of Last 28, But Down 5 of Last 7

MONDAY
D 52.4
S 61.9
N 66.7
11

If we did all the things we are capable of doing, we would literally astound ourselves.
— Thomas Alva Edison (American inventor, 1093 patents, 1847–1931)

TUESDAY
D 52.4
S 61.9
N 66.7
12

The stock market is a device for transferring money from the impatient to the patient.
— Warren Buffett (CEO Berkshire Hathaway, investor & philanthropist, b. 1930)

January Expiration Week, Dow Down 11 of Last 22, But Up 8 of Last 10

WEDNESDAY
D 47.6
S 38.1
N 42.9
13

Any fool can buy. It is the wise man who knows how to sell.
— Albert W. Thomas (Trader, investor, *Over My Shoulder*, mutualfundmagic.com, *If It Doesn't Go Up, Don't Buy It!*, b. 1927)

THURSDAY
D 47.6
S 52.4
N 47.6
14

You know you're right when the other side starts to shout.
— I. A. O'Shaughnessy (American oilman, 1885–1973)

January Expiration Day Improving Since 2011, Dow Up 10 Years in a Row

FRIDAY
D 57.1
S 57.1
N 42.9
15

Never tell people how to do things. Tell them what to do and they will surprise you with their ingenuity.
— General George S. Patton, Jr. (U.S. Army field commander WWII, 1885–1945)

SATURDAY
16

SUNDAY
20

JANUARY BAROMETER IN GRAPHIC FORM

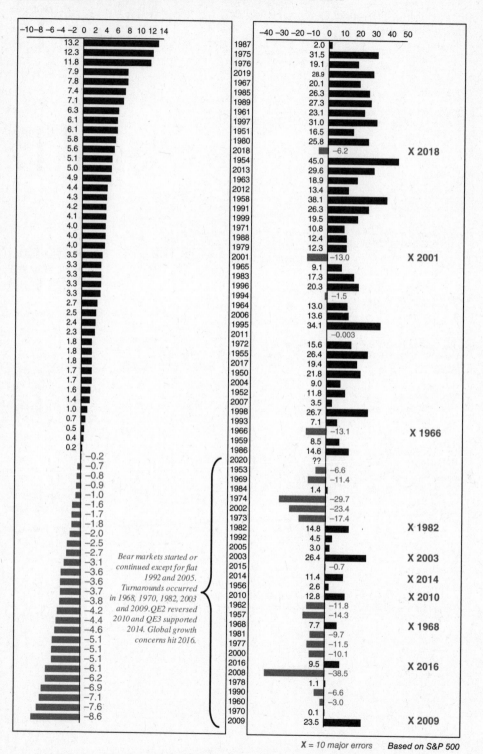

-10-8 -6 -4 -2 0 2 4 6 8 10 12 14		-40 -30 -20 -10 0 10 20 30 40 50	
13.2	1987	2.0	
12.3	1975	31.5	
11.8	1976	19.1	
7.9	2019	28.9	
7.8	1967	20.1	
7.4	1985	26.3	
7.1	1989	27.3	
6.3	1961	23.1	
6.1	1997	31.0	
6.1	1951	16.5	
5.8	1980	25.8	
5.6	2018	−6.2	X 2018
5.1	1954	45.0	
5.0	2013	29.6	
4.9	1963	18.9	
4.4	2012	13.4	
4.3	1958	38.1	
4.2	1991	26.3	
4.1	1999	19.5	
4.0	1971	10.8	
4.0	1988	12.4	
4.0	1979	12.3	
3.5	2001	−13.0	X 2001
3.3	1965	9.1	
3.3	1983	17.3	
3.3	1996	20.3	
3.3	1994	−1.5	
2.7	1964	13.0	
2.5	2006	13.6	
2.4	1995	34.1	
2.3	2011	−0.003	
1.8	1972	15.6	
1.8	1955	26.4	
1.8	2017	19.4	
1.7	1950	21.8	
1.7	2004	9.0	
1.6	1952	11.8	
1.4	2007	3.5	
1.0	1998	26.7	
0.7	1993	7.1	
0.5	1966	−13.1	X 1966
0.4	1959	8.5	
0.2	1986	14.6	
−0.2	2020	??	
−0.7	1953	−6.6	
−0.8	1969	−11.4	
−0.9	1984	1.4	
−1.0	1974	−29.7	
−1.6	2002	−23.4	
−1.7	1973	−17.4	
−1.8	1982	14.8	X 1982
−2.0	1992	4.5	
−2.5	2005	3.0	
−2.7	2003	26.4	X 2003
−3.1	2015	−0.7	
−3.6	2014	11.4	X 2014
−3.6	1956	2.6	
−3.7	2010	12.8	X 2010
−3.8	1962	−11.8	
−4.2	1957	−14.3	
−4.4	1968	7.7	X 1968
−4.6	1981	−9.7	
−5.1	1977	−11.5	
−5.1	2000	−10.1	
−5.1	2016	9.5	X 2016
−6.1	2008	−38.5	
−6.2	1978	1.1	
−6.9	1990	−6.6	
−7.1	1960	−3.0	
−7.6	1970	0.1	
−8.6	2009	23.5	X 2009

Bear markets started or continued except for flat 1992 and 2005. Turnarounds occurred in 1968, 1970, 1982, 2003 and 2009. QE2 reversed 2010 and QE3 supported 2014. Global growth concerns hit 2016.

X = 10 major errors   *Based on S&P 500*

Martin Luther King Jr. Day *(Market Closed)*

MONDAY
18

The measure of success is not whether you have a tough problem to deal with, but whether it's the same problem you had last year.
— John Foster Dulles (Secretary of State under Eisenhower, 1888–1959)

TUESDAY
D 52.4
S 66.7
N 71.4
19

The man who can master his time can master nearly anything.
— Winston Churchill (British statesman, 1874–1965)

WEDNESDAY
D 38.1
S 47.6
N 52.4
20

Securities pricing is, in every sense a psychological phenomenon that arises from the interaction of human beings with fear. Why not greed and fear as the equation is usually stated? Because greed is simply fear of not having enough.
— John Bollinger (Bollinger Capital Management, BollingerBands.com)

January Ends "Best Three-Month Span" (Pages 50, 58, 147 and 148)

THURSDAY
D 42.9
S 47.6
N 42.9
21

He who wants to persuade should put his trust not in the right argument, but in the right word. The power of sound has always been greater than the power of sense.
— Joseph Conrad (Polish/British novelist, 1857–1924)

FRIDAY
D 33.3
S 47.6
N 38.1
22

The world has changed! You can't be an 800-pound gorilla; you need to be an economic gazelle. You've got to be able to change directions quickly.
— Mark Breier (*The 10-Second Internet Manager*)

SATURDAY
23

SUNDAY
24

DOWN JANUARYS: A REMARKABLE RECORD

In the first third of the 20th century, there was no correlation between January markets and the year as a whole. Then, in 1972, Yale Hirsch discovered that the 1933 "Lame Duck" Amendment to the Constitution changed the political calendar, and the January Barometer was born—its record has been quite accurate (page 16).

Down Januarys are harbingers of trouble ahead in the economic, political, or military arena. Eisenhower's heart attack in 1955 cast doubt on whether he could run in 1956—a flat year. Two other election years with down Januarys were also flat (1984 & 1992). Thirteen bear markets began, and ten continued into second years with poor Januarys. 1968 started down, as we were mired in Vietnam, but Johnson's "bombing halt" changed the climate. Imminent military action in Iraq held January 2003 down before the market triple-bottomed in March. After Baghdad fell, pre-election and recovery forces fueled 2003 into a banner year. 2005 was flat, registering the narrowest Dow trading range on record. 2008 was the worst January on record and preceded the worst bear market since the Great Depression. A negative reading in 2015 and 2016 preceded an official Dow bear market declaration in February 2016. In 2020 the shortest bear market in history began after the close on February 19.

Unfortunately, bull and bear markets do not start conveniently at the beginnings and ends of months or years. Though some years ended higher, **every down January since 1950 was followed by a new or continuing bear market, a 10% correction, or a flat year. Down Januarys were followed by substantial declines averaging** *minus* **12.9%,** providing excellent buying opportunities later in most years.

FROM DOWN JANUARY S&P CLOSES TO LOW NEXT 11 MONTHS

Year	January Close	% Change	11-Month Low	Date of Low	Jan Close to Low %	% Feb to Dec	Year % Change	
1953	26.38	−0.7%	22.71	14-Sep	−13.9%	−6.0%	−6.6%	bear
1956	43.82	−3.6	43.42	14-Feb	−0.9	6.5	2.6	FLAT/bear
1957	44.72	−4.2	38.98	22-Oct	−12.8	−10.6	−14.3	Cont. bear
1960	55.61	−7.1	52.30	25-Oct	−6.0	4.5	−3.0	bear
1962	68.84	−3.8	52.32	26-Jun	−24.0	−8.3	−11.8	bear
1968	92.24	−4.4	87.72	5-Mar	−4.9	12.6	7.7	−10%/bear
1969	103.01	−0.8	89.20	17-Dec	−13.4	−10.6	−11.4	Cont. bear
1970	85.02	−7.6	69.20	26-May	−18.6	8.4	0.1	Cont. bear
1973	116.03	−1.7	92.16	5-Dec	−20.6	−15.9	−17.4	bear
1974	96.57	−1.0	62.28	3-Oct	−35.5	−29.0	−29.7	Cont. bear
1977	102.03	−5.1	90.71	2-Nov	−11.1	−6.8	−11.5	bear
1978	89.25	−6.2	86.90	6-Mar	−2.6	7.7	1.1	Cont. bear/bear
1981	129.55	−4.6	112.77	25-Sep	−13.0	−5.4	−9.7	bear
1982	120.40	−1.8	102.42	12-Aug	−14.9	16.8	14.8	Cont. bear
1984	163.42	−0.9	147.82	24-Jul	−9.5	2.3	1.4	Cont. bear/FLAT
1990	329.07	−6.9	295.46	11-Oct	−10.2	0.4	−6.6	bear
1992	408.79	−2.0	394.50	8-Apr	−3.5	6.6	4.5	FLAT
2000	1394.46	−5.1	1264.74	20-Dec	−9.3	−5.3	−10.1	bear
2002	1130.20	−1.6	776.76	9-Oct	−31.3	−22.2	−23.4	bear
2003	855.70	−2.7	800.73	11-Mar	−6.4	29.9	26.4	Cont. bear
2005	1181.27	−2.5	1137.50	20-Apr	−3.7	5.7	3.0	FLAT
2008	1378.55	−6.1	752.44	20-Nov	−45.4	−34.5	−38.5	bear
2009	825.88	−8.6	676.53	9-Mar	−18.1	35.0	23.5	Cont. bear
2010	1073.87	−3.7	1022.58	2-Jul	−4.8	17.1	12.8	−10%/no bear
2014	1782.59	−3.6	1741.89	3-Feb	−2.3	15.5	11.4	−10% intraday
2015	1994.99	−3.1	1867.61	25-Aug	−6.4	2.5	−0.7	bear
2016	1940.24	−5.1	1829.08	11-Feb	−5.7	15.4	9.5	Cont. bear
2020*	3225.52	−0.2	2237.40	23-Mar	−30.6	??	??	bear
				Totals	**−348.8%**	**32.3%**	**−76.0%**	
				Average	**−12.9%**	**1.2%**	**−2.8%**	

*As of June 30, 2020. Not included in averages.

MONDAY

D 66.7
S 66.7
N 57.1

25

Never will a man penetrate deeper into error than when he is continuing on a road that has led him to great success.
— Friedrich Hayek (Austrian-British economist & philosopher, 1899–1992)

TUESDAY

D 61.9
S 47.6
N 66.7

26

So much hangs on the decisions of a small number of poorly educated people. That's Democracy. A terrible way to run a country, but every other system is worse.
— Kenneth Martin Follett (Welsh author, *Fall of Giants,* b. 1949)

FOMC Meeting (2 Days)

WEDNESDAY

D 47.6
S 42.9
N 52.4

27

It is tact that is golden, not silence.
— Samuel Butler (English writer, 1600–1680)

THURSDAY

D 42.9
S 47.6
N 42.9

28

Small business has been the first rung on the ladder upward for every minority group in the nation's history.
— S. I. Hayakawa (1947, U.S. Senator California 1977-1983, 1906–1992)

"January Barometer" 85.7% Accurate (Page 16)
Almanac Investor Subscribers Emailed Official Results (See Insert)

FRIDAY

D 52.4
S 57.1
N 57.1

29

The reasonable man adapts himself to the world; the unreasonable one persists in trying to adapt the world to himself. Therefore, all progress depends on the unreasonable man.
— George Bernard Shaw (Irish dramatist, 1856–1950)

SATURDAY

30

SUNDAY

31

FEBRUARY ALMANAC

FEBRUARY						
S	M	T	W	T	F	S
	1	2	3	4	5	6
7	8	9	10	11	12	13
14	15	16	17	18	19	20
21	22	23	24	25	26	27
28						

MARCH						
S	M	T	W	T	F	S
	1	2	3	4	5	6
7	8	9	10	11	12	13
14	15	16	17	18	19	20
21	22	23	24	25	26	27
28	29	30	31			

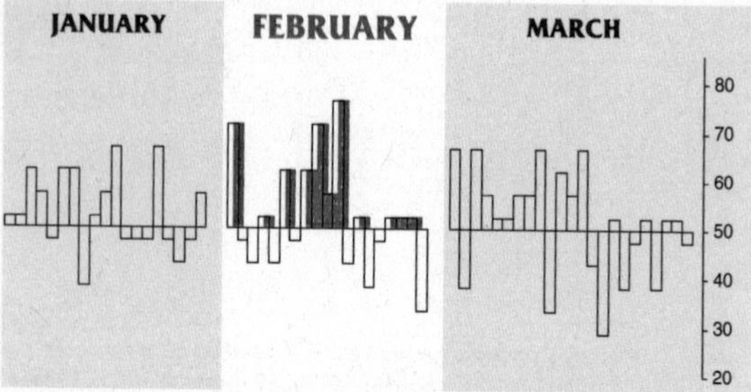

Market Probability Chart above is a graphic representation of the S&P 500 Recent Market Probability Calendar on page 124.

◆ February is the weak link in "Best Six Months" (pages 50, 52 & 147) ◆ RECENT RECORD: S&P up 9, down 6, average change — 0.1% last 15 years ◆ Worst NASDAQ month in post–presidential election years average loss 3.3% up 4 down 8 (page 158), #10 Dow, up 8 down 9 and #12 S&P, up 8, down 9 (pages 153 & 156) ◆ Day before Presidents' Day weekend S&P down 17 of 29, 11 straight 1992–2002, day after up 8 of last 10 (see page 98 & 133) ◆ Many technicians modify market predictions based on January's market

February Vital Statistics

	DJIA	S&P 500	NASDAQ	Russell 1K	Russell 2K
Rank	8	10	9	11	6
Up	42	39	27	25	24
Down	29	32	23	17	18
Average % Change	0.1%	–0.04%	0.6%	0.2%	1.0%
Post-Election Year	–1.1%	–1.5%	–3.3%	–1.3%	–1.6%
Best & Worst February					
	% Change	% Change	% Change	% Change	% Change
Best	1986 8.8	1986 7.1	2000 19.2	1986 7.2	2000 16.4
Worst	2009 –11.7	2009 –11.0	2001 –22.4	2009 –10.7	2009 –12.3
Best & Worst February Weeks					
Best	02/01/2008 4.4	02/06/2009 5.2	02/04/2000 9.2	02/06/2009 5.3	02/01/1991 6.6
Worst	02/28/2020 –12.4	02/28/2020 –11.5	02/28/2020 –10.5	02/28/2020 –11.6	02/28/2020 –12.0
Best & Worst February Days					
Best	02/24/2009 3.3	02/24/2009 4.0	02/11/1999 4.2	02/24/2009 4.1	02/24/2009 4.5
Worst	02/10/2009 –4.6	02/10/2009 –4.9	02/16/2001 –5.0	02/10/2009 –4.8	02/10/2009 –4.7
First Trading Day of Expiration Week: 1980–2020					
Record (#Up – #Down)	24–17	29–12	25–16	29–12	25–16
Current Streak	D2	D1	U7	D1	D1
Avg % Change	0.31	0.28	0.13	0.26	0.17
Options Expiration Day: 1980–2020					
Record (#Up – #Down)	21–20	18–23	17–24	19–22	20–21
Current Streak	D1	D1	D1	D1	D1
Avg % Change	–0.02	–0.11	–0.25	–0.11	–0.04
Options Expiration Week: 1980–2020					
Record (#Up – #Down)	25–16	23–18	23–18	23–18	27–14
Current Streak	D1	D1	D1	D1	D1
Avg % Change	0.54	0.35	0.29	0.36	0.49
Week After Options Expiration: 1980–2020					
Record (#Up – #Down)	20–21	20–21	24–17	20–21	22–19
Current Streak	D1	D1	D1	D1	D1
Avg % Change	–0.49	–0.40	–0.34	–0.37	–0.30
First Trading Day Performance					
% of Time Up	63.4	62.0	70.0	66.7	66.7
Avg % Change	0.15	0.16	0.33	0.20	0.33
Last Trading Day Performance					
% of Time Up	46.5	52.1	48.0	50.0	50.0
Avg % Change	–0.05	–0.05	–0.10	–0.12	–0.04

Dow & S&P 1950-June 19, 2020, NASDAQ 1971-June 19, 2020, Russell 1K & 2K 1979-June 19, 2020.

Either go short, or stay away the day before Presidents' Day.

First Day Trading in February, Dow Up 15 of Last 18

MONDAY

D 76.2
S 71.4
N 76.2

1

It wasn't raining when Noah built the ark.
— Warren Buffett (CEO Berkshire Hathaway, investor & philanthropist, b. 1930)

TUESDAY

D 38.1
S 47.6
N 47.6

2

The best minds are not in government. If any were, business would hire them away.
— Ronald Reagan (40th U.S. President, 1911–2004)

WEDNESDAY

D 52.4
S 42.9
N 38.1

3

If you destroy a free market you create a black market. If you have ten thousand regulations you destroy all respect for the law.
— Winston Churchill (British statesman, 1874–1965)

THURSDAY

D 52.4
S 52.4
N 57.1

4

There is only one side of the market and it is not the bull side or the bear side, but the right side.
— Jesse Livermore (Early 20th century stock trader and speculator, *How to Trade in Stocks*, 1877–1940)

FRIDAY

D 42.9
S 42.9
N 47.6

5

Don't compete. Create. Find out what everyone else is doing and then don't do it.
— Joel Weldon

SATURDAY

6

SUNDAY

7

MARKET BEHAVIOR UNDER NEW PRESIDENTS

For 54 annual editions of this Almanac we have had to look ahead six to eighteen months and try to anticipate what the stock market will do in the year to come. Predictable effects on the economy and stock market from quadrennial presidential and biennial congressional elections have steered us well over the years. Also, bear markets lasting about a year on average tended to consume the first year of Republican and second of Democratic terms (page 28).

Prognosticating was tougher in the 1990s during the greatest bull cycle in history. Being bullish and staying bullish was the best course. Bear markets were few and far between and when they did come, were swift and over in a few months. Market timers and fundamentalists, as a result, did not keep pace with the momentum players. The market has come back to earth and many of these patterns have reemerged.

POST-ELECTION MARKETS WHEN PARTY IN POWER IS OUSTED

New Democrats		Dow %	New Republicans		Dow %
Wilson	1913	— 10.3%	Harding	1921	12.7%
Roosevelt	1933	66.7	Eisenhower	1953	— 3.8
Kennedy	1961	18.7	Nixon	1969	— 15.2
Carter	1977	— 17.3	Reagan	1981	— 9.2
Clinton	1993	13.7	G.W. Bush	2001	— 7.1
Obama	2009	23.5	Trump	2017	25.1

WHEN INCUMBENT PARTY RETAINS POWER WITH NEW PRESIDENT

Succeeding Democrats			Succeeding Republicans		
Truman	1949	12.9%	Hoover	1929	— 17.2%
			G.H.W. Bush	1989	27.0

Looking at the past you can see that new and succeeding Democrats fared better in post-election years than Republicans. Democrats have tended to come to power following economic and market woes. Republicans often reclaimed the White House after foreign entanglements initiated by Democrats. Both have fallen to scandal and party division.

Wilson won after the Republican Party split in two, Carter after the Watergate scandal and G.W. Bush after the Lewinsky affair. Roosevelt, Kennedy, Clinton and Obama won elections during bad economies. Republicans took over after major wars were begun under Democrats, benefiting Harding, Eisenhower and Nixon. Reagan ousted Carter following the late 1970s stagflation and the Iran hostage crisis.

Truman held the White House after 16 years of effective Democratic rule. Hoover and G.H.W. Bush were passed the torch after eight years of Republican led peace and prosperity.

An ongoing global pandemic, the aftermath of an economic shutdown in response to the pandemic and continued uncertainty make handicapping this November's winner elusive at press time. Historically, incumbent administrations have the advantage, but growing angst from the electorate as the pandemic continues is beginning to erode that edge.

FEBRUARY 2021

MONDAY
D 42.9
S 61.9
N 61.9
8

Why is it right-wing [conservatives] always stand shoulder to shoulder in solidarity, while liberals always fall out among themselves?
— Yevgeny Yevtushenko (Russian poet, Babi Yar, quoted in *London Observer* December 15, 1991, b. 1933)

TUESDAY
D 52.4
S 47.6
N 47.6
9

In a study of 3000 companies, researchers at the University of Pennsylvania found that spending 10% of revenue on capital improvements boosts productivity by 3.9%, but a similar investment in developing human capital increases productivity by 8.5%.
— John A. Byrne (Editor-in-Chief, *Fast Company* Magazine)

Week Before February Expiration Week, NASDAQ Down 11 of Last 20, But Up 8 of Last 11

WEDNESDAY
D 52.4
S 61.9
N 61.9
10

We are like tenant farmers chopping down the fence around our house for fuel when we should be using Nature's inexhaustible sources of energy—sun, wind and tide. I'd put my money on the sun and solar energy. What a source of power! I hope we don't have to wait until oil and coal run out before we tackle that.
— Thomas Alva Edison (American inventor, 1093 patents, 1847–1931)

THURSDAY
D 61.9
S 71.4
N 71.4
11

Take care of your employees and they'll take care of your customers.
— John W. Marriott (Founder Marriott International, 1900–1985)

Day Before Presidents' Day Weekend, S&P Up 9 of Last 10

FRIDAY
D 52.4
S 57.1
N 76.2
12

The very purpose of existence is to reconcile the glowing opinion we hold of ourselves with the appalling things that other people think about us.
— Quentin Crisp (Author, performer, 1908–1999)

SATURDAY
13

Valentine's Day ♥

SUNDAY
14

MARKET CHARTS OF POST-PRESIDENTIAL ELECTION YEARS

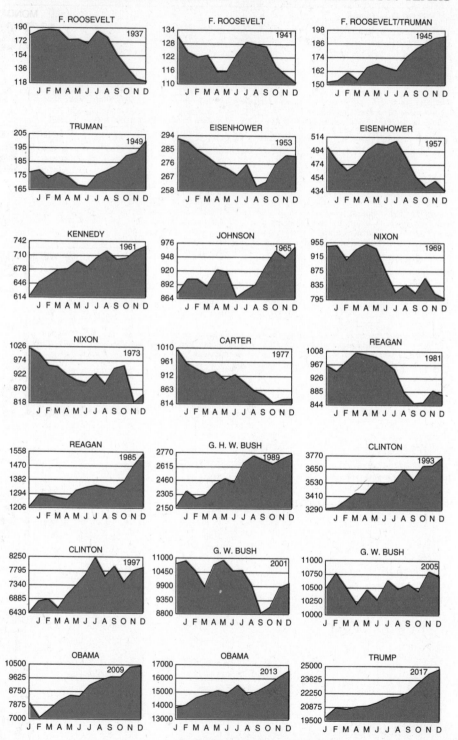

Based on Dow Jones Industial Average monthly closing prices

26

Presidents' Day *(Market Closed)*

If you could kick the person in the pants responsible for most of your trouble, you wouldn't sit for a month.
— Theodore Roosevelt (26th U.S. President, 1858–1919)

Day After Presidents Day, NASDAQ Down 15 of Last 26, But Up 7 of Last 8
First Trading Day of February Expiration Week, Dow Down 9 of Last 16

D 71.4
S 76.2
N 66.7

Age is a question of mind over matter. If you don't mind, it doesn't matter.
— Leroy Robert "Satchel" Paige (Negro League and Hall of Fame Pitcher, 1906–1982)

Ash Wednesday

D 52.4
S 42.9
N 42.9

A good manager is a man who isn't worried about his own career but rather the careers of those who work for him…
Don't worry about yourself! Take care of those who work for you and you'll float to greatness on their achievements.
— H.S.M. Burns (Scottish CEO Shell Oil 1947-1960, 1900–1971)

D 47.6
S 52.4
N 52.4

If a battered stock refuses to sink any lower no matter how many negative articles appear in the papers,
that stock is worth a close look.
— James L. Fraser (Contrary Investor)

February Expiration Day, NASDAQ Down 14 of Last 21

D 38.1
S 38.1
N 38.1

News on stocks is not important. How the stock reacts to it is important.
— Michael L. Burke (Investors Intelligence)

POST-ELECTION YEAR PERFORMANCE BY PARTY

From the table on page 130 it is clear that during the first two years of a president's term market performance lags well behind the latter two. After a president wins the election the first two years are spent pushing through as much policy as possible. Frequently the market, economy and country experience bear markets, recessions and war. Conversely, as presidents and their parties get anxious about holding on to power, they begin to prime the pump in the third year, fostering bull markets, prosperity and peace.

There is a dramatic difference in market performance under the two parties in post-election and midterm years the last seventeen election cycles. Since 1953 there have been twenty-one confirmed bull and twenty bear markets. Only eight bear markets have bottomed in the pre-election or election year and eleven tops have occurred in these years; the bulk of the declines were relegated to the post-election and midterm years. However, more bear markets and negative market action have plagued Republican administrations in the post-election year whereas the midterm year has been worse under Democrats.

Republicans have mostly taken over after foreign entanglements and personal transgressions during boom times and administered tough action right away, knocking the market down: 1953 (Korea), 1969 (Vietnam), 1981 (Iran hostage crisis) and 2001 (Lewinsky affair). Democrats have usually reclaimed power after economic duress or political scandal during leaner times and addressed more favorable policy moves the first year, buoying the market: 1961 (recession), 1977 (Watergate), 1993 (recession) and 2009 (financial crisis).

MARKET ACTION UNDER REPUBLICANS & DEMOCRATS SINCE 1953
Annual % Change in Dow Jones Industrial Average [1]

4-Year Cycle Beginning		Post-Election Year	Mid-Term Year	Pre-Election Year	Election Year	Totals
		REPUBLICANS				
1953*	Eisenhower (R)	−3.8	44.0	20.8	2.3	
1957	Eisenhower (R)	−12.8	34.0	16.4	−9.3	
1969*	Nixon (R)	−15.2	4.8	6.1	14.6	
1973	Nixon (R)***	−16.6	−27.6	38.3	17.9	
1981*	Reagan (R)	−9.2	19.6	20.3	−3.7	
1985	Reagan (R)	27.7	22.6	2.3	11.8	
1989	G. H. W. Bush (R)	27.0	−4.3	20.3	4.2	
2001*	G. W. Bush (R)	−7.1	−16.8	25.3	3.1	
2005	G. W. Bush (R)	−0.6	16.3	6.4	−33.8	
2017*	Trump (R)	25.1	−5.6	22.3		
	Total % Gain	**14.5**	**87.0**	**178.5**	**7.1**	**287.1**
	Average % Gain	**1.5**	**8.7**	**17.9**	**0.8**	**6.8**
	# Up	3	6	10	6	23
	# Down	7	4	0	3	13
		DEMOCRATS				
1961*	Kennedy (D)**	18.7	−10.8	17.0	14.6	
1965	Johnson (D)	10.9	−18.9	15.2	4.3	
1977*	Carter (D)	−17.3	−3.1	4.2	14.9	
1993*	Clinton (D)	13.7	2.1	33.5	26.0	
1997	Clinton (D)	22.6	16.1	25.2	−6.2	
2009*	Obama (D)	18.8	11.0	5.5	7.3	
2013	Obama (D)	26.5	7.5	−2.2	13.4	
	Total % Gain	**93.9**	**3.9**	**98.4**	**74.3**	**270.5**
	Average % Gain	**13.4**	**0.6**	**14.1**	**10.6**	**9.7**
	# Up	6	4	6	6	22
	# Down	1	3	1	1	6
		BOTH PARTIES				
	Total % Gain	**108.4**	**90.9**	**276.9**	**81.4**	**557.6**
	Average % Gain	**6.4**	**5.3**	**16.3**	**5.1**	**8.3**
	# Up	9	10	16	12	47
	# Down	8	7	1	4	20

*Party in power ousted , **Death in office, ***Resigned, D—Democrat, R—Republican, [1] Based on annual close

28

MONDAY

D 52.4
S 47.6
N 52.4

22

If I have seen further, it is by standing upon the shoulders of giants.
— Sir Isaac Newton (English physicist, mathematician, Laws of Gravity, letter to
Robert Hooke 2/15/1676, 1643–1727)

TUESDAY

D 47.6
S 52.4
N 61.9

23

*Banking establishments are more dangerous than standing armies; and that the principle of spending money
to be paid by posterity, under the name of funding, is but swindling futurity on a large scale.*
— Thomas Jefferson (3rd U.S. President, 1743-7/4/1826, 1816 letter to John Taylor of Caroline)

*Week After February Expiration Week, Dow Down 12 of Last 22
But Up 7 of Last 9, 2020 Down 12.4%, 5th Worst Week Since 1950*

WEDNESDAY

D 52.4
S 52.4
N 61.9

24

*Never doubt that a small group of thoughtful, committed citizens can change the world:
indeed it's the only thing that ever has.*
— Margaret Mead (American anthropologist)

THURSDAY

D 47.6
S 52.4
N 57.1

25

*Pretend that every single person you meet has a sign around his or her neck that says, "Make me feel
important." Not only will you succeed in sales, you will succeed in life.*
— Mary Kay Ash (Mary Kay Cosmetics)

End of February Miserable in Recent Years (Pages 22 and 133)

FRIDAY

D 33.3
S 33.3
N 23.8

26

Fortune favors the brave.
— Virgil (Roman Poet, *Aeneid*, 70-19 B.C.)

SATURDAY

27

March Almanac Investor Sector Seasonalities: See Pages 92, 94 and 96

SUNDAY

28

MARCH ALMANAC

MARCH						
S	M	T	W	T	F	S
	1	2	3	4	5	6
7	8	9	10	11	12	13
14	15	16	17	18	19	20
21	22	23	24	25	26	27
28	29	30	31			

APRIL						
S	M	T	W	T	F	S
				1	2	3
4	5	6	7	8	9	10
11	12	13	14	15	16	17
18	19	20	21	22	23	24
25	26	27	28	29	30	

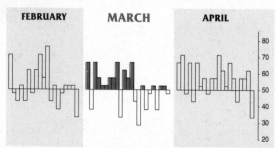

Market Probability Chart above is a graphic representation of the S&P 500 Recent Market Probability Calendar on page 124.

◆ Mid-month strength and late-month weakness are most evident above ◆ RECENT RECORD: S&P 12 up, 9 down, average gain 0.9%, fourth best ◆ Rather turbulent in recent years, with wild fluctuations and large gains and losses ◆ March 2020 Dow declined 13.7%, worst March loss since 1938 ◆ March has been taking some mean end-of-quarter hits (page 134), down 1469 Dow points March 9–22, 2001 ◆ Last three or four days Dow a net loser 20 out of last 31 years ◆ NASDAQ hard hit in 2001, down 14.5% after 22.4% drop in February ◆ Fourth worst NASDAQ month during post–presidential election years average loss 0.2%, up 6, down 6 ◆ Third Dow month to gain more than 1000 points in 2016

March Vital Statistics

	DJIA		S&P 500		NASDAQ		Russell 1K		Russell 2K	
Rank	6		6		8		8		7	
Up	45		45		31		27		29	
Down	26		26		19		15		13	
Average % Change	0.8%		1.0%		0.6%		0.8%		0.8%	
Post-Election Year	0.3%		0.6%		−0.2%		0.7%		1.1%	
Best & Worst March										
	% Change		% Change		% Change		% Change		% Change	
Best	2000	7.8	2000	9.7	2009	10.9	2000	8.9	1979	9.7
Worst	2020	−13.7	2020	−12.5	1980	−17.1	2020	−13.4	2020	−21.9
Best & Worst March Weeks										
Best	03/27/2020	12.8	03/13/2009	10.7	03/13/2009	10.6	03/13/2009	10.7	03/13/2009	12.0
Worst	03/20/2020	−17.3	03/20/2020	−15.0	03/20/2020	−12.6	03/20/2020	−15.3	03/13/2020	−16.5
Best & Worst March Days										
Best	03/24/2020	11.4	03/24/2020	9.4	03/13/2020	9.4	03/24/2020	9.5	03/24/2020	9.4
Worst	03/16/2020	−12.9	03/16/2020	−12.0	03/16/2020	−12.3	03/16/2020	−12.2	03/16/2020	−14.3
First Trading Day of Expiration Week: 1980–2020										
Record (#Up − #Down)	26–15		26–15		21–20		24–17		22–19	
Current Streak	D1		D1		D1		D1		D1	
Avg % Change	−0.13		−0.19		−0.47		−0.25		−0.58	
Options Expiration Day: 1980–2020										
Record (#Up − #Down)	22–19		24–17		21–20		22–19		20–20	
Current Streak	D1		D1		D1		D1		D1	
Avg % Change	−0.01		−0.06		−0.10		−0.06		−0.09	
Options Expiration Week: 1980–2020										
Record (#Up − #Down)	28–12		27–14		25–16		26–15		23–18	
Current Streak	D1		D1		D1		D1		D1	
Avg % Change	0.44		0.39		−0.14		0.33		−0.09	
Week After Options Expiration: 1980–2020										
Record (#Up − #Down)	17–24		13–28		19–22		13–28		18–23	
Current Streak	U1		U1		U1		U1		U1	
Avg % Change	−0.13		−0.10		0.01		−0.10		−0.05	
First Trading Day Performance										
% of Time Up	67.6		64.8		64.0		61.9		66.9	
Avg % Change	0.24		0.25		0.36		0.27		0.33	
Last Trading Day Performance										
% of Time Up	42.3		40.8		64.0		47.6		81.0	
Avg % Change	−0.10		−0.001		0.18		0.08		0.38	

Dow & S&P 1950–June 19, 2020 NASDAQ 1971–June 19, 2020, Russell 1K & 2K 1979–June 19, 2020.

March has Ides and St. Patrick's Day;
Begins bullishly, then fades away.

First Trading Day in March, S&P Up 17 of Last 25

MONDAY
D 61.9
S 66.7
N 66.7

1

Methodology is the last refuge of a sterile mind.
— Marianne L. Simmel (Psychologist)

TUESDAY
D 38.1
S 38.1
N 38.1

2

The more feted by the media, the worse a pundit's accuracy.
— Sharon Begley (Senior editor *Newsweek*, 2/23/2009, referencing
Philip E. Tetlock's 2005 *Expert Political Judgment*)

March Historically Strong Early in the Month (Pages 30 and 134)

WEDNESDAY
D 57.1
S 66.7
N 61.9

3

Little minds are tamed and subdued by misfortune; but great minds rise above them.
— Washington Irving (American essayist, historian, novelist, *The Legend of Sleepy Hollow*,
U.S. ambassador to Spain 1842–46, 1783–1859)

THURSDAY
D 52.4
S 57.1
N 47.6

4

I don't know where speculation got such a bad name, since I know of no forward leap which was not fathered by speculation.
— John Steinbeck

FRIDAY
D 52.4
S 52.4
N 38.1

5

Resentment is like taking poison and waiting for the other person to die.
— Malachy McCourt *(A Monk Swimming: A Memoir)*

SATURDAY

6

SUNDAY

7

POST-ELECTION YEARS: PAYING THE PIPER

Politics being what it is, incumbent administrations during election years try to make the economy look good to impress the electorate and tend to put off unpopular decisions until the votes are counted. This produces an American phenomenon—the Post–Election Year Syndrome. The year begins with an inaugural ball, after which the piper must be paid, and we Americans have often paid dearly in the past 107 years.

Victorious candidates rarely succeed in fulfilling campaign promises of "peace and prosperity." In the past 27 post-election years, three major wars began: World War I (1917), World War II (1941), and Vietnam (1965); four drastic bear markets started in 1929, 1937, 1969 and 1973; 9/11, recession and continuing bear markets in 2001 and 2009; less severe bear markets occurred or were in progress in 1913, 1917, 1921, 1941, 1949, 1953, 1957, 1977 and 1981. Only in 1925, 1985, 1989, 1993, 1997, 2013 and 2017 were Americans blessed with peace and prosperity.

THE RECORD SINCE 1913

1913	Wilson (D)	Minor bear market.
1917	Wilson (D)	World War I and a bear market.
1921	Harding (R)	Post-war depression and bear market.
1925	Coolidge (R)	Peace and prosperity. Hallelujah!
1929	Hoover (R)	Worst market crash in history until 1987.
1933	Roosevelt (D)	Devaluation, bank failures, Depression still on but market strong.
1937	Roosevelt (D)	Another crash, 20% unemployment rate.
1941	Roosevelt (D)	World War II and a continuing bear.
1945	Roosevelt (D)	Post-war industrial contraction, strong market precedes 1946 crash.
1949	Truman (D)	Minor bear market.
1953	Eisenhower (R)	Minor post-war (Korea) bear market.
1957	Eisenhower (R)	Major bear market.
1961	Kennedy (D)	Bay of Pigs fiasco, strong market precedes 1962 crash.
1965	Johnson (D)	Vietnam escalation. Bear came in 1966.
1969	Nixon (R)	Start of worst bear market since 1937.
1973	Nixon, Ford (R)	Start of worst bear market since 1929.
1977	Carter (D)	Bear market in blue chip stocks.
1981	Reagan (R)	Bear strikes again.
1985	Reagan (R)	No bear in sight.
1989	Bush (R)	Effect of 1987 Crash wears off.
1993	Clinton (D)	S&P up 7.1%, next year off 1.5%.
1997	Clinton (D)	S&P up 31.0%, next year up 26.7%.
2001	Bush, GW (R)	9/11, recession, bear market intensifies.
2005	Bush, GW (R)	Flat year, narrowest range, Dow off –0.6%.
2009	Obama (D)	Financial crisis, bear bottom, Dow up 18.8%.
2013	Obama (D)	Fed QE, Dow up, 26.5%.
2017	Trump (R)	Major corporate tax cuts, Dow up, 25.1%

Republicans took back the White House following foreign involvements under Democrats in 1921 (WWI), 1953 (Korea), 1969 (Vietnam), and 1981 (Iran); and scandal in 2001. Bear markets occurred in these post-election years. Democrats recaptured power after domestic problems under Republicans: in 1913 (GOP split), 1933 (Crash and Depression), 1961 (recession), 1977 (Watergate), 1993 (sluggish economy) and 2009 (financial crisis). Post-election years have been better under Democrats (page 28).

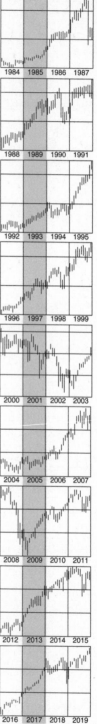

Graph shows Post-Election years screened
Based on Dow Jones industial average monthly ranges

PROBABILITIES FUND

PROBABILITIES
FUND MANAGEMENT, LLC

Category: Liquid Alternative - Class A: PROAX Class I: PROTX Class C: PROCX

September 2020

Cumulative Growth Chart (1/1/2008 – 9/30/2020)

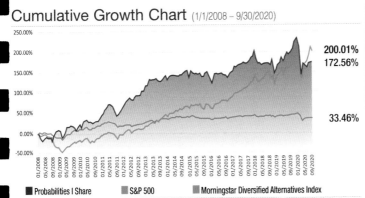

200.01%
172.56%

33.46%

- ■ Probabilities I Share
- ■ S&P 500
- ■ Morningstar Diversified Alternatives Index

Past Performance is no indication of future returns. Since inception, January 1, 2008 to present. The Morningstar Diversified Alternatives Index is comprised of seven alternative asset classes that broadly represent the alternative landscape, hedge funds, long/short equity, merger arbitrage, managed futures, breakeven Inflation, global Infrastructure, and listed private equity. The hypothetical scenario does not take into account federal, state or municipal takes. If taxes were taken into account, the hypothetical values shown would have been lower.

Using historical trends and patterns to obtain dynamic exposure to the US stock market.

Statistical Analysis vs S&P 500

	Probabilities I Share	MDAI	S&P 500
Cumulative Performance	172.56%	34.46%	200.01%
Annualized Alpha	3.14%	-1.37%	0.00%
Beta	0.61	0.35	1.00
Sharpe Ratio	0.52	0.28	0.59
Standard Deviation	17.02%	6.92%	15.76%
Maximum Drawdown	-27.33%	-15.25%	-48.45%
Correlation	0.57	0.81	1.00
Up Capture of S&P 500	77.45%	33.79%	100%
Down Capture of S&P 500	71.31%	38.65%	100%

Standardized Returns As of 9/30/2020 (Greater than one year, annualized)

Updated Quarterly	YTD	1 Year	3 Years	5 Years	10 Years	Since Inception
Probabilities Fund I Share (Inception 01/01/2008)	-17.31%	-8.17%	0.22%	2.70%	7.88%	8.19%
Probabilities Fund A at NAV (Inception 01/16/2014)	-17.49%	-8.45%	-0.06%	2.45%	N/A	1.68%
Probabilities Fund A at Maximum Load	-22.24%	-13.75%	-2.01%	1.24%	N/A	0.78%
Probabilities Fund C (Inception 01/16/2014)	-17.90%	-9.04%	-0.77%	1.70%	N/A	0.93%
S&P 500 Total Return	5.57%	15.15%	12.28%	14.15%	13.74%	9.00%

Disclosures

Historical Performance (PROTX)

	Jan	Feb	Mar	Apr	May	Jun	Jul	Aug	Sep	Oct	Nov	Dec	YTD	MDAI*	S&P 500	ITD
2020	0.74%	-7.04%	-21.83%	11.60%	-1.51%	-2.56%	4.63%	-0.10%	0.91%				-17.31%	-7.62%	5.57%	172.56%
2019	2.92%	5.68%	2.09%	5.56%	-3.97%	4.81%	3.76%	-2.03%	1.44%	2.76%	6.49%	1.49%	35.10%	7.42%	31.49%	229.62%
2018	4.40%	-6.50%	-4.13%	1.18%	-1.94%	0.69%	0.39%	0.29%	-0.49%	-1.65%	5.47%	-12.73%	-15.21%	-3.49%	-4.38%	143.98%
2017	1.05%	4.26%	-0.27%	2.27%	0.18%	0.98%	0.79%	-0.61%	0.26%	1.84%	2.67%	1.65%	16.03%	2.70%	21.83%	187.76%
2016	-6.02%	-1.36%	9.89%	0.19%	-0.48%	0.78%	0.10%	-1.64%	-0.39%	-2.85%	3.74%	1.95%	3.16%	2.31%	11.96%	148.01%
2015	-7.56%	7.58%	-1.95%	-1.14%	0.29%	-0.95%	1.35%	-3.61%	0.39%	3.83%	1.04%	-3.93%	-5.35%	-3.66%	1.38%	140.42%
2014	-4.46%	2.98%	1.35%	0.19%	0.10%	-0.47%	0.00%	1.62%	-0.66%	2.27%	1.85%	0.61%	5.30%	3.04%	13.69%	154.02%
2013	5.91%	0.53%	6.57%	-0.24%	0.62%	0.28%	0.71%	-2.23%	-0.35%	0.71%	2.53%	2.61%	18.73%	8.64%	32.39%	141.29%
2012	6.19%	5.83%	2.04%	2.38%	-2.80%	0.18%	4.19%	1.77%	-0.26%	0.70%	5.13%	0.07%	28.07%	6.82%	16.00%	103.17%
2011	4.16%	7.75%	2.12%	6.09%	0.81%	-3.26%	-0.49%	-8.86%	-6.67%	5.79%	4.38%	2.54%	13.65%	-3.67%	2.11%	58.64%
2010	-6.75%	10.41%	4.41%	2.16%	-3.56%	0.62%	-2.97%	1.22%	1.70%	0.62%	3.09%	5.45%	16.43%	11.83%	15.06%	39.48%
2009	-0.94%	-15.90%	1.44%	10.98%	15.15%	0.75%	3.01%	-1.84%	-1.82%	-7.96%	8.31%	5.76%	13.88%	21.73%	26.46%	19.89%
2008	1.68%	-15.28%	-8.28%	5.59%	6.07%	-0.61%	-0.07%	-2.56%	-2.33%	10.19%	11.65%	2.30%	5.27%	-12.21%	-37.00%	5.28%

Morningstar Diversified Alternatives Index.

Important Disclosures

Investors should carefully consider the investment objectives, risks, charges and expenses of the Probabilities Fund. This and other importantinformation about the Fund is contained in the Prospectus, which can be obtained by contacting your financial advisor, or by calling 1.888.868.9501. The Prospectus should be read carefully before investing. Probabilities Fund is distributed by Northern Lights Distributors, LLC member FINRA/SIPC. Probabilities Fund Management, LLC and Northern Lights Distributors are not affiliated.

Performance shown before the inception date of the mutual fund, December 12, 2013, is for the Fund's predecessor limited partnership. The prior performance is net of management fee and other expenses, including the effect of the performance fee. The Fund's investment goals, policies, guidelines and restrictions are similar to the predecessor limited partnership. From its inception date, the predecessor limited partnership was not subject to certain investment restrictions,diversification requirements and other restrictions of the Investment Company Act of 1940 which if they had been applicable, it might have adversely affected its performance. In addition, the predecessor limited partnership was not subject to sales loads that would have adversely affected performance. Performance of the predecessor fund is not an indicator of future results.

Mutual Funds involve risk including the possible loss of principal.

The Fund's advisor has contractually agreed to reduce the fees and/or absorb expenses of the Fund, at least until January 31, 2021, to ensure that the net annual fund operating expenses will not exceed 2.14% for Class A, 2.89% for Class C and 1.89% for Class I, subject to possible recoupment from the Fund in future years.

ETFs are subject to investment advisory and other expenses, which will be indirectly paid by the Fund. As a result, your cost of investing in the Fund will behigher than the cost of investing directly in the ETFs and may be higher than other mutual funds that invest directly in stocks and bonds. Each ETF is subject to specific risks, depending on its investments. Leveraged ETFs employ leverage, which magnifies the changes in the value of the Leveraged ETFs, which could result in significant losses to the Fund. The Fund invests in Leveraged ETFs in an effort to deliver daily performance at twice the rate of the underlying index and if held over long periods of time, particularly in volatile markets, the ETFs may not achieve their objective and may, in fact, perform contrary to expectations. Inverse ETFs are designed to rise in price when stock prices are falling.

Inverse ETFs tend to limit the Fund's participation in overall market-wide gains. Accordingly, their performance over longer terms can perform very differently than underlying assets and benchmarks, and volatile markets can amplify this effect.

The advisor's judgment about the attractiveness, value and potential appreciation of particular security or derivative in which the Fund invests or sells short may prove to be incorrect and may not produce the desired results. Equity prices can fall rapidly in response to developments affecting a specific company or industry, or to changing economic, political or market conditions. A higher portfolio turnover may result in higher transactional and brokerage costs. The indices shown are for informational purposes only and are not reflective of any investment. As it is not possible to invest in the indices, the data shown does not reflect or compare features of an actual investment, such as its objectives, costs and expenses, liquidity, safety, guarantees or insurance, fluctuation of principal or return, or tax features. Past performance does not guaranteed future results. The S&P 500 Index is an unmanaged composite of 500 large capitalization companies. This index is widely used by professional investors as a performance benchmark for large-cap stocks.

Alpha (Jensen's alpha) is a risk-adjusted performance measure that represents the average return on an investment, above or below that predicted by the capital asset pricing model (CAPM), given the investment's beta and the average market return. This metric is also commonly referred to as simply alpha. Beta is a measure of a fund's volatility relative to market movements. Sharpe Ratio is a measure of risk adjusted performance calculated by subtracting the risk-free rate from the rate of return of the portfolio and dividing the result by the standard deviation of the portfolio returns. The 3 month T-Bill rate was used in the calculation.

Standard Deviation is a statistical measurement of volatility risk based on historical returns. Maximum Drawdown represents the largest peak-to-trough decline during a specific period of time. Correlation is a statistical measure of how two investments move inrelation to each other.

Up and Down Capture ratios reflect how a particular investment performed when a specific index has either risen or fallen. Long positions entail buying asecurity such as a stock, commodity or currency, with the expectation that the asset will rise in value. Short positions entail a sale that is completed by the delivery of a security borrowed by the seller. Short sellers assume they will be able to buy the stock at a lower amount that the price at which they sold short.

MONDAY

D 47.6
S 52.4
N 52.4

8

Don't be the last bear or last bull standing, let history guide you, be contrary to the crowd, and let the tape tell you when to act.
— Jeffrey A. Hirsch (Editor, *Stock Trader's Almanac*, b. 1966)

Dow Down 1469 Points March 9–22 in 2001

TUESDAY

D 57.1
S 57.1
N 47.6

9

The four most expensive words in the English language, "This time it's different."
— Sir John Templeton (Founder Templeton Funds, philanthropist, 1912–2008)

WEDNESDAY

D 52.4
S 57.1
N 52.4

10

I will never knowingly buy any company that has a real-time quote of their stock price in the building lobby.
— Robert Mahan (A trader commenting on Enron)

THURSDAY

D 61.9
S 66.7
N 66.7

11

There is always plenty of capital for those who can create practical plans for using it.
— Napoleon Hill (Author, *Think and Grow Rich*, 1883–1970)

FRIDAY

D 57.1
S 33.3
N 38.1

12

You must automate, emigrate, or evaporate.
— James A. Baker (General Electric)

SATURDAY

13

Daylight Saving Time Begins

SUNDAY

14

THE DECEMBER LOW INDICATOR: A USEFUL PROGNOSTICATING TOOL

When the Dow closes below its December closing low in the first quarter, it is frequently an excellent warning sign. Jeffrey Saut, Market Strategist and Board Member at Capital Wealth Planning, brought this to our attention years ago. The December Low Indicator was originated by Lucien Hooper, a *Forbes* columnist and Wall Street analyst back in the 1970s. Hooper dismissed the importance of January and January's first week as reliable indicators. He noted that the trend could be random or even manipulated during a holiday-shortened week. Instead, said Hooper, "Pay much more attention to the December low. If that low is violated during the first quarter of the New Year, watch out!"

Twenty of the 36 occurrences were followed by gains for the rest of the year—and 18 full-year gains—after the low for the year was reached. For perspective we've included the January Barometer readings for the selected years. Hooper's "Watch Out" warning was absolutely correct, though. All but two of the instances since 1952 experienced further declines, as the Dow fell an additional 11% on average when December's low was breached in Q1.

Only three significant drops occurred (not shown) when December's low was not breached in Q1 (1974, 1981 and 1987). Both indicators were wrong seven times and nine years ended flat. If the December low is not crossed, turn to our January Barometer for guidance (page 16).

YEARS DOW FELL BELOW DECEMBER LOW IN FIRST QUARTER

Year	Previous Dec Low	Date Crossed	Crossing Price	Subseq. Low	% Change Cross-Low	Rest of Year % Change	Full Year % Change	Jan Bar
1952	262.29	2/19/52	261.37	256.35	−1.9%	11.7%	8.4%	1.6%[2]
1953	281.63	2/11/53	281.57	255.49	−9.3	−0.2	−3.8	−0.7[3]
1956	480.72	1/9/56	479.74	462.35	−3.6	4.1	2.3	−3.6[1, 2, 3]
1957	480.61	1/18/57	477.46	419.79	−12.1	−8.7	−12.8	−4.2
1960	661.29	1/12/60	660.43	566.05	−14.3	−6.7	−9.3	−7.1
1962	720.10	1/5/62	714.84	535.76	−25.1	−8.8	−10.8	−3.8
1966	939.53	3/1/66	938.19	744.32	−20.7	−16.3	−18.9	0.5[1]
1968	879.16	1/22/68	871.71	825.13	−5.3	8.3	4.3	−4.4[1, 2, 3]
1969	943.75	1/6/69	936.66	769.93	−17.8	−14.6	−15.2	−0.8
1970	769.93	1/26/70	768.88	631.16	−17.9	9.1	4.8	−7.6[2, 3]
1973	1000.00	1/29/73	996.46	788.31	−20.9	−14.6	−16.6	−1.7
1977	946.64	2/7/77	946.31	800.85	−15.4	−12.2	−17.3	−5.1
1978	806.22	1/5/78	804.92	742.12	−7.8	0.01	−3.1	−6.2[3]
1980	819.62	3/10/80	818.94	759.13	−7.3	17.7	14.9	5.8[2]
1982	868.25	1/5/82	865.30	776.92	−10.2	20.9	19.6	−1.8[1, 2]
1984	1236.79	1/25/84	1231.89	1086.57	−11.8	−1.6	−3.7	−0.9[3]
1990	2687.93	1/15/90	2669.37	2365.10	−11.4	−1.3	−4.3	−6.9[3]
1991	2565.59	1/7/91	2522.77	2470.30	−2.1	25.6	20.3	4.2[2]
1993	3255.18	1/8/93	3251.67	3241.95	−0.3	15.5	13.7	0.7[2]
1994	3697.08	3/30/94	3626.75	3593.35	−0.9	5.7	2.1	3.3[2, 3]
1996	5059.32	1/10/96	5032.94	5032.94	NC	28.1	26.0	3.3[2]
1998	7660.13	1/9/98	7580.42	7539.07	−0.5	21.1	16.1	1.0[2]
2000	10998.39	1/4/00	10997.93	9796.03	−10.9	−1.9	−6.2	−5.1
2001	10318.93	3/12/01	10208.25	8235.81	−19.3	−1.8	−7.1	3.5[1]
2002	9763.96	1/16/02	9712.27	7286.27	−25.0	−14.1	−16.8	−1.6
2003	8303.78	1/24/03	8131.01	7524.06	−7.5	28.6	25.3	−2.7[1, 2]
2005	10440.58	1/21/05	10392.99	10012.36	−3.7	3.1	−0.6	−2.5[3]
2006	10717.50	1/20/06	10667.39	10667.39	NC	16.8	16.3	2.5
2007	12194.13	3/2/07	12114.10	12050.41	−0.5	9.5	6.4	1.4[2]
2008	13167.20	1/2/08	13043.96	7552.29	−42.1	−32.7	−33.8	−6.1
2009	8149.09	1/20/09	7949.09	6547.05	−17.6	31.2	18.8	−8.6[1, 2]
2010	10285.97	1/22/10	10172.98	9686.48	−4.8	13.8	11.0	−3.7[1, 2]
2014	15739.43	1/31/14	15698.85	15372.80	−2.1	13.5	7.5	−3.6[1, 2]
2016	17128.55	1/6/16	16906.51	15660.18	−7.4	16.9	13.4	−5.1[1, 2]
2018	24140.91	2/8/18	23860.46	21792.20	−8.7	−2.2	−5.6	5.6[1]
2020	27502.81	2/25/20	27081.36	18591.93	−31.3	??	??	−0.2
				Average Drop	**−11.0%**			

[1] January Barometer wrong. [2] December Low Indicator wrong. [3] Year Flat.

Monday Before March Triple Witching, Dow Up 23 of Last 33
2020 Down 12.9% 2nd Worst Dow Day Since 1901

MONDAY

D 76.2
S 61.9
N 47.6

15

Chance favors the informed mind.
— Louis Pasteur (French chemist, founder of microbiology, 1822–1895)

TUESDAY

D 52.4
S 57.1
N 66.7

16

Good luck is what happens when preparation meets opportunity, bad luck is what happens when lack
of preparation meets a challenge.
— Paul Krugman (Economist, *NY Times* 3/3/2006)

St. Patrick's Day ♣
FOMC Meeting (2 Days)

WEDNESDAY

D 61.9
S 66.7
N 71.4

17

A cynic is a man who knows the price of everything and the value of nothing.
— Oscar Wilde (Irish-born writer and wit, 1845–1900)

THURSDAY

D 57.1
S 42.9
N 66.7

18

A leader has the ability to create infectious enthusiasm.
— Ted Turner (Billionaire, *New Yorker* Magazine, April 23, 2001)

March Triple-Witching Day Mixed Last 30 Years,
But Dow and S&P Up 4 of Last 6, NASDAQ Up 5 of Last 6

FRIDAY

D 33.3
S 28.6
N 38.1

19

It's better to have your enemies inside the tent pissing out than outside pissing in.
— Lyndon B. Johnson (36th U.S. President, 1908–1973)

SATURDAY

20

SUNDAY

21

HOW TO TRADE BEST MONTHS SWITCHING STRATEGIES

Our Best Months Switching Strategies found on pages 52, 54, 60 and 62 are simple and reliable, with a proven 70-year track record. Thus far we have failed to find a similar trading strategy that even comes close over the past six decades. And to top it off, the strategy has only been improving since we first discovered it in 1986.

Exogenous factors and cultural shifts must be considered. "Backward" tests that go back to 1925 or even 1896 and conclude that the pattern does not work are best ignored. They do not take into account these factors. Farming made August the best month from 1900 to 1951. Since 1987 it is the worst month of the year for the Dow and S&P. Panic caused by the financial crisis in 2007–08 caused every asset class aside from U.S. Treasuries to decline substantially. But the bulk of the major decline in equities in the worst months of 2008 was sidestepped using these strategies.

Our Best Months Switching Strategy will not make you an instant millionaire as other strategies claim they can do. What it will do is steadily build wealth over time with probably less risk than a buy-and-hold approach.

A sampling of tradable funds for the best and worst months appears in the table below. These are just a starting point and only skim the surface of possible trading vehicles currently available to take advantage of these strategies. Your specific situation and risk tolerance will dictate a suitable choice. If you are trading in a tax-advantaged account such as a company-sponsored 401(k) or Individual Retirement Account (IRA), your investment options may be limited to what has been selected by your employer or IRA administrator. But if you are a self-directed trader with a brokerage account, then you likely have unlimited choices (perhaps too many).

TRADABLE BEST AND WORST MONTHS SWITCHING STRATEGY FUNDS

Best Months Exchange Traded Funds (ETF)		Worst Months Exchange Traded Funds (ETF)	
Symbol	Name	Symbol	Name
DIA	SPDR Dow Jones Industrial Average	SHY	iShares 1–3 Year Treasury Bond
SPY	SPDR S&P 500	IEI	iShares 3–7 Year Treasury Bond
QQQ	Invesco QQQ	IEF	iShares 7–10 Year Treasury Bond
IWM	iShares Russell 2000	TLT	iShares 20+ Year Treasury Bond
Mutual Funds		**Mutual Funds**	
Symbol	Name	Symbol	Name
VWNDX	Vanguard Windsor Fund	VFSTX	Vanguard Short-Term Investment-Grade Bond Fund
FMAGX	Fidelity Magellan Fund	FBNDX	Fidelity Investment Grade Bond Fund
AMCPX	American Funds AMCAP Fund	ABNDX	American Funds Bond Fund of America
FCGAX	Franklin Growth Fund	FKUSX	Franklin U.S. Government Securities Fund
SECEX	Guggenheim Large Cap Core Fund	SIUSX	Guggenheim Investment Grade Bond Fund

Generally speaking, during the best months you want to be invested in equities that offer similar exposure to the companies that constitute the Dow, S&P 500, and NASDAQ indices. These would typically be large-cap growth and value stocks as well as technology concerns. Reviewing the holdings of a particular ETF or mutual fund and comparing them to the index members is an excellent way to correlate.

During the Worst Months switch into Treasury bonds, money market funds or a bear/short fund. **Grizzly Short** (GRZZX) and **AdvisorShares Ranger Equity Bear** (HDGE) are two possible choices. Money market funds will be the safest, but are likely to offer the smallest return, while bear/short funds offer potentially greater returns, but more risk. If the market moves sideways or higher during the Worst Months, a bear/short fund is likely to lose money. Treasuries can offer a combination of fair returns with limited risk.

Additional Worst Month possibilities include precious metals and the companies that mine them. **SPDR Gold Shares** (GLD), **VanEck Vectors Gold Miners** (GDX) and **ETF Securities Physical Swiss Gold** (SGOL) are a few well-recognized names available from the ETF universe.

BECOME AN ALMANAC INVESTOR

Almanac Investor subscribers receive specific buy and sell trade ideas based upon the Best Months Switching Strategies online and via email. Sector Index Seasonalities, found on page 92, are also put into action throughout the year with corresponding ETF trades. Buy limits, stop losses, and auto-sell price points for the majority of seasonal trades are delivered directly to your inbox. Visit *www.stocktradersalmanac.com* or see the insert for details and a special offer for new subscribers.

MARCH 2021

Dow Lost 4012 Points (17.3%) on the Week Ending 3/20/2020
Worst Dow Weekly Point Loss and 2nd Worst Percent Loss Overall

MONDAY
D 47.6
S 52.4
N 61.9
22

A man should always hold something in reserve, a surprise to spring when things get tight.
— Christy Mathewson (MLB Hall of Fame Pitcher, first 5 elected, 3rd most wins, 1880–1925)

TUESDAY
D 42.9
S 38.1
N 47.6
23

Inflation is the modern way that governments default on their debt.
— Mike Epstein (MTA, MIT/Sloan Lab for Financial Engineering)

Week After Triple Witching, Dow Down 22 of Last 33, 2000 Up 4.9%, 2007 Up 3.1%,
2009 Up 6.8%, 2011 Up 3.1%, 2020 Up 12.8% Best Week Since 1950

WEDNESDAY
D 28.6
S 47.6
N 52.4
24

Education is our passport to the future, for tomorrow belongs only to the people who prepare for it today.
— Malcom X (Minister, human rights activist and civil rights leader, 1925–1965)

THURSDAY
D 57.1
S 52.4
N 66.7
25

How a minority, Reaching majority, Seizing authority, Hates a minority.
— Leonard H. Robbins

March Historically Weak Later in the Month (Pages 30 and 134)

FRIDAY
D 38.1
S 38.1
N 28.6
26

A person's greatest virtue is his ability to correct his mistakes and continually make a new person of himself.
— Yang-Ming Wang (Chinese philosopher, 1472-1529)

SATURDAY
27

Passover
April Almanac Investor Sector Seasonalities: See Pages 92, 94 and 96

SUNDAY
28

APRIL ALMANAC

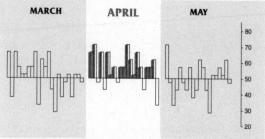

APRIL						
S	M	T	W	T	F	S
					1	2	3
4	5	6	7	8	9	10
11	12	13	14	15	16	17
18	19	20	21	22	23	24
25	26	27	28	29	30	

MAY						
S	M	T	W	T	F	S
						1
2	3	4	5	6	7	8
9	10	11	12	13	14	15
16	17	18	19	20	21	22
23	24	25	26	27	28	29
30	31					

Market Probability Chart above is a graphic representation of the S&P 500 Recent Market Probability Calendar on page 124.

◆ April is still the best Dow month (average 2.0%) since 1950 (page 50) ◆ April 1999 first month ever to gain 1000 Dow points, 856 in 2001, knocked off its high horse in 2002 down 458, 2003 up 488 ◆ Up fifteen straight, average gain 2.9% ◆ April 2020 Dow +11.1%, best April since 1938 ◆ Prone to weakness after mid-month tax deadline ◆ Stocks anticipate great first quarter earnings by rising sharply before earnings are reported, rather than after ◆ Rarely a dangerous month, recent exceptions are 2002, 2004 and 2005 ◆ "Best Six Months" of the year end with April (page 52) ◆ Post–presidential election year Aprils since 1950 (Dow 1.9%, S&P 1.5%, NASDAQ –2.4%) ◆ End of April NASDAQ strength fading (pages 125 & 126)

April Vital Statistics

	DJIA		S&P 500		NASDAQ		Russell 1K		Russell 2K	
Rank	1		1		2		1		3	
Up	49		51		33		30		27	
Down	22		20		17		12		15	
Average % Change	2.0%		1.6%		1.7%		1.8%		1.8%	
Post-Election Year	1.9%		1.5%		2.4%		2.4%		2.1%	
	Best & Worst April									
	% Change		% Change		% Change		% Change		% Change	
Best	2020	11.1	2020	12.7	2020	15.4	2020	13.1	2009	15.3
Worst	1970	–6.3	1970	–9.0	2000	–15.6	2002	–5.8	2000	–6.1
	Best & Worst April Weeks									
Best	4/9/2020	12.7	4/9/2020	12.1	4/12/2001	14.0	4/9/2020	12.6	4/9/2020	18.5
Worst	4/14/2000	–7.3	4/14/2000	–10.5	4/14/2000	–25.3	4/14/2000	–11.2	4/14/2000	–16.4
	Best & Worst April Days									
Best	4/6/2020	7.7	4/6/2020	7.0	4/5/2001	8.9	4/6/2020	7.1	4/6/2020	8.2
Worst	4/14/2000	–5.7	4/14/2000	–5.8	4/14/2000	–9.7	4/14/2000	–6.0	4/14/2000	–7.3
	First Trading Day of Expiration Week: 1980-2020									
Record (#Up – #Down)	24–17		22–19		22–19		21–20		18–23	
Current Streak	D2		D2		U1		D2		D2	
Avg % Change	0.17		0.11		0.13		0.09		–0.06	
	Options Expiration Day: 1980-2020									
Record (#Up – #Down)	26–15		26–15		23–18		26–15		25–16	
Current Streak	U2		U2		U2		U2		U1	
Avg % Change	0.22		0.19		–0.03		0.19		0.26	
	Options Expiration Week: 1980-2020									
Record (#Up – #Down)	33–8		29–12		28–13		27–14		29–12	
Current Streak	U5		U1		U5		U1		D2	
Avg % Change	1.06		0.89		1.02		0.87		0.74	
	Week After Options Expiration: 1980-2020									
Record (#Up – #Down)	26–15		27–14		28–13		27–14		28–13	
Current Streak	D3		D1		D1		D1		U2	
Avg % Change	0.38		0.43		0.70		0.43		0.84	
	First Trading Day Performance									
% of Time Up	57.7		60.6		46.0		571.0		47.6	
Avg % Change	0.09		0.06		–0.20		0.03		–0.27	
	Last Trading Day Performance									
% of Time Up	49.3		53.5		60.0		52.4		59.5	
Avg % Change	0.05		0.04		0.08		–0.003		–0.09	

Dow & S&P 1950-June 19, 2020, NASDAQ 1971-June 19, 2020, Russell 1K & 2K 1979-June 19, 2020.

April "Best Month" for Dow since 1950;
Day-before-Good Friday gains are nifty.

Start Looking for Dow and S&P MACD SELL Signal on April 1 (Pages 52 & 54)
Almanac Investor Subscribers Emailed When It Triggers (See Insert)

MONDAY
D 47.6
S 52.4
N 47.6
29

Life is an illusion. You are what you think you are.
— Yale Hirsch (Creator of *Stock Trader's Almanac*, b. 1923)

TUESDAY
D 61.9
S 52.4
N 61.9
30

The heights by great men reached and kept, were not attained by sudden flight, but they, while their companions slept, were toiling upward in the night.
— Henry Wadsworth Longfellow

Last Day of March, Dow Down 19 of Last 31, Russell 2000 Up 23 of Last 31

WEDNESDAY
D 42.9
S 47.6
N 57.1
31

Executives owe it to the organization and to their fellow workers not to tolerate nonperforming individuals in important jobs.
— Peter Drucker (Austrian-born pioneer management theorist, 1909–2005)

First Trading Day in April, Dow and S&P Up 18 of Last 26
NASDAQ Up 19 of Last 20 Days Before Good Friday

THURSDAY
D 66.7
S 66.7
N 61.9
1

You don't learn to hold your own in the world by standing on guard, but by attacking and getting well hammered yourself.
— George Bernard Shaw (Irish dramatist, 1856–1950)

Good Friday *(Market Closed)*

FRIDAY
2

Friendship renders prosperity more brilliant, while it lightens adversity by sharing it and making its burden common.
— Marcus Tullius Cicero (Great Roman Orator, Politician, 106-43 B.C.)

SATURDAY
3

Easter

SUNDAY
4

DOW JONES INDUSTRIALS ONE-YEAR SEASONAL PATTERN CHARTS SINCE 1901

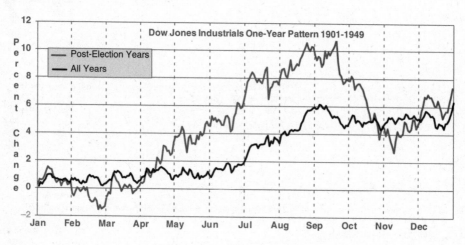

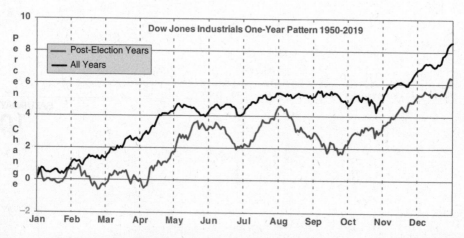

Day After Easter, Second Worst Post-Holiday (Page 98)

MONDAY
5

D 66.7
S 71.4
N 66.7

The government would not look fondly on Caesar's Palace if it opened a table for wagering on corporate failure.
It should not give greater encouragement for Goldman Sachs [et al] to do so.
— Roger Lowenstein (Financial journalist and author, *End of Wall Street, NY Times* OpEd 4/20/2010, b. 1954)

April is the Best Month for the Dow, Average 1.9% Gain Since 1950

TUESDAY
6

D 47.6
S 47.6
N 61.9

What people in the Middle East tell you in private is irrelevant.
All that matters is what they will defend in public in their language.
— Thomas L. Friedman (*NY Times* Foreign Affairs columnist, "Meet the Press" 12/17/06)

WEDNESDAY
7

D 66.7
S 66.7
N 57.1

Buy when others are despondently selling and sell when others are greedily buying.
— Mark Mobius (Fund manager Templeton Investments, on investing in foreign countries)

April is now Best Month for S&P, 2nd Best for NASDAQ (Since 1971)

THURSDAY
8

D 42.9
S 42.9
N 33.3

The worst crime against working people is a company that fails to make a profit.
— Samuel Gompers

FRIDAY
9

D 57.1
S 66.7
N 66.7

Each day is a building block to the future. Who I am today is dependent on who I was yesterday.
— Matthew McConaughey (Actor, *Parade* magazine)

SATURDAY
10

SUNDAY
11

S&P 500 ONE-YEAR SEASONAL PATTERN CHARTS SINCE 1930

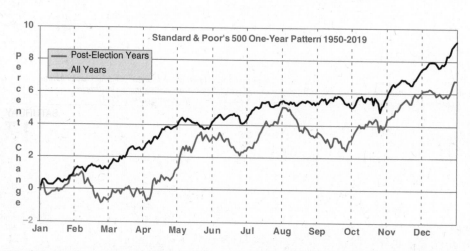

Monday Before Expiration, Dow Up 20 of Last 32, Down 9 of Last 15

MONDAY
D 57.1
S 52.4
N 47.6
12

The highest reward for a person's toil is not what they get for it, but what they become by it.
— John Ruskin (English writer)

TUESDAY
D 57.1
S 57.1
N 61.9
13

Buy when you are scared to death; sell when you are tickled to death.
— Market Maxim (*The Cabot Market Letter*, April 12, 2001)

WEDNESDAY
D 47.6
S 47.6
N 38.1
14

Technology will gradually strengthen democracies in every country and at every level.
— William H. Gates (Microsoft founder)

Income Tax Deadline
April Exhibits Strength After Tax Deadline Recent Years (Pages 38 and 134)

THURSDAY
D 71.4
S 57.1
N 47.6
15

In a bear market everyone loses. And the winner is the one who loses the least.
— Richard Russell (*Dow Theory Letters* 1924–2015)

April Expiration Day Dow Up 16 of Last 24, But Down 5 of Last 7

FRIDAY
D 61.9
S 57.1
N 47.6
16

A good general [or trader] plans in two ways: for an absolute victory and for absolute defeat. The one enables him to squeeze the last ounce of success out of a triumph; the other keeps a failure from turning into a catastrophe.
— Frederick Schiller Faust (AKA Max Brand, American author, *Way of the Lawless*, 1892–1944)

SATURDAY
17

SUNDAY
18

NASDAQ, RUSSELL 1000 & 2000 ONE-YEAR SEASONAL PATTERN CHARTS SINCE 1971

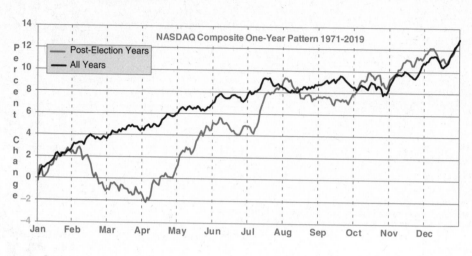

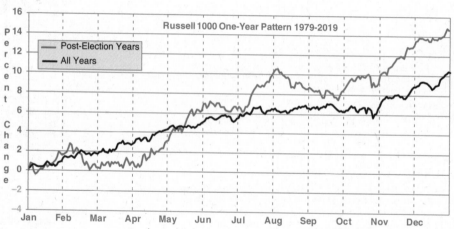

MONDAY
D 61.9
S 71.4
N 71.4
19

Over the last 25 years, computer processing capacity has risen more than a millionfold, while communication capacity has risen over a thousandfold.
— Richard Worzel (Futurist, *Facing the Future*, b. 1950)

TUESDAY
D 57.1
S 61.9
N 47.6
20

Don't delay! A good plan, violently executed now, is better than a perfect plan next week. War is a very simple thing, [like stock trading] and the determining characteristics are self-confidence, speed, and audacity.
— General George S. Patton, Jr. (U.S. Army field commander WWII, 1885–1945)

April 1999 First Month Ever to Gain 1000 Dow Points

WEDNESDAY
D 61.9
S 52.4
N 52.4
21

America, this brash and noble container of dreams, this muse to artists and inventors and entrepreneurs, this beacon of optimism, this dynamo of energy, this trumpet blare of liberty.
— Peter Jennings (Canadian-born anchor ABC World News Tonight, July 2003 after gaining U.S. citizenship in May, 1938–2005)

THURSDAY
D 61.9
S 66.7
N 61.9
22

It is the growth of total government spending as a percentage of gross national product—not the way it is financed—that crowds out the private sector.
— Paul Craig Roberts (*Business Week*, 1984)

FRIDAY
D 57.1
S 57.1
N 47.6
23

You may not have started out life in the best of circumstances. But if you can find a mission in life worth working for and believe in yourself, nothing can stop you from achieving success.
— Kemmons Wilson (Holiday Inn founder)

SATURDAY
24

May Almanac Investor Sector Seasonalities: See Pages 92, 94 and 96

SUNDAY
25

MAY ALMANAC

MAY						
S	M	T	W	T	F	S
						1
2	3	4	5	6	7	8
9	10	11	12	13	14	15
16	17	18	19	20	21	22
23	24	25	26	27	28	29
30	31					

JUNE						
S	M	T	W	T	F	S
		1	2	3	4	5
6	7	8	9	10	11	12
13	14	15	16	17	18	19
20	21	22	23	24	25	26
27	28	29	30			

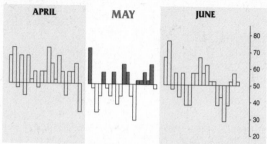

Market Probability Chart above is a graphic representation of the S&P 500 Recent Market Probability Calendar on page 124.

◆ "May/June disaster area" between 1965 and 1984 with S&P down 15 out of 20 Mays ◆ Between 1985 and 1997 May was the best month with 13 straight gains, gaining 3.3% per year on average, up 14, down 9 since ◆ Worst six months of the year begin with May (page 52) ◆ A $10,000 investment compounded to $960,943 for November–April in 70 years compared to a $1,656 gain for May–October ◆ Dow Memorial Day week record: up 12 years in a row (1984–1995), down 15 of the last 25 years ◆ Since 1950 post–presidential election year Mays #4 Dow, #3 S&P and #2 NASDAQ

May Vital Statistics

	DJIA		S&P 500		NASDAQ		Russell 1K		Russell 2K	
Rank	9		8		5		5		5	
Up	38		42		31		29		27	
Down	33		29		19		13		15	
Average % Change	−0.04%		0.2%		1.0%		0.9%		1.3%	
Post-Election Year	1.3%		1.7%		3.4%		3.0%		3.9%	
	Best & Worst May									
	% Change		% Change		% Change		% Change		% Change	
Best	1990	8.3	1990	9.2	1997	11.1	1990	8.9	1997	11.0
Worst	2010	−7.9	1962	−8.6	2000	−11.9	2010	−8.1	2019	−7.9
	Best & Worst May Weeks									
Best	05/29/1970	5.8	05/02/1997	6.2	05/17/2002	8.8	05/02/1997	6.4	05/22/2020	7.8
Worst	05/25/1962	−6.0	05/25/1962	−6.8	05/07/2010	−8.0	05/07/2010	−6.6	05/07/2010	−8.9
	Best & Worst May Days									
Best	05/27/1970	5.1	05/27/1970	5.0	05/30/2000	7.9	05/10/2010	4.4	05/18/2020	6.1
Worst	05/28/1962	−5.7	05/28/1962	−6.7	05/23/2000	−5.9	05/20/2010	−3.9	05/20/2010	−5.1
	First Trading Day of Expiration Week: 1980–2020									
Record (#Up – #Down)	25–16		27–14		23–18		26–16		20–21	
Current Streak	D2		U1		U1		U1		D3	
Avg % Change	0.11		0.12		0.11		0.09		−0.06	
	Options Expiration Day: 1980–2020									
Record (#Up – #Down)	21–20		23–18		20–21		23–18		21–20	
Current Streak	U1		U1		U1		U1		U1	
Avg % Change	−0.07		−0.07		−0.08		−0.06		0.04	
	Options Expiration Week: 1980–2020									
Record (#Up – #Down)	19–22		19–22		23–21		18–23		21–20	
Current Streak	D5		D4		D4		D4		D2	
Avg % Change	−0.05		−0.06		0.09		−0.06		−0.29	
	Week After Options Expiration: 1980–2020									
Record (#Up – #Down)	23–18		26–15		28–13		26–15		30–11	
Current Streak	U1		U1		U1		U1		U1	
Avg % Change	0.11		0.24		0.33		0.27		0.34	
	First Trading Day Performance									
% of Time Up	54.9		57.7		62.0		57.1		59.5	
Avg % Change	15.00		0.19		0.26		0.17		0.16	
	Last Trading Day Performance									
% of Time Up	56.3		59.2		64.0		51.2		59.5	
Avg % Change	0.13		0.22		0.17		0.15		0.24	

Dow & S&P 1950–June 19, 2020, NASDAQ 1971–June 19, 2020, Russell 1K & 2K 1979–June 19, 2020.

Trading in May used to be a disaster
Now it's prime time for portfolio masters

MONDAY
D 47.6
S 42.9
N 47.6
26

When someone told me "We're going with you guys because no one ever got fired for buying Cisco (products)." That's what they used to say in IBM's golden age.
— Mark Dickey (Former Cisco sales exec, then at SmartPipes, *Fortune* 5/15/00).

TUESDAY
D 61.9
S 57.1
N 42.9
27

We were fairly arrogant, until we realized the Japanese were selling quality products for what it cost us to make them.
— Paul A. Allaire (former Chairman of Xerox)

FOMC Meeting (2 Days)

WEDNESDAY
D 71.4
S 57.1
N 47.6
28

There are very few instances in history when any government has ever paid off debt.
— Walter Wriston (Retired CEO of Citicorp and Citibank)

THURSDAY
D 61.9
S 61.9
N 71.4
29

It isn't as important to buy as cheap as possible as it is to buy at the right time.
— Jesse Livermore (Early 20th century stock trader and speculator, *How to Trade in Stocks*, 1877–1940)

End of "Best Six Months" of the Year (Pages 52, 54, 62 and 147)

FRIDAY
D 28.6
S 33.3
N 42.9
30

There are two kinds of people who lose money: those who know nothing and those who know everything.
— Henry Kaufman (German-American economist, b. 1927, to Robert Lenzner in *Forbes* 10/19/98 who added, "With two Nobel Prize winners in the house, Long-Term Capital clearly fits the second case.")

SATURDAY
1

SUNDAY
2

SUMMER MARKET VOLUME DOLDRUMS DRIVE WORST SIX MONTHS

In recent years, Memorial Day weekend has become the unofficial start of summer. Not long afterward trading activity typically begins to slowly decline (barring any external event triggers) toward a later summer low. We refer to this summertime slowdown in trading as the doldrums due to the anemic volume and uninspired trading on Wall Street. The individual trader, if he is looking to sell a stock, is generally met with disinterest from The Street. It becomes difficult to sell a stock at a good price. That is also why many summer rallies tend to be short lived and are quickly followed by a pullback or correction.

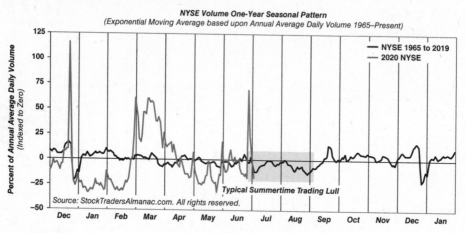

NYSE Volume One-Year Seasonal Pattern
(Exponential Moving Average based upon Annual Average Daily Volume 1965–Present)

Source: StockTradersAlmanac.com. All rights reserved.

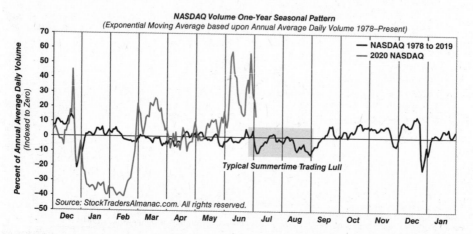

NASDAQ Volume One-Year Seasonal Pattern
(Exponential Moving Average based upon Annual Average Daily Volume 1978–Present)

Source: StockTradersAlmanac.com. All rights reserved.

Above are plotted the one-year seasonal volume patterns since 1965 for the NYSE and since 1978 for NASDAQ against the annual average daily volume moving average for 2020 as of the close on June 2, 2020. The typical summer lull is highlighted in the shaded box. A prolonged surge in volume during the typically quiet summer months, especially when accompanied by gains, can be an encouraging sign that the bull market will continue. However, should traders lose their conviction and participate in the annual summer exodus from The Street, a market pullback or correction could quickly unfold.

MAY 2021

First Trading Day in May, S&P Up 16 of Last 23

MONDAY
D 61.9
S 71.4
N 71.4
3

Today we deal with 65,000 more pieces of information each day than did our ancestors 100 years ago.
— Dr. Jean Houston (A founder of the Human Potential Movement, b. 1937)

TUESDAY
D 57.1
S 47.6
N 52.4
4

All there is to investing is picking good stocks at good times and staying with them as long as they remain good companies.
— Warren Buffett (CEO Berkshire Hathaway, investor & philanthropist, b. 1930)

WEDNESDAY
D 38.1
S 33.3
N 38.1
5

Every age has a blind eye and sees nothing wrong in practices and institutions, which its successors view with just horror.
— Sir Richard Livingstone (*On Education*, 1880–1960)

THURSDAY
D 38.1
S 42.9
N 47.6
6

In Wall Street, the man who does not change his mind will soon have no change to mind.
— William D. Gann (Trader, technical analyst, author, publisher, 1878–1955)

Friday Before Mother's Day, Dow Up 18 of Last 26

FRIDAY
D 61.9
S 57.1
N 52.4
7

The number one thing that has made us successful, by far, is obsessive, compulsive focus on the customer, as opposed to obsession over the competitor.
— Jeff Bezos (Founder & CEO Amazon, technology entrepreneur, investor & philanthropist, b. 1964)

SATURDAY
8

Mother's Day

SUNDAY
9

TOP PERFORMING MONTHS:
STANDARD & POOR'S 500 AND DOW JONES INDUSTRIALS

Monthly performance of the S&P and the Dow is ranked over the past 70 1/2 years. NASDAQ monthly performance is shown on page 58.

April, November and December still hold the top three positions in both the Dow and the S&P. March has reclaimed the fourth spot on the S&P. Disastrous Januarys in 2008, 2009 and 2016 knocked January into fifth. This, in part, led to our discovery in 1986 of the market's most consistent seasonal pattern. You can divide the year into two sections and have practically all the gains in one six-month section and very little in the other. September is the worst month on both lists. (See "Best Six Months" on page 52.)

MONTHLY % CHANGES (JANUARY 1950–MAY 2020)

Standard & Poor's 500					Dow Jones Industrials				
Month	Total % Change	Avg. % Change	# Up	# Down	Month	Total % Change	Avg. % Change	# Up	# Down
Jan	77.9%	1.1%	43	28	Jan	70.2%	1.0%	45	26
Feb	−2.5	−0.03	39	32	Feb	8.2	0.1	42	29
Mar	70.0	1.0	45	26	Mar	59.6	0.8	45	26
Apr	116.6	1.6	51	20	Apr	142.8	2.0	49	22
May	15.8	0.2	42	29	May	−2.5	−0.04	38	33
Jun	5.8	0.1	38	32	Jun	−12.9	−0.2	33	37
Jul	74.9	1.1	40	30	Jul	86.9	1.2	45	25
Aug	−4.8	−0.1	38	32	Aug	−11.4	−0.2	39	31
Sep*	−30.3	−0.4	32	37	Sep	−44.7	−0.6	29	41
Oct	57.7	0.8	42	28	Oct	42.1	0.6	42	28
Nov	110.4	1.6	48	22	Nov	113.7	1.6	48	22
Dec	103.2	1.5	52	18	Dec	105.9	1.5	49	21
%					**%**				
Rank					**Rank**				
Apr	116.6%	1.6%	51	20	Apr	142.8%	2.0%	49	22
Nov	110.4	1.6	48	22	Nov	113.7	1.6	48	22
Dec	103.2	1.5	52	18	Dec	105.9	1.5	49	21
Jan	77.9	1.1	43	28	Jul	86.9	1.2	45	25
Jul	74.9	1.1	40	30	Jan	70.2	1.0	45	26
Mar	70.0	1.0	45	26	Mar	59.6	0.8	45	26
Oct	57.7	0.8	42	28	Oct	42.1	0.6	42	28
May	15.8	0.2	42	29	Feb	8.2	0.1	42	29
Jun	5.8	0.1	38	32	May	−2.5	−0.04	38	33
Feb	−2.5	−0.03	39	32	Aug	−11.4	−0.2	39	31
Aug	−4.8	−0.1	38	32	Jun	−12.9	−0.2	33	37
Sep*	−30.3	−0.4	32	37	Sep	−44.7	−0.6	29	41
Totals	**594.7%**	**8.5%**			**Totals**	**557.9%**	**7.8%**		
Average		**0.71%**			**Average**		**0.65%**		

*No change 1979

Anticipators, shifts in cultural behavior and faster information flow have altered seasonality in recent years. Here is how the months ranked over the past 15 years (186 months) using total percentage gains on the S&P 500: April 42.7, July 29.2, November 15.3, March 12.8, September 8.0, December 7.7, October 7.0, May 1.7, February 0.3, January −0.1, June −5.5 and August −5.9.

January has declined in 10 of the last 21 years. Sizable turnarounds in "bear killing" October were a common occurrence from 1999 to 2007. Recent big Dow losses in the 21-year period were: September 2001 (9/11 attack), off 11.1%; September 2002 (Iraq war drums), off 12.4%; June 2008, off 10.2%; October 2008, off 14.1%; and February 2009, off 11.7% (financial crisis) and March 2020, off 13.7% (coronavirus pandemic shutdown).

Monday After Mother's Day, Dow Up 17 of Last 26

D 66.7
S 47.6
N 71.4

MONDAY
10

The first panacea for a mismanaged nation is inflation of the currency; the second is war. Both bring a temporary prosperity; both bring a permanent ruin. But both are the refuge of political and economic opportunists.
— Ernest Hemingway (American writer, 1954 Nobel Prize, 1899–1961)

D 42.9
S 42.9
N 47.6

TUESDAY
11

The authority of a thousand is not worth the humble reasoning of a single individual.
— Galileo Galilei (Italian physicist and astronomer, 1564–1642)

D 61.9
S 57.1
N 47.6

WEDNESDAY
12

Short-term volatility is greatest at turning points and diminishes as a trend becomes established.
— George Soros (Financier, philanthropist, political activist, author and philosopher, b. 1930)

D 38.1
S 38.1
N 42.9

THURSDAY
13

Bear markets don't act like a medicine ball rolling down a smooth hill. Instead, they behave like a basketball bouncing down a rock-strewn mountainside; there's lots of movement up and sideways before the bottom is reached.
— Daniel Turov (*Turov on Timing, Barron's* May 21, 2001, b. 1947)

D 52.4
S 42.9
N 47.6

FRIDAY
14

There have been three great inventions since the beginning of time: Fire, the wheel, and central banking.
— Will Rogers (American humorist and showman, 1879–1935)

SATURDAY
15

SUNDAY
16

"BEST SIX MONTHS": STILL AN EYE-POPPING STRATEGY

Our Best Six Months Switching Strategy consistently delivers. Investing in the Dow Jones Industrial Average between November 1 and April 30 each year and then switching into fixed income for the other six months has produced reliable returns with reduced risk since 1950.

The chart on page 147 shows November, December, January, March and April to be the top months since 1950. Add February, and an excellent strategy is born! These six consecutive months gained 20353.44 Dow points in 70 years, while the remaining May-through-October months gained 3777.95 points. The S&P gained 2283.57 points in the same best six months versus 610.79 points in the worst six.

Percentage changes are shown along with a compounding $10,000 investment. The November–April $960,943 gain overshadows May–October's $1,656 gain. (S&P results are $788,997 to $10,145.) Just four November–April losses were double-digit: April 1970 (Cambodian invasion), 1973 (OPEC oil embargo), 2008 (financial crisis) and March 2020 (coronavirus economic shutdown). Similarly, Iraq muted the Best Six and inflated the Worst Six in 2003. When we discovered this strategy in 1986, November–April outperformed May–October by $88,163 to minus $1,522. Results improved substantially these past 33 years, $872,780 to $3,178. A simple timing indicator nearly triples results (page 54).

	SIX-MONTH SWITCHING STRATEGY			
	DJIA % Change May 1–Oct 31	Investing $10,000	DJIA % Change Nov 1–Apr 30	Investing $10,000
1950	5.0%	$10,500	15.2%	$11,520
1951	1.2	10,626	−1.8	11,313
1952	4.5	11,104	2.1	11,551
1953	0.4	11,148	15.8	13,376
1954	10.3	12,296	20.9	16,172
1955	6.9	13,144	13.5	18,355
1956	−7.0	12,224	3.0	18,906
1957	−10.8	10,904	3.4	19,549
1958	19.2	12,998	14.8	22,442
1959	3.7	13,479	−6.9	20,894
1960	−3.5	13,007	16.9	24,425
1961	3.7	13,488	−5.5	23,082
1962	−11.4	11,950	21.7	28,091
1963	5.2	12,571	7.4	30,170
1964	7.7	13,539	5.6	31,860
1965	4.2	14,108	−2.8	30,968
1966	−13.6	12,189	11.1	34,405
1967	−1.9	11,957	3.7	35,678
1968	4.4	12,483	−0.2	35,607
1969	−9.9	11,247	−14.0	30,622
1970	2.7	11,551	24.6	38,155
1971	−10.9	10,292	13.7	43,382
1972	0.1	10,302	−3.6	41,820
1973	3.8	10,693	−12.5	36,593
1974	−20.5	8,501	23.4	45,156
1975	1.8	8,654	19.2	53,826
1976	−3.2	8,377	−3.9	51,727
1977	−11.7	7,397	2.3	52,917
1978	−5.4	6,998	7.9	57,097
1979	−4.6	6,676	0.2	57,211
1980	13.1	7,551	7.9	61,731
1981	−14.6	6,449	−0.5	61,422
1982	16.9	7,539	23.6	75,918
1983	−0.1	7,531	−4.4	72,578
1984	3.1	7,764	4.2	75,626
1985	9.2	8,478	29.8	98,163
1986	5.3	8,927	21.8	119,563
1987	−12.8	7,784	1.9	121,835
1988	5.7	8,228	12.6	137,186
1989	9.4	9,001	0.4	137,735
1990	−8.1	8,272	18.2	162,803
1991	6.3	8,793	9.4	178,106
1992	−4.0	8,441	6.2	189,149
1993	7.4	9,066	0.03	189,206
1994	6.2	9,628	10.6	209,262
1995	10.0	10,591	17.1	245,046
1996	8.3	11,470	16.2	284,743
1997	6.2	12,181	21.8	346,817
1998	−5.2	11,548	25.6	435,602
1999	−0.5	11,490	0.04	435,776
2000	2.2	11,743	−2.2	426,189
2001	−15.5	9,923	9.6	467,103
2002	−15.6	8,375	1.0	471,774
2003	15.6	9,682	4.3	492,060
2004	−1.9	9,498	1.6	499,933
2005	2.4	9,726	8.9	544,427
2006	6.3	10,339	8.1	588,526
2007	6.6	11,021	−8.0	541,444
2008	−27.3	8,012	−12.4	474,305
2009	18.9	9,526	13.3	537,388
2010	1.0	9,621	15.2	619,071
2011	−6.7	8,976	10.5	684,073
2012	−0.9	8,895	13.3	775,055
2013	4.8	9,322	6.7	826,984
2014	4.9	9,779	2.6	848,486
2015	−1.0	9,681	0.6	853,577
2016	2.1	$9,884	15.4	$985,223
2017	11.6	$11,031	3.4	$1,018,721
2018	3.9	$11,461	5.9	$1,078,826
2019	1.7	$11,656	−10.0	$970,943
Average/Gain	0.6%	$1,656	7.2%	$950,943
# Up/Down	43/27		55/15	

52

Monday Before May Expiration, Dow Up 24 of Last 33, Down 6 of Last 10

MONDAY
D 57.1
S 61.9
N 57.1
17

There's no trick to being a humorist when you have the whole government working for you.
— Will Rogers (American humorist and showman, 1879–1935)

TUESDAY
D 52.4
S 57.1
N 61.9
18

We always live in an uncertain world. What is certain is that the United States will go forward over time.
— Warren Buffett (CEO Berkshire Hathaway, investor & philanthropist, CNBC 9/22/2010, b. 1930)

WEDNESDAY
D 42.9
S 42.9
N 47.6
19

We may face more inflation pressure than currently shows up in formal data.
— William Poole (Economist, president Federal Reserve Bank St. Louis 1998–2008, June 2006 speech, b. 1937)

THURSDAY
D 33.3
S 28.6
N 28.6
20

Pullbacks near the 30-week moving average are often good times to take action.
— Michael L. Burke (Investors Intelligence)

May Expiration Day, Dow Up 13 of Last 20

FRIDAY
D 47.6
S 52.4
N 52.4
21

Life does not consist mainly of facts and happenings. It consists mainly of the storm of thoughts that are forever blowing through one's mind.
— Mark Twain (1835-1910, pen name of Samuel Longhorne Clemens, American novelist and satirist)

SATURDAY
22

SUNDAY
23

MACD-TIMING TRIPLES "BEST SIX MONTHS" RESULTS

Using the simple MACD (Moving Average Convergence Divergence) indicator developed by our friend Gerald Appel to better time entries and exits into and out of the Best Six Months (page 52) period nearly triples the results. Several years ago, Sy Harding (RIP) enhanced our Best Six Months Switching Strategy with MACD triggers, dubbing it the "best mechanical system ever." In 2006, we improved it even more, achieving similar results with just four trades every four years (page 60).

Our *Almanac Investor eNewsletter* (see ad insert) implements this system with quite a degree of success. Starting on the first trading day of October, we look to catch the market's first hint of an up-trend after the summer doldrums, and beginning on the first trading day of April, we prepare to exit these seasonal positions as soon as the market falters.

In up-trending markets, MACD signals get you in earlier and keep you in longer. But if the market is trending down, entries are delayed until the market turns up, and exit points can come a month earlier.

The results are astounding, applying the simple MACD signals. Instead of $10,000 gaining $960,943 over the 70 recent years when invested only during the Best Six Months (page 52), the gain nearly tripled to $2,617,071. The $1,656 gain during the Worst Six Months became a loss of $5,800.

Impressive results for being invested during only 6.3 months of the year on average! For the rest of the year consider money markets, bonds, puts, bear funds, covered calls, or credit call spreads.

Updated signals are emailed to our *Almanac Investor eNewsletter* subscribers as soon as they are triggered. Visit *www.stocktradersalmanac.com,* or see the ad insert for details and a special offer for new subscribers.

BEST SIX-MONTH SWITCHING STRATEGY+TIMING

	DJIA % Change May 1–Oct 31*	DJIA Investing $10,000	DJIA % Change Nov 1–Apr 30*	DJIA Investing $10,000
1950	7.3%	$10,730	13.3%	$11,330
1951	0.1	10,741	1.9	11,545
1952	1.4	10,891	2.1	11,787
1953	0.2	10,913	17.1	13,803
1954	13.5	12,386	16.3	16,053
1955	7.7	13,340	13.1	18,156
1956	−6.8	12,433	2.8	18,664
1957	−12.3	10,904	4.9	19,579
1958	17.3	12,790	16.7	22,849
1959	1.6	12,995	−3.1	22,141
1960	−4.9	12,358	16.9	25,883
1961	2.9	12,716	−1.5	25,495
1962	−15.3	10,770	22.4	31,206
1963	4.3	11,233	9.6	34,202
1964	6.7	11,986	6.2	36,323
1965	2.6	12,298	−2.5	35,415
1966	−16.4	10,281	14.3	40,479
1967	−2.1	10,065	5.5	42,705
1968	3.4	10,407	0.2	42,790
1969	−11.9	9,169	−6.7	39,923
1970	−1.4	9,041	20.8	48,227
1971	−11.0	8,046	15.4	55,654
1972	−0.6	7,998	−1.4	54,875
1973	−11.0	7,118	0.1	54,930
1974	−22.4	5,524	28.2	70,420
1975	0.1	5,530	18.5	83,448
1976	−3.4	5,342	−3.0	80,945
1977	−11.4	4,733	0.5	81,350
1978	−4.5	4,520	9.3	88,916
1979	−5.3	4,280	7.0	95,140
1980	9.3	4,678	4.7	99,612
1981	−14.6	3,995	0.4	100,010
1982	15.5	4,614	23.5	123,512
1983	2.5	4,729	−7.3	114,496
1984	3.3	4,885	3.9	118,961
1985	7.0	5,227	38.1	164,285
1986	−2.8	5,081	28.2	210,613
1987	−14.9	4,324	3.0	216,931
1988	6.1	4,588	11.8	242,529
1989	9.8	5,038	3.3	250,532
1990	−6.7	4,700	15.8	290,116
1991	4.8	4,926	11.3	322,899
1992	−6.2	4,621	6.6	344,210
1993	5.5	4,875	5.6	363,486
1994	3.7	5,055	13.1	411,103
1995	7.2	5,419	16.7	479,757
1996	9.2	5,918	21.9	584,824
1997	3.6	6,131	18.5	693,016
1998	−12.4	5,371	39.9	969,529
1999	−6.4	5,027	5.1	1,018,975
2000	−6.0	4,725	5.4	1,074,000
2001	−17.3	3,908	15.8	1,243,692
2002	−25.2	2,923	6.0	1,318,314
2003	16.4	3,402	7.8	1,421,142
2004	−0.9	3,371	1.8	1,446,723
2005	−0.5	3,354	7.7	1,558,121
2006	4.7	3,512	14.4	1,782,490
2007	5.6	3,709	−12.7	1,556,114
2008	−24.7	2,793	−14.0	1,338,258
2009	23.8	3,458	10.8	1,482,790
2010	4.6	3,617	7.3	1,591,034
2011	−9.4	3,277	18.7	1,888,557
2012	0.3	3,287	10.0	2,077,413
2013	4.1	3,422	7.1	2,224,909
2014	2.3	3,501	7.4	2,389,552
2015	−6.0	3,291	4.9	2,506,640
2016	3.5	3,406	13.1	2,835,010
2017	15.7	3,941	0.4	2,846,350
2018	5.0	4,138	5.2	2,994,360
2019	1.5	4,200	−12.6	2,617,071
Average	−0.7%		8.8%	
# Up	39		60	
# Down	31		10	
70-Year Gain (Loss)	($5,800)			$2,607,071

*MACD generated entry and exit points (earlier or later) can lengthen or shorten six-month periods.

54

MONDAY

D 47.6
S 52.4
N 47.6

24

The only function of economic forecasting is to make astrology look respectable.
— John Kenneth Galbraith (Canadian/American economist and diplomat, 1908–2006)

TUESDAY

D 52.4
S 57.1
N 57.1

25

Give me a stock clerk with a goal and I will give you a man who will make history.
Give me a man without a goal, and I will give you a stock clerk.
— James Cash Penney (J.C. Penney founder)

Start Looking for NASDAQ MACD Sell Signal on June 1 (Page 60)
Almanac Investor Subscribers Emailed When It Triggers (See Insert)

WEDNESDAY

D 47.6
S 52.4
N 57.1

26

In nature there are no rewards or punishments; there are consequences.
— Horace Annesley Vachell (English writer, *The Face of Clay*, 1861–1955)

THURSDAY

D 61.9
S 61.9
N 71.4

27

Being uneducated is sometimes beneficial. Then you don't know what can't be done.
— Michael Ott (Venture capitalist)

Friday Before Memorial Day Tends to Be Lackluster with Light Trading,
Dow Down 12 of Last 21, Average -0.2%

FRIDAY

D 38.1
S 47.6
N 47.6

28

Everyone times the market. Some people buy when they have money, and sell when they need money,
while others use methods that are more sophisticated.
— Marian McClellan (Co-creator of the McClellan Oscillator and Summation Index, 1934–2003)

June Almanac Investor Sector Seasonalities: See Pages 92, 94 and 96

SATURDAY

29

SUNDAY

30

JUNE ALMANAC

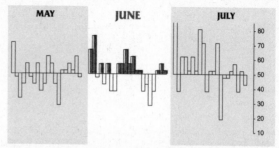

MAY JUNE JULY

Market Probability Chart above is a graphic representation of the S&P 500 Recent Market Probability Calendar on page 124.

JUNE							JULY						
S	M	T	W	T	F	S	S	M	T	W	T	F	S
				1	2	3						1	2
4	5	6	7	8	9	10	3	4	5	6	7	8	9
11	12	13	14	15	16	17	10	11	12	13	14	15	16
18	19	20	21	22	23	24	17	18	19	20	21	22	23
25	26	27	28	29	30		24	25	26	27	28	29	30
							31						

◆ The "summer rally" in most years is the weakest rally of all four seasons (page 74) ◆ Week after June Triple-Witching Day Dow down 27 of last 31 (page 106) ◆ RECENT RECORD: S&P up 12, down 9, average loss 0.5%, ranks tenth ◆ Stronger for NASDAQ, average gain 0.7% last 21 years ◆ Watch out for end-of-quarter "portfolio pumping" on last day of June, Dow down 17 of last 30, NASDAQ up 9 of last 10 ◆ Post–presidential election year Junes: #10 S&P, #11 Dow, #8 NASDAQ ◆ June ends NASDAQ's Best Eight Months

June Vital Statistics

	DJIA		S&P 500		NASDAQ		Russell 1K		Russell 2K	
Rank	11		9		6		9		8	
Up	33		38		27		25		26	
Down	37		32		22		16		15	
Average % Change	−0.2%		0.1%		0.8%		0.3%		0.8%	
Post-Election Year	−1.1%		−0.6%		0.4%		0.1%		1.2%	
	Best & Worst June									
	% Change		% Change		% Change		% Change		% Change	
Best	2019	7.2	1955	8.2	2000	16.6	2019	6.9	2000	8.6
Worst	2008	−10.2	2008	−8.6	2002	−9.4	2008	−8.5	2010	−7.9
	Best & Worst June Weeks									
Best	6/5/2020	6.8	6/2/2000	7.2	6/2/2000	19.0	6/2/2000	8.0	6/2/2000	12.2
Worst	6/30/1950	−6.8	6/30/1950	−7.6	6/15/2001	−8.4	6/12/2020	−4.2	6/12/2020	−4.9
	Best & Worst June Days									
Best	6/28/1962	3.8	6/28/1962	3.4	6/2/2000	6.4	6/10/2010	3.0	6/2/2000	4.2
Worst	6/11/2020	−6.9	6/11/2020	−5.9	6/11/2020	−5.3	6/11/2020	−5.9	6/11/2020	−7.6
	First Trading Day of Expiration Week: 1980–2020									
Record (#Up – #Down)	22–19		24–17		19–22		22–19		17–23	
Current Streak	U3		U3		U3		U3		U3	
Avg % Change	−0.02		−0.08		−0.20		−0.09		−0.24	
	Options Expiration Day: 1980–2020									
Record (#Up – #Down)	23–18		24–17		21–20		24–17		21–20	
Current Streak	D3		D3		U1		D3		D6	
Avg % Change	−0.08		0.003		−0.04		−0.02		−0.03	
	Options Expiration Week: 1980–2020									
Record (#Up – #Down)	24–17		23–18		19–22		21–20		20–21	
Current Streak	U2		U4		U3		U4		U3	
Avg % Change	0.01		0.003		−0.11		−0.05		−0.15	
	Week After Options Expiration: 1980–2020									
Record (#Up – #Down)	12–28		18–22		22–18		18–22		21–19	
Current Streak	D2		D2		D2		D2		U3	
Avg % Change	−0.50		−0.21		0.11		−0.18		−0.06	
	First Trading Day Performance									
% of Time Up	57.7		54.9		60.0		61.9		66.7	
Avg % Change	0.16		0.13		0.13		0.10		0.20	
	Last Trading Day Performance									
% of Time Up	55.7		52.9		69.4		56.1		65.9	
Avg % Change	0.06		0.11		0.33		0.07		0.42	

Dow & S&P 1950-June 19, 2020, NASDAQ 1971-June 19, 2020, Russell 1K & 2K 1979-June 19, 2020.

Last Day of June not hot for the Dow;
Down 17 of 30, WOW!

Memorial Day *(Market Closed)*

The test of success is not what you do when you are on top. Success is how high you bounce when you hit bottom.
— General George S. Patton, Jr. (U.S. Army field commander WWII, 1885–1945)

First Trading Day in June, Dow Up 26 of Last 33, Down 4 of 5 2008–2012
Day After Memorial Day, Dow Up 22 of Last 35, But Down 5 of Last 6

TUESDAY

D 76.2
S 66.7
N 57.1

1

In Washington people tell the truth off the record and lie on the record.
In the Middle East they lie off the record and tell the truth on the record.
— Thomas L. Friedman (*NY Times* Foreign Affairs columnist, "Meet the Press" 12/17/06)

WEDNESDAY

D 57.1
S 76.2
N 71.4

2

The most valuable executive is one who is training somebody to be a better man than he is.
— Robert G. Ingersoll (American lawyer, politician and orator, "The Great Agnostic," 1833–1899)

Memorial Day Week Dow Down 15 of Last 25, Up 12 Straight 1984–1995

THURSDAY

D 47.6
S 47.6
N 52.4

3

The thing you do obsessively between age 13 and 18 that's the thing you have the most chance of being world class at.
— William H. Gates (Microsoft founder, "Charlie Rose" interview 2/22/2016, b. 1955)

FRIDAY

D 57.1
S 57.1
N 57.1

4

There's nothing wrong with cash. It gives you time to think.
— Robert Prechter, Jr. (*Elliott Wave Theorist*)

SATURDAY

5

SUNDAY

6

TOP PERFORMING NASDAQ MONTHS

NASDAQ stocks continue to run away during three consecutive months, November, December and January, with an average gain of 6.1% despite the slaughter of November 2000, −22.9%, December 2000, −4.9%, December 2002, −9.7%, November 2007, −6.9%, January 2008, −9.9%, November 2008, −10.8%, January 2009, −6.4%, January 2010, −5.4%, January 2016, −7.9%, and December 2018, −9.5%. Solid gains in November and December 2004 offset January 2005's 5.2% Iraq turmoil–fueled drop.

You can see the months graphically on page 148. January by itself is impressive, up 2.8% on average. April, May and June also shine, creating our NASDAQ Best Eight Months strategy. What appears as a Death Valley abyss occurs during NASDAQ's leanest months: July, August and September. NASDAQ's Best Eight Months seasonal strategy using MACD timing is displayed on page 60.

MONTHLY % CHANGES (JANUARY 1971–MAY 2020)

NASDAQ Composite*						Dow Jones Industrials			
Month	Total % Change	Avg. % Change	# Up	# Down		Month	Total % Change	Avg. % Change	# Up	# Down
Jan	139.0%	2.8%	33	17		Jan	60.5%	1.2%	31	19
Feb	29.5	0.6	27	23		Feb	13.8	0.3	30	20
Mar	32.3	0.6	31	19		Mar	38.4	0.8	32	18
Apr	84.3	1.7	33	17		Apr	111.8	2.2	34	16
May	50.1	1.0	31	19		May	10.9	0.2	28	22
Jun	38.5	0.8	27	22		Jun	4.3	0.1	25	24
Jul	23.8	0.5	27	22		Jul	43.4	0.9	29	20
Aug	9.8	0.2	27	22		Aug	−14.1	−0.3	27	22
Sep	−23.6	−0.5	27	22		Sep	−40.8	−0.8	19	30
Oct	32.5	0.7	27	22		Oct	30.7	0.6	30	19
Nov	81.5	1.7	34	15		Nov	69.7	1.4	34	15
Dec	79.2	1.6	29	20		Dec	69.6	1.4	34	15
% Rank						**% Rank**				
Jan	139.0%	2.8%	33	17		Apr	111.8%	2.2%	34	16
Apr	84.3	1.7	33	17		Nov	69.7	1.4	34	15
Nov	81.5	1.7	34	15		Dec	69.6	1.4	34	15
Dec	79.2	1.6	29	20		Jan	60.5	1.2	31	19
May	50.1	1.0	31	19		Jul	43.4	0.9	29	20
Jun	38.5	0.8	27	22		Mar	38.4	0.8	32	18
Oct	32.5	0.7	27	22		Oct	30.7	0.6	30	19
Mar	32.3	0.6	31	19		Feb	13.8	0.3	30	20
Feb	29.5	0.6	27	23		May	10.9	0.2	28	22
Jul	23.8	0.5	27	22		Jun	4.3	0.1	25	24
Aug	9.8	0.2	27	22		Aug	−14.1	−0.3	27	22
Sep	−23.6	−0.5	27	22		Sep	−40.8	−0.8	19	30
Totals	**576.9%**	**11.7%**				**Totals**	**398.2%**	**8.0%**		
Average		**0.98%**				**Average**		**0.67%**		

Based on NASDAQ composite, prior to Feb. 5, 1971 based on National Quotation Bureau indices.

For comparison, Dow figures are shown. During this period, NASDAQ averaged a 0.98% gain per month, 46.3% more than the Dow's 0.67% per month. Between January 1971 and January 1982, NASDAQ's composite index doubled in 12 years, while the Dow stayed flat. But while NASDAQ plummeted 77.9% from its 2000 highs to the 2002 bottom, the Dow only lost 37.8%. The Great Recession and bear market of 2007–2009 spread its carnage equally across the Dow and NASDAQ. Recent market moves are increasingly more correlated, but NASDAQ still has an advantage.

MONDAY
D 66.7
S 42.9
N 42.9
7

The incestuous relationship between government and big business thrives in the dark.
— Jack Anderson (Washington journalist and author, *Peace, War and Politics*, 1922–2005)

June Ends NASDAQ's "Best Eight Months" (Pages 58, 60 and 148)

TUESDAY
D 61.9
S 57.1
N 42.9
8

Never attribute to malevolence what is merely due to incompetence.
— Arthur C. Clarke (British sci-fi writer, *3001: The Final Odyssey*, 1917–2008)

WEDNESDAY
D 38.1
S 38.1
N 38.1
9

Big Business breeds bureaucracy and bureaucrats exactly as big government does.
— T.K. Quinn

2008 Second Worst June Ever, Dow -10.2%, S&P -8.6%,
Only 1930 Was Worse, NASDAQ June 2008 -9.1%, June 2002 -9.4%

THURSDAY
D 38.1
S 38.1
N 33.3
10

The two most abundant elements in the universe are hydrogen and stupidity.
— Harlan Ellison (Science fiction writer, b. 1934)

FRIDAY
D 57.1
S 57.1
N 52.4
11

The job of central banks: To take away the punch bowl just as the party is getting going.
— William McChesney Martin (Federal Reserve Chairman 1951–1970, 1906–1998)

SATURDAY
12

SUNDAY
13

GET MORE OUT OF NASDAQ'S "BEST EIGHT MONTHS" WITH MACD TIMING

NASDAQ's amazing eight-month run from November through June is hard to miss on pages 58 and 148. A $10,000 investment in these eight months since 1971 gained $746,487 versus a loss of $336 during the void that is the four-month period July–October (as of July 2, 2020).

Using the same MACD timing indicators on the NASDAQ as is done for the Dow (page 54) has enabled us to capture much of October's improved performance, pumping up NASDAQ's results considerably. Over the 49 years since NASDAQ began, the gain on the same $10,000 more than doubles to $2,431,987 and the loss during the four-month void increases to $6,459. Only four sizable losses occurred during the favorable period, and the bulk of NASDAQ's bear markets were avoided, including the worst of the 2000–2002 bear.

Updated signals are emailed to our monthly newsletter subscribers as soon as they are triggered. Visit *www.stocktradersalmanac.com*, or see the ad insert for details and a special offer for new subscribers.

BEST EIGHT MONTHS STRATEGY + TIMING

MACD Signal Date	Worst 4 Months July 1–Oct 31* NASDAQ	% Change	Investing $10,000	MACD Signal Date	Best 8 Months Nov 1–June 30* NASDAQ	% Change	Investing $10,000
22-Jul-71	109.54	−3.6	$9,640	4-Nov-71	105.56	24.1	$12,410
7-Jun-72	131.00	−1.8	9,466	23-Oct-72	128.66	−22.7	9,593
25-Jun-73	99.43	−7.2	8,784	7-Dec-73	92.32	−20.2	7,655
3-Jul-74	73.66	−23.2	6,746	7-Oct-74	56.57	47.8	11,314
11-Jun-75	83.60	−9.2	6,125	7-Oct-75	75.88	20.8	13,667
22-Jul-76	91.66	−2.4	5,978	19-Oct-76	89.45	13.2	15,471
27-Jun-77	101.25	−4.0	5,739	4-Nov-77	97.21	26.6	19,586
7-Jun-78	123.10	−6.5	5,366	6-Nov-78	115.08	19.1	23,327
3-Jul-79	137.03	−1.1	5,307	30-Oct-79	135.48	15.5	26,943
20-Jun-80	156.51	26.2	6,697	9-Oct-80	197.53	11.2	29,961
4-Jun-81	219.68	−17.6	5,518	1-Oct-81	181.09	−4.0	28,763
7-Jun-82	173.84	12.5	6,208	7-Oct-82	195.59	57.4	45,273
1-Jun-83	307.95	−10.7	5,544	3-Nov-83	274.86	−14.2	38,844
1-Jun-84	235.90	5.0	5,821	15-Oct-84	247.67	17.3	45,564
3-Jun-85	290.59	−3.0	5,646	1-Oct-85	281.77	39.4	63,516
10-Jun-86	392.83	−10.3	5,064	1-Oct-86	352.34	20.5	76,537
30-Jun-87	424.67	−22.7	3,914	2-Nov-87	328.33	20.1	91,921
8-Jul-88	394.33	−6.6	3,656	29-Nov-88	368.15	22.4	112,511
13-Jun-89	450.73	0.7	3,682	9-Nov-89	454.07	1.9	114,649
11-Jun-90	462.79	−23.0	2,835	2-Oct-90	356.39	39.3	159,706
11-Jun-91	496.62	6.4	3,016	1-Oct-91	528.51	7.4	171,524
11-Jun-92	567.68	1.5	3,061	14-Oct-92	576.22	20.5	206,686
7-Jun-93	694.61	9.9	3,364	1-Oct-93	763.23	−4.4	197,592
17-Jun-94	729.35	5.0	3,532	11-Oct-94	765.57	13.5	224,267
1-Jun-95	868.82	17.2	4,140	13-Oct-95	1018.38	21.6	272,709
3-Jun-96	1238.73	1.0	4,181	7-Oct-96	1250.87	10.3	300,798
4-Jun-97	1379.67	24.4	5,201	3-Oct-97	1715.87	1.8	306,212
1-Jun-98	1746.82	−7.8	4,795	15-Oct-98	1611.01	49.7	458,399
1-Jun-99	2412.03	18.5	5,682	6-Oct-99	2857.21	35.7	622,047
29-Jun-00	3877.23	−18.2	4,648	18-Oct-00	3171.56	−32.2	421,748
1-Jun-01	2149.44	−31.1	3,202	1-Oct-01	1480.46	5.5	444,944
3-Jun-02	1562.56	−24.0	2,434	2-Oct-02	1187.30	38.5	616,247
20-Jun-03	1644.72	15.1	2,802	6-Oct-03	1893.46	4.3	642,746
21-Jun-04	1974.38	−1.6	2,757	1-Oct-04	1942.20	6.1	681,954
8-Jun-05	2060.18	1.5	2,798	19-Oct-05	2091.76	6.1	723,553
1-Jun-06	2219.86	3.9	2,907	5-Oct-06	2306.34	9.5	792,291
7-Jun-07	2541.38	7.9	3,137	1-Oct-07	2740.99	−9.1	724,796
2-Jun-08	2491.53	−31.3	2,155	17-Oct-08	1711.29	6.1	769,009
15-Jun-09	1816.38	17.8	2,539	9-Oct-09	2139.28	1.6	781,313
7-Jun-10	2173.90	18.6	3,011	4-Nov-10	2577.34	7.4	839,130
1-Jun-11	2769.19	−10.5	2,695	7-Oct-11	2479.35	10.8	929,756
1-Jun-12	2747.48	9.6	2,954	6-Nov-12	3011.93	16.2	1,080,376
4-Jun-13	3445.26	10.1	3,252	15-Oct-13	3794.01	15.4	1,227,442
26-Jun-14	4379.05	0.9	3,281	21-Oct-14	4419.48	14.5	1,405,421
4-Jun-15	5059.12	−5.5	3,101	5-Oct-15	4781.26	1.4	1,425,097
13-Jun-16	4848.44	9.5	3,396	24-Oct-16	5309.83	18.8	1,693,015
9-Jun-17	6207.92	11.3	3,780	28-Nov-17	6912.36	11.6	1,859,187
21-Jun-18	7712.95	−5.3	3,580	31-Oct-18	7305.90	7.9	2,006,063
19-Jul-19	8146.49	−1.1	3,541	11-Oct-19	8057.04	17.8	2,441,987
11-Jun-20	9492.73						
	49-Year Loss		**($6,459)**		**49-Year Gain**		**$2,431,987**

* *MACD-generated entry and exit points (earlier or later) can lengthen or shorten eight-month periods.*

Monday of Triple-Witching Week, Dow Down 13 of Last 24

MONDAY
D 57.1
S 57.1
N 52.4
14

If buying equities seem the most hazardous and foolish thing you could possibly do,
then you are near the bottom that will end the bear market.
— Joseph E. Granville

TUESDAY
D 57.1
S 66.7
N 66.7
15

If investing is entertaining, if you're having fun, you're probably not making any money. Good investing is boring.
— George Soros (Financier, philanthropist, political activist, author and philosopher, b. 1930)

FOMC Meeting (2 Days)

WEDNESDAY
D 61.9
S 57.1
N 57.1
16

A weakened White House creates uncertainty on Wall Street.
— Robert D. Hormats (Under Secretary of State for Economic Growth, Energy, and the Environment
2009-2013, Goldman Sachs 1982-2009, CNN 10/28/2005, b.1943)

Triple Witching Week Often Up in Bull Markets, Down in Bears (Page 106)

THURSDAY
D 57.1
S 61.9
N 66.7
17

Don't fritter away your time. Create, act, take a place wherever you are and be somebody.
— Theodore Roosevelt (26th U.S. President, 1858–1919)

June Triple-Witching Day, Dow Up 10 of Last 18, But Down 5 of Last 6

FRIDAY
D 52.4
S 52.4
N 52.4
18

I keep hearing "Should I buy? Should I buy?" When I start hearing "Should I sell?" that's the bottom.
— Nick Moore (portfolio manager, Jurika & Voyles, *TheStreet.com* Mar. 12, 2001)

SATURDAY
19

Father's Day

SUNDAY
20

TRIPLE RETURNS, FEWER TRADES: BEST 6 + 4–YEAR CYCLE

We first introduced this strategy to *Almanac Investor* newsletter subscribers in October 2006. Recurring seasonal stock market patterns and the four-year Presidential Election/ Stock Market Cycle (page 130) have been integral to our research since the first Almanac more than 50 years ago. Yale Hirsch discovered the Best Six Months in 1986 (page 52), and it has been a cornerstone of our seasonal investment analysis and strategies ever since.

Most of the market's gains have occurred during the Best Six Months, and the market generally hits a low point every four years in the first (post-election) or second (midterm) year and exhibits the greatest gains in the third (pre-election) year. This strategy combines the best of these two market phenomena, the Best Six Months and the 4-Year Cycle, timing entries and exits with MACD (pages 54 and 60).

We've gone back to 1949 to include the full four-year cycle that began with post-election year 1949. Only four trades every four years are needed to nearly triple the results of the Best Six Months. Buy and sell during the post-election and midterm years and then hold from the midterm MACD seasonal buy signal sometime after October 1 until the post-election MACD seasonal sell signal sometime after April 1, approximately 2.5 years: solid returns, less effort, lower transaction fees and fewer taxable events.

FOUR TRADES EVERY FOUR YEARS		
	Worst Six Months	Best Six Months
Year	May–Oct	Nov–April
Post-election	Sell	Buy
Midterm	Sell	Buy
Pre-election	Hold	Hold
Election	Hold	Hold

BEST SIX MONTHS+TIMING+4-YEAR CYCLE STRATEGY

Year	DJIA % Change May 1–Oct 31*	Investing $10,000	DJIA % Change Nov 1–Apr 30*	Investing $10,000
1949	3.0%	$10,300	17.5%	$11,750
1950	7.3	11,052	19.7	14,065
1951		11,052		14,065
1952		11,052		14,065
1953	0.2	11,074	17.1	16,470
1954	13.5	12,569	35.7	22,350
1955		12,569		22,350
1956		12,569		22,350
1957	−12.3	11,023	4.9	23,445
1958	17.3	12,930	27.8	29,963
1959		12,930		29,963
1960		12,930		29,963
1961	2.9	13,305	−1.5	29,514
1962	−15.3	11,269	58.5	46,780
1963		11,269		46,780
1964		11,269		46,780
1965	2.6	11,562	−2.5	45,611
1966	−16.4	9,666	22.2	55,737
1967		9,666		55,737
1968		9,666		55,737
1969	−11.9	8,516	−6.7	52,003
1970	−1.4	8,397	21.5	63,184
1971		8,397		63,184
1972		8,397		63,184
1973	−11.0	7,473	0.1	63,247
1974	−22.4	5,799	42.5	90,127
1975		5,799		90,127
1976		5,799		90,127
1977	−11.4	5,138	0.5	90,578
1978	−4.5	4,907	26.8	114,853
1979		4,907		114,853
1980		4,907		114,853
1981	−14.6	4,191	0.4	115,312
1982	15.5	4,841	25.9	145,178
1983		4,841		145,178
1984		4,841		145,178
1985	7.0	5,180	38.1	200,491
1986	−2.8	5,035	33.2	267,054
1987		5,035		267,054
1988		5,035		267,054
1989	9.8	5,528	3.3	275,867
1990	−6.7	5,158	35.1	372,696
1991		5,158		372,696
1992		5,158		372,696
1993	5.5	5,442	5.6	393,455
1994	3.7	5,643	88.2	740,482
1995		5,643		740,482
1996		5,643		740,482
1997	3.6	5,846	18.5	877,471
1998	−12.4	5,121	36.3	1,195,993
1999		5,121		1,195,993
2000		5,121		1,195,993
2001	−17.3	4,235	15.8	1,384,960
2002	−25.2	3,168	34.2	1,858,616
2003		3,168		1,858,616
2004		3,168		1,858,616
2005	−0.5	3,152	7.7	2,001,729
2006	4.7	3,300	−31.7	1,367,181
2007		3,300		1,367,181
2008		3,300		1,367,181
2009	23.8	4,085	10.8	1,514,738
2010	4.6	4,273	27.4	1,929,777
2011		4,273		1,929,777
2012		4,273		1,929,777
2013	4.1	4,448	7.1	2,066,791
2014	2.3	4,550	24.0	2,562,820
2015		4,550		2,562,820
2016		4,550		2,562,820
2017*	15.7	$5,265	0.4	$2,573,072
2018*	5.0	$5,528	2.8	$2,645,118
Average	−0.5%		9.4%	
# Up	20		32	
# Down	16		4	
71-Year Gain (Loss)	($4,472)			$2,635,118

* MACD and 2.5-year hold lengthen and shorten six-month periods.
* As of July 2, 2020, close.

MONDAY

D 38.1
S 52.4
N 61.9

21

Analysts are supposed to be critics of corporations. They often end up being public relations spokesmen for them.
— Ralph Wanger (Chief Investment Officer, Acorn Fund)

TUESDAY

D 33.3
S 38.1
N 38.1

22

Throughout the centuries there were men who took first steps down new roads armed with nothing but their own vision.
— Ayn Rand (Russian-born American novelist and philosopher, *The Fountainhead*, 1957, 1905–1982)

*Week After June Triple Witching, Dow Down 27 of Last 31
Average Loss Since 1990, 1.1%*

WEDNESDAY

D 38.1
S 42.9
N 38.1

23

*To succeed in the markets, it is essential to make your own decisions.
Numerous traders cited listening to others as their worst blunder.*
— Jack D. Schwager (Investment manager, author, *Stock Market Wizards: Interviews with America's
Top Stock Traders*, b. 1948)

THURSDAY

D 28.6
S 28.6
N 23.8

24

Market risk tends to be poorly rewarded when market valuations are rich and interest rates are rising.
— John P. Hussman, Ph.D. (Hussman Funds, 5/22/06)

FRIDAY

D 38.1
S 38.1
N 47.6

25

Regulatory agencies within five years become controlled by industries they were set up to regulate.
— Gabriel Kolko (American historian and author, 1932-2014)

SATURDAY

26

July Almanac Investor Sector Seasonalities: See Pages 92, 94 and 96

SUNDAY

27

JULY ALMANAC

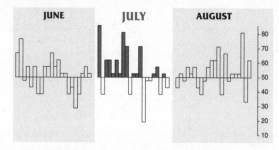

JULY								AUGUST						
S	M	T	W	T	F	S		S	M	T	W	T	F	S
					1	2	3			1	2	3	4	5	6	7
4	5	6	7	8	9	10		8	9	10	11	12	13	14
11	12	13	14	15	16	17		15	16	17	18	19	20	21
18	19	20	21	22	23	24		22	23	24	25	26	27	28
25	26	27	28	29	30	31		29	30	31				

Market Probability Chart above is a graphic representation of the S&P 500 Recent Market Probability Calendar on page 124.

◆ July is the best month of the third quarter (page 66) ◆ Start of 2nd half brings an inflow of retirement funds ◆ First trading day Dow up 26 of last 32 ◆ Graph above shows strength in the first half of July ◆ Huge gain in July usually provides better buying opportunity over next 4 months ◆ Start of NASDAQ's worst four months of the year (page 58) ◆ Post–presidential election Julys are ranked #1 Dow (up 14, down 3), #1 S&P (up 11, down 6), and #1 NASDAQ (up 10, down 2)

July Vital Statistics

	DJIA		S&P 500		NASDAQ		Russell 1K		Russell 2K	
Rank	4		5		10		7		10	
Up	45		40		27		21		21	
Down	25		30		22		20		20	
Average % Change	1.2%		1.1%		0.5%		0.8%		−0.2%	
Post-Election Year	2.2%		2.1%		3.4%		3.2%		2.8%	
Best & Worst July										
	% Change		% Change		% Change		% Change		% Change	
Best	1989	9.0	1989	8.8	1997	10.5	1989	8.2	1980	11.0
Worst	1969	−6.6	2002	−7.9	2002	−9.2	2002	−7.5	2002	−15.2
Best & Worst July Weeks										
Best	7/17/2009	7.3	7/17/2009	7.0	7/17/2009	7.4	7/17/2009	7.0	7/17/2009	8.0
Worst	7/19/2002	−7.7	7/19/2002	−8.0	7/28/2000	−10.5	7/19/2002	−7.4	7/2/2010	−7.2
Best & Worst July Days										
Best	7/24/2002	6.4	7/24/2002	5.7	7/29/2002	5.8	7/24/2002	5.6	7/29/2002	4.9
Worst	7/19/2002	−4.6	7/19/2002	−3.8	7/28/2000	−4.7	7/19/2002	−3.6	7/23/2002	−4.1
First Trading Day of Expiration Week: 1980–2020										
Record (#Up – #Down)	25–15		25–15		27–13		25–15		22–18	
Current Streak	U2		U1		U1		U1		D2	
Avg % Change	0.13		0.05		0.07		0.03		−0.04	
Options Expiration Day: 1980–2020										
Record (#Up – #Down)	17–21		19–21		16–24		19–21		15–25	
Current Streak	D3		D4		D4		D4		D3	
Avg % Change	−0.23		−0.27		−0.40		−0.29		−0.44	
Options Expiration Week: 1980–2020										
Record (#Up – #Down)	25–15		23–17		21–19		23–17		22–18	
Current Streak	D1		D1		D2		D1		D1	
Avg % Change	0.44		0.16		0.12		0.11		−0.06	
Week After Options Expiration: 1980–2020										
Record (#Up – #Down)	22–18		20–20		18–22		21–19		15–25	
Current Streak	U4		U2		U1		U2		U1	
Avg % Change	0.02		−0.10		−0.36		−0.12		−0.36	
First Trading Day Performance										
% of Time Up	67.1		72.9		63.3		75.6		68.3	
Avg % Change	0.27		0.27		0.15		0.32		0.14	
Last Trading Day Performance										
% of Time Up	50.0		60.0		49.0		56.1		63.4	
Avg % Change	0.01		0.05		−0.05		−0.04		−0.01	

Dow & S&P 1950–June 19, 2020, NASDAQ 1971–June 19, 2020, Russell 1K & 2K 1979–June 19, 2020.

When Dow and S&P in July are inferior, NASDAQ days tend to be even drearier.

Those who study market history are bound to profit from it!

"I'm a mechanical engineer, and an investment advisor, and been in this business for over 30 years, throughout the years I subscribed to the most expensive newsletters in the country, and never made (a) profit because of the momentum stocks they all recommend, and most of their recommendations made (a) round trip no exception. In 8 weeks I followed your recommendations regarding the seasonality trends (and) I made over $135,000.00." – Sam C. from Mississippi

ACT NOW! Visit www.STOCKTRADERSALMANAC.com
CALL 845-875-9582. <u>TWO WAYS TO SAVE:</u>

▶ **1-Year @ $150 – 48% Off** vs. Monthly – Use promo code **1YRSTA21**

▶ **2-Years @ $250 – BEST DEAL,** 57% Off – Use promo code **2YRSTA21**

Now you can find out which seasonal trends are on schedule and which are not, and how to take advantage of them. You will be kept abreast of upcoming market-moving events and what our indicators are saying about the next major market move. Every week you will receive timely dispatches about bullish and bearish seasonal patterns.

Our digital subscription service, *Almanac Investor*, provides all this plus unusual investing opportunities – exciting small-, mid- and large-cap stocks; seasoned, under-valued equities; timely sector ETF trades and more. Our **Data-Rich and Data-Driven Market Cycle Analysis** is the only investment tool of its kind that helps traders and investors forecast market trends with accuracy and confidence.

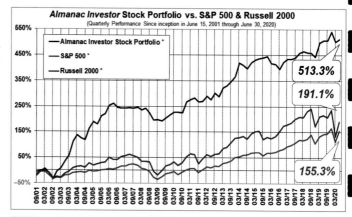

Almanac Investor Stock Portfolio vs. S&P 500 & Russell 2000
(Quarterly Performance Since inception in June 15, 2001 through June 30, 2020)
— Almanac Investor Stock Portfolio *
— S&P 500 *
— Russell 2000 *
513.3%
191.1%
155.3%

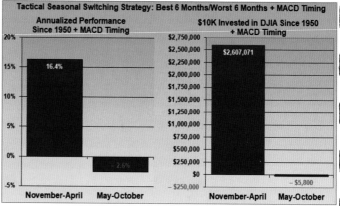

Tactical Seasonal Switching Strategy: Best 6 Months/Worst 6 Months + MACD Timing
Annualized Performance Since 1950 + MACD Timing — November-April 16.4%, May-October −2.6%
$10K Invested in DJIA Since 1950 + MACD Timing — November-April $2,607,071, May-October −$5,800

JUNE/JULY 2021

MONDAY
D 57.1
S 52.4
N 71.4
28

If the models are telling you to sell, sell, sell, but only buyers are out there, don't be a jerk. Buy!
— William Silber, Ph.D. (New York University, *Newsweek*, 1986)

TUESDAY
D 52.4
S 57.1
N 61.9
29

The punishment of wise men who refuse to take part in the affairs of government is to live under the government of unwise men.
— Plato (Greek philosopher, 427-347 BC)

Last Day of Q2 Bearish for Dow, Down 17 of Last 30, But Up 8 of Last 10, Bullish for NASDAQ, Up 21 of 29

WEDNESDAY
D 52.4
S 52.4
N 61.9
30

It's no coincidence that three of the top five stock option traders in a recent trading contest were all former Marines.
— Robert Prechter, Jr. (*Elliott Wave Theorist*)

First Trading Day in July, S&P Up 28 of Last 32, Average Gain 0.5%

THURSDAY
D 81.0
S 85.7
N 76.2
1

Your emotions are often a reverse indicator of what you ought to be doing.
— John F. Hindelong (Dillon, Reed)

July Begins NASDAQ's "Worst Four Months" (Pages 58, 60 and 148)

FRIDAY
D 33.3
S 38.1
N 38.1
2

Between two evils, I always pick the one I never tried before.
— Mae West (American actress and playwright, 1893-1980)

SATURDAY
3

Independent Day

Independence Day

SUNDAY
4

FIRST MONTH OF QUARTERS IS THE MOST BULLISH

We have observed over the years that the investment calendar reflects the annual, semiannual and quarterly operations of institutions during January, April and July. The opening month of the first three quarters produces the greatest gains in the Dow Jones Industrials, the S&P 500 and NASDAQ.

The fourth quarter had behaved quite differently, since it is affected by year-end portfolio adjustments and presidential and congressional elections in even-numbered years. Since 1991, major turnarounds have helped October join the ranks of bullish first months of quarters. October transformed into a bear-killing-turnaround month, posting Dow gains in 16 of the last 22 years; 2008 was a significant exception. (See pages 152–163.)

After experiencing the most powerful bull market of all time during the 1990s, followed by two ferocious bear markets early in the millennium, we divided the monthly average percentage changes into two groups: before 1991 and after. Comparing the month-by-month quarterly behavior of the three major U.S. averages in the table, you'll see that first months of the first three quarters perform best overall. Nasty sell-offs in April 2000, 2002, 2004 and 2005, and July 2000–2002 and 2004 hit the NASDAQ hardest. The bear market of October 2007–March 2009, which cut the markets more than in half, took a toll on every first month except April. October 2008 was the worst month in a decade. January was also a difficult month in seven of the last thirteen years, pulling its performance lower. (See pages 152–163.)

Between 1950 and 1990, the S&P 500 gained 1.3% (Dow, 1.4%) on average in first months of the first three quarters. Second months barely eked out any gain, while third months, thanks to March, moved up 0.23% (Dow, 0.07%) on average. NASDAQ's first month of the first three quarters averages 1.67% from 1971 to 1990, with July being a negative drag.

DOW JONES INDUSTRIALS, S&P 500 AND NASDAQ
AVERAGE MONTHLY % CHANGES BY QUARTER

	DJIA 1950–1990			S&P 500 1950–1990			NASDAQ 1971–1990		
	1st Mo	2nd Mo	3rd Mo	1st Mo	2nd Mo	3rd Mo	1st Mo	2nd Mo	3rd Mo
1Q	1.5%	−0.01%	1.0%	1.5%	−0.1%	1.1%	3.8%	1.2%	0.9%
2Q	1.6	−0.4	0.1	1.3	−0.1	0.3	1.7	0.8	1.1
3Q	1.1	0.3	−0.9	1.1	0.3	−0.7	−0.5	0.1	−1.6
Tot	**4.2%**	**−0.1%**	**0.2%**	**3.9%**	**0.1%**	**0.7%**	**5.0%**	**2.1%**	**0.4%**
Avg	**1.40%**	**−0.04%**	**0.07%**	**1.30%**	**0.03%**	**0.23%**	**1.67%**	**0.70%**	**0.13%**
4Q	−0.1%	1.4%	1.7%	0.4%	1.7%	1.6%	−1.4%	1.6%	1.4%

	DJIA 1991–June 2020			S&P 500 1991–June 2020			NASDAQ 1991–June 2020		
1Q	0.3%	0.3%	0.6%	0.6%	0.03%	0.8%	2.1%	0.2%	0.5%
2Q	2.5	0.5	−0.5	2.1	0.7	−0.1	1.7	1.1	0.8
3Q	1.4	−0.8	−0.3	1.0	−0.5	−0.1	1.2	0.3	0.3
Tot	**4.2%**	**−0.01%**	**−0.2%**	**3.7%**	**0.2%**	**0.6%**	**5.0%**	**1.6%**	**1.6%**
Avg	**1.40%**	**−0.003%**	**−0.07%**	**1.23%**	**0.07%**	**0.20%**	**1.67%**	**0.52%**	**0.53%**
4Q	1.6%	1.9%	1.3%	1.5%	1.5%	1.3%	2.1%	1.7%	1.7%

	DJIA 1950–June 2020			S&P 500 1950–June 2020			NASDAQ 1971–June 2020		
1Q	1.0%	0.1%	0.8%	1.1%	−0.03%	1.0%	2.8%	0.6%	0.6%
2Q	2.0	−0.04	−0.2	1.6	0.2	0.1	1.7	1.0	0.9
3Q	1.2	−0.2	−0.6	1.1	−0.07	−0.4	0.5	0.2	−0.5
Tot	**4.2%**	**−0.1%**	**0.0%**	**3.8%**	**0.1%**	**0.7%**	**5.0%**	**1.8%**	**1.0%**
Avg	**1.40%**	**−0.05%**	**0.00%**	**1.27%**	**0.03%**	**0.24%**	**1.66%**	**0.60%**	**0.33%**
4Q	0.6%	1.6%	1.5%	0.8%	1.6%	1.5%	0.7%	1.7%	1.6%

(Market Closed – Independence Day Observed)

MONDAY

5

Nothing gives one person so much advantage over another as to remain always cool and unruffled under all circumstances.
— Thomas Jefferson (3rd U.S. President, 1743-7/4/1826)

Market Subject to Elevated Volatility After July 4th

TUESDAY

6

D 52.4
S 61.9
N 57.1

If you don't profit from your investment mistakes, someone else will.
— Yale Hirsch (Creator of *Stock Trader's Almanac*, b. 1923)

WEDNESDAY

7

D 61.9
S 61.9
N 66.7

In all recorded history, there has not been one economist who has had to worry about where the next meal would come from.
— Peter Drucker (Austrian-born pioneer management theorist, 1909–2005)

July Is Best-Performing Dow & S&P Month of Third Quarter (Page 66)

THURSDAY

8

D 57.1
S 52.4
N 57.1

The average bottom-of-the-ladder person is potentially as creative as the top executive who sits in the big office. The problem is that the person on the bottom of the ladder doesn't trust his own brilliance and doesn't, therefore, believe in his own ideas.
— Robert Schuller (Minister)

FRIDAY

9

D 61.9
S 61.9
N 66.7

A weak currency is the sign of a weak economy, and a weak economy leads to a weak nation.
— H. Ross Perot (American businessman, *The Dollar Crisis*, 2X 3rd-party presidential candidate 1992/1996, b. 1930)

SATURDAY

10

SUNDAY

11

2019 DAILY DOW POINT CHANGES
(DOW JONES INDUSTRIAL AVERAGE)

Week #		Monday**	Tuesday	Wednsday	Thursday	Friday** 2018 Close	Weekly Dow Close 23327.46	Net Point Change
1		Holiday	18.78	−660.02	746.94	23433.16	105.70
2	J	98.19	256.10	91.67	122.80	−5.97	23995.95	562.79
3	A	−86.11	155.75	141.57	162.94	336.25	24706.35	710.40
4	N	Holiday	−301.87	171.14	−22.38	183.96	24737.20	30.85
5		−208.98	51.74	434.90	−15.19	64.22	25063.89	326.69
6		175.48	172.15	−21.22	−220.77	−63.20	25106.33	42.44
7	F	−53.22	372.65	117.51	−103.88	443.86	25883.25	776.92
8	E B	Holiday	8.07	63.12	−103.81	181.18	26031.81	148.56
9		60.14	−33.97	−72.82	−69.16	110.32	26026.32	−5.49
10		−206.67	−13.02	−133.17	−200.23	−22.99	25450.24	−576.08
11	M	200.64	−96.22	148.23	7.05	138.93	25848.87	398.63
12	A R	65.23	−26.72	−141.71	216.84	−460.19	25502.32	−346.55
13		14.51	140.90	−32.14	91.87	211.22	25928.68	426.36
14		329.74	−79.29	39.00	166.50	40.36	26424.99	496.31
15	A	−83.97	−190.44	6.58	−14.11	269.25	26412.30	−12.69
16	P R	−27.53	67.89	−3.12	110.00	Holiday	26559.54	147.24
17		−48.49	145.34	−59.34	−134.97	81.25	26543.33	−16.21
18		11.06	38.52	−162.77	−122.35	197.16	26504.95	−38.38
19	M	−66.47	−473.39	2.24	−138.97	114.01	25942.37	−562.58
20	A Y	−617.38	207.06	115.97	214.66	−98.68	25764.00	−178.37
21		−84.10	197.43	−100.72	−286.14	95.22	25585.69	−178.31
22		Holiday	−237.92	−221.36	43.47	−354.84	24815.04	−770.65
23		4.74	512.40	207.39	181.09	263.28	25983.94	1168.90
24	J U	78.74	−14.17	−43.68	101.94	−17.16	26089.61	105.67
25	N	22.92	353.01	38.46	249.17	−34.04	26719.13	629.52
26		8.41	−179.32	−11.40	−10.24	73.38	26599.96	−119.17
27		117.47	69.25	179.32*	Holiday	−43.88	26922.12	322.16
28	J	−115.98	−22.65	76.71	227.88	243.95	27332.03	409.91
29	U L	27.13	−23.53	−115.78	3.12	−68.77	27154.20	−177.83
30		17.70	177.29	−79.22	−128.99	51.47	27192.45	38.25
31		28.90	−23.33	−333.75	−280.85	−98.41	26485.01	−707.44
32	A	−767.27	311.78	−22.45	371.12	−90.75	26287.44	−197.57
33	U G	−380.07	372.54	−800.49	99.97	306.62	25886.01	−401.43
34		249.78	−173.35	240.29	49.51	−623.34	25628.90	−257.11
35		269.93	−120.93	258.20	326.15	41.03	26403.28	774.38
36		Holiday	−285.26	237.45	372.68	69.31	26797.46	394.18
37	S	38.05	73.92	227.61	45.41	37.07	27219.52	422.06
38	E P	−142.70	33.98	36.28	−52.29	−159.72	26935.07	−284.45
39		14.92	−142.22	162.94	−79.59	−70.87	26820.25	−114.82
40		96.58	−343.79	−494.42	122.42	372.68	26573.72	−246.53
41	O	−95.70	−313.98	181.97	150.66	319.92	26816.59	242.87
42	C	−29.23	237.44	−22.82	23.90	−255.68	26770.20	−46.39
43	T	57.44	−39.54	45.85	−28.42	152.53	26958.06	187.86
44		132.66	−19.26	115.23	−140.46	301.13	27347.36	389.30
45		114.75	30.52	−0.07	182.24	6.44	27681.24	333.88
46	N	10.25	0.00	92.10	−1.63	222.93	28004.89	323.65
47	O V	31.33	−102.20	−112.93	−54.80	109.33	27875.62	−129.27
48		190.85	55.21	42.32	Holiday	−112.59 *	28051.41	175.79
49		−268.37	−280.23	146.97	28.01	337.27	28015.06	−36.35
50	D	−105.46	−27.88	29.58	220.75	3.33	28135.38	120.32
51	E C	100.51	31.27	−27.88	137.68	78.13	28455.09	319.71
52		96.44	−36.08*	Holiday	105.94	23.87	28645.26	190.17
53		−183.12	76.30				28538.44	−106.82
TOTALS		**−1723.31**	**1364.93**	**656.12**	**1156.52**	**3756.72**		**5210.98**

Outline Bold Color: Down Friday, Down Monday
Shortened trading day: July 3, Nov 29, Dec 24
** Monday denotes first trading day of week, Friday denotes last trading day of week

MONDAY

D 52.4
S 52.4
N 57.1

12

Change is the law of life. And those who look only to the past or present are certain to miss the future.
— John F. Kennedy (35th U.S. President, 1917–1963)

TUESDAY

D 76.2
S 81.0
N 66.7

13

The principles of successful stock speculation are based on the supposition that people will continue in the future to make the mistakes that they have made in the past.
— Thomas F. Woodlock (*Wall Street Journal* editor/columnist, quoted in *Reminiscences of a Stock Operator*, 1866–1945)

WEDNESDAY

D 71.4
S 71.4
N 76.2

14

Awareness of competition and ability to react to it is a fundamental competence every business must have if it is to be long lived.
— Paul Allen (Microsoft founder)

THURSDAY

D 52.4
S 38.1
N 52.4

15

Selling a soybean contract short is worth two years at the Harvard Business School.
— Robert Stovall (60-year veteran Wall Street analyst and strategist, Father of Sam, b. 1926)

FRIDAY

D 52.4
S 52.4
N 57.1

16

We are handicapped by policies based on old myths rather than current realities.
— James William Fulbright (U.S. Senator Arkansas 1944–1974, 1905–1995)

SATURDAY

17

SUNDAY

18

DON'T SELL STOCKS ON MONDAY OR FRIDAY

Since 1989, Monday*, Tuesday and Wednesday have been the most consistently bullish days of the week for the Dow, and Thursday and Friday* the least bullish, as traders have become reluctant to stay long going into the weekend. Since 1989 Mondays and Tuesdays gained 16,398.16 Dow points, while Thursdays and Fridays have gained 2,087.55 points. Also broken out are the last nineteen and a half years to illustrate Monday's and Friday's poor performance in bear market years 2001–2002, 2008–2009 and early 2020. See pages 68, 76 and 141–144 for more.

ANNUAL DOW POINT CHANGES FOR DAYS OF THE WEEK SINCE 1953

Year	Monday*	Tuesday	Wednesday	Thursday	Friday*	Year's DJIA Closing	Year's Point Change
1953	-36.16	-7.93	19.63	5.76	7.70	280.90	-11.00
1954	15.68	3.27	24.31	33.96	46.27	404.39	123.49
1955	-48.36	26.38	46.03	-0.66	60.62	488.40	84.01
1956	-27.15	-9.36	-15.41	8.43	64.56	499.47	11.07
1957	-109.50	-7.71	64.12	3.32	-14.01	435.69	-63.78
1958	17.50	23.59	29.10	22.67	55.10	583.65	147.96
1959	-44.48	29.04	4.11	13.60	93.44	679.36	95.71
1960	-111.04	-3.75	-5.62	6.74	50.20	615.89	-63.47
1961	-23.65	10.18	87.51	-5.96	47.17	731.14	115.25
1962	-101.60	26.19	9.97	-7.70	-5.90	652.10	-79.04
1963	-8.88	47.12	16.23	22.39	33.99	762.95	110.85
1964	-0.29	-17.94	39.84	5.52	84.05	874.13	111.18
1965	-73.23	39.65	57.03	3.20	68.48	969.26	95.13
1966	-153.24	-27.73	56.13	-46.19	-12.54	785.69	-183.57
1967	-68.65	31.50	25.42	92.25	38.90	905.11	119.42
1968†	6.41	34.94	25.16	-72.06	44.19	943.75	38.64
1969	-164.17	-36.70	18.33	23.79	15.36	800.36	-143.39
1970	-100.05	-46.09	116.07	-3.48	72.11	838.92	38.56
1971	-2.99	9.56	13.66	8.04	23.01	890.20	51.28
1972	-87.40	-1.23	65.24	8.46	144.75	1020.02	129.82
1973	-174.11	10.52	-5.94	36.67	-36.30	850.86	-169.16
1974	-149.37	47.51	-20.31	-13.70	-98.75	616.24	-234.62
1975	39.46	-109.62	56.93	124.00	125.40	852.41	236.17
1976	70.72	71.76	50.88	-33.70	-7.42	1004.65	152.24
1977	-65.15	-44.89	-79.61	-5.62	21.79	831.17	-173.48
1978	-31.29	-70.84	71.33	-64.67	69.31	805.01	-26.16
1979	-32.52	9.52	-18.84	75.18	0.39	838.74	33.73
1980	-86.51	135.13	137.67	-122.00	60.96	963.99	125.25
1981	-45.68	-49.51	-13.95	-14.67	34.82	875.00	-88.99
1982	5.71	86.20	28.37	-1.47	52.73	1046.54	171.54
1983	30.51	-30.92	149.68	61.16	1.67	1258.64	212.10
1984	-73.80	78.02	-139.24	92.79	-4.84	1211.57	-47.07
1985	80.36	52.70	51.26	46.32	104.46	1546.67	335.10
1986	-39.94	97.63	178.65	29.31	83.63	1895.95	349.28
1987	-559.15	235.83	392.03	139.73	-165.56	1938.83	42.88
1988	268.12	166.44	-60.48	-230.84	86.50	2168.57	229.74
1989	-53.31	143.33	233.25	90.25	171.11	2753.20	584.63
Subtotal	*-1937.20*	*941.79*	*1708.54*	*330.82*	*1417.35*		*2461.30*
1990	219.90	-25.22	47.96	-352.55	-9.63	2633.66	-119.54
1991	191.13	47.97	174.53	254.79	-133.25	3168.83	535.17
1992	237.80	-49.67	3.12	108.74	-167.71	3301.11	132.28
1993	322.82	-37.03	243.87	4.97	-81.65	3754.09	452.98
1994	206.41	-95.33	29.98	-168.87	108.16	3834.44	80.35
1995	262.97	210.06	357.02	140.07	312.56	5117.12	1282.68
1996	626.41	155.55	-34.24	268.52	314.91	6448.27	1331.15
1997	1136.04	1989.17	-590.17	-949.80	-125.26	7908.25	1459.98
1998	649.10	679.95	591.63	-1579.43	931.93	9181.43	1273.18
1999	980.49	-1587.23	826.68	735.94	1359.81	11497.12	2315.69
2000	2265.45	306.47	-1978.34	238.21	-1542.06	10786.85	-710.27
Subtotal	*7098.52*	*1594.69*	*-327.96*	*-1299.41*	*967.81*		*8033.65*
2001	-389.33	336.86	-396.53	976.41	-1292.76	10021.50	-765.35
2002	-1404.94	-823.76	1443.69	-428.12	-466.74	8341.63	-1679.87
2003	978.87	482.11	-425.46	566.22	510.55	10453.92	2112.29
2004	201.12	523.28	358.76	-409.72	-344.35	10783.01	329.09
2005	316.23	-305.62	27.67	-128.75	24.96	10717.50	-65.51
2006	95.74	573.98	1283.87	193.34	-401.28	12463.15	1745.65
2007	278.23	-157.97	1316.74	-766.63	131.26	13264.82	801.67
2008	-1387.20	1704.51	-3073.72	-940.88	-791.14	8776.39	-4488.43
2009	-45.22	161.76	617.56	932.68	-15.12	10428.05	1651.66
2010	1236.88	-421.80	1019.66	-76.73	-608.55	11577.51	1149.46
2011	-571.02	1423.66	-776.05	246.27	317.19	12217.56	640.05
2012	254.59	-49.28	-456.37	847.34	299.30	13104.14	886.58
2013	-79.63	1091.75	170.93	653.64	1635.83	16576.66	3472.52
2014	-171.63	817.56	265.07	-337.48	672.89	17823.07	1246.41
2015	308.28	-879.14	926.70	982.16	-1736.04	17425.03	-398.04
2016	602.00	594.09	636.92	678.40	-173.84	19762.60	2337.57
2017	1341.29	1184.32	882.40	445.43	1103.18	24719.22	4956.62
2018	-1694.23	252.29	754.24	-47.39	-656.67	23327.46	-1391.76
2019	-1723.31	1364.93	656.12	1156.52	3756.72	28538.44	5210.98
2020‡	-1073.17	2757.83	-306.82	-3228.08	-860.87		
Subtotal	*-2926.45*	*10631.40*	*4925.38*	*1314.63*	*1104.52*		*17751.59*
Totals	**2234.87**	**13167.88**	**6305.96**	**346.04**	**3489.68**		**28246.54**

* Monday denotes first trading day of week, Friday denotes last trading day of week
† Most Wednesdays closed last 7 months of 1968 ‡ Partial year through July 2, 2020

MONDAY
D 57.1
S 52.4
N 57.1
19

There is one thing stronger than all the armies in the world, and this is an idea whose time has come.
— Victor Hugo (French novelist, playwright, *The Hunchback of Notre Dame* and *Les Misérables*, 1802-1885)

Week After July Expiration Prone to Wild Swings, Dow Up 13 of Last 18
1998 –4.3%, 2002 +3.1%, 2006 +3.2%, 2007 –4.2%, 2009 +4.0%, 2010 +3.2
TUESDAY
D 71.4
S 71.4
N 71.4
20

Eighty percent of success is showing up.
— Woody Allen (Filmaker, b. 1935)

WEDNESDAY
D 14.3
S 19.0
N 14.3
21

Six words that spell business success: create concept, communicate concept, sustain momentum.
— Yale Hirsch (Creator of Stock Trader's Almanac, b. 1923)

Beware the "Summer Rally" Hype
Historically the Weakest Rally of All Seasons (Page 74)
THURSDAY
D 42.9
S 47.6
N 47.6
22

Pretending to know everything closes the door to finding out what's really there.
— Neil deGrasse Tyson (American astrophysicist, cosmologist, Director Hayden Planetarium,
Cosmos: A Spacetime Odyssey, b. 1958)

FRIDAY
D 33.3
S 47.6
N 47.6
23

Successful innovation is not a feat of intellect, but of will.
— Joseph A. Schumpeter (Austrian-American economist, *Theory of Economic Development*, 1883-1950)

SATURDAY
24

August Almanac Investor Sector Seasonalities: See Pages 92, 94 and 96
SUNDAY
25

AUGUST ALMANAC

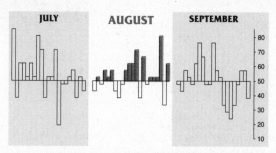

Market Probability Chart above is a graphic representation of the S&P 500 Recent Market Probability Calendar on page 124.

Market Probability Chart above is a graphic representation of the S&P 500 Recent Market Probability Calendar on page 124.

◆ Harvesting made August the best stock market month 1901–1951 ◆ Now that about 2% farm, August is the worst Dow, S&P, and NASDAQ (2000 up 11.7%, 2001 down 10.9) month since 1987 ◆ The second-shortest bear in history (45 days) caused by turmoil in Russia, currency crisis and hedge fund debacle ended here in 1998, 1344.22-point drop in the Dow, second worst behind October 2008, off 15.1% ◆ Saddam Hussein triggered a 10.0% slide in 1990 ◆ Best Dow gains: 1982 (11.5%) and 1984 (9.8%) as bear markets ended ◆ Next to last day S&P up only seven times last 24 years ◆ Post-presidential election year Augusts' rankings #11 S&P, #12 Dow, and #11 NASDAQ

August Vital Statistics

	DJIA	S&P 500	NASDAQ	Russell 1K	Russell 2K
Rank	10	11	11	10	9
Up	39	38	27	25	23
Down	31	32	22	16	18
Average % Change	−0.2%	−0.1%	0.2%	0.2%	0.2%
Post-Election Year	−1.7%	−1.4%	−1.2%	−1.4%	−0.8%
Best & Worst August					
	% Change	% Change	% Change	% Change	% Change
Best	1982 11.5	1982 11.6	2000 11.7	1982 11.3	1984 11.5
Worst	1998 −15.1	1998 −14.6	1998 −19.9	1998 −15.1	1998 −19.5
Best & Worst August Weeks					
Best	08/20/1982 10.3	08/20/1982 8.8	08/03/1984 7.4	08/20/1982 8.5	08/03/1984 7.0
Worst	08/23/1974 −6.1	08/05/2011 −7.2	08/28/1998 −8.8	08/05/2011 −7.7	08/05/2011 −10.3
Best & Worst August Days					
Best	08/17/1982 4.9	08/17/1982 4.8	08/09/1974 5.3	08/09/2011 5.0	08/09/2011 6.9
Worst	08/31/1998 −6.4	08/31/1998 −6.8	08/31/1998 −8.6	08/08/2011 −6.9	08/08/2011 −8.9
First Trading Day of Expiration Week: 1980–2020					
Record (#Up − #Down)	25−15	28−12	29−11	28−12	25−15
Current streak	D2	D2	D2	D2	D2
Avg % Change	0.22	0.25	0.31	0.23	0.27
Options Expiration Day: 1980-2020					
Record (#Up − #Down)	20−20	21−19	22−18	22−18	23−17
Current streak	U2	U2	U2	U2	U2
Avg % Change	−0.10	−0.04	−0.10	−0.04	0.12
Options Expiration Week: 1980-2020					
Record (#Up − #Down)	19−21	22−18	21−19	22−18	24−16
Current streak	D1	D1	D3	D1	D1
Avg % Change	0.00	0.17	0.30	0.18	0.38
Week After Options Expiration: 1980-2020					
Record (#Up − #Down)	24−16	26−14	25−15	26−14	26−14
Current streak	D1	D1	D1	D1	D1
Avg % Change	0.27	0.30	0.50	0.30	0.12
First Trading Day Performance					
% of Time Up	45.7	48.6	53.1	43.9	46.3
Avg % Change	0.004	0.04	−0.06	0.07	−0.05
Last Trading Day Performance					
% of Time Up	60.0	64.3	65.3	61.0	68.3
Avg % Change	0.12	0.12	0.05	−0.03	0.07

Dow & S&P 1950-June 19, 2020, NASDAQ 1971-June 19, 2020, Russell 1K & 2K 1979-June 19, 2020.

August's a good month to go on vacation;
Trading stocks will likely lead to frustration.

MONDAY

D 57.1
S 52.4
N 52.4

26

If you are ready to give up everything else to study the whole history of the market as carefully as a medical student studies anatomy and you have the cool nerves of a great gambler, the sixth sense of a clairvoyant, and the courage of a lion, you have a ghost of a chance.
— Bernard Baruch (Financier, speculator, statesman, presidential adviser, 1870–1965)

TUESDAY

D 57.1
S 57.1
N 61.9

27

Nobody can be a great economist who is only an economist—and I am even tempted to add that the economist who is only an economist is likely to become a nuisance if not a positive danger.
— Friedrich Hayek (Austrian-British economist & philosopher, 1899–1992)

FOMC Meeting (2 Days)

WEDNESDAY

D 42.9
S 38.1
N 38.1

28

Those who cannot remember the past are condemned to repeat it.
— George Santayana (American philosopher, poet, 1863–1952)

THURSDAY

D 33.3
S 52.4
N 57.1

29

All free governments are managed by the combined wisdom and folly of the people.
— James A. Garfield (20th U.S. President, 1831–1881)

Last Trading Day in July, NASDAQ Down 11 of Last 15
Dow Down 12 of Last 15

FRIDAY

D 38.1
S 42.9
N 38.1

30

Keep me away from the wisdom which does not cry, the philosophy which does not laugh and the greatness which does not bow before children.
— Kahlil Gibran (Lebanese-born American mystic, poet and artist, 1883–1931)

SATURDAY

31

SUNDAY

1

A RALLY FOR ALL SEASONS

Most years, especially when the market sells off during the first half, prospects for the perennial summer rally become the buzz on the Street. Parameters for this "rally" were defined by the late Ralph Rotnem as the lowest close in the Dow Jones Industrials in May or June to the highest close in July, August, or September. Such a big deal is made of the "summer rally" that one might get the impression the market puts on its best performance in the summertime. Nothing could be further from the truth! Not only does the market "rally" in every season of the year, but it does so with more gusto in the winter, spring and fall than in the summer.

Winters in 57 years averaged a 12.9% gain as measured from the low in November or December to the first quarter closing high. Spring rose 11.8%, followed by fall with 11.0%. Last and least was the average 9.2% "summer rally." Even 2009's impressive 19.7% "summer rally" was outmatched by spring. Nevertheless, no matter how thick the gloom or grim the outlook, don't despair! There's always a rally for all seasons, statistically.

SEASONAL GAINS IN DOW JONES INDUSTRIALS

	WINTER RALLY Nov/Dec Low to Q1 High	SPRING RALLY Feb/Mar Low to Q2 High	SUMMER RALLY May/Jun Low to Q3 High	FALL RALLY Aug/Sep Low to Q4 High
1964	15.3%	6.2%	9.4%	8.3%
1965	5.7	6.6	11.6	10.3
1966	5.9	4.8	3.5	7.0
1967	11.6	8.7	11.2	4.4
1968	7.0	11.5	5.2	13.3
1969	0.9	7.7	1.9	6.7
1970	5.4	6.2	22.5	19.0
1971	21.6	9.4	5.5	7.4
1972	19.1	7.7	5.2	11.4
1973	8.6	4.8	9.7	15.9
1974	13.1	8.2	1.4	11.0
1975	36.2	24.2	8.2	8.7
1976	23.3	6.4	5.9	4.6
1977	8.2	3.1	2.8	2.1
1978	2.1	16.8	11.8	5.2
1979	11.0	8.9	8.9	6.1
1980	13.5	16.8	21.0	8.5
1981	11.8	9.9	0.4	8.3
1982	4.6	9.3	18.5	37.8
1983	15.7	17.8	6.3	10.7
1984	5.9	4.6	14.1	9.7
1985	11.7	7.1	9.5	19.7
1986	31.1	18.8	9.2	11.4
1987	30.6	13.6	22.9	5.9
1988	18.1	13.5	11.2	9.8
1989	15.1	12.9	16.1	5.7
1990	8.8	14.5	12.4	8.6
1991	21.8	11.2	6.6	9.3
1992	14.9	6.4	3.7	3.3
1993	8.9	7.7	6.3	7.3
1994	9.7	5.2	9.1	5.0
1995	13.6	19.3	11.3	13.9
1996	19.2	7.5	8.7	17.3
1997	17.7	18.4	18.4	7.3
1998	20.3	13.6	8.2	24.3
1999	15.1	21.6	8.2	12.6
2000	10.8	15.2	9.8	3.5
2001	6.4	20.8	1.7	23.1
2002	14.8	7.9	2.8	17.6
2003	6.5	23.9	14.3	15.7
2004	11.6	5.2	4.4	10.6
2005	9.0	2.1	5.6	5.3
2006	8.8	8.3	9.5	13.0
2007	6.7	13.5	6.6	10.3
2008	2.5	11.2	3.8	4.5
2009	19.6	34.4	19.7	15.5
2010	11.6	13.1	11.1	16.0
2011	12.6	10.3	7.0	14.7
2012	18.0	4.5	12.4	5.7
2013	16.2	11.8	6.9	12.2
2014	6.0	10.2	5.5	10.3
2015	7.1	5.5	3.0	14.4
2016	3.4	15.6	8.7	10.8
2017	18.0	8.3	8.8	14.6
2018	14.4	7.6	11.8	6.6
2019	19.7	6.8	10.3	12.4
2020	8.1	48.3	11.1*	
Totals	**734.9%**	**675.4%**	**521.6%**	**614.6%**
Average	**12.9%**	**11.8%**	**9.2%**	**11.0%**

*As of July 2, 2019

First Trading Day in August, Dow Down 16 of Last 23

MONDAY

D 33.3
S 42.9
N 47.6

2

Liberties voluntarily forfeited are not easily retrieved. All the more so for those that are removed surreptitiously.
— Ted Koppel (Newsman, managing editor Discovery Channel, *NY Times* 11/6/06, b. 1940)

TUESDAY

D 52.4
S 52.4
N 38.1

3

In the course of evolution and a higher civilization we might be able to get along comfortably without Congress, but without Wall Street, never.
— Henry Clews (1900)

First Nine Trading Days of August Are Historically Weak (Pages 72 and 124)

WEDNESDAY

D 52.4
S 47.6
N 47.6

4

Victory goes to the player who makes the next-to-last mistake.
— Savielly Grigorievitch Tartakower (Chess master, 1887–1956)

THURSDAY

D 52.4
S 57.1
N 52.4

5

If you can buy more of your best idea, why put [the money] into your 10th-best idea or your 20th-best idea? The more positions you have, the more average you are.
— Bruce Berkowitz (Fairholme Fund, *Barron's* 3/17/08)

August Worst Dow and S&P Month 1988–2019
Harvesting Made August Best Dow Month 1901–1951

FRIDAY

D 52.4
S 52.4
N 42.9

6

The reading of all good books is indeed like a conversation with the noblest men of past centuries, in which they reveal to us the best of their thoughts.
— René Descartes (French philosopher, mathematician & scientist, 1596–1650)

SATURDAY

7

SUNDAY

8

TAKE ADVANTAGE OF DOWN FRIDAY/
DOWN MONDAY WARNING

Fridays and Mondays are the most important days of the week. Friday is the day for squaring positions—trimming longs or covering shorts before taking off for the weekend. Traders want to limit their exposure (particularly to stocks that are not acting well) since there could be unfavorable developments before trading resumes two or more days later.

Monday is important because the market then has the chance to reflect any weekend news, plus what traders think after digesting the previous week's action and the many Monday morning research and strategy comments.

For over 30 years, a down Friday followed by down Monday has frequently corresponded to important market inflection points that exhibit a clearly negative bias, often coinciding with market tops and, on a few climactic occasions, such as in October 2002, March 2009 and March 2020, near-major market bottoms.

One simple way to get a quick reading on which way the market may be heading is to keep track of the performance of the Dow Jones Industrial Average on Fridays and the following Mondays. Since 1995, there have been 257 occurrences of Down Friday/ Down Monday (DF/DM), with 74 falling in the bear market years of 2001, 2002, 2008, 2011, 2015 and 2020, producing an average decline of 14.7%.

To illustrate how Down Friday/ Down Monday can telegraph market inflection points we created the chart below of the Dow Jones Industrials from November 2018 to July 2, 2020, with arrows pointing to occurrences of DF/ DM. Use DF/DM as a warning to examine market conditions carefully.

DOW FRIDAY/DOWN MONDAY

Year	Total Number Down Friday/ Down Monday	Subsequent Average % Dow Loss*	Average Number of Days it took
1995	8	−1.2%	18
1996	9	−3.0%	28
1997	6	−5.1%	45
1998	9	−6.4%	47
1999	9	−6.4%	39
2000	11	−6.6%	32
2001	13	−13.5%	53
2002	18	−11.9%	54
2003	9	−3.0%	17
2004	9	−3.7%	51
2005	10	−3.0%	37
2006	11	−2.0%	14
2007	8	−6.0%	33
2008	15	−17.0%	53
2009	10	−8.7%	15
2010	7	−3.1%	10
2011	11	−9.0%	53
2012	11	−4.0%	38
2013	7	−2.4%	15
2014	7	−2.5%	8
2015	12	−9.2%	44
2016	10	−2.7%	25
2017	11	−1.2%	18
2018	14	−5.8%	45
2019	7	−4.3%	32
2020**	5	−27.7%	27
Average	**10**	**−6.5%**	**33**

* Over next 3 months, ** Ending July 2, 2020

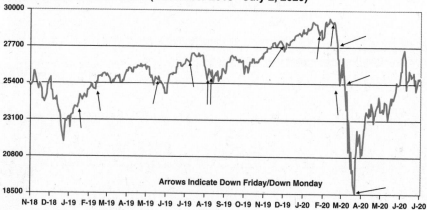

DOW JONES INDUSTRIALS (November 2018 - July 2, 2020)

Arrows Indicate Down Friday/Down Monday

N-18 D-18 J-19 F-19 M-19 A-19 M-19 J-19 J-19 A-19 S-19 O-19 N-19 D-19 J-20 F-20 M-20 A-20 M-20 J-20 J-20

MONDAY
D 52.4
S 57.1
N 42.9
9

Those heroes of finance are like beads on a string, when one slips off, the rest follow.
— Henrik Ibsen (Norwegian playwright, 1828–1906)

TUESDAY
D 42.9
S 42.9
N 47.6
10

Keep away from people who try to belittle your ambitions. Small people always do that,
but the really great make you feel that you, too, can become great.
— Mark Twain (1835–1910, pen name of Samuel Longhorne Clemens, American novelist and satirist)

WEDNESDAY
D 33.3
S 38.1
N 38.1
11

The CROWD is always wrong at market turning points but often times right once a trend sets in. The reason many
market fighters go broke is they believe the CROWD is always wrong. There is nothing further from the truth.
Unless volatility is extremely low or very high one should think twice before betting against the CROWD.
— Shawn Andrew (Trader, Ricercar Fund /SA, 12/21/01)

THURSDAY
D 52.4
S 47.6
N 52.4
12

Every man with a new idea is a crank until the idea succeeds.
— Mark Twain (American novelist and satirist, pen name of Samuel Longhorne Clemens, 1835–1910)

Mid-August Stronger Than Beginning and End

FRIDAY
D 61.9
S 57.1
N 61.9
13

The price of a stock varies inversely with the thickness of its research file.
— Martin Sosnoff (Atalanta Sosnoff Capital, *Silent Investor, Silent Loser*)

SATURDAY
14

SUNDAY
15

MARKET FARES BETTER UNDER DEMOCRATS; DOLLAR HOLDS UP UNDER REPUBLICANS

Does the market perform better under Republicans or Democrats? The market surge under Reagan and Bush I after Vietnam, OPEC and Iran inflation helped Republicans even up the score in the 20th century as opposed to the Democrats, who benefited when Roosevelt came in following an 89.2% drop by the Dow. However, under Clinton, the Democrats took the lead again. Both parties were more evenly matched in the last half of the 20th century. Under Obama, the Dow gained 90.5%, while the dollar lost 10.3%. Under Trump, the Dow has gained 40.9% while the dollar has lost 6.8%.

THE STOCK MARKET UNDER REPUBLICANS AND DEMOCRATS

Republican Eras		% Change	Democratic Eras		% Change
1901-1912	12 Years	48.3%	1913-1920	8 Years	29.2%
1921-1932	12 Years	−24.5%	1933-1952	20 Years	318.4%
1953-1960	8 Years	121.2%	1961-1968	8 Years	58.3%
1969-1976	8 Years	2.1%	1977-1980	4 Years	−3.0%
1981-1992	12 Years	247.0%	1993-2000	8 Years	236.7%
2001-2008	8 Years	−12.1%	2009-2016	8 Years	90.5%
2017-2020*	4 Years	40.9%			
Totals	**64 Years***	**422.9%**	**Totals**	**56 Years**	**730.2%**
Average Annual Change		**6.6%**	**Average Annual Change**		**13.0%**

Based on Dow Jones Industrial Average on previous year's Election Day or day before when closed
*Through July 2, 2020

A $10,000 investment compounded during Democratic eras would have grown to $532,739 in 56 years. The same investment during 64* Republican years would have appreciated to $108,725. After lagging for many years, performance under the Republicans improved under Reagan and Bush. Under Clinton, Democratic performance surged ahead. Under Trump, Republicans have reclaimed ground.

DECLINE OF THE DOLLAR UNDER REPUBLICANS AND DEMOCRATS

Republican Eras		Loss in Purch. Power	Value of Dollar	Democratic Eras		Loss in Purch. Power	Value of Dollar
1901–1912	12 Years	− 23.6%	$0.76	1913–1920	8 Years	− 51.4%	$0.49
1921–1932	12 Years	+ 46.9%	$1.12	1933–1952	20 Years	− 48.6%	$0.25
1953–1960	8 Years	− 10.2%	$1.01	1961–1968	8 Years	− 15.0%	$0.21
1969–1976	8 Years	− 38.9%	$0.62	1977–1980	4 Years	− 30.9%	$0.15
1981–1992	12 Years	− 41.3%	$0.36	1993–2000	8 Years	− 18.5%	$0.12
2001–2008	8 Years	− 20.0%	$0.29	2009–2016	8 Years	− 10.3%	$0.11
2017–2020*	4 Years	− 6.8%	$0.27				

The Republican Dollar declined to $0.27 in 64 years.

The Democratic Dollar declined to $0.11 in 56 years.

Based on average annual Consumer Price Index 1982-1984 = 100
*Through July 2, 2020

Adjusting stock market performance for loss of purchasing power reduced the Democrats' $532,739 to $57,105 and the Republicans' $108,725 to $29,338. Republicans may point out that all four major wars of the 20th century began while the Democrats were in power. Democrats can counter that the 46.7 percent increase in purchasing power occurred during the Depression and was not very meaningful to the 25 percent who were unemployed.

For the record, there have been 16 recessions and 21 bear markets under the Republicans and 7 recessions and 16 bear markets under the Democrats.

Monday Before August Expiration, Dow Up 16 of Last 25, Average Gain 0.3%

MONDAY
D 57.1
S 61.9
N 61.9
16

I measure what's going on, and I adapt to it. I try to get my ego out of the way. The market is smarter than I am so I bend.
— Martin Zweig (Fund manager, *Winning on Wall Street*, 1943–2013)

TUESDAY
D 57.1
S 61.9
N 66.7
17

The choice of starting a war this [pre-election] spring was made for political as well as military reasons…
[The president] cleary does not want to have a war raging on the eve of his presumed reelection campaign.
— Senior European diplomat (*NY Times* 3/14/03)

WEDNESDAY
D 71.4
S 71.4
N 66.7
18

Investors operate with limited funds and limited intelligence, they don't need to know everything.
As long as they understand something better than others, they have an edge.
— George Soros (Financier, philanthropist, political activist, author and philosopher, b. 1930)

THURSDAY
D 42.9
S 38.1
N 38.1
19

When teachers held high expectations of their students that alone was enough to cause an increase of 25 points in the students' IQ scores.
— Warren Bennis (Author, *The Unconscious Conspiracy: Why Leaders Can't Lead*, 1976)

August Expiration Day Less Bullish Lately, Dow Down 7 of Last 10
Down 531 Points (3.1%) in 2015

FRIDAY
D 61.9
S 66.7
N 81.0
20

If there is something you really want to do, make your plan and do it. Otherwise, you'll just regret it forever.
— Richard Rocco (PostNet franchisee, *Entrepreneur* magazine 12/2006, b. 1946)

SATURDAY
21

SUNDAY
22

REPUBLICAN CONGRESS & DEMOCRATIC PRESIDENT IS BEST FOR THE MARKET

Six possible political alignments exist in Washington: Republican President with a Republican congress, Democratic congress or split Congress; and a Democratic President with a Democratic Congress, Republican Congress or split Congress. Data presented in the chart below begin in 1949 with the first full presidential term following WWII. Lopsided market moves during the first half of the 20th Century prior to latter-day improvements to financial systems, including the Depression, have been omitted to focus on the modern era.

First looking at just the historical performance of the Dow under Democratic and Republican Presidents we see a pattern that is contrary to popular belief. Under a Democrat, the Dow has performed better than under a Republican. The Dow has historically returned 10.1% under Democrats compared to 7.4% under a Republican executive. Congressional results are the opposite and much more dramatic. Republican Congresses since 1949 have yielded an average 14.6% gain in the Dow compared to a 6.1% return when Democrats have controlled the Hill.

With total Republican control of Washington, the Dow has been up on average 13.0%. Democrats in power of the two branches have produced an average Dow gain of 7.4%. When power is split, with a Republican President and a Democratic Congress or a split Congress, the Dow has not done well averaging only a 5.9% gain. With a Democratic President and a Republican Congress or a split Congress, Dow has performed well averaging an 14.7% gain. The best scenario for all investors has been a Democrat in the White House and Republican control of Congress with average gains of 16.4%.

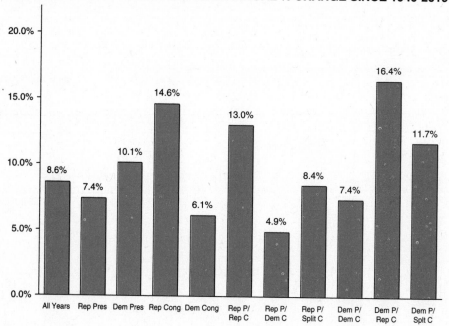

DOW JONES INDUSTRIALS AVERAGE ANNUAL % CHANGE SINCE 1949-2019

MONDAY

D 52.4
S 47.6
N 47.6

23

An economist is someone who sees something happen, and then wonders if it would work in theory.
— Ronald Reagan (40th U.S. President, 1911–2004)

TUESDAY

D 52.4
S 52.4
N 52.4

24

I've learned that only through focus can you do world-class things, no matter how capable you are.
— William H. Gates (Microsoft founder, *Fortune*, July 8, 2002)

Week After August Expiration Mixed, Dow Down 8 of Last 15

WEDNESDAY

D 52.4
S 52.4
N 52.4

25

I'd be a bum on the street with a tin cup, if the markets were always efficient.
— Warren Buffett (CEO Berkshire Hathaway, investor & philanthropist, b. 1930)

THURSDAY

D 42.9
S 52.4
N 52.4

26

Under capitalism man exploits man: under socialism the reverse is true.
— Polish proverb

FRIDAY

D 76.2
S 81.0
N 81.0

27

We can guarantee cash benefits as far out and at whatever size you like, but we cannot guarantee their purchasing power.
— Alan Greenspan (Fed Chairman 1987–2006, on funding Social Security to Senate Banking Committee 2/15/05)

SATURDAY

28

September Almanac Investor Sector Seasonalities: See Pages 92, 94 and 96

SUNDAY

29

SEPTEMBER ALMANAC

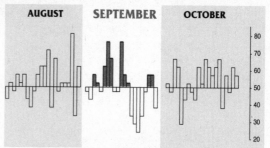

SEPTEMBER						
S	M	T	W	T	F	S
				1	2	3	4
5	6	7	8	9	10	11
12	13	14	15	16	17	18
19	20	21	22	23	24	25
26	27	28	29	30		

OCTOBER						
S	M	T	W	T	F	S
					1	2
3	4	5	6	7	8	9
10	11	12	13	14	15	16
17	18	19	20	21	22	23
24	25	26	27	28	29	30
31						

Market Probability Chart above is a graphic representation of the S&P 500 Recent Market Probability Calendar on page 124.

◆ Start of business year, end of vacations, and back to school made September a leading barometer month in first 60 years of 20th century; now portfolio managers back after Labor Day tend to clean house ◆ Biggest % loser on the S&P, Dow and NASDAQ since 1950 (pages 50 & 58) ◆ Streak of four great Dow Septembers averaging 4.2% gains ended in 1999 with six losers in a row averaging –5.9% (see page 152), up three straight 2005–2007, down 6% in 2008 and 2011 ◆ Day after Labor Day Dow up 16 of last 26 ◆ S&P opened strong 14 of last 25 years but tends to close weak due to end-of-quarter mutual fund portfolio restructuring, last trading day: S&P down 17 of past 27 ◆ September Triple-Witching Week can be dangerous, week after is pitiful (see page 106)

September Vital Statistics

	DJIA		S&P 500		NASDAQ		Russell 1K		Russell 2K	
Rank	12		12		12		12		11	
Up	29		32		27		21		23	
Down	41		37		22		20		18	
Average % Change	–0.6%		–0.4%		–0.5%		–0.5%		–0.4%	
Post-Election Year	–0.5%		–0.5%		–0.2%		–0.5%		–0.04%	
				Best & Worst September						
	% Change		% Change		% Change		% Change		% Change	
Best	2010	7.7	2010	8.8	1998	13.0	2010	9.0	2010	12.3
Worst	2002	–12.4	1974	–11.9	2001	–17.0	2002	–10.9	2001	–13.6
				Best & Worst September Weeks						
Best	09/28/2001	7.4	09/28/2001	7.8	09/16/2011	6.3	09/28/2001	7.6	09/28/2001	6.9
Worst	09/21/2001	–14.3	09/21/2001	–11.6	09/21/2001	–16.1	09/21/2001	–11.7	09/21/2001	–14.0
				Best & Worst September Days						
Best	09/08/1998	5.0	09/30/2008	5.4	09/08/1998	6.0	09/30/2008	5.3	09/18/2008	7.0
Worst	09/17/2001	–7.1	09/29/2008	–8.8	09/29/2008	–9.1	09/29/2008	–8.7	09/29/2008	–6.7
			First Trading Day of Expiration Week: 1980–2020							
Record (#Up - #Down)	25–15		21–19		15–25		21–19		17–23	
Current streak	D2		D2		D2		D2		U1	
Avg % Change	–0.04		–0.08		–0.28		–0.10		–0.18	
			Options Expiration Day: 1980–2020							
Record (#Up - #Down)	20–20		20–20		24–16		21–19		24–16	
Current streak	D1		D2		D2		D2		D2	
Avg % Change	–0.05		0.07		0.07		0.05		0.10	
			Options Expiration Week: 1980–2020							
Record (#Up - #Down)	22–18		24–16		23–17		24–16		21–19	
Current streak	D1		D1		D2		D1		D2	
Avg % Change	–0.11		0.09		0.11		0.08		0.13	
			Week After Options Expiration: 1980–2020							
Record (#Up - #Down)	14–26		12–28		17–23		12–27		14–26	
Current streak	D2		D2		D1		D2		D2	
Avg % Change	–0.68		–0.73		–0.85		–0.75		–1.27	
			First Trading Day Performance							
% of Time Up	58.6		58.6		55.1		51.2		48.8	
Avg % Change	–0.02		–0.03		–0.07		–0.09		–0.040	
			Last Trading Day Performance							
% of Time Up	41.4		42.9		51.0		51.2		63.4	
Avg % Change	–0.10		–0.04		0.04		0.07		0.26	

Dow & S&P 1950–June 19, 2020, NASDAQ 1971–June 19, 2020, Russell 1K & 2K 1979–June 19, 2020.

September is when leaves and stocks tend to fall;
On Wall Street it's the worst month of all.

August's Next-to-Last Trading Day, S&P Down 17 of Last 24 Years

MONDAY
30

D 33.3
S 33.3
N 57.1

To find one man in a thousand who is your true friend from unselfish motives is to find one of the great wonders of the world.
— Leopold Mozart (Quoted by Maynard Solomon, *Mozart*)

TUESDAY
31

D 57.1
S 61.9
N 57.1

By the law of nature the father continues master of his child no longer than the child stands in need of his assistance; after that term they become equal, and then the son entirely independent of the father, owes him no obedience, but only respect.
— Jean-Jacques Rousseau (Swiss philosopher, *The Social Contract*, 1712–1778)

September First Trading Day, S&P Up 14 of Last 25, But Down 9 of Last 12

WEDNESDAY
1

D 47.6
S 47.6
N 57.1

In this game, the market has to keep pitching, but you don't have to swing.
You can stand there with the bat on your shoulder for six months until you get a fat pitch.
— Warren Buffett (CEO Berkshire Hathaway, investor and philanthropist, b. 1930)

THURSDAY
2

D 71.4
S 42.9
N 42.9

When you get into a tight place and everything goes against you, till it seems as though you could not hang on a minute longer, never give up then, for that is just the place and time that the tide will turn.
— Harriet Beecher Stowe (American writer and abolitionist)

FRIDAY
3

D 66.7
S 57.1
N 52.4

Bill Gates' One-Minus Staffing: For every project, figure out the bare minimum of people needed to staff it.
Cut to the absolute muscle and bones, then take out one more. When you understaff, people jump on the loose ball.
You find out who the real performers are. Not so when you're overstaffed. People sit around waiting for somebody else to do it.
— Quoted by Rich Karlgaard (Publisher, *Forbes* Dec. 25, 2000)

SATURDAY
4

SUNDAY
5

MARKET GAINS MORE ON SUPER-8 DAYS EACH MONTH THAN ON ALL 13 REMAINING DAYS COMBINED

For many years, the last day plus the first four days were the best days of the month. The market currently exhibits greater bullish bias from the last three trading days of the previous month through the first two days of the current month, and now shows significant bullishness during the middle three trading days, 9 to 11, due to 401(k) cash inflows (see pages 145 & 146). This pattern was not as pronounced during the boom years of the 1990s, with market strength all month long. Since the 2009 market bottom, the Super-8 advantage has been sporadic. In 2012 and 2015, the "Super Eight" had a clear advantage. The "Super Eight" have been destroyed in 2020 through the end of June. When compared to the last twenty-one and half year record (at the bottom of the page), the "Super Eight" edge has dulled recently.

SUPER-8 DAYS* DOW % CHANGES VS. REST OF MONTH

	Super 8 Days	Rest of Month		Super 8 Days	Rest of Month		Super 8 Days	Rest of Month
	2012			**2013**			**2014**	
Jan	1.90%	1.66%		2.28%	3.47%		0.92%	−4.26%
Feb	−0.39	2.33		−0.27	−0.41		−1.99	3.66
Mar	2.22	−0.55		2.93	1.82		0.77	−0.21
Apr	1.00	−1.80		0.11	1.65		2.44	−1.82
May	−0.38	−4.52		1.93	2.81		−0.56	2.50
Jun	−1.30	2.08		−0.27	−3.96		−0.09	1.24
Jul	5.11	−2.22		1.11	4.23		1.79	−1.10
Aug	−0.40	2.09		−1.35	−3.75		−1.81	2.61
Sep	−0.24	2.98		2.55	0.83		0.32	−1.26
Oct	0.77	−3.60		−0.64	2.60		−3.28	3.82
Nov	−2.01	0.55		1.79	1.41		2.42	2.28
Dec	0.49	1.35		−0.72	3.30		−1.66	3.14
Totals	**6.77%**	**0.35%**		**9.45%**	**14.00%**		**−0.73%**	**10.60%**
Average	**0.56%**	**0.03%**		**0.79%**	**1.17%**		**−0.06%**	**0.88%**
	2015			**2016**			**2017**	
Jan	−3.64%	−0.07%		−2.95%	−4.93%		−0.44%	1.24%
Feb	2.65	2.00		1.69	0.30		0.62	2.90
Mar	1.91	−4.78		4.02	2.21		1.16	−1.66
Apr	1.20	0.83		2.14	0.43		−0.39	1.83
May	1.31	−1.28		−1.33	0.57		−0.03	0.45
Jun	−1.32	0.49		−1.33	−2.68		1.18	−0.09
Jul	−0.11	−1.31		4.97	2.66		0.89	0.98
Aug	0.37	−8.02		−0.11	−0.30		2.12	−1.65
Sep	2.27	−2.04		0.84	−1.72		0.53	1.65
Oct	1.03	6.57		−0.65	0.49		1.97	2.96
Nov	0.68	0.68		−0.71	5.93		−0.15	0.93
Dec	−0.74	−0.86		0.38	3.73		3.61	1.27
Totals	**5.61%**	**−7.79%**		**6.96%**	**6.69%**		**11.07%**	**10.81%**
Average	**0.47%**	**−0.65%**		**0.58%**	**0.56%**		**0.92%**	**0.90%**
	2018			**2019**			**2020**	
Jan	2.83%	4.54%		0.04%	7.10%		1.40%	−1.01%
Feb	−1.68	−3.17		4.70	1.54		−0.78	−4.78
Mar	−4.26	−0.09		0.11	−1.77		−18.59	2.59
Apr	0.89	−1.34		2.90	0.21		−4.42	11.77
May	−0.79	3.59		−1.71	−2.56		−1.92	5.59
Jun	−0.67	−1.17		0.35	4.32		−1.56	4.78
Jul	0.33	4.72		1.81	0.60			
Aug	−1.39	3.53		−3.87	−1.41			
Sep	0.05	1.59		1.98	2.62			
Oct	−0.30	−6.62		−1.32	1.85			
Nov	1.97	−1.68		2.50	1.05			
Dec	−2.63	−5.08		−0.85	2.85			
Totals	**−5.65%**	**−1.18%**		**6.64%**	**16.40%**		**−25.87%**	**18.94%**
Average	**−0.47%**	**−0.10%**		**0.55%**	**1.37%**		**−4.31%**	**3.16%**

		Super Eight Days		Rest of Month (13 days)	
258	Net % Changes	103.89%	Net % Changes	29.15%
Month	Average Period	0.40%	Average Period	0.11%
Totals	Average Day	0.05%	Average Day	0.01%

* Super 8 Days = Last 3 + First 2 + Middle 3

Labor Day *(Market Closed)*

MONDAY

6

Leadership is the ability to hide your panic from others.
— Lao Tzu (Chinese philosopher, Shaolin monk, founder of Taoism, 6th century BCE)

Rosh Hashanah
Day After Labor Day, Dow Up 16 of Last 26, But Down 7 of Last 10

TUESDAY

D 42.9
S 52.4
N 52.4

7

Drawing on my fine command of language, I said nothing.
— Robert Benchley (American writer, actor and humorist, 1889–1945)

WEDNESDAY

D 57.1
S 47.6
N 52.4

8

Government is like fire—useful when used legitimately, but dangerous when not.
— David Brooks (*NY Times* columnist, 10/5/07)

THURSDAY

D 57.1
S 61.9
N 57.1

9

The only things that evolve by themselves in an organization are disorder, friction and malperformance.
— Peter Drucker (Austrian-born pioneer management theorist, 1909–2005)

2001 4-Day Closing, Longest Since 9-Day Banking Moratorium in March 1933

FRIDAY

D 76.2
S 76.2
N 66.7

10

The mind is not a vessel to be filled but a fire to be kindled.
— Plutarch (Greek biographer and philosopher, Parallel Lives, 46–120 AD)

SATURDAY

11

"In Memory"

SUNDAY

12

A CORRECTION FOR ALL SEASONS

While there's a rally for every season (page 74), almost always there's a decline or correction, too. Fortunately, corrections tend to be smaller than rallies, and that's what gives the stock market its long-term upward bias. In each season the average bounce outdoes the average setback. On average, the net gain between the rally and the correction is smallest in summer and fall.

The summer setback tends to be slightly outdone by the average correction in the fall. Tax selling and portfolio cleaning are the usual explanations—individuals sell to register a tax loss, and institutions like to get rid of their losers before preparing year-end statements. The October jinx also plays a major part. Since 1964, there have been 19 fall declines of over 10%, and in 10 of them (1966, 1974, 1978, 1979, 1987, 1990, 1997, 2000, 2002, 2008 and 2018) much damage was done in October, where so many bear markets end. Recent October lows were also seen in 1998, 1999, 2004, 2005 and 2011. Most often, it has paid to buy after fourth quarter or late third quarter "waterfall declines" for a rally that may continue into January or even beyond. Anticipation of war in Iraq put the market down in 2003 Q1. Quick success rallied stocks through Q3. The coronavirus economic shutdown in late Q1 of 2020 caused the worst winter and spring slumps since 1932. Easy monetary policy and strong corporate earnings spared Q1 2011 and 2012 from a seasonal slump. Tax cut expectations lifted the market in Q4 2017.

SEASONAL CORRECTIONS IN DOW JONES INDUSTRIALS

	WINTER SLUMP Nov/Dec High to Q1 Low	SPRING SLUMP Feb/Mar High to Q2 Low	SUMMER SLUMP May/Jun High to Q3 Low	FALL SLUMP Aug/Sep High to Q4 Low
1964	−0.1%	−2.4%	−1.0%	−2.1%
1965	−2.5	−7.3	−8.3	−0.9
1966	−6.0	−13.2	−17.7	−12.7
1967	−4.2	−3.9	−5.5	−9.9
1968	−8.8	−0.3	−5.5	+0.4
1969	−8.7	−8.7	−17.2	−8.1
1970	−13.8	−20.2	−8.8	−2.5
1971	−1.4	−4.8	−10.7	−13.4
1972	−0.5	−2.6	−6.3	−5.3
1973	−11.0	−12.8	−10.9	−17.3
1974	−15.3	−10.8	−29.8	−27.6
1975	−6.3	−5.5	−9.9	−6.7
1976	−0.2	−5.1	−4.7	−8.9
1977	−8.5	−7.2	−11.5	−10.2
1978	−12.3	−4.0	−7.0	−13.5
1979	−2.5	−5.8	−3.7	−10.9
1980	−10.0	−16.0	−1.7	−6.8
1981	−6.9	−5.1	−18.6	−12.9
1982	−10.9	−7.5	−10.6	−3.3
1983	−4.1	−2.8	−6.8	−3.6
1984	−11.9	−10.5	−8.4	−6.2
1985	−4.8	−4.4	−2.8	−2.3
1986	−3.3	−4.7	−7.3	−7.6
1987	−1.4	−6.6	−1.7	−36.1
1988	−6.7	−7.0	−7.6	−4.5
1989	−1.7	−2.4	−3.1	−6.6
1990	−7.9	−4.0	−17.3	−18.4
1991	−6.3	−3.6	−4.5	−6.3
1992	+0.1	−3.3	−5.4	−7.6
1993	−2.7	−3.1	−3.0	−2.0
1994	−4.4	−9.6	−4.4	−7.1
1995	−0.8	−0.1	−0.2	−2.0
1996	−3.5	−4.6	−7.5	+0.2
1997	−1.8	−9.8	−2.2	−13.3
1998	−7.0	−3.1	−18.2	−13.1
1999	−2.7	−1.7	−8.0	−11.5
2000	−14.8	−7.4	−4.1	−11.8
2001	−14.5	−13.6	−27.4	−16.2
2002	−5.1	−14.2	−26.7	−19.5
2003	−15.8	−5.3	−3.1	−2.1
2004	−3.9	−7.7	−6.3	−5.7
2005	−4.5	−8.5	−3.3	−4.5
2006	−2.4	−5.4	−7.8	−0.4
2007	−3.7	−3.2	−6.1	−8.4
2008	−14.5	−11.0	−20.6	−35.9
2009	−32.0	−6.3	−7.4	−3.5
2010	−6.1	−10.4	−13.1	−1.0
2011	+0.2	−4.0	−16.3	−12.2
2012	+0.5	−8.7	−5.3	−7.8
2013	−0.2	−0.3	−4.1	−5.7
2014	−7.3	−2.6	−3.4	−6.7
2015	−4.9	−3.8	−14.4	−7.6
2016	−12.6	−3.3	−0.9	−4.0
2017	−1.2	−3.4	−1.0	+0.6
2018	−5.3	−9.7	−4.5	−18.5
2019	−13.4	−4.9	−4.8	−4.2
2020	−35.1	−29.1	−6.7*	
Totals	−397.4%	−387.3%	−485.1%	−495.6%
Average	−7.0%	−6.8%	−8.5%	−8.9%

* As of July 2, 2020

Monday Before September Triple Witching, Russell 2000 Down 13 of Last 21 🐗 **MONDAY**

D 61.9
S 66.7
N 66.7

13

Every time everyone's talking about something, that's the time to sell.
— George Lindemann (Billionaire, *Forbes*)

TUESDAY

D 47.6
S 47.6
N 66.7

14

When a country lives on borrowed time, borrowed money and borrowed energy, it is just begging the markets to discipline it in their own way at their own time. Usually the markets do it in an orderly way—except when they don't.
— Thomas L. Friedman (*NY Times* Foreign Affairs columnist, 2/24/05)

Expiration Week 2001, Dow Lost 1370 Points (14.3%)
8th Worst Weekly Point Loss Ever, 6th Worst Week Overall

WEDNESDAY

D 52.4
S 47.6
N 33.3

15

For a country, everything will be lost when the jobs of an economist and a banker become highly respected professions.
— Montesquieu

Yom Kippur

🐗 **THURSDAY**

D 76.2
S 76.2
N 76.2

16

The difference between life and the movies is that a script has to make sense, and life doesn't.
— Joseph L. Mankiewicz (Film director, writer, producer, 1909–1993)

September Triple Witching, Dow Up 11 of Last 16

🐗 🐗 🐗 **FRIDAY**

D 52.4
S 57.1
N 52.4

17

Financial markets will find and exploit hidden flaws, particularly in untested new innovations—and do so at a time that will inflict the most damage to the most people.
— Raymond F. DeVoe, Jr. (Market strategist Jesup & Lamont, The DeVoe Report, 3/30/07 1929–2014)

SATURDAY

18

SUNDAY

19

FIRST-TRADING-DAY-OF-THE-MONTH PHENOMENON

While the Dow Jones Industrial Average has gained 17983.12 points between September 2, 1997 (7622.42) and June 12, 2020 (25605.54), it is incredible that 6739.24 points were gained on the first trading days of these 274 months. The remaining 5459 trading days combined gained 11862.13 points during the period. This averages out to gains of 24.60 points on first days, in contrast to just 2.06 points on all others.

Note September 1997 through October 2000 racked up a total gain of 2632.39 Dow points on the first trading days of these 38 months (winners except for 7 occasions). But between November 2000 and September 2002, when the 2000–2002 bear markets did the bulk of their damage, frightened investors switched from pouring money into the market on that day to pulling it out, 14 months out of 23, netting a 404.80 Dow point loss. The 2007–2009 bear market lopped off 964.14 Dow points on first days in 17 months November 2007–March 2009. First days had their worst year in 2014, declining eight times for a total loss of 820.86 Dow points.

First days of August have performed worst, declining 15 times in the last 22 years. July's first trading day is third best by points but best based upon frequency of gains with only four declines in the last 22 years. In rising market trends, first days tend to perform much better, as institutions are likely anticipating strong performance at each month's outset. S&P 500 and NASDAQ first days differ slightly from Dow's pattern with losses in four months; April, August, September and October.

DOW POINTS GAINED FIRST DAY OF MONTH
SEPTEMBER 1997–JUNE 21, 2019

	Jan	Feb	Mar	Apr	May	Jun	Jul	Aug	Sep	Oct	Nov	Dec	Totals
1997									257.36	70.24	232.31	189.98	749.89
1998	56.79	201.28	4.73	68.51	83.70	22.42	96.65	−96.55	288.36	−210.09	114.05	16.99	646.84
1999	2.84	−13.13	18.20	46.35	225.65	36.52	95.62	−9.19	108.60	−63.95	−81.35	120.58	486.74
2000	−139.61	100.52	9.62	300.01	77.87	129.87	112.78	84.97	23.68	49.21	−71.67	−40.95	636.30
2001	−140.70	96.27	−45.14	−100.85	163.37	78.47	91.32	−12.80	47.74	−10.73	188.76	−87.60	268.11
2002	51.90	−12.74	262.73	−41.24	113.41	−215.46	−133.47	−229.97	−355.45	346.86	120.61	−33.52	−126.34
2003	265.89	56.01	−53.22	77.73	−25.84	47.55	55.51	−79.83	107.45	194.14	57.34	116.59	819.32
2004	−44.07	11.11	94.22	15.63	88.43	14.20	−101.32	39.45	−5.46	112.38	26.92	162.20	413.69
2005	−53.58	62.00	63.77	−99.46	59.19	82.39	28.47	−17.76	−21.97	−33.22	−33.30	106.70	143.23
2006	129.91	89.09	60.12	35.62	−23.85	91.97	77.80	−59.95	83.00	−8.72	−49.71	−27.80	397.48
2007	11.37	51.99	−34.29	27.95	73.23	40.47	126.81	150.38	91.12	191.92	−362.14	−57.15	311.66
2008	−220.86	92.83	−7.49	391.47	189.87	−134.50	32.25	−51.70	−26.63	−19.59	−5.18	−679.95	−439.48
2009	258.30	−64.03	−299.64	152.68	44.29	221.11	57.06	114.95	−185.68	−203.00	76.71	126.74	299.49
2010	155.91	118.20	78.53	70.44	143.22	−112.61	−41.49	208.44	254.75	41.63	6.13	249.76	1172.91
2011	93.24	148.23	−168.32	56.99	−3.18	−279.65	168.43	−10.75	−119.96	−258.08	−297.05	−25.65	−695.75
2012	179.82	83.55	28.23	52.45	65.69	−274.88	−8.70	−37.62	−54.90	77.98	136.16	−59.98	187.80
2013	308.41	149.21	35.17	−5.69	−138.85	138.46	65.36	128.48	23.65	62.03	69.80	−77.64	758.39
2014	−135.31	−326.05	−153.68	74.95	−21.97	26.46	129.47	−69.93	−30.89	−238.19	−24.28	−51.44	−820.86
2015	9.92	196.09	155.93	−77.94	185.54	29.69	138.40	−91.66	−469.68	−11.99	165.22	168.43	395.95
2016	−276.09	−17.12	348.58	107.66	117.52	2.47	19.38	−27.73	18.42	−54.30	−105.32	68.35	201.82
2017	119.16	26.85	303.31	−13.01	−27.05	135.53	129.64	72.80	39.46	152.51	57.77	−40.76	956.21
2018	104.79	37.32	−420.22	−458.92	−64.10	219.37	35.77	−81.37	−12.34	192.90	264.98	287.97	106.15
2019	18.78	64.22	110.32	329.74	−162.77	4.74	117.47	−280.85	−285.26	−343.79	301.13	−268.37	−394.64
2020	330.36	143.78	1293.96	−973.65	−622.03	91.91							264.33
Totals	1087.17	1295.48	1685.42	37.42	539.34	396.50	1293.21	−358.19	−224.63	36.15	787.89	163.48	6739.24

SUMMARY FIRST DAYS VS. OTHER DAYS OF MONTH

	# of Days	Total Points Gained	Average Daily Point Gain
First days	274	6739.24	24.60
Other days	5459	11243.88	2.06

MONDAY

D 57.1
S 52.4
N 57.1

20

First-rate people hire first-rate people; second-rate people hire third-rate people.
— Leo Rosten (American author, 1908–1997)

TUESDAY

D 52.4
S 33.3
N 38.1

21

From very early on, I understood that you can touch a piece of paper once…if you touch it twice, you're dead. Therefore, paper only touches my hand once. After that, it's either thrown away, acted on or given to somebody else.
— Manuel Fernandez (Businessman, *Investor's Business Daily*)

FOMC Meeting (2 days)

WEDNESDAY

D 33.3
S 28.6
N 28.6

22

If a man has no talents, he is unhappy enough; but if he has, envy pursues him in proportion to his ability.
— Leopold Mozart (to his son Wolfgang Amadeus, 1768)

THURSDAY

D 28.6
S 23.8
N 33.3

23

The true mystery of the world is the visible, not the invisible.
— Oscar Wilde (Irish-born writer and wit, 1845–1900)

Week After September Triple Witching, Dow Down 23 of Last 30
Average Loss Since 1990, 1.0%

FRIDAY

D 33.3
S 33.3
N 42.9

24

In my experience, selling a put is much safer than buying a stock.
— Kyle Rosen (Boston Capital Mgmt., *Barron's* 8/23/04)

SATURDAY

25

October Almanac Investor Sector Seasonalities: See Pages 92, 94 and 96

SUNDAY

26

OCTOBER ALMANAC

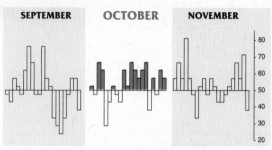

OCTOBER						
S	M	T	W	T	F	S
					1	2
3	4	5	6	7	8	9
10	11	12	13	14	15	16
17	18	19	20	21	22	23
24	25	26	27	28	29	30
31						

NOVEMBER						
S	M	T	W	T	F	S
	1	2	3	4	5	6
7	8	9	10	11	12	13
14	15	16	17	18	19	20
21	22	23	24	25	26	27
28	29	30				

Market Probability Chart above is a graphic representation of the S&P 500 Recent Market Probability Calendar on page 124.

◆ Known as the jinx month because of crashes in 1929 and 1987, the 554-point drop on October 27, 1997, back-to-back massacres in 1978 and 1979, Friday the 13th in 1989 and the meltdown in 2008 ◆ Yet October is a "bear killer" and turned the tide in 12 post–WWII bear markets: 1946, 1957, 1960, 1962, 1966, 1974, 1987, 1990, 1998, 2001, 2002 and 2011 ◆ First October Dow top in 2007, 20-year 1987 Crash anniversary –2.6% ◆ Worst six months of the year ends with October (page 52) ◆ No longer worst month (pages 50 & 58) ◆ Best Dow, S&P and NASDAQ month from 1993 to 2007 ◆ Post–presidential election year Octobers since 1950, #6 Dow (0.9%), #5 S&P (1.0%) and #6 NASDAQ (1.4%) ◆ October is a great time to buy ◆ Big October gains five years 1999–2003 after atrocious Septembers ◆ Can get into Best Six Months earlier using MACD (page 54) ◆ October 2011, second month to gain 1000 Dow points and again in 2015

October Vital Statistics

	DJIA	S&P 500	NASDAQ	Russell 1K	Russell 2K
Rank	7	7	7	6	12
Up	42	42	27	26	23
Down	28	28	22	15	18
Average % Change	0.6%	0.8%	0.7%	0.8%	−0.4%
Post-Election Year	0.9%	1.0%	1.4%	0.9%	0.3%

Best & Worst October										
	% Change		% Change		% Change		% Change		% Change	
Best	1982	10.7	1974	16.3	1974	17.2	1982	11.3	2011	15.0
Worst	1987	−23.2	1987	−21.8	1987	−27.2	1987	−21.9	1987	−30.8

Best & Worst October Weeks										
Best	10/11/1974	12.6	10/11/1974	14.1	10/31/2008	10.9	10/31/2008	10.8	10/31/2008	14.1
Worst	10/10/2008	−18.2	10/10/2008	−18.2	10/23/1987	−19.2	10/10/2008	−18.2	10/23/1987	−20.4

Best & Worst October Days										
Best	10/13/2008	11.1	10/13/2008	11.6	10/13/2008	11.8	10/13/2008	11.7	10/13/2008	9.3
Worst	10/19/1987	−22.6	10/19/1987	−20.5	10/19/1987	−11.4	10/19/1987	−19.0	10/19/1987	−12.5

First Trading Day of Expiration Week: 1980–2020				
Record (#Up - #Down)	30–10	28–12	26–14	29–11	28–12
Current streak	D2	D2	D2	D2	D1
Avg % Change	0.65	0.61	0.48	0.59	0.36

Options Expiration Day: 1980–2020				
Record (#Up - #Down)	19–21	20–20	22–18	20–20	16–24
Current streak	D1	D2	D2	D2	D2
Avg % Change	−0.14	−0.19	−0.11	−0.19	−0.20

Options Expiration Week: 1980–2020				
Record (#Up - #Down)	28–12	29–11	23–17	28–12	24–16
Current streak	D1	U5	U1	U1	U1
Avg % Change	0.60	0.64	0.66	0.63	0.42

Week After Options Expiration: 1980–2020				
Record (#Up - #Down)	20-20	18–22	21–19	18-22	18–22
Current streak	U1	U1	U1	U1	U1
Avg % Change	−0.32	−0.36	−0.32	−0.38	−0.62

First Trading Day Performance				
% of Time Up	48.6	50.0	46.9	53.7	46.3
Avg % Change	0.05	0.04	−0.16	0.18	−0.29

Last Trading Day Performance				
% of Time Up	52.9	54.3	63.3	63.4	70.7
Avg % Change	0.07	0.15	0.50	0.33	0.56

Dow & S&P 1950–June 19, 2020 NASDAQ 1971–June 19, 2020, Russell 1K & 2K 1979–June 19, 2020.

October has killed many a bear;
Buy techs and small caps and soon wear a grin ear to ear.

End of September Prone to Weakness
From End-of-Q3 Institutional Portfolio Restructuring

MONDAY

D 52.4
S 47.6
N 52.4

27

On [TV financial news programs], if the stock is near its high, 90% of the guests like it,
if it is near its lows, 90% of the guests hate it.
— Michael L. Burke (*Investors Intelligence*, May 2002)

TUESDAY

D 57.1
S 57.1
N 42.9

28

Look for an impending crash in the economy when the best seller lists are filled with books on business
strategies and quick-fix management ideas.
— Peter Drucker (Austrian-born pioneer management theorist, 1909–2005)

WEDNESDAY

D 57.1
S 57.1
N 42.9

29

While markets often make double bottoms, three pushes to a high is the most common topping pattern.
— John Bollinger (Bollinger Capital Management, BollingerBands.com)

Last Day of Q3, S&P Down 15 of Last 23, Massive 5.4% Rally in 2008

THURSDAY

D 42.9
S 38.1
N 47.6

30

The greatest lie ever told: Build a better mousetrap and the world will beat a path to your door.
— Yale Hirsch (Creator of *Stock Trader's Almanac*, b. 1923)

First Trading Day in October, Dow Down 9 of Last 15, Off 2.4% in 2011

FRIDAY

D 47.6
S 52.4
N 42.9

1

Spend at least as much time researching a stock as you would choosing a refrigerator.
— Peter Lynch (Fidelity Investments, *One Up On Wall Street*, b. 1944)

SATURDAY

2

SUNDAY

3

SECTOR SEASONALITY: SELECTED PERCENTAGE PLAYS

Sector seasonality was featured in the first *Almanac* in 1968. A Merrill Lynch study showed that buying seven sectors around September or October and selling in the first few months of 1954–1964 tripled the gains of holding them for 10 years. Over the years we have honed this strategy significantly and now devote a significant portion of our time and resources to investing and trading during positive and negative seasonal periods for the different sector indexes below with highly correlated Exchange Traded Funds (ETFs).

Updated seasonalities appear in the table below. We specify whether the seasonality starts or finishes in the beginning third (B), middle third (M), or last third (E) of the month. These selected percentage plays are geared to take advantage of the bulk of seasonal sector strength or weakness.

By design, entry points are in advance of the major seasonal moves, providing traders ample opportunity to accumulate positions at favorable prices. Conversely, exit points have been selected to capture the majority of the move.

From the major seasonalities in the table below, we created the Sector Index Seasonality Strategy Calendar on pages 94 and 96. Note the concentration of bullish sector seasonalities during the Best Six Months, November to April, and bearish sector seasonalities during the Worst Six Months, May to October.

Almanac Investor eNewsletter subscribers receive specific entry and exit points for highly correlated ETFs and detailed analysis in ETF Trade Alerts. Visit *www.stocktradersalmanac.com*, or see the ad insert for additional details and a special offer for new subscribers.

SECTOR INDEX SEASONALITY TABLE

Ticker	Sector Index	Type	Start		Finish		15-Year	10-Year	5-Year
							\multicolumn{3}{Average % Return[†]}		
XCI	Computer Tech	Short	January	B	March	B	−3.1	1.1	0.3
XNG	Natural Gas	Long	February	E	June	B	13.8	11.5	19.3
MSH	High-Tech	Long	March	M	July	B	6.8	3.6	6.4
UTY	Utilities	Long	March	M	October	B	7.7	6.3	6.6
XCI	Computer Tech	Long	April	M	July	M	7.1	5.9	7.4
BKX	Banking	Short	May	B	July	B	−7.8	−4.7	−3.4
XAU	Gold & Silver	Short	May	M	June	E	−4.8	−3.6	−2.0
S5MATR	Materials	Short	May	M	October	M	−4.5	−1.5	−2.8
XNG	Natural Gas	Short	June	M	July	E	−5.0	−4.1	−7.3
XAU	Gold & Silver	Long	July	E	December	E	4.7	0.1	0.8
S5INDU	Industrials	Short	July	M	October	B	−3.5	−3.2	−2.2
DJT	Transports	Short	July	M	October	M	−4.2	−3.2	−2.4
BTK	Biotech	Long	August	B	March	B	14.7	17.8	4.2
MSH	High-Tech	Long	August	M	January	M	9.5	12.8	9.5
SOX	Semiconductor	Short	August	M	October	E	−4.4	−0.02	1.2
XOI	Oil	Short	September	B	November	E	−4.3	−1.9	−4.3
BKX	Banking	Long	October	B	May	B	8.8	11.1	3.2
XBD	Broker/Dealer	Long	October	B	April	M	13.4	16.7	8.6
XCI	Computer Tech	Long	October	B	January	B	8.2	8.2	7.2
S5COND	Consumer Discretionary	Long	October	B	June	B	14.1	16.4	12.8
S5CONS	Consumer Staples	Long	October	B	June	B	7.9	9.4	5.9
S5HLTH	Healthcare	Long	October	B	May	B	8.7	11.7	5.0
S5INDU	Industrials	Long	October	E	May	M	10.8	11.5	3.2
S5MATR	Materials	Long	October	B	May	B	13.8	12.2	6.2
DRG	Pharmaceutical	Long	October	M	January	B	5.9	5.3	3.5
RMZ	Real Estate	Long	October	E	May	B	8.1	6.1	−0.9
SOX	Semiconductor	Long	October	E	December	B	8.4	9.0	7.7
XTC	Telecom	Long	October	M	December	E	6.0	4.8	7.1
DJT	Transports	Long	October	B	May	B	14.1	12.2	1.2
XOI	Oil	Long	December	M	July	B	5.7	5.0	−0.5

[†] Average % Return based on full seasonality completion through July 2, 2020

Start Looking for MACD BUY Signals on October 1 (Pages 52, 54 and 60)
Almanac Investor Subscribers Emailed When It Triggers (See Insert)

MONDAY
4

D 47.6
S 47.6
N 52.4

The riskiest moment is when you are right. That's when you're in the most trouble,
because you tend to overstay the good decisions.
— Peter L. Bernstein (Economist, *Money* magazine 10/15/2004, 1919–2009)

TUESDAY
5

D 66.7
S 66.7
N 76.2

There is a perfect inverse correlation between inflation rates and price/earnings ratios...
When inflation has been very high…P/E has been [low].
— Liz Ann Sonders (Chief Investment Strategist Charles Schwab, June 2006)

October Ends Dow & S&P "Worst Six Months" (Pages 50, 52, 54, 62 &
147) And NASDAQ "Worst Four Months" (Pages 58, 60 and 148)

WEDNESDAY
6

D 61.9
S 61.9
N 57.1

Entrepreneurs who believe they're in business to vanquish the competition are less successful than those
who believe their goal is to maximize profits or increase their company's value.
— Kaihan Krippendorff (Business consultant, strategist, author, *The Art of the Advantage*, b. 1971)

THURSDAY
7

D 28.6
S 28.6
N 42.9

The reason the market did so well in the last several years is because the Federal Reserve drove interest
rates down to extraordinary low levels—like 1%.
— George Roche (Chairman, T. Rowe Price, *Barron's* 12/18/06)

Dow Lost 1874 Points (18.2%) on the Week Ending 10/10/2008
Worst Dow Week in the History of Wall Street

FRIDAY
8

D 47.6
S 42.9
N 52.4

If a man can see both sides of a problem, you know that none of his money is tied up in it.
— Verda Ross

SATURDAY
9

SUNDAY
10

SECTOR INDEX SEASONALITY STRATEGY CALENDAR*

* Graphic representation of the Sector Index Seasonality Percentage Plays on page 92.
L = Long Trade, S = Short Trade, ⟶ = Start of Trade

(continued on page 96)

94

Columbus Day *(Bond Market Closed)*
Monday Before October Expiration, Dow Up 29 of 37

MONDAY
D 52.4
S 52.4
N 57.1
11

Success is going from failure to failure without loss of enthusiasm.
— Winston Churchill (British statesman, 1874–1965)

TUESDAY
D 47.6
S 47.6
N 52.4
12

Wise men are instructed by reason, men of less understanding by experience, the most ignorant by necessity, the beasts by nature.
— Marcus Tullius Cicero (Great Roman Orator, Politician, 106–43 B.C.)

October 2011, Second Dow Month to Gain 1000 Points

WEDNESDAY
D 38.1
S 42.9
N 52.4
13

I sold enough papers last year of high school to pay cash for a BMW.
— Michael Dell (Founder Dell Computer, *Forbes*)

THURSDAY
D 66.7
S 61.9
N 71.4
14

What's money? A man is a success if he gets up in the morning and goes to bed at night and in between does what he wants to do.
— Bob Dylan (American singer-songwriter, musician and artist, b. 1941)

October Expiration Day, Dow Down 6 Straight 2005–2010 and 10 of Last 17

FRIDAY
D 52.4
S 52.4
N 47.6
15

When everbody thinks alike, everyone is likely to be wrong.
— Humphrey B. Neill (Investor, analyst, author, *Art of Contrary Thinking* 1954, 1895–1977)

SATURDAY
16

SUNDAY
17

(continued from page 94)

SECTOR INDEX SEASONALITY STRATEGY CALENDAR*

* Graphic representation of the Sector Index Seasonality Percentage Plays on page 92.
L = Long Trade, S = Short Trade, —→ = Start of Trade

MONDAY

D 57.1
S 66.7
N 57.1

18

When everybody starts looking really smart, and not realizing that a lot of it was luck, I get scared.
— Raphael Yavneh (President Forbes Investors Advisory Institute, 1930–1990)

Crash of October 19, 1987, Dow Down 22.6% in One Day

TUESDAY

D 52.4
S 61.9
N 52.4

19

The greatest discovery of my generation is that human beings can alter their lives by altering their attitudes.
— William James (Philosopher, psychologist, 1842–1910)

WEDNESDAY

D 52.4
S 57.1
N 57.1

20

Some men see things as they are and say "why?" I dream things that never were and say "why not?"
— George Bernard Shaw (Irish dramatist, 1856–1950)

Late October Is Time to Buy Depressed Stocks
Especially Techs and Small Caps

THURSDAY

D 57.1
S 61.9
N 61.9

21

On Wall Street, to know what everyone else knows is to know nothing.
— Newton Zinder (Investment advisor and analyst, E.F. Hutton, b. 1927)

FRIDAY

D 57.1
S 66.7
N 57.1

22

Successful investing is anticipating the anticipations of others.
— John Maynard Keynes (British economist, 1883–1946)

SATURDAY

23

November Almanac Investor Sector Seasonalities: See Pages 92, 94 and 96

SUNDAY

24

MARKET BEHAVIOR THREE DAYS BEFORE AND THREE DAYS AFTER HOLIDAYS

The *Stock Trader's Almanac* has tracked holiday seasonality annually since the first edition in 1968. Stocks used to rise on the day before holidays and sell off the day after, but nowadays, each holiday moves to its own rhythm. Eight holidays are separated into six groups. Average percentage changes for the Dow, S&P 500, NASDAQ, and Russell 2000 are shown.

The Dow and S&P consist of blue chips and the largest cap stocks, whereas NASDAQ and the Russell 2000 would be more representative of smaller-cap stocks. This is evident on the last day of the year, with NASDAQ and the Russell 2000 having a field day, while their larger brethren in the Dow and S&P are showing losses on average.

Thanks to the Santa Claus Rally, the three days before and after New Year's Day and Christmas are best. NASDAQ and the Russell 2000 average gains of 1.1% to 1.5% over the six-day spans. However, trading around the first day of the year has been mixed recently. Traders have been selling more the first trading day of the year, pushing gains and losses into the New Year.

Bullishness before Labor Day and after Memorial Day is affected by strength the first day of September and June. The second worst day after a holiday is the day after Easter. Surprisingly, the following day is the best second day after a holiday, eclipsing the second day after New Year's Day.

Presidents' Day is the least bullish of all the holidays, bearish the day before and three days after. NASDAQ has dropped 20 of the last 31 days before Presidents' Day (Dow, 17 of 31; S&P, 18 of 31; Russell 2000, 15 of 31).

HOLIDAYS: 3 DAYS BEFORE, 3 DAYS AFTER (Average % change 1980–June 2020)

	−3	−2	−1		+1	+2	+3
S&P 500	0.05	0.17	−0.11	**New Year's**	0.23	0.20	0.09
DJIA	0.03	0.12	−0.16	**Day**	0.32	0.18	0.19
NASDAQ	0.09	0.20	0.14	1/1/21	0.25	0.44	0.23
Russell 2K	0.05	0.33	0.36	Mixed	0.05	0.16	0.11
S&P 500	0.36	0.04	−0.10	**Presidents'**	−0.15	−0.03	−0.13
DJIA	0.34	0.01	−0.02	**Day**	−0.11	−0.06	−0.14
NASDAQ	0.56	0.30	−0.24	2/15/21	−0.40	−0.002	−0.11
Russell 2K	0.44	0.19	0.002	Negative Before & After	−0.29	−0.12	−0.07
S&P 500	0.11	0.01	0.40	**Good Friday**	−0.23	0.41	0.06
DJIA	0.10	0.0005	0.32	4/2/21	−0.17	0.38	0.06
NASDAQ	0.28	0.21	0.48	Positive Before &	−0.31	0.48	0.18
Russell 2K	0.16	0.11	0.58	Negative After	−0.39	0.36	0.05
S&P 500	0.10	0.01	0.01	**Memorial**	0.26	0.16	0.22
DJIA	0.08	−0.03	−0.05	**Day**	0.30	0.16	0.12
NASDAQ	0.16	0.17	0.06	5/31/21	0.22	0.01	0.43
Russell 2K	0.03	0.23	0.14	Positive After	0.28	0.13	0.33
S&P 500	0.17	0.14	0.08	**Independence**	−0.12	0.04	0.07
DJIA	0.14	0.13	0.09	**Day**	−0.07	0.06	0.06
NASDAQ	0.30	0.16	0.05	7/4/21	−0.12	−0.09	0.23
Russell 2K	0.31	0.05	0.03	Negative After	−0.22	−0.05	0.05
S&P 500	0.23	−0.15	0.13	**Labor**	0.07	0.08	−0.04
DJIA	0.20	−0.21	0.13	**Day**	0.08	0.14	−0.11
NASDAQ	0.44	0.05	0.15	9/6/21	0.003	−0.05	0.09
Russell 2K	0.52	0.09	0.13	Positive Before & After	0.04	0.13	0.05
S&P 500	0.12	−0.01	0.25	**Thanksgiving**	0.16	−0.39	0.30
DJIA	0.12	−0.01	0.24	11/25/21	0.12	−0.33	0.31
NASDAQ	0.06	−0.19	0.41		0.40	−0.39	0.12
Russell 2K	0.18	−0.06	0.41		0.27	−0.50	0.26
S&P 500	0.15	0.15	0.13	**Christmas**	0.27	0.02	0.22
DJIA	0.21	0.19	0.16	12/25/21	0.30	0.04	0.18
NASDAQ	−0.08	0.31	0.31		0.27	0.05	0.26
Russell 2K	0.20	0.28	0.29		0.30	0.03	0.41

🐻 **MONDAY**
D 42.9
S 38.1
N 47.6
25

Based on my own personal experience—both as an investor in recent years and an expert witness in years past—rarely do more than three or four variables really count. Everything else is noise.
— Martin J. Whitman (Founder Third Avenue Funds, b. 1924)

TUESDAY
D 66.7
S 57.1
N 47.6
26

In this age of instant information, investors can experience both fear and greed at the exact same moment.
— Sam Stovall (Chief Investment Strategist CFRA Research, October 2003)

WEDNESDAY
D 52.4
S 47.6
N 52.4
27

The investor who concentrated on the 50 stocks in the S&P 500 that are followed by the fewest Wall Street analysts wound up with a rousing 24.6% gain in [2006 versus] 13.6% [for] the S&P 500.
— Rich Bernstein (Chief Investment Strategist, Merrill Lynch, *Barron's* 1/8/07)

🐂 **THURSDAY**
D 61.9
S 61.9
N 57.1
28

But how do we know when irrational exuberance has unduly escalated asset values, which then become subject to unexpected and prolonged contractions as they have in Japan over the past decade?
— Alan Greenspan (Fed Chairman 1987-2006, 12/5/96 speech to American Enterprise Institute, b. 1926)

88th Anniversary of 1929 Crash, Dow Down 23.0% in 2 Days, October 28-29

FRIDAY
D 52.4
S 57.1
N 57.1
29

Sight and Sound function differently in the mind, with sound being the surer investment.
WIN THE EARS OF THE PEOPLE, THEIR EYES WILL FOLLOW.
— Roy H. Williams (The Wizard of Ads)

SATURDAY
30

Halloween 🎃

SUNDAY
31

NOVEMBER ALMANAC

NOVEMBER						
S	M	T	W	T	F	S
			1	2	3	4
7	8	9	10	11	12	13
14	15	16	17	18	19	20
21	22	23	24	25	26	27
28	29	30				

DECEMBER						
S	M	T	W	T	F	S
				1	2	3	4
5	6	7	8	9	10	11
12	13	14	15	16	17	18
19	20	21	22	23	24	25
26	27	28	29	30	31	

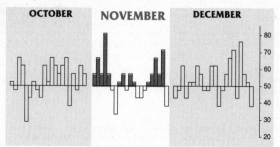

Market Probability Chart above is a graphic representation of the S&P 500 Recent Market Probability Calendar on page 124.

◆ #2 S&P and Dow month since 1950, #3 on NASDAQ since 1971 (pages 50 & 58) ◆ Start of the "Best Six Months" of the year (page 52), NASDAQ's Best Eight Months and Best Three Months (pages 147 & 148) ◆ Simple timing indicator almost triples "Best Six Months" strategy (page 54), doubles NASDAQ's Best Eight (page 60) ◆ Day before and after Thanksgiving Day combined, only 17 losses in 68 years (page 104) ◆ Week before Thanksgiving Dow up 19 of last 27 ◆ Post–presidential election year Novembers rank #3 Dow and #2 S&P, NASDAQ #3

November Vital Statistics

	DJIA		S&P 500		NASDAQ		Russell 1K		Russell 2K	
Rank	2		2		3		2		2	
Up	48		48		34		31		28	
Down	22		22		15		10		13	
Average % Change	1.6%		1.6%		1.7%		1.8%		2.1%	
Post-Election Year	1.9%		1.8%		2.4%		3.7%		2.8%	
				Best & Worst November						
	% Change		% Change		% Change		% Change		% Change	
Best	1962	10.1	1980	10.2	2001	14.2	1980	10.1	2016	11.0
Worst	1973	−14.0	1973	−11.4	2000	−22.9	2000	−9.3	2008	−12.0
				Best & Worst November Weeks						
Best	11/28/2008	9.7	11/28/2008	12.0	11/28/2008	10.9	11/28/2008	12.5	11/28/2008	16.4
Worst	11/21/2008	−5.3	11/21/2008	−8.4	11/10/2000	−12.2	11/21/2008	−8.8	11/21/2008	−11.0
				Best & Worst November Days						
Best	11/13/2008	6.7	11/13/2008	6.9	11/13/2008	6.5	11/13/2008	7.0	11/13/2008	8.5
Worst	11/20/2008	−5.6	11/20/2008	−6.7	11/19/2008	−6.5	11/20/2008	−6.9	11/19/2008	−7.9
			First Trading Day of Expiration Week: 1980-2020							
Record (#Up − #Down)	22–18		18–22		15–25		20–20		17–23	
Current streak	U1		D2		D2		D2		D3	
Avg % Change	−0.06		−0.09		−0.19		−0.09		−0.11	
				Options Expiration Day: 1980-2020						
Record (#Up − #Down)	26–14		24–16		21–19		24–16		23–16	
Current streak	U2		U2		U1		U2		U10	
Avg % Change	0.24		0.18		0.05		0.17		0.16	
				Options Expiration Week: 1980-2020						
Record (#Up − #Down)	26–14		24–16		22–18		23–17		20–20	
Current streak	U1		U1		U1		U1		D2	
Avg % Change	0.29		0.10		0.07		0.09		−0.15	
			Week After Options Expiration: 1980-2020							
Record (#Up − #Down)	23–17		25–15		26–14		25–15		24–16	
Current streak	D2		D2		D2		D2		D2	
Avg % Change	0.54		0.55		0.66		0.56		0.75	
				First Trading Day Performance						
% of Time Up	64.3		64.3		65.3		73.2		61.0	
Avg % Change	0.29		0.31		0.32		0.40		0.26	
				Last Trading Day Performance						
% of Time Up	55.7		52.9		63.3		46.3		65.9	
Avg % Change	0.12		0.13		−0.07		0.03		0.13	

Dow & S&P 1950–June 19, 2020, NASDAQ 1971–June 19, 2020, Russell 1K & 2K 1979–June 19, 2020.

Astute investors always smile and remember,
When stocks seasonally start soaring, and salute November.

First Trading Day in November, Dow Up 8 of Last 11

MONDAY

D 57.1
S 57.1
N 61.9

1

Early in March (1960), Dr. Arthur F. Burns called on me…Burns' conclusion was that unless some decisive action was taken, and taken soon, we were heading for another economic dip which would hit its low point in October, just before the elections.
— Richard M. Nixon (37th U.S. President, *Six Crises*, 1913–1994)

Election Day

TUESDAY

D 57.1
S 66.7
N 61.9

2

The political problem of mankind is to combine three things: economic efficiency, social justice, and individual liberty.
— John Maynard Keynes (British economist, 1883–1946)

FOMC Meeting (2 Days)

WEDNESDAY

D 61.9
S 57.1
N 61.9

3

Today's Ponzi-style acute fragility and speculative dynamics dictate that he who panics first panics best.
— Doug Noland (Prudent Bear Funds, *Credit Bubble Bulletin*, 10/26/07)

THURSDAY

D 76.2
S 81.0
N 66.7

4

Cooperation is essential to address 21st-century challenges; you can't fire cruise missiles at the global financial crisis.
— Nicholas D. Kristof (*NY Times* columnist, 10/23/2008)

FRIDAY

D 66.7
S 57.1
N 61.9

5

The Stone Age didn't end for lack of stone, and the oil age will end long before the world runs out of oil.
— Sheik Ahmed Zaki Yamani (Saudi oil minister 1962-1986, b. 1930)

SATURDAY

6

Daylight Saving Time Ends

SUNDAY

7

FOURTH-QUARTER MARKET MAGIC

Examining market performance on a quarterly basis reveals several intriguing and helpful patterns. Fourth-quarter market gains have been magical, providing the greatest and most consistent gains over the years. First-quarter performance runs a respectable second. This should not be surprising, as cash inflows, trading volume, and buying bias are generally elevated during these two quarters.

Positive market psychology hits a fever pitch as the holiday season approaches, and does not begin to wane until spring. Professionals drive the market higher, as they make portfolio adjustments to maximize year-end numbers. Bonuses are paid and invested around the turn of the year.

The market's sweet spot of the four-year cycle begins in the fourth quarter of the midterm year. The best two-quarter span runs from the fourth quarter of the midterm year through the first quarter of the pre-election year, averaging 13.7% for the Dow, 14.4% for the S&P 500 and an amazing 19.9% for NASDAQ. Pre-election Q2 is smoking, too, the third best quarter of the cycle, creating a three-quarter sweet spot from midterm Q4 to pre-election Q2.

Quarterly strength fades in the latter half of the pre-election year, but stays impressively positive through the election year. Losses dominate the first quarter of post-election years and the second and third quarters of midterm years.

QUARTERLY % CHANGES

	Q1	Q2	Q3	Q4	Year	Q2–Q3	Q4–Q1
Dow Jones Industrials (1949–June 2020)							
Average	2.0%	1.8%	0.6%	3.9%	8.6%	2.2%	6.0%
Post Election	−0.1%	1.7%	0.5%	4.2%	6.7%	2.3%	5.5%
Midterm	1.2%	−1.4%	0.1%	6.1%	6.0%	−1.2%	13.7%
Pre-Election	7.3%	4.8%	1.0%	2.7%	16.2%	5.8%	2.3%
Election	−0.5%	1.9%	0.7%	2.3%	5.3%	1.8%	2.4%
S&P 500 (1949–June 2020)							
Average	2.1%	1.9%	0.8%	4.0%	9.2%	2.5%	6.3%
Post Election	−0.2%	2.2%	0.9%	3.6%	7.0%	3.2%	4.7%
Midterm	0.9%	−2.1%	0.5%	6.6%	6.0%	−1.5%	14.4%
Pre-Election	7.4%	4.9%	0.6%	3.5%	16.8%	5.5%	3.7%
Election	0.2%	2.8%	1.1%	2.0%	6.7%	2.9%	2.0%
NASDAQ Composite (1971–June 2020)							
Average	4.1%	3.7%	0.4%	4.2%	12.9%	3.8%	8.5%
Post Election	−1.2%	6.3%	2.5%	5.0%	12.6%	8.8%	6.9%
Midterm	2.0%	−1.9%	−3.5%	6.4%	2.2%	−5.0%	19.9%
Pre-Election	13.2%	7.2%	0.9%	5.9%	29.3%	8.1%	8.3%
Election	2.0%	3.0%	1.8%	−0.6%	6.0%	2.8%	−1.3%

NOVEMBER 2021

November Begins Dow & S&P "Best Six Months" (Pages 50, 52, 54, 62 & 147)
And NASDAQ "Best Eight Months" (Pages 58, 60 and 148)

MONDAY
8

D 57.1
S 47.6
N 52.4

It is better to be out wishing you were in, than in wishing you were out.
— Albert W. Thomas (Trader, investor, *Over My Shoulder*, mutualfundmagic.com,
If It Doesn't Go Up, Don't Buy It!, b. 1927)

TUESDAY
9

D 42.9
S 33.3
N 33.3

*The market is a voting machine, whereon countless individuals register choices which are the product partly
of reason and partly of emotion.*
— Graham & Dodd

WEDNESDAY
10

D 38.1
S 52.4
N 61.9

Washington is run by people who think there is a 1% difference between 2% growth and 3% growth.
— George Will (American political commentator & journalist, b. 1941)

Veterans' Day

THURSDAY
11

D 61.9
S 57.1
N 66.7

*There are no secrets to success. Don't waste your time looking for them. Success is the result of perfection,
hard work, learning from failure, loyalty to those for whom you work, and persistence.*
— General Colin Powell (Chairman Joint Chiefs 1989-1993,
Secretary of State 2001–2005, *NY Times*, 10/22/2008, b. 1937)

FRIDAY
12

D 47.6
S 47.6
N 42.9

I don't think education has a lot to do with the number of years you're incarcerated in a brick building being talked down to.
— Tom Peters (American writer, *In Search of Excellence*, *Fortune*, 11/13/2000, b. 1942)

SATURDAY
13

SUNDAY
14

TRADING THE THANKSGIVING MARKET

For 35 years, the "holiday spirit" gave the Wednesday before Thanksgiving and the Friday after a great track record, except for two occasions. Publishing it in the 1987 *Almanac* was the kiss of death. Since 1988, Wednesday–Friday gained 18 of 32 times, with a total Dow point gain of 531.05 versus Monday's total Dow point loss of 814.56, down 15 of 22 since 1998. The best strategy appears to be coming into the week long and exiting into strength Friday.

DOW JONES INDUSTRIALS BEFORE AND AFTER THANKSGIVING

	Tuesday Before	Wednesday Before		Friday After	Total Gain Dow Points	Dow Close	Next Monday
1952	−0.18	1.54		1.22	2.76	283.66	0.04
1953	1.71	0.65		2.45	3.10	280.23	1.14
1954	3.27	1.89		3.16	5.05	387.79	0.72
1955	4.61	0.71		0.26	0.97	482.88	−1.92
1956	−4.49	−2.16		4.65	2.49	472.56	−2.27
1957	−9.04	10.69		3.84	14.53	449.87	−2.96
1958	−4.37	8.63		8.31	16.94	557.46	2.61
1959	2.94	1.41	T	1.42	2.83	652.52	6.66
1960	−3.44	1.37		4.00	5.37	606.47	−1.04
1961	−0.77	1.10	H	2.18	3.28	732.60	−0.61
1962	6.73	4.31		7.62	11.93	644.87	−2.81
1963	32.03	−2.52	A	9.52	7.00	750.52	1.39
1964	−1.68	−5.21		−0.28	−5.49	882.12	−6.69
1965	2.56	N/C	N	−0.78	−0.78	948.16	−1.23
1966	−3.18	1.84		6.52	8.36	803.34	−2.18
1967	13.17	3.07	K	3.58	6.65	877.60	4.51
1968	8.14	−3.17		8.76	5.59	985.08	−1.74
1969	−5.61	3.23	S	1.78	5.01	812.30	−7.26
1970	5.21	1.98		6.64	8.62	781.35	12.74
1971	−5.18	0.66	G	17.96	18.62	816.59	13.14
1972	8.21	7.29		4.67	11.96	1025.21	−7.45
1973	−17.76	10.08	I	−0.98	9.10	854.00	−29.05
1974	5.32	2.03		−0.63	1.40	618.66	−15.64
1975	9.76	3.15	V	2.12	5.27	860.67	−4.33
1976	−6.57	1.66		5.66	7.32	956.62	−6.57
1977	6.41	0.78	I	1.12	1.90	844.42	−4.85
1978	−1.56	2.95		3.12	6.07	810.12	3.72
1979	−6.05	−1.80	N	4.35	2.55	811.77	16.98
1980	3.93	7.00		3.66	10.66	993.34	−23.89
1981	18.45	7.90	G	7.80	15.70	885.94	3.04
1982	−9.01	9.01		7.36	16.37	1007.36	−4.51
1983	7.01	−0.20		1.83	1.63	1277.44	−7.62
1984	9.83	6.40		18.78	25.18	1220.30	−7.95
1985	0.12	18.92		−3.56	15.36	1472.13	−14.22
1986	6.05	4.64		−2.53	2.11	1914.23	−1.55
1987	40.45	−16.58		−36.47	−53.05	1910.48	−76.93
1988	11.73	14.58		−17.60	−3.02	2074.68	6.76
1989	7.25	17.49	N	18.77	36.26	2675.55	19.42
1990	−35.15	9.16		−12.13	−2.97	2527.23	5.94
1991	14.08	−16.10	G	−5.36	−21.46	2894.68	40.70
1992	25.66	17.56		15.94	33.50	3282.20	22.96
1993	3.92	13.41		−3.63	9.78	3683.95	−6.15
1994	−91.52	−3.36		33.64	30.28	3708.27	31.29
1995	40.46	18.06		7.23*	25.29	5048.84	22.04
1996	−19.38	−29.07	D	22.36*	−6.71	6521.70	N/C
1997	41.03	−14.17		28.35*	14.18	7823.13	189.98
1998	−73.12	13.13	A	18.80*	31.93	9333.08	−216.53
1999	−93.89	12.54		−19.26*	−6.72	10988.91	−40.99
2000	31.85	−95.18	Y	70.91*	−24.27	10470.23	75.84
2001	−75.08	−66.70		125.03*	58.33	9959.71	23.04
2002	−172.98	255.26		−35.59*	219.67	8896.09	−33.52
2003	16.15	15.63		2.89*	18.52	9782.46	116.59
2004	3.18	27.71		1.92*	29.63	10522.23	−46.33
2005	51.15	44.66		15.53*	60.19	10931.62	−40.90
2006	5.05	5.36		−46.78*	−41.42	12280.17	−158.46
2007	51.70	−211.10		181.84*	−29.26	12980.88	−237.44
2008	36.08	247.14		102.43*	349.57	8829.04	−679.95
2009	−17.24	30.69		−154.48*	−123.79	10309.92	34.92
2010	−142.21	150.91		−95.28*	55.63	11092.00	−39.51
2011	−53.59	−236.17		−25.77*	−261.94	11231.78	291.23
2012	−7.45	48.38		172.79*	221.17	13009.68	−42.31
2013	0.26	24.53		−10.92*	13.61	16086.41	−77.64
2014	−2.96	−2.69		15.99*	13.30	17828.24	−51.44
2015	19.51	1.20		−14.90*	−13.70	17798.49	−78.57
2016	67.18	59.31		68.96*	128.27	19152.14	−54.24
2017	160.50	−64.65		31.81*	−32.84	23557.99	22.79
2018	−551.80	−0.95		−178.74*	−179.69	24285.95	354.29
2019	55.21	42.32		−112.59	−70.27	28051.41	−268.37

*Shortened trading day

104

Monday Before November Expiration, Dow Up 11 of Last 16
2008 –2.6%, 2018 –2.3%

MONDAY

D 66.7
S 57.1
N 47.6

15

Only those who will risk going too far can possibly find out how far one can go.
— T.S. Eliot (English poet, essayist and critic, *The Wasteland*, 1888–1965)

TUESDAY

D 57.1
S 52.4
N 57.1

16

It has been said that politics is the second oldest profession. I have learned that it bears a striking resemblance to the first.
— Ronald Reagan (40th U.S. President, 1911–2004)

Week Before Thanksgiving, Dow Up 19 of Last 27, 2003 –1.4%, 2004 –0.8%,
2008 –5.3%, 2011 –2.9%, 2012 –1.8%, 2018 –2.2%

WEDNESDAY

D 38.1
S 42.9
N 42.9

17

What counts more than luck, is determination and perseverance. If the talent is there, it will come through.
Don't be too impatient.
— Fred Astaire (The report from his first screen test stated, "Can't act. Can't sing. Balding. Can dance a little.")

THURSDAY

D 42.9
S 42.9
N 47.6

18

Don't worry about people stealing your ideas. If the ideas are any good, you'll have to ram them down people's throats.
— Howard Aiken (U.S. computer scientist, 1900–1973)

November Expiration Day, Dow Up 14 of Last 18
Dow Surged in 2008, Up 494 Points (6.5%)

FRIDAY

D 42.9
S 47.6
N 47.6

19

At a time of war, we need you to work for peace. At a time of inequality, we need you to work for opportunity.
At a time of so much cynicism and so much doubt, we need you to make us believe again.
— Barack H. Obama (44th U.S. President, Commencement Wesleyan University 5/28/2008, b. 1961)

SATURDAY

20

SUNDAY

21

AURA OF THE TRIPLE WITCH—4TH QUARTER MOST BULLISH: DOWN WEEKS TRIGGER MORE WEAKNESS WEEK AFTER

Standard options expire the third Friday of every month, but in March, June, September, and December, a powerful coven gathers. Since the S&P index futures began trading on April 21, 1982, stock options, index options, and index futures all expire at the same time four times each year—known as Triple Witching. Traders have long sought to understand and master the magic of this quarterly phenomenon.

The market for single-stock and ETF futures and weekly options continues to grow. However, their impact on the market has thus far been subdued. As their availability continues to expand, trading volumes and market influence could broaden. Until such time, we do not believe the term "quadruple witching" is applicable just yet.

We have analyzed what the market does prior to, during, and following Triple-Witching expirations in search of consistent trading patterns. Here are some of our findings of how the Dow Jones Industrials perform around Triple-Witching Week (TWW).

- TWWs have become more bullish since 1990, except in the second quarter.
- Following weeks have become more bearish. Since Q1 2000, only 30 of 81 were up, and 15 occurred in December, 8 in March, 5 in September, 2 in June.
- TWWs have tended to be down in flat periods and dramatically so during bear markets.
- DOWN WEEKS TEND TO FOLLOW DOWN TWWs is a most interesting pattern. Since 1991, of 39 down TWWs, 27 following weeks were also down. This is surprising, inasmuch as the previous decade had an exactly opposite pattern: There were 13 down TWWs then, but 12 up weeks followed them.
- TWWs in the second and third quarter (Worst Six Months May through October) are much weaker, and the weeks following, horrendous. But in the first and fourth quarter (Best Six Months period November through April), only the week after Q1 expiration is negative.

Throughout the *Almanac* you will also see notations on the performance of Mondays and Fridays of TWW, as we place considerable significance on the beginnings and ends of weeks (pages 70, 76 and 141–144).

TRIPLE-WITCHING WEEK AND WEEK AFTER DOW POINT CHANGES

	Expiration Week Q1	Week After	Expiration Week Q2	Week After	Expiration Week Q3	Week After	Expiration Week Q4	Week After
1991	−6.93	−89.36	−34.98	−58.81	33.54	−13.19	20.12	167.04
1992	40.48	−44.95	−69.01	−2.94	21.35	−76.73	9.19	12.97
1993	43.76	−31.60	−10.24	−3.88	−8.38	−70.14	10.90	6.15
1994	32.95	−120.92	3.33	−139.84	58.54	−101.60	116.08	26.24
1995	38.04	65.02	86.80	75.05	96.85	−33.42	19.87	−78.76
1996	114.52	51.67	55.78	−50.60	49.94	−15.54	179.53	76.51
1997	−130.67	−64.20	14.47	−108.79	174.30	4.91	−82.01	−76.98
1998	303.91	−110.35	−122.07	231.67	100.16	133.11	81.87	314.36
1999	27.20	−81.31	365.05	−303.00	−224.80	−524.30	32.73	148.33
2000	666.41	517.49	−164.76	−44.55	−293.65	−79.63	−277.95	200.60
2001	−821.21	−318.63	−353.36	−19.05	−1369.70	611.75	224.19	101.65
2002	34.74	−179.56	−220.42	−10.53	−326.67	−284.57	77.61	−207.54
2003	662.26	−376.20	83.63	−211.70	173.27	−331.74	236.06	46.45
2004	−53.48	26.37	6.31	−44.57	−28.61	−237.22	106.70	177.20
2005	−144.69	−186.80	110.44	−325.23	−36.62	−222.35	97.01	7.68
2006	203.31	0.32	122.63	−25.46	168.66	−52.67	138.03	−102.30
2007	−165.91	370.60	215.09	−279.22	377.67	75.44	110.80	−84.78
2008	410.23	−144.92	−464.66	−496.18	−33.55	−245.31	−50.57	−63.56
2009	54.40	497.80	−259.53	−101.34	214.79	−155.01	−142.61	191.21
2010	117.29	108.38	239.57	−306.83	145.08	252.41	81.59	81.58
2011	−185.88	362.07	52.45	−69.78	516.96	−737.61	−317.87	427.61
2012	310.60	−151.89	212.97	−126.39	−13.90	−142.34	55.83	−252.73
2013	117.04	−2.08	−270.78	110.20	75.03	−192.85	465.78	257.27
2014	237.10	20.29	171.34	−95.24	292.23	−166.59	523.97	248.91
2015	378.34	−414.99	117.11	−69.27	−48.51	−69.91	−136.66	423.62
2016	388.99	−86.57	−190.18	−274.41	38.35	137.65	86.56	90.40
2017	11.64	−317.90	112.31	10.48	470.55	81.25	322.58	102.32
2018	−389.23	−1413.31	−226.05	−509.59	588.83	−285.19	−1655.14	617.03
2019	398.63	−346.55	629.52	−119.17	−284.45	−114.82	319.71	190.17
2020	−4011.64	2462.80	265.92	−855.91				
Up	21	11	18	4	18	7	22	22
Down	9	19	12	26	11	22	7	7

Trading Thanksgiving Market: Long into Weakness Prior,
Exit into Strength After (Page 104)

MONDAY
D 57.1
S 52.4
N 66.7
22

It is impossible to please all the world and one's father.
— Jean de La Fontaine (French poet, 1621–1695)

TUESDAY
D 61.9
S 57.1
N 61.9
23

As for it being different this time, it is different every time. The question is in what way, and to what extent.
— Tom McClellan (*The McClellan Market Report*)

WEDNESDAY
D 76.2
S 66.7
N 66.7
24

Nothing will improve a person's hearing more than sincere praise.
— Harvey Mackay (*Pushing the Envelope*, 1999)

Thanksgiving *(Market Closed)*

THURSDAY
25

Everyone wants to make the same three things: money, a name, and a difference.
What creates diversity in the human race is how we prioritize the three.
— Roy H. Williams (*The Wizard of Ads*)

(Shortened Trading Day)

FRIDAY
D 61.9
S 57.1
N 57.1
26

The death of contrarians has been greatly exaggerated. The reason is that the crowd is the market for
most of any cycle. You cannot be contrarian all the time, otherwise you end up simply fighting the tape the
whole way up (or down), therefore being wildly wrong.
— Barry L. Ritholtz (Founder/CIO Ritholtz Wealth Management, *Bailout Nation*,
The Big Picture blog, *Bloomberg View* 12/20/2013, b. 1961)

SATURDAY
27

December Almanac Investor Sector Seasonalities: See Pages 92, 94 and 96

SUNDAY
28

DECEMBER ALMANAC

DECEMBER						
S	M	T	W	T	F	S
				1	2	3	4
5	6	7	8	9	10	11
12	13	14	15	16	17	18
19	20	21	22	23	24	25
26	27	28	29	30	31	

JANUARY						
S	M	T	W	T	F	S
						1
2	3	4	5	6	7	8
9	10	11	12	13	14	15
16	17	18	19	20	21	22
23	24	25	26	27	28	29
30	31					

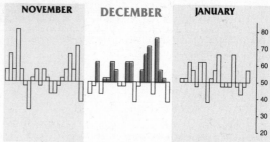

Market Probability Chart above is a graphic representation of the S&P 500 Recent Market Probability Calendar on page 124.

◆ #3 S&P (+1.5%) and Dow (+1.5%) month since 1950 (page 50), #4 NASDAQ 1.6% since 1971 (page 58) ◆ 2018 worst December since 1931, down over 8% Dow and S&P, –9.5% on NASDAQ (pages 152, 155 and 158) ◆ "Free lunch" served on Wall Street before Christmas (page 114) ◆ Small caps start to outperform larger caps near middle of month (pages 110 and 112) ◆ "Santa Claus Rally" visible in graph above and on page 116 ◆ In 1998 was part of best fourth quarter since 1928 (page 170) ◆ Fourth-quarter expiration week most bullish triple-witching week, Dow up 22 of last 29 (page 106) ◆ Post–presidential election years Decembers rankings: #5 Dow, #7 S&P and #7 NASDAQ

December Vital Statistics

	DJIA	S&P 500	NASDAQ	Russell 1K	Russell 2K
Rank	3	3	4	3	1
Up	49	52	29	31	31
Down	21	18	20	10	10
Average % Change	1.5%	1.5%	1.6%	1.3%	2.2%
Post-Election Year	1.0%	0.6%	0.9%	1.3%	2.2%
Best & Worst December					
	% Change	% Change	% Change	% Change	% Change
Best	1991 9.5	1991 11.2	1999 22.0	1991 11.2	1999 11.2
Worst	2018 –8.7	2018 –9.2	2002 –9.7	2018 –9.3	2018 –12.0
Best & Worst December Weeks					
Best	12/2/2011 7.0	12/2/2011 7.4	12/8/2000 10.3	12/2/2011 7.4	12/2/2011 10.3
Worst	12/4/1987 –7.5	12/6/1974 –7.1	12/15/2000 –9.1	12/21/2018 –7.1	12/21/2018 –8.4
Best & Worst December Days					
Best	12/26/2018 5.0	12/16/2008 5.1	12/5/2000 10.5	12/16/2008 5.2	12/16/2008 6.7
Worst	12/1/2008 –7.7	12/1/2008 –8.9	12/1/2008 –9.0	12/1/2008 –9.1	12/1/2008 –11.9
First Trading Day of Expiration Week: 1980-2020					
Record (#Up – #Down)	24–16	24–16	18–22	24–16	17–23
Current Streak	U1	U1	U1	U1	U1
Avg % Change	0.13	0.10	–0.08	0.06	–0.22
Options Expiration Day: 1980-2020					
Record (#Up – #Down)	25–15	28–12	27–13	28–12	25–15
Current Streak	U1	U1	U1	U1	U1
Avg % Change	0.21	0.28	0.24	0.27	0.34
Options Expiration Week: 1980-2020					
Record (#Up – #Down)	30–10	28–12	23–17	27–13	21–19
Current Streak	U1	U1	U1	U1	U1
Avg % Change	0.57	0.58	0.13	0.53	0.42
Week After Options Expiration: 1980-2020					
Record (#Up – #Down)	29–10	26–14	27–13	26–14	28–12
Current Streak	U7	U7	U7	U7	D1
Avg % Change	0.83	0.59	0.77	0.61	0.91
First Trading Day Performance					
% of Time Up	47.1	48.6	57.1	48.8	48.8
Avg % Change	–0.04	–0.03	0.09	–0.04	–0.15
Last Trading Day Performance					
% of Time Up	52.9	60.0	69.4	51.2	65.9
Avg % Change	0.06	0.09	0.28	–0.06	0.36

Dow & S&P 1950-June 19, 2020, NASDAQ 1971-June 19, 2020, Russell 1K & 2K 1979-June 19, 2020.

If Santa Claus should fail to call,
Bears may come to Broad and Wall.

Chanukah

MONDAY
29
D 61.9
S 71.4
N 61.9

The soul is dyed the color of its thoughts. Think only on those things that are in line with your principles and can bear the light of day. The content of your character is your choice. Day by day, what you do is who you become.
— Heraclitus (Greek philosopher, 535–475 BC)

Last Trading Day of November, S&P Down 14 of Last 22

TUESDAY
30
D 52.4
S 38.1
N 42.9

You have to keep digging, keep asking questions, because otherwise you'll be seduced or brainwashed into the idea that it's somehow a great privilege, an honor, to report the lies they've been feeding you.
— David Halberstam (Amercian writer, war reporter, 1964 Pulitzer Prize, 1934–2007)

First Trading Day in December, NASDAQ Up 21 of 33, But Down 9 of Last 14

WEDNESDAY
1
D 42.9
S 42.9
N 52.4

I hate to be wrong. That has aborted many a tempting error, but not all of them. But I hate much more to stay wrong.
— Paul A. Samuelson (American economist, 12/23/03 University of Kansas interview, 1915–2009)

THURSDAY
2
D 38.1
S 47.6
N 52.4

[The Fed] is very smart, but [it] doesn't run the markets. In the end, the markets will run [the Fed]. The markets are bigger than any man or any group of men. The markets can even break a president…
— Richard Russell (Dow Theory Letters, 8/4/04)

FRIDAY
3
D 66.7
S 61.9
N 66.7

A day will come when all nations on our continent will form a European brotherhood…A day will come when we shall see…the United States of Europe…reaching out for each other across the seas.
— Victor Hugo (French novelist, playwright, *The Hunchback of Notre Dame* and *Les Misérables*, 1802–1885)

SATURDAY
4

SUNDAY
5

MOST OF THE SO-CALLED JANUARY EFFECT TAKES PLACE IN THE LAST HALF OF DECEMBER

Over the years we have reported annually on the fascinating January Effect, showing that small-cap stocks handily outperformed large-cap stocks during January 40 out of 43 years between 1953 and 1995. Readers saw that "Cats and Dogs" on average quadrupled the returns of blue chips in this period. Then the January Effect disappeared over the next four years.

Looking at the graph on page 112, comparing the Russell 1000 index of large-capitalization stocks to the Russell 2000 smaller-capitalization stocks, shows small-cap stocks beginning to outperform the blue chips in mid-December. Narrowing the comparison down to half-month segments was an inspiration and proved to be quite revealing, as you can see in the table below.

33-YEAR AVERAGE RATES OF RETURN (DEC 1987 – FEB 2020)

From mid-Dec*	Russell 1000		Russell 2000	
	Change	Annualized	Change	Annualized
12/15–12/31	1.6%	43.9%	2.9%	92.5%
12/15–01/15	2.1	26.9	3.4	46.7
12/15–01/31	2.3	20.3	3.5	32.3
12/15–02/15	3.4	22.2	5.2	35.5
12/15–02/28	2.5	13.3	4.7	26.0
end-Dec*				
12/31–01/15	0.5	11.0	0.5	11.0
12/31–01/31	0.7	8.7	0.6	7.4
12/31–02/15	1.8	15.1	2.2	18.7
12/31–02/28	0.9	5.8	1.7	11.2

41-YEAR AVERAGE RATES OF RETURN (DEC 1979 – FEB 2020)

From mid-Dec*	Russell 1000		Russell 2000	
	Change	Annualized	Change	Annualized
12/15–12/31	1.5%	40.6%	2.7%	84.1%
12/15–01/15	2.2	28.3	3.8	53.3
12/15–01/31	2.5	22.2	4.1	38.6
12/15–02/15	3.5	22.9	5.6	38.7
12/15–02/28	2.9	15.2	5.3	29.1
end-Dec*				
12/31–01/15	0.8	18.2	1.1	25.8
12/31–01/31	1.1	14.0	1.4	18.2
12/31–02/15	2.0	16.9	2.9	25.2
12/31–02/28	1.4	9.2	2.5	16.8

* Mid-month dates are the 11th trading day of the month, month end dates are monthly closes.

Small-cap strength in the last half of December became even more magnified after the 1987 market crash. Note the dramatic shift in gains in the last half of December during the 33-year period starting in 1987, versus the 41 years from 1979 to 2020. With all the beaten-down small stocks being dumped for tax-loss purposes, it generally pays to get a head start on the January Effect in mid-December. You don't have to wait until December either; the small-cap sector often begins to turn around toward the beginning of November.

MONDAY

D 42.9
S 42.9
N 61.9

6

It is totally unproductive to think the world has been unfair to you. Every tough stretch is an opportunity.
— Charlie Munger (Vice-Chairman Berkshire Hathaway, 2007 Wesco Annual Meeting, b. 1924)

TUESDAY

D 57.1
S 52.4
N 47.6

7

In the business world, everyone is paid in two coins: cash and experience. Take the experience first; the cash will come later.
— Harold S. Geneen (British-American businessman, CEO ITT Corp, 1910–1977)

Small Cap Strength Starts in Mid-December (Pages 110 and 112)

WEDNESDAY

D 52.4
S 52.4
N 57.1

8

The whole secret to our success is being able to con ourselves into believing that we're going to change the world [even though] we are unlikely to do it.
— Tom Peters (American writer, *In Search of Excellence, Fortune*, 11/13/2000, b. 1942)

THURSDAY

D 57.1
S 61.9
N 71.4

9

A man will fight harder for his interests than his rights.
— Napoleon Bonaparte (Emperor of France 1804–1815, 1769–1821)

FRIDAY

D 61.9
S 57.1
N 47.6

10

I look at the future from the standpoint of probabilities. It's like a branching stream of probabilities, and there are actions that we can take that affect those probabilities or that accelerate one thing or slow down another thing.
— Elon Musk (South African engineer & industrialist, CEO Tesla, Founder SpaceX, b. 1971)

SATURDAY

11

SUNDAY

12

JANUARY EFFECT NOW STARTS IN MID-DECEMBER

Small-cap stocks tend to outperform big caps in January. Known as the "January Effect," the tendency is clearly revealed by the graph below. Thirty-nine of daily data for the Russell 2000 index of smaller companies are divided by the Russell 1000 index of largest companies, and then compressed into a single year to show an idealized yearly pattern. When the graph is descending, big blue chips are outperforming smaller companies; when the graph is rising, smaller companies are moving up faster than their larger brethren.

In a typical year, the smaller fry stay on the sidelines while the big boys are on the field. Then, around early November, small stocks begin to wake up, and in mid-December they take off. Anticipated year-end dividends, payouts and bonuses could be a factor. Other major moves are quite evident just before Labor Day—possibly because individual investors are back from vacation. Small caps hold the lead through the beginning of June, though the bulk of the move is complete by early March.

RUSSELL 2000/RUSSELL 1000 ONE-YEAR SEASONAL PATTERN

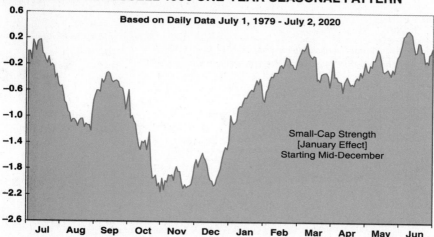

The bottom graph shows the actual ratio of the Russell 2000 divided by the Russell 1000 from 1979. Smaller companies had the upper hand for five years into 1983, as the last major bear trend wound to a close and the nascent bull market logged its first year. After falling behind for about eight years, they came back after the Persian Gulf War bottom in 1990, moving up until 1994, when big caps ruled the latter stages of the millennial bull. For six years, the picture was bleak for small fry, as the blue chips and tech stocks moved to stratospheric PE ratios. Small caps spiked in late 1999 and early 2000 and reached a peak in early 2006, as the four-year-old bull entered its final year. Note how the small-cap advantage has waned during major bull moves and intensified during weak market times.

RUSSELL 2000/RUSSELL 1000 (1979–JUNE 2020)

Monday Before December Triple Witching, S&P Up 13 of Last 20, 2018 -2.1%

MONDAY

D 57.1
S 47.6
N 47.6

13

*New indicator: CFO Magazine gave Excellence awards to WorldCom's Scott Sullivan (1998),
Enron's Andrew Fastow (1999), and to Tyco's Mark Swartz (2000). All were subsequently indicted.*
— Roger Lowenstein (Financial journalist and author, *Origins Of The Crash*, b. 1954)

TUESDAY

D 52.4
S 47.6
N 47.6

14

One determined person can make a significant difference; a small group of determined people can change the course of history.
— Sonia Johnson (author, lecturer)

FOMC Meeting (2 Days)

WEDNESDAY

D 61.9
S 61.9
N 61.9

15

...those inquirers who desire an exact knowledge of the past as an aid to the interpretation of the future...
— Thucydides (Greek aristocrat and historian, *The Peloponnesian War*, 460–400 BC)

December Triple Witching Week, S&P Up 27 of 38, Avg 0.5%, 2018 -7.1%

THURSDAY

D 57.1
S 61.9
N 57.1

16

History must repeat itself because we pay such little attention to it the first time.
— Blackie Sherrod (Sportswriter, b. 1919)

December Triple Witching Day, S&P Up 26 of Last 38, 2018 -2.1%

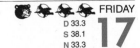

FRIDAY

D 33.3
S 38.1
N 33.3

17

*Whatever method you use to pick stocks..., your ultimate success or failure will depend on your ability to
ignore the worries of the world long enough to allow your investments to succeed. It isn't the head but the
stomach that determines the fate of the stockpicker.*
— Peter Lynch (Fidelity Investments, *Beating the Street*, 1994)

*The Only FREE LUNCH on Wall Street Is Served (Page 114)
Almanac Investors Emailed Alert Before the Open, Monday (See Insert)*

SATURDAY

18

SUNDAY

19

WALL STREET'S ONLY "FREE LUNCH" SERVED BEFORE CHRISTMAS

Investors tend to get rid of their losers near year-end for tax purposes, often hammering these stocks down to bargain levels. Over the years, the *Almanac* has shown that NYSE stocks selling at their lows on December 15 will usually outperform the market by February 15 in the following year. Preferred stocks, closed-end funds, splits and new issues are eliminated.

BARGAIN STOCKS VS. THE MARKET*

Short Span* Late Dec–Jan/Feb	New Lows Late Dec	% Change Jan/Feb	% Change NYSE Composite	Bargain Stocks Advantage
1974–75	112	48.9%	22.1%	26.8%
1975–76	21	34.9	14.9	20.0
1976–77	2	1.3	–3.3	4.6
1977–78	15	2.8	–4.5	7.3
1978–79	43	11.8	3.9	7.9
1979–80	5	9.3	6.1	3.2
1980–81	14	7.1	–2.0	9.1
1981–82	21	–2.6	–7.4	4.8
1982–83	4	33.0	9.7	23.3
1983–84	13	–3.2	–3.8	0.6
1984–85	32	19.0	12.1	6.9
1985–86	4	–22.5	3.9	–26.4
1986–87	22	9.3	12.5	–3.2
1987–88	23	13.2	6.8	6.4
1988–89	14	30.0	6.4	23.6
1989–90	25	–3.1	–4.8	1.7
1990–91	18	18.8	12.6	6.2
1991–92	23	51.1	7.7	43.4
1992–93	9	8.7	0.6	8.1
1993–94	10	–1.4	2.0	–3.4
1994–95	25	14.6	5.7	8.9
1995–96	5	–11.3	4.5	–15.8
1996–97	16	13.9	11.2	2.7
1997–98	29	9.9	5.7	4.2
1998–99	40	–2.8	4.3	–7.1
1999–00	26	8.9	–5.4	14.3
2000–01	51	44.4	0.1	44.3
2001–02	12	31.4	–2.3	33.7
2002–03	33	28.7	3.9	24.8
2003–04	15	16.7	2.3	14.4
2004–05	36	6.8	–2.8	9.6
2005–06	71	12.0	2.6	9.4
2006–07	43	5.1	–0.5	5.6
2007–08	71	–3.2	–9.4	6.2
2008–09	88	11.4	–2.4	13.8
2009–10	25	1.8	–3.0	4.8
2010–11	20	8.3	3.4	4.9
2011–12	65	18.1	6.1	12.0
2012–13	17	20.9	3.4	17.5
2013–14	18	25.7	1.7	24.0
2014–15	17	0.2	–0.4	0.6
2015–16	38	–9.2	5.6	–14.8
2016–17	19	2.8	0.6	2.2
2017–18	18	3.3	1.2	2.1
2018–19	23	24.9	15.1	9.8
2019–2020	13	–1.1%	–0.3%	–0.7%
46-Year Totals		548.7%	146.4%	402.3%
Average		11.9%	3.2%	8.7%

Dec 15–Feb 15 (1974–1999), Dec 1999–2019 based on actual newsletter portfolio

In response to changing market conditions, we tweaked the strategy the last 21 years, adding selections from NASDAQ and AMEX, and selling in mid-January some years. We email the list of stocks to our *Almanac Investor eNewsletter* subscribers. Visit *www.stocktradersalmanac.com*, or see the ad insert for additional details and a special offer for new subscribers.

We have come to the conclusion that the most prudent course of action is to compile our list from the stocks making new lows on Triple-Witching Friday before Christmas, capitalizing on the Santa Claus Rally (page 116). This also gives us the weekend to evaluate the issues in greater depth and weed out any glaringly problematic stocks. Subscribers will receive the list of stocks selected from the new lows made on December 18, 2020 and December 17, 2021 via email.

This "Free Lunch" strategy is an extremely short-term strategy reserved for the nimblest traders. It has performed better after market corrections and when there are more new lows to choose from. The object is to buy bargain stocks near their 52-week lows and sell after any quick, generous gains, as these issues can be real dogs.

Week After December Triple Witching, Dow Up 22 of Last 29
Average Gain Since 1991, 0.9%

MONDAY
D 47.6
S 47.6
N 47.6
20

We pay the debts of the last generation by issuing bonds payable by the next generation.
— Lawrence J. Peter

TUESDAY
D 61.9
S 57.1
N 52.4
21

It's a lot of fun finding a country nobody knows about. The only thing better is finding a country everybody's bullish on and shorting it.
— Jim Rogers (Financier, *Investment Biker*, b. 1942)

WEDNESDAY
D 66.7
S 66.7
N 61.9
22

Financial genius is a rising stock market.
— John Kenneth Galbraith (Canadian/American economist and diplomat, 1908–2006)

Last Trading Day Before Christmas, NASDAQ Up 9 of Last 13 Years, 2018 -2.2%

THURSDAY
D 71.4
S 71.4
N 66.7
23

If the market does not rally, as it should during bullish seasonal periods, it is a sign that other forces are stronger and that when the seasonal period ends those forces will really have their say.
— Edson Gould (Stock market analyst, *Findings & Forecasts*, 1902–1987)

(Market Closed – Christmas Day Observed)

FRIDAY
24

If more of us valued food and cheer and song above hoarded gold, it would be a merrier world.
— J. R. R. Tolkien (English writer, poet, philologist, and academic, *The Hobbit*, 1892–1973)

Christmas Day

SATURDAY
25

January Almanac Investor Sector Seasonalities: See Pages 92, 94 and 96

SUNDAY
26

IF SANTA CLAUS SHOULD FAIL TO CALL, BEARS MAY COME TO BROAD AND WALL

Santa Claus tends to come to Wall Street nearly every year, bringing a short, sweet, respectable rally within the last five days of the year and the first two in January. This has been good for an average 1.3% gain since 1969 (1.3% since 1950 as well). Santa's failure to show tends to precede bear markets, or times stocks could be purchased later in the year at much lower prices. We discovered this phenomenon in 1972.

DAILY % CHANGE IN S&P 500 AT YEAR END

	Trading Days Before Year End						First Days in January			Rally %
	6	5	4	3	2	1	1	2	3	Change
1969	−0.4	1.1	0.8	−0.7	0.4	0.5	1.0	0.5	−0.7	3.6
1970	0.1	0.6	0.5	1.1	0.2	−0.1	−1.1	0.7	0.6	1.9
1971	−0.4	0.2	1.0	0.3	−0.4	0.3	−0.4	0.4	1.0	1.3
1972	−0.3	−0.7	0.6	0.4	0.5	1.0	0.9	0.4	−0.1	3.1
1973	−1.1	−0.7	3.1	2.1	−0.2	0.01	0.1	2.2	−0.9	6.7
1974	−1.4	1.4	0.8	−0.4	0.03	2.1	2.4	0.7	0.5	7.2
1975	0.7	0.8	0.9	−0.1	−0.4	0.5	0.8	1.8	1.0	4.3
1976	0.1	1.2	0.7	−0.4	0.5	0.5	−0.4	−1.2	−0.9	0.8
1977	0.8	0.9	N/C	0.1	0.2	0.2	−1.3	−0.3	−0.8	−0.3
1978	0.03	1.7	1.3	−0.9	−0.4	−0.2	0.6	1.1	0.8	3.3
1979	−0.6	0.1	0.1	0.2	−0.1	0.1	−2.0	−0.5	1.2	−2.2
1980	−0.4	0.4	0.5	−1.1	0.2	0.3	0.4	1.2	0.1	2.0
1981	−0.5	0.2	−0.2	−0.5	0.5	0.2	0.2	−2.2	−0.7	−1.8
1982	0.6	1.8	−1.0	0.3	−0.7	0.2	−1.6	2.2	0.4	1.2
1983	−0.2	−0.03	0.9	0.3	−0.2	0.05	−0.5	1.7	1.2	2.1
1984	−0.5	0.8	−0.2	−0.4	0.3	0.6	−1.1	−0.5	−0.5	−0.6
1985	−1.1	−0.7	0.2	0.9	0.5	0.3	−0.8	0.6	−0.1	1.1
1986	−1.0	0.2	0.1	−0.9	−0.5	−0.5	1.8	2.3	0.2	2.4
1987	1.3	−0.5	−2.6	−0.4	1.3	−0.3	3.6	1.1	0.1	2.2
1988	−0.2	0.3	−0.4	0.1	0.8	−0.6	−0.9	1.5	0.2	0.9
1989	0.6	0.8	−0.2	0.6	0.5	0.8	1.8	−0.3	−0.9	4.1
1990	0.5	−0.6	0.3	−0.8	0.1	0.5	−1.1	−1.4	−0.3	−3.0
1991	2.5	0.6	1.4	0.4	2.1	0.5	0.04	0.5	−0.3	5.7
1992	−0.3	0.2	−0.1	−0.3	0.2	−0.7	−0.1	−0.2	0.04	−1.1
1993	0.01	0.7	0.1	−0.1	−0.4	−0.5	−0.2	0.3	0.1	−0.1
1994	0.01	0.2	0.4	−0.3	0.1	−0.4	−0.03	0.3	−0.1	0.2
1995	0.8	0.2	0.4	0.04	−0.1	0.3	0.8	0.1	−0.6	1.8
1996	−0.3	0.5	0.6	0.1	−0.4	−1.7	−0.5	1.5	−0.1	0.1
1997	−1.5	−0.7	0.4	1.8	1.8	−0.04	0.5	0.2	−1.1	4.0
1998	2.1	−0.2	−0.1	1.3	−0.8	−0.2	−0.1	1.4	2.2	1.3
1999	1.6	−0.1	0.04	0.4	0.1	0.3	−1.0	−3.8	0.2	−4.0
2000	0.8	2.4	0.7	1.0	0.4	−1.0	−2.8	5.0	−1.1	5.7
2001	0.4	−0.02	0.4	0.7	0.3	−1.1	0.6	0.9	0.6	1.8
2002	0.2	−0.5	−0.3	−1.6	0.5	0.05	3.3	−0.05	2.2	1.2
2003	0.3	−0.2	0.2	1.2	0.01	0.2	−0.3	1.2	0.1	2.4
2004	0.1	−0.4	0.7	−0.01	0.01	−0.1	−0.8	−1.2	−0.4	−1.8
2005	0.4	0.04	−1.0	0.1	−0.3	−0.5	1.6	0.4	0.002	0.4
2006	−0.4	−0.5	0.4	0.7	−0.1	−0.5	−0.1	0.1	−0.6	0.003
2007	1.7	0.8	0.1	−1.4	0.1	−0.7	−1.4	N/C	−2.5	−2.5
2008	−1.0	0.6	0.5	−0.4	2.4	1.4	3.2	−0.5	0.8	7.4
2009	0.2	0.5	0.1	−0.1	0.02	−1.0	1.6	0.3	0.05	1.4
2010	−0.2	0.1	0.1	0.1	−0.2	−0.02	1.1	−0.1	0.5	1.1
2011	0.8	0.9	0.01	−1.3	1.1	−0.4	1.6	0.02	0.3	1.9
2012	−0.9	−0.2	−0.5	−0.1	−1.1	1.7	2.5	−0.2	0.5	2.0
2013	0.5	0.3	0.5	−0.03	−0.02	0.4	−0.9	−0.03	−0.3	0.2
2014	0.2	−0.01	0.3	0.1	−0.5	−1.0	−0.03	−1.8	−0.9	−3.0
2015	1.2	−0.2	−0.2	1.1	−0.7	−0.9	−1.5	0.2	−1.3	−2.3
2016	−0.2	0.1	0.2	−0.8	−0.03	−0.5	0.9	0.6	−0.1	0.4
2017	0.2	−0.05	−0.1	0.1	0.2	−0.5	0.8	0.6	0.4	1.1
2018	−2.1	−2.7	5.0	0.9	−0.1	0.9	0.1	−2.5	3.4	1.3
2019	0.1	−0.02	0.5	0.003	−0.6	0.3	0.8	−0.7	0.4	0.3
Avg	0.08	0.23	0.35	0.07	0.14	0.01	0.24	0.28	0.07	1.3

The couplet above was certainly on the mark in 1999, as the period suffered a horrendous 4.0% loss. On January 14, 2000, the Dow started its 33-month 37.8% slide to the October 2002 midterm election year bottom. NASDAQ cracked eight weeks later, falling 37.3% in 10 weeks, eventually dropping 77.9% by October 2002. Energy prices and Middle East terror woes may have grounded Santa in 2004. In 2007, the third worst reading since 1950 was recorded, as a full-blown financial crisis led to the second worst bear market in history. In 2016, the period was hit again as global growth concerns escalated and the market digested the first interest rate hike in nearly a decade.

DECEMBER 2021/JANUARY 2022

Santa Claus Rally Begins December 27 (Page 116)

MONDAY

D 38.1
S 42.9
N 61.9

27

Intellect and Emotion are partners who do not speak the same language. The intellect finds logic to justify what the emotions have decided. WIN THE HEARTS OF PEOPLE, THEIR MINDS WILL FOLLOW.
— Roy H. Williams (*The Wizard of Ads*)

TUESDAY

D 71.4
S 76.2
N 61.9

28

The power to tax involves the power to destroy.
— John Marshall (U. S. Supreme Court, 1819)

WEDNESDAY

D 52.4
S 57.1
N 52.4

29

A market is the combined behavior of thousands of people responding to information, misinformation and whim.
— Kenneth Chang (*NY Times* journalist)

THURSDAY

D 42.9
S 52.4
N 42.9

30

A good new chairman of the Federal Reserve Bank is worth a $10 billion tax cut.
— Paul H. Douglas (U.S. Senator Illinois 1949–1967, 1892–1976)

Last Trading Day of the Year, NASDAQ Down 15 of last 20
NASDAQ Was Up 29 Years in a Row 1971–1999

FRIDAY

D 42.9
S 38.1
N 28.6

31

The fear of capitalism has compelled socialism to widen freedom,
and the fear of socialism has compelled capitalism to increase equality.
— Will and Ariel Durant (The Lessons of History, 1885–1981, 1898–1981)

New Year's Day

SATURDAY

1

SUNDAY

2

2022 STRATEGY CALENDAR

(Option expiration dates circled)

	MONDAY	TUESDAY	WEDNESDAY	THURSDAY	FRIDAY	SATURDAY	SUNDAY
JANUARY	27	28	29	30	31	1 **JANUARY** New Year's Day	2
	3	4	5	6	7	8	9
	10	11	12	13	14	15	16
	17 Martin Luther King Day	18	19	20	(21)	22	23
	24	25	26	27	28	29	30
FEBRUARY	31	1 FEBRUARY	2	3	4	5	6
	7	8	9	10	11	12	13
	14 ♥	15	16	17	(18)	19	20
	21 Presidents' Day	22	23	24	25	26	27
MARCH	28	1 MARCH	2 Ash Wednesday	3	4	5	6
	7	8	9	10	11	12	13 Daylight Saving Time Begins
	14	15	16	17 ♣ St. Patrick's Day	(18)	19	20
	21	22	23	24	25	26	27
APRIL	28	29	30	31	1 APRIL	2	3
	4	5	6	7	8	9	10
	11	12	13	(14)	15 Good Friday	16 Passover	17 Easter
	18 Tax Deadline	19	20	21	22	23	24
MAY	25	26	27	28	29	30	1 MAY
	2	3	4	5	6	7	8 Mother's Day
	9	10	11	12	13	14	15
	16	17	18	19	(20)	21	22
	23	24	25	26	27	28	29
JUNE	30 Memorial Day	31	1 JUNE	2	3	4	5
	6	7	8	9	10	11	12
	13	14	15	16	(17)	18	19 Father's Day
	20	21	22	23	24	25	26

Market closed on shaded weekdays; closes early when half-shaded.

2022 STRATEGY CALENDAR

(Option expiration dates circled)

MONDAY	TUESDAY	WEDNESDAY	THURSDAY	FRIDAY	SATURDAY	SUNDAY	
27	28	29	30	1 JULY	2	3	JULY
4 Independence Day	5	6	7	8	9	10	
11	12	13	14	(15)	16	17	
18	19	20	21	22	23	24	
25	26	27	28	29	30	31	
1 AUGUST	2	3	4	5	6	7	AUGUST
8	9	10	11	12	13	14	
15	16	17	18	(19)	20	21	
22	23	24	25	26	27	28	
29	30	31	1 SEPTEMBER	2	3	4	SEPTEMBER
5 Labor Day	6	7	8	9	10	11	
12	13	14	15	(16)	17	18	
19	20	21	22	23	24	25	
26 Rosh Hashanah	27	28	29	30	1 OCTOBER	2	OCTOBER
3	4	5 Yom Kippur	6	7	8	9	
10 Columbus Day	11	12	13	14	15	16	
17	18	19	20	(21)	22	23	
24	25	26	27	28	29	30	
31 🎃	1 NOVEMBER	2	3	4	5	6 Daylight Saving Time Ends	NOVEMBER
7	8 Election Day	9	10	11 Veterans' Day	12	13	
14	15	16	17	(18)	19	20	
21	22	23	24 Thanksgiving Day	25	26	27	
28	29	30	1 DECEMBER	2	3	4	DECEMBER
5	6	7	8	9	10	11	
12	13	14	15	(16)	17	18	
19 Chanukah	20	21	22	23	24	25 Christmas	
26	27	28	29	30	31	1 JANUARY New Year's Day	

DIRECTORY OF TRADING PATTERNS AND DATABANK

CONTENTS

DOW JONES INDUSTRIALS MARKET PROBABILITY CALENDAR 2021

THE % CHANCE OF THE MARKET RISING ON ANY TRADING DAY OF THE YEAR*

(Based on the number of times the DJIA rose on a particular trading day during January 1953–December 2019)

Date	Jan	Feb	Mar	Apr	May	Jun	Jul	Aug	Sep	Oct	Nov	Dec
1	H	61.2	65.7	59.7	S	59.7	67.2	S	56.7	47.8	62.7	44.8
2	S	53.7	61.2	H	S	53.7	56.7	43.3	61.2	S	53.7	50.7
3	S	41.8	58.2	S	55.2	50.7	S	44.8	61.2	S	67.2	62.7
4	59.7	55.2	50.7	S	62.7	58.2	S	49.3	S	56.7	58.2	S
5	71.6	46.3	46.3	59.7	50.7	S	H	52.2	S	55.2	50.7	S
6	47.8	S	S	52.2	46.3	S	61.2	53.7	H	61.2	S	56.7
7	56.7	S	S	59.7	47.8	55.2	56.7	S	44.8	43.3	S	50.7
8	44.8	40.3	53.7	50.7	S	47.8	61.2	S	49.3	52.2	61.2	44.8
9	S	47.8	61.2	59.7	S	37.3	58.2	46.3	46.3	S	53.7	53.7
10	S	59.7	52.2	S	55.2	52.2	S	44.8	61.2	S	55.2	58.2
11	49.3	49.3	55.2	S	49.3	59.7	S	44.8	S	44.8	49.3	S
12	47.8	50.7	52.2	61.2	52.2	S	50.7	49.3	S	41.8	46.3	S
13	47.8	S	S	61.2	44.8	S	46.3	62.7	59.7	50.7	S	46.3
14	56.7	S	S	55.2	53.7	56.7	67.2	S	47.8	59.7	S	50.7
15	55.2	H	62.7	71.6	S	49.3	50.7	S	55.2	52.2	59.7	50.7
16	S	56.7	61.2	61.2	S	50.7	47.8	56.7	58.2	S	53.7	56.7
17	S	43.3	56.7	S	55.2	52.2	S	52.2	43.3	S	47.8	46.3
18	H	49.3	52.2	S	44.8	46.3	S	49.3	S	53.7	47.8	S
19	59.7	49.3	41.8	56.7	50.7	S	52.2	53.7	S	46.3	56.7	S
20	40.3	S	S	55.2	43.3	S	53.7	58.2	50.7	58.2	S	55.2
21	41.8	S	S	53.7	35.8	49.3	37.3	S	46.3	43.3	S	56.7
22	41.8	40.3	41.8	50.7	S	46.3	46.3	S	41.8	50.7	64.2	58.2
23	S	47.8	47.8	52.2	S	43.3	44.8	49.3	38.8	S	59.7	52.2
24	S	61.2	35.8	S	52.2	35.8	S	50.7	47.8	S	67.2	H
25	58.2	46.3	49.3	S	44.8	47.8	S	49.3	S	29.9	H	S
26	58.2	47.8	46.3	50.7	43.3	S	58.2	44.8	S	53.7	61.2	S
27	49.3	S	S	58.2	56.7	S	55.2	62.7	53.7	53.7	S	58.2
28	58.2	S	S	58.2	55.2	47.8	46.3	S	52.2	59.7	S	70.1
29	56.7		53.7	50.7	S	53.7	56.7	S	49.3	52.2	53.7	49.3
30	S		46.3	49.3	S	55.2	49.3	41.8	41.8	S	53.7	53.7
31	S		43.3		H		S	59.7		S		53.7

See new trends developing on pages 70, 84, 141-146

THE % CHANCE OF THE MARKET RISING ON ANY TRADING DAY OF THE YEAR*
(Based on the number of times the DJIA rose on a particular trading day during January 1999–December 2019**)

Date	Jan	Feb	Mar	Apr	May	Jun	Jul	Aug	Sep	Oct	Nov	Dec
1	H	76.2	61.9	66.7	S	76.2	81.0	S	47.6	47.6	57.1	42.9
2	S	38.1	38.1	H	S	57.1	33.3	33.3	71.4	S	57.1	38.1
3	S	52.4	57.1	S	61.9	47.6	S	52.4	66.7	S	61.9	66.7
4	66.7	52.4	52.4	S	57.1	57.1	S	52.4	S	47.6	76.2	S
5	61.9	42.9	52.4	66.7	38.1	S	H	52.4	S	66.7	66.7	S
6	52.4	S	S	47.6	38.1	S	52.4	52.4	H	61.9	S	42.9
7	52.4	S	S	66.7	61.9	66.7	61.9	S	42.9	28.6	S	57.1
8	38.1	42.9	47.6	42.9	S	61.9	57.1	S	57.1	47.6	57.1	52.4
9	S	52.4	57.1	57.1	S	38.1	61.9	52.4	57.1	S	42.9	57.1
10	S	52.4	52.4	S	66.7	38.1	S	42.9	76.2	S	38.1	61.9
11	52.4	61.9	61.9	S	42.9	57.1	S	33.3	S	52.4	61.9	S
12	52.4	52.4	57.1	57.1	61.9	S	52.4	52.4	S	47.6	47.6	S
13	47.6	S	S	57.1	38.1	S	76.2	61.9	61.9	38.1	S	57.1
14	47.6	S	S	47.6	52.4	57.1	71.4	S	47.6	66.7	S	52.4
15	57.1	H	76.2	71.4	S	57.1	52.4	S	52.4	52.4	66.7	61.9
16	S	71.4	52.4	61.9	S	61.9	52.4	57.1	76.2	S	57.1	57.1
17	S	52.4	61.9	S	57.1	57.1	S	57.1	52.4	S	38.1	33.3
18	H	47.6	57.1	S	52.4	52.4	S	71.4	S	57.1	42.9	S
19	52.4	38.1	33.3	61.9	42.9	S	57.1	42.9	S	52.4	42.9	S
20	38.1	S	S	57.1	33.3	S	71.4	61.9	57.1	52.4	S	47.6
21	42.9	S	S	61.9	47.6	38.1	14.3	S	52.4	57.1	S	61.9
22	33.3	52.4	47.6	61.9	S	33.3	42.9	S	33.3	57.1	57.1	66.7
23	S	47.6	42.9	57.1	S	38.1	33.3	52.4	28.6	S	61.9	71.4
24	S	52.4	28.6	S	47.6	28.6	S	52.4	33.3	S	76.2	H
25	66.7	47.6	57.1	S	52.4	38.1	S	52.4	S	42.9	H	S
26	61.9	33.3	38.1	47.6	47.6	S	57.1	42.9	S	66.7	61.9	S
27	47.6	S	S	61.9	61.9	S	57.1	76.2	52.4	52.4	S	38.1
28	42.9	S	S	71.4	38.1	57.1	42.9	S	57.1	61.9	S	71.4
29	52.4		47.6	61.9	S	52.4	33.3	S	57.1	52.4	61.9	52.4
30	S		61.9	28.6	S	52.4	38.1	33.3	42.9	S	52.4	42.9
31	S		42.9		H		S	57.1		S		42.9

*See new trends developing on pages 70, 84, 141–146   ** Based on most recent 21-year period

S&P 500 MARKET PROBABILITY CALENDAR 2021

THE % CHANCE OF THE MARKET RISING ON ANY TRADING DAY OF THE YEAR*
(Based on the number of times the S&P 500 rose on a particular trading day during January 1953–December 2019)

Date	Jan	Feb	Mar	Apr	May	Jun	Jul	Aug	Sep	Oct	Nov	Dec
1	H	61.2	62.7	62.7	S	56.7	73.1	S	58.2	49.3	62.7	46.3
2	S	58.2	58.2	H	S	62.7	55.2	46.3	53.7	S	56.7	50.7
3	S	47.8	61.2	S	58.2	52.2	S	44.8	59.7	S	67.2	61.2
4	49.3	50.7	49.3	S	65.7	56.7	S	49.3	S	64.2	56.7	S
5	68.7	49.3	47.8	61.2	53.7	S	H	53.7	S	56.7	49.3	S
6	52.2	S	S	53.7	43.3	S	56.7	55.2	H	61.2	S	56.7
7	52.2	S	S	56.7	46.3	47.8	59.7	S	46.3	44.8	S	46.3
8	44.8	44.8	55.2	52.2	S	46.3	61.2	S	49.3	49.3	58.2	49.3
9	S	43.3	61.2	62.7	S	40.3	56.7	46.3	53.7	S	58.2	55.2
10	S	62.7	52.2	S	52.2	53.7	S	50.7	61.2	S	56.7	49.3
11	52.2	56.7	64.2	S	47.8	62.7	S	44.8	S	43.3	47.8	S
12	53.7	47.8	43.3	61.2	53.7	S	52.2	47.8	S	46.3	47.8	S
13	52.2	S	S	53.7	43.3	S	53.7	62.7	64.2	50.7	S	47.8
14	59.7	S	S	52.2	50.7	56.7	71.6	S	49.3	55.2	S	43.3
15	61.2	H	61.2	62.7	S	55.2	50.7	S	53.7	52.2	52.2	50.7
16	S	56.7	62.7	59.7	S	49.3	46.3	61.2	58.2	S	52.2	58.2
17	S	38.8	55.2	S	55.2	56.7	S	55.2	49.3	S	52.2	43.3
18	H	52.2	49.3	S	49.3	43.3	S	55.2	S	58.2	50.7	S
19	58.2	43.3	41.8	59.7	52.2	S	47.8	50.7	S	46.3	56.7	S
20	49.3	S	S	55.2	38.8	S	53.7	59.7	53.7	64.2	S	47.8
21	50.7	S	S	53.7	44.8	50.7	37.3	S	46.3	43.3	S	50.7
22	47.8	43.3	46.3	55.2	S	50.7	47.8	S	46.3	47.8	62.7	55.2
23	S	43.3	41.8	47.8	S	46.3	46.3	46.3	35.8	S	59.7	49.3
24	S	58.2	49.3	S	52.2	34.3	S	49.3	46.3	S	67.2	H
25	55.2	50.7	41.8	S	49.3	41.8	S	47.8	S	32.8	H	S
26	52.2	53.7	47.8	47.8	46.3	S	55.2	46.3	S	58.2	61.2	S
27	44.8	S	S	58.2	56.7	S	55.2	62.7	50.7	56.7	S	58.2
28	61.2	S	S	52.2	56.7	50.7	46.3	S	58.2	59.7	S	71.6
29	62.7		55.2	49.3	S	58.2	62.7	S	50.7	53.7	59.7	53.7
30	S		40.3	55.2	S	52.2	59.7	44.8	43.3	S	50.7	59.7
31	S		41.8		H		S	64.2		S		61.2

* See new trends developing on pages 70, 84, 141–146

RECENT S&P 500 MARKET PROBABILITY CALENDAR 2021

THE % CHANCE OF THE MARKET RISING ON ANY TRADING DAY OF THE YEAR*

(Based on the number of times the S&P 500 rose on a particular trading day during January 1999–December 2019**)

Date	Jan	Feb	Mar	Apr	May	Jun	Jul	Aug	Sep	Oct	Nov	Dec
1	H	71.4	66.7	66.7	S	66.7	85.7	S	47.6	52.4	57.1	42.9
2	S	47.6	38.1	H	S	76.2	38.1	42.9	42.9	S	66.7	47.6
3	S	42.9	66.7	S	71.4	47.6	S	52.4	57.1	S	57.1	61.9
4	52.4	52.4	57.1	S	47.6	57.1	S	47.6	S	47.6	81.0	S
5	52.4	42.9	52.4	71.4	33.3	S	H	57.1	S	66.7	57.1	S
6	61.9	S	S	47.6	42.9	S	61.9	52.4	H	61.9	S	42.9
7	57.1	S	S	66.7	57.1	42.9	61.9	S	52.4	28.6	S	52.4
8	47.6	61.9	52.4	42.9	S	57.1	52.4	S	47.6	42.9	47.6	52.4
9	S	47.6	57.1	66.7	S	38.1	61.9	57.1	61.9	S	33.3	61.9
10	S	61.9	57.1	S	47.6	38.1	S	42.9	76.2	S	52.4	57.1
11	61.9	71.4	66.7	S	42.9	57.1	S	38.1	S	52.4	57.1	S
12	61.9	57.1	33.3	52.4	57.1	S	52.4	47.6	S	47.6	47.6	S
13	38.1	S	S	57.1	38.1	S	81.0	57.1	66.7	42.9	S	47.6
14	52.4	S	S	47.6	42.9	57.1	71.4	S	47.6	61.9	S	47.6
15	57.1	H	61.9	57.1	S	66.7	38.1	S	47.6	52.4	57.1	61.9
16	S	76.2	57.1	57.1	S	57.1	52.4	61.9	76.2	S	52.4	61.9
17	S	42.9	66.7	S	61.9	61.9	S	61.9	57.1	S	42.9	38.1
18	H	52.4	42.9	S	57.1	52.4	S	71.4	S	66.7	42.9	S
19	66.7	38.1	28.6	71.4	42.9	S	52.4	38.1	S	61.9	47.6	S
20	47.6	S	S	61.9	28.6	S	71.4	66.7	52.4	57.1	S	47.6
21	47.6	S	S	52.4	52.4	52.4	19.0	S	33.3	61.9	S	57.1
22	47.6	47.6	52.4	66.7	S	38.1	47.6	S	28.6	66.7	52.4	66.7
23	S	52.4	38.1	57.1	S	42.9	47.6	47.6	23.8	S	57.1	71.4
24	S	52.4	47.6	S	52.4	28.6	S	52.4	33.3	S	66.7	H
25	66.7	52.4	52.4	S	57.1	38.1	S	52.4	S	38.1	H	S
26	47.6	33.3	38.1	42.9	52.4	S	52.4	52.4	S	57.1	57.1	S
27	42.9	S	S	57.1	61.9	S	57.1	81.0	47.6	47.6	S	42.9
28	47.6	S	S	57.1	47.6	52.4	38.1	S	57.1	61.9	S	76.2
29	57.1		52.4	61.9	S	57.1	52.4	S	57.1	57.1	71.4	57.1
30	S		52.4	33.3	S	52.4	42.9	33.3	38.1	S	38.1	52.4
31	S		47.6		H		S	61.9		S		38.1

* See new trends developing on pages 70, 84, 141–146   ** Based on most recent 21-year period

NASDAQ COMPOSITE MARKET PROBABILITY CALENDAR 2021

THE % CHANCE OF THE MARKET RISING ON ANY TRADING DAY OF THE YEAR*
(Based on the number of times the NASDAQ rose on a particular trading day during January 1971–December 2019)

Date	Jan	Feb	Mar	Apr	May	Jun	Jul	Aug	Sep	Oct	Nov	Dec
1	H	69.4	63.3	46.9	S	59.2	63.3	S	55.1	46.9	65.3	57.1
2	S	65.3	55.1	H	S	73.5	46.9	53.1	59.2	S	53.1	59.2
3	S	55.1	67.3	S	63.3	57.1	S	40.8	59.2	S	67.3	65.3
4	57.1	63.3	51.0	S	67.3	61.2	S	51.0	S	59.2	57.1	S
5	63.3	53.1	49.0	65.3	55.1	S	H	59.2	S	61.2	51.0	S
6	59.2	S	S	63.3	51.0	S	49.0	57.1	H	61.2	S	59.2
7	65.3	S	S	55.1	55.1	51.0	55.1	S	57.1	55.1	S	46.9
8	57.1	53.1	57.1	44.9	S	49.0	61.2	S	55.1	57.1	55.1	55.1
9	S	51.0	59.2	65.3	S	40.8	67.3	42.9	49.0	S	55.1	51.0
10	S	65.3	51.0	S	63.3	51.0	S	51.0	55.1	S	61.2	42.9
11	61.2	63.3	71.4	S	55.1	61.2	S	46.9	S	51.0	55.1	S
12	59.2	67.3	49.0	61.2	44.9	S	61.2	57.1	S	51.0	49.0	S
13	57.1	S	S	59.2	53.1	S	69.4	61.2	63.3	67.3	S	44.9
14	61.2	S	S	51.0	57.1	61.2	75.5	S	57.1	63.3	S	40.8
15	61.2	H	53.1	59.2	S	55.1	61.2	38.8	S	51.0	44.9	51.0
16	S	63.3	65.3	51.0	S	51.0	51.0	57.1	55.1	S	51.0	57.1
17	S	49.0	59.2	S	55.1	53.1	S	53.1	53.1	S	51.0	49.0
18	H	55.1	67.3	S	57.1	49.0	S	59.2	S	53.1	51.0	S
19	71.4	38.8	38.8	63.3	49.0	S	53.1	49.0	S	44.9	51.0	S
20	57.1	S	S	55.1	40.8	S	61.2	69.4	63.3	63.3	S	53.1
21	46.9	S	S	55.1	51.0	61.2	34.7	S	49.0	49.0	S	55.1
22	49.0	49.0	46.9	59.2	S	46.9	49.0	S	46.9	49.0	67.3	59.2
23	S	55.1	55.1	53.1	S	49.0	53.1	51.0	42.9	S	59.2	63.3
24	S	63.3	51.0	S	53.1	38.8	S	51.0	51.0	S	61.2	H
25	49.0	59.2	49.0	S	55.1	46.9	S	53.1	S	36.7	H	S
26	65.3	46.9	44.9	51.0	59.2	S	55.1	57.1	S	42.9	69.4	S
27	57.1	S	S	46.9	59.2	S	51.0	67.3	46.9	55.1	S	67.3
28	53.1	S	S	65.3	63.3	59.2	42.9	S	49.0	59.2	S	71.4
29	65.3		53.1	65.3	S	67.3	55.1	S	46.9	63.3	65.3	51.0
30	S		57.1	61.2	S	69.4	49.0	59.2	51.0	S	63.3	61.2
31	S		65.3		H		S	65.3		S		69.4

See new trends developing on pages 70, 84, 141–146
Based on NASDAQ composite, prior to Feb. 5, 1971 based on National Quotation Bureau indices

RECENT NASDAQ COMPOSITE MARKET PROBABILITY CALENDAR 2021

THE % CHANCE OF THE MARKET RISING ON ANY TRADING DAY OF THE YEAR*
(Based on the number of times the NASDAQ rose on a particular trading day during January 1999–December 2019**)

Date	Jan	Feb	Mar	Apr	May	Jun	Jul	Aug	Sep	Oct	Nov	Dec
1	H	76.2	66.7	61.9	S	57.1	76.2	S	57.1	42.9	61.9	52.4
2	S	47.6	38.1	H	S	71.4	38.1	47.6	42.9	S	61.9	52.4
3	S	38.1	61.9	S	71.4	52.4	S	38.1	52.4	S	61.9	66.7
4	71.4	57.1	47.6	S	52.4	57.1	S	47.6	S	52.4	66.7	S
5	47.6	47.6	38.1	66.7	38.1	S	H	52.4	S	76.2	61.9	S
6	57.1	S	S	61.9	47.6	S	57.1	42.9	H	57.1	S	61.9
7	57.1	S	S	57.1	52.4	42.9	66.7	S	52.4	42.9	S	47.6
8	66.7	61.9	52.4	33.3	S	42.9	57.1	S	52.4	52.4	52.4	57.1
9	S	47.6	47.6	66.7	S	38.1	66.7	42.9	57.1	S	33.3	71.4
10	S	61.9	52.4	S	71.4	33.3	S	47.6	66.7	S	61.9	47.6
11	66.7	71.4	66.7	S	47.6	52.4	S	38.1	S	57.1	66.7	S
12	66.7	76.2	38.1	47.6	47.6	S	57.1	52.4	S	52.4	42.9	S
13	42.9	S	S	61.9	42.9	S	66.7	61.9	66.7	52.4	S	47.6
14	47.6	S	S	38.1	47.6	52.4	76.2	S	66.7	71.4	S	47.6
15	42.9	H	47.6	47.6	S	66.7	52.4	S	33.3	47.6	47.6	61.9
16	S	66.7	66.7	47.6	S	57.1	57.1	61.9	76.2	S	57.1	57.1
17	S	42.9	71.4	S	57.1	66.7	S	66.7	52.4	S	42.9	33.3
18	H	52.4	66.7	S	61.9	52.4	S	66.7	S	57.1	47.6	S
19	71.4	38.1	38.1	71.4	47.6	S	57.1	38.1	S	52.4	47.6	S
20	52.4	S	S	47.6	28.6	S	71.4	81.0	57.1	57.1	S	47.6
21	42.9	S	S	52.4	52.4	61.9	14.3	S	38.1	61.9	S	52.4
22	38.1	52.4	61.9	61.9	S	38.1	47.6	S	28.6	57.1	66.7	61.9
23	S	61.9	47.6	47.6	S	38.1	47.6	47.6	33.3	S	61.9	66.7
24	S	61.9	52.4	S	47.6	23.8	S	52.4	42.9	S	66.7	H
25	57.1	57.1	66.7	S	57.1	47.6	S	52.4	S	47.6	H	S
26	66.7	23.8	28.6	47.6	57.1	S	52.4	52.4	S	47.6	57.1	S
27	52.4	S	S	42.9	71.4	S	61.9	81.0	52.4	52.4	S	61.9
28	42.9	S	S	47.6	47.6	71.4	38.1	S	42.9	57.1	S	61.9
29	57.1		47.6	71.4	S	61.9	57.1	S	42.9	57.1	61.9	52.4
30	S		61.9	42.9	S	61.9	38.1	57.1	47.6	S	42.9	42.9
31	S		57.1		H		S	57.1		S		28.6

* See new trends developing on pages 70, 84, 141–146   ** Based on most recent 21-year period

RUSSELL 1000 INDEX MARKET PROBABILITY CALENDAR 2021

THE % CHANCE OF THE MARKET RISING ON ANY TRADING DAY OF THE YEAR*
(Based on the number of times the RUSSELL 1000 rose on a particular trading day during January 1979–December 2019)

Date	Jan	Feb	Mar	Apr	May	Jun	Jul	Aug	Sep	Oct	Nov	Dec
1	H	65.9	61.0	58.5	S	61.0	75.6	S	51.2	53.7	73.2	48.8
2	S	58.5	48.8	H	S	61.0	41.5	43.9	48.8	S	56.1	51.2
3	S	56.1	61.0	S	58.5	51.2	S	41.5	56.1	S	58.5	61.0
4	46.3	53.7	43.9	S	61.0	58.5	S	48.8	S	56.1	61.0	S
5	58.5	53.7	43.9	63.4	51.2	S	H	51.2	S	58.5	48.8	S
6	58.5	S	S	53.7	39.0	S	48.8	56.1	H	58.5	S	43.9
7	56.1	S	S	58.5	46.3	39.0	58.5	S	43.9	39.0	S	48.8
8	51.2	51.2	56.1	43.9	S	46.3	58.5	S	48.8	51.2	56.1	48.8
9	S	46.3	58.5	68.3	S	41.5	53.7	56.1	56.1	S	48.8	53.7
10	S	73.2	46.3	S	56.1	48.8	S	43.9	68.3	S	56.1	46.3
11	65.9	68.3	63.4	S	56.1	56.1	S	43.9	S	39.0	56.1	S
12	56.1	48.8	39.0	56.1	53.7	S	58.5	46.3	S	43.9	53.7	S
13	53.7	S	S	51.2	51.2	S	68.3	61.0	68.3	58.5	S	46.3
14	58.5	S	S	48.8	51.2	56.1	80.5	S	56.1	63.4	S	41.5
15	65.9	H	58.5	56.1	S	58.5	48.8	S	51.2	56.1	53.7	58.5
16	S	65.9	61.0	61.0	S	53.7	53.7	63.4	53.7	S	48.8	58.5
17	S	41.5	56.1	S	58.5	63.4	S	61.0	51.2	S	58.5	46.3
18	H	46.3	48.8	S	56.1	43.9	S	65.9	S	56.1	46.3	S
19	65.9	39.0	36.6	61.0	51.2	S	48.8	61.0	S	48.8	53.7	S
20	41.5	S	S	51.2	43.9	S	61.0	68.3	48.8	68.3	S	46.3
21	43.9	S	S	53.7	43.9	51.2	34.1	S	39.0	46.3	S	51.2
22	48.8	46.3	48.8	56.1	S	51.2	46.3	S	43.9	46.3	61.0	68.3
23	S	46.3	43.9	56.1	S	46.3	43.9	46.3	36.6	S	63.4	58.5
24	S	58.5	41.5	S	61.0	31.7	S	53.7	36.6	S	65.9	H
25	56.1	56.1	48.8	S	61.0	39.0	S	46.3	S	34.1	H	S
26	61.0	51.2	41.5	46.3	53.7	S	70.7	53.7	S	56.1	73.2	S
27	51.2	S	S	56.1	56.1	S	53.7	61.0	48.8	53.7	S	58.5
28	56.1	S	S	58.5	51.2	51.2	41.5	S	63.4	63.4	S	70.7
29	58.5		48.8	56.1	S	61.0	63.4	S	56.1	63.4	65.9	58.5
30	S		46.3	53.7	S	56.1	56.1	48.8	51.2	S	46.3	61.0
31	S		48.8		H		S	61.0		S		51.2

* See new trends developing on pages 70, 84, 141–146

RUSSELL 2000 INDEX MARKET PROBABILITY CALENDAR 2021

THE % CHANCE OF THE MARKET RISING ON ANY TRADING DAY OF THE YEAR*
(Based on the number of times the RUSSELL 2000 rose on a particular trading day during January 1979–December 2019)

Date	Jan	Feb	Mar	Apr	May	Jun	Jul	Aug	Sep	Oct	Nov	Dec
1	H	65.9	65.9	48.8	S	65.9	68.3	S	48.8	46.3	61.0	48.8
2	S	61.0	58.5	H	S	70.7	46.3	46.3	58.5	S	70.7	58.5
3	S	53.7	63.4	S	61.0	51.2	S	43.9	56.1	S	61.0	63.4
4	48.8	65.9	53.7	S	65.9	56.1	S	48.8	S	48.8	61.0	S
5	63.4	58.5	58.5	58.5	56.1	S	H	53.7	S	53.7	56.1	S
6	58.5	S	S	48.8	56.1	S	46.3	48.8	H	65.9	S	61.0
7	61.0	S	S	56.1	56.1	58.5	58.5	S	61.0	39.0	S	48.8
8	56.1	58.5	48.8	43.9	S	43.9	51.2	S	58.5	46.3	56.1	53.7
9	S	48.8	56.1	58.5	S	46.3	61.0	46.3	58.5	S	51.2	51.2
10	S	70.7	46.3	S	53.7	53.7	S	56.1	63.4	S	68.3	46.3
11	63.4	65.9	63.4	S	63.4	58.5	S	43.9	S	46.3	46.3	S
12	56.1	68.3	48.8	61.0	51.2	S	53.7	48.8	S	48.8	46.3	S
13	65.9	S	S	63.4	51.2	S	61.0	73.2	63.4	63.4	S	43.9
14	63.4	S	S	48.8	46.3	61.0	65.9	S	56.1	58.5	S	39.0
15	63.4	H	51.2	56.1	S	58.5	53.7	S	39.0	61.0	51.2	43.9
16	S	61.0	63.4	61.0	S	51.2	51.2	58.5	51.2	S	26.8	56.1
17	S	56.1	65.9	S	48.8	46.3	S	61.0	43.9	S	61.0	58.5
18	H	43.9	53.7	S	58.5	46.3	S	58.5	S	46.3	46.3	S
19	70.7	41.5	46.3	61.0	53.7	S	48.8	48.8	S	51.2	36.6	S
20	65.9	S	S	51.2	53.7	S	56.1	68.3	43.9	63.4	S	61.0
21	39.0	S	S	56.1	53.7	51.2	34.1	S	43.9	46.3	S	61.0
22	51.2	51.2	46.3	63.4	S	46.3	41.5	S	48.8	46.3	63.4	65.9
23	S	53.7	61.0	53.7	S	48.8	48.8	46.3	39.0	S	65.9	65.9
24	S	58.5	46.3	S	61.0	36.6	S	58.5	43.9	S	61.0	H
25	51.2	65.9	53.7	S	53.7	46.3	S	61.0	S	34.1	H	S
26	65.9	51.2	46.3	51.2	61.0	S	61.0	58.5	S	41.5	65.9	S
27	53.7	S	S	58.5	63.4	S	63.4	68.3	36.6	56.1	S	75.6
28	53.7	S	S	65.9	61.0	56.1	46.3	S	53.7	53.7	S	68.3
29	73.2		51.2	56.1	S	70.7	56.1	S	53.7	70.7	68.3	53.7
30	S		56.1	61.0	S	65.9	63.4	63.4	63.4	S	65.9	61.0
31	S		82.9		H		S	68.3		S		65.9

* See new trends developing on pages 70, 84, 141–146

DECENNIAL CYCLE: A MARKET PHENOMENON

By arranging each year's market gain or loss so that the first and succeeding years of each decade fall into the same column, certain interesting patterns emerge—strong fifth and eighth years; weak first, seventh, and zero years.

This fascinating phenomenon was first presented by Edgar Lawrence Smith in *Common Stocks and Business Cycles* (William-Frederick Press, 1959). Anthony Gaubis co-pioneered the decennial pattern with Smith.

When Smith first cut graphs of market prices into 10-year segments and placed them above one another, he observed that each decade tended to have three bull market cycles and that the longest and strongest bull markets seemed to favor the middle years of a decade.

Don't place too much emphasis on the decennial cycle nowadays, other than the extraordinary fifth and zero years, as the stock market is more influenced by the quadrennial presidential election cycle, shown on page 130. Also, the last half-century, which has been the most prosperous in U.S. history, has distributed the returns among most years of the decade. Interestingly, NASDAQ suffered its worst bear market ever in a zero year.

First years have the third-worst record of the decennial cycle. The year is also a post-election year which has the weakest record in the four-year presidential election cycle. Covid-19 triggered the shortest bear market on record in 2020, the ensuing recovery was notably quick as well. However, great uncertainty remains for the balance of 2020 and into 2021 as a vaccine has yet to be discovered and distributed.

THE 10-YEAR STOCK MARKET CYCLE
Annual % Change in Dow Jones Industrial Average
Year of Decade

DECADES	1st	2nd	3rd	4th	5th	6th	7th	8th	9th	10th
1881–1890	3.0%	−2.9%	−8.5%	−18.8%	20.1%	12.4%	−8.4%	4.8%	5.5%	−14.1%
1891–1900	17.6	−6.6	−24.6	−0.6	2.3	−1.7	21.3	22.5	9.2	7.0
1901–1910	−8.7	−0.4	−23.6	41.7	38.2	−1.9	−37.7	46.6	15.0	−17.9
1911–1920	0.4	7.6	−10.3	−5.4	81.7	−4.2	−21.7	10.5	30.5	−32.9
1921–1930	12.7	21.7	−3.3	26.2	30.0	0.3	28.8	48.2	−17.2	−33.8
1931–1940	−52.7	−23.1	66.7	4.1	38.5	24.8	−32.8	28.1	−2.9	−12.7
1941–1950	−15.4	7.6	13.8	12.1	26.6	−8.1	2.2	−2.1	12.9	17.6
1951–1960	14.4	8.4	−3.8	44.0	20.8	2.3	−12.8	34.0	16.4	−9.3
1961–1970	18.7	−10.8	17.0	14.6	10.9	−18.9	15.2	4.3	−15.2	4.8
1971–1980	6.1	14.6	−16.6	−27.6	38.3	17.9	−17.3	−3.1	4.2	14.9
1981–1990	−9.2	19.6	20.3	−3.7	27.7	22.6	2.3	11.8	27.0	−4.3
1991–2000	20.3	4.2	13.7	2.1	33.5	26.0	22.6	16.1	25.2	−6.2
2001–2010	−7.1	−16.8	25.3	3.1	−0.6	16.3	6.4	−33.8	18.8	11.0
2011–2020	5.5	7.3	26.5	7.5	−2.2	13.4	25.1	−5.6	22.3	
Total % Change	5.6%	30.4%	92.6%	99.3%	365.8%	101.2%	−6.8%	182.3%	151.7%	−75.9%
Avg % Change	0.4%	2.2%	6.6%	7.1%	26.1%	7.2%	−0.5%	13.0%	10.8%	−5.8%
Up Years	9	8	7	9	12	9	8	10	11	5
Down Years	5	6	7	5	2	5	6	4	3	8

Based on annual close; Cowles indices 1881–1885; 12 Mixed Stocks, 10 Rails, 2 Inds 1886–1889;

20 Mixed Stocks, 18 Rails, 2 Inds 1890–1896; Railroad average 1897 (First industrial average published May 26, 1896).

PRESIDENTIAL ELECTION/STOCK MARKET CYCLE: THE 187-YEAR SAGA CONTINUES

It is no mere coincidence that the last two years (pre-election year and election year) of the 45 administrations since 1833 produced a total net market gain of 764.8%, dwarfing the 326.6% gain of the first two years of these administrations.

Presidential elections every four years have a profound impact on the economy and the stock market. Wars, recessions, and bear markets tend to start or occur in the first half of the term; prosperous times and bull markets, in the latter half. After nine straight annual Dow gains during the millennial bull, the four-year election cycle reasserted its overarching domination of market behavior until 2008. Recovery from the worst recession since the Great Depression produced six straight annual gains, until 2015, when the Dow suffered its first pre-election year loss since 1939.

STOCK MARKET ACTION SINCE 1833
Annual % Change in Dow Jones Industrial Average[1]

4-Year Cycle Beginning	President Elected	Post-Election Year	Mid-Term Year	Pre-Election Year	Election Year
1833	Jackson (D)	–0.9	13.0	3.1	–11.7
1837	Van Buren (D)	–11.5	1.6	–12.3	5.5
1841*	W.H. Harrison (W)**	–13.3	–18.1	45.0	15.5
1845*	Polk (D)	8.1	–14.5	1.2	–3.6
1849*	Taylor (W)	N/C	18.7	–3.2	19.6
1853*	Pierce (D)	–12.7	–30.2	1.5	4.4
1857	Buchanan (D)	–31.0	14.3	–10.7	14.0
1861*	Lincoln (R)	–1.8	55.4	38.0	6.4
1865	Lincoln (R)**	–8.5	3.6	1.6	10.8
1869	Grant (R)	1.7	5.6	7.3	6.8
1873	Grant (R)	–12.7	2.8	–4.1	–17.9
1877	Hayes (R)	–9.4	6.1	43.0	18.7
1881	Garfield (R)**	3.0	–2.9	–8.5	–18.8
1885*	Cleveland (D)	20.1	12.4	–8.4	4.8
1889*	B. Harrison (R)	5.5	–14.1	17.6	–6.6
1893*	Cleveland (D)	–24.6	–0.6	2.3	–1.7
1897*	McKinley (R)	21.3	22.5	9.2	7.0
1901	McKinley (R)**	–8.7	–0.4	–23.6	41.7
1905	T. Roosevelt (R)	38.2	–1.9	–37.7	46.6
1909	Taft (R)	15.0	–17.9	0.4	7.6
1913*	Wilson (D)	–10.3	–5.4	81.7	–4.2
1917	Wilson (D)	–21.7	10.5	30.5	–32.9
1921*	Harding (R)**	12.7	21.7	–3.3	26.2
1925	Coolidge (R)	30.0	0.3	28.8	48.2
1929	Hoover (R)	–17.2	–33.8	–52.7	–23.1
1933*	F. Roosevelt (D)	66.7	4.1	38.5	24.8
1937	F. Roosevelt (D)	–32.8	28.1	–2.9	–12.7
1941	F. Roosevelt (D)	–15.4	7.6	13.8	12.1
1945	F. Roosevelt (D)**	26.6	–8.1	2.2	–2.1
1949	Truman (D)	12.9	17.6	14.4	8.4
1953*	Eisenhower (R)	–3.8	44.0	20.8	2.3
1957	Eisenhower (R)	–12.8	34.0	16.4	–9.3
1961*	Kennedy (D)**	18.7	–10.8	17.0	14.6
1965	Johnson (D)	10.9	–18.9	15.2	4.3
1969*	Nixon (R)	–15.2	4.8	6.1	14.6
1973	Nixon (R)***	–16.6	–27.6	38.3	17.9
1977*	Carter (D)	–17.3	–3.1	4.2	14.9
1981*	Reagan (R)	–9.2	19.6	20.3	–3.7
1985	Reagan (R)	27.7	22.6	2.3	11.8
1989	G. H. W. Bush (R)	27.0	–4.3	20.3	4.2
1993*	Clinton (D)	13.7	2.1	33.5	26.0
1997	Clinton (D)	22.6	16.1	25.2	–6.2
2001*	G. W. Bush (R)	–7.1	–16.8	25.3	3.1
2005	G. W. Bush (R)	–0.6	16.3	6.4	–33.8
2009*	Obama (D)	18.8	11.0	5.5	7.3
2013	Obama (D)	26.5	7.5	–2.2	13.4
2017*	Trump (R)	25.1	–5.6	22.3	
Total % Gain		137.7	188.9	489.6	275.2
Average % Gain		3.0	4.0	10.4	6.0
# Up		22	28	35	31
# Down		24	19	12	15

*Party in power ousted   **Died in office   ***Resigned   **D**–Democrat, **W**–Whig, **R**–Republican
[1] Based on annual close; prior to 1886 based on Cowles and other indices; 12 Mixed Stocks, 10 Rails, 2 Inds 1886–1889; 20 Mixed Stocks, 18 Rails, 2 Inds 1890–1896; Railroad average 1897 (First industrial average published May 26, 1896).

DOW JONES INDUSTRIALS BULL AND BEAR MARKETS SINCE 1900

Bear markets begin at the end of one bull market and end at the start of the next bull market (10/9/07 to 3/9/09 as an example). The longest bull market on record ended on 7/17/98, and the shortest bear market on record ended on 3/23/2020, when the new bull market began. The greatest bull super cycle in history that began 8/12/82 ended in 2000 after the Dow gained 1409% and NASDAQ climbed 3072%. The Dow gained only 497% in the eight-year super bull from 1921 to the top in 1929. NASDAQ suffered its worst loss ever from the 2000 top to the 2002 bottom, down 77.9%, nearly as much as the 89.2% drop in the Dow from the 1929 top to the 1932 bottom. The third-longest Dow bull since 1900 that began 10/9/02 ended on its fifth anniversary. The ensuing bear market was the second worst bear market since 1900, slashing the Dow 53.8%. At press time, the Dow is currently trading above 26,000 after a swift recovery from its bear market low but struggling as Covid-19 cases spike threatening to stall the economic reopening. (See page 132 for S&P 500 and NASDAQ bulls and bears.)

DOW JONES INDUSTRIALS BULL AND BEAR MARKETS SINCE 1900

— Beginning —		— Ending —		Bull		Bear	
Date	DJIA	Date	DJIA	% Gain	Days	% Change	Days
9/24/00	38.80	6/17/01	57.33	47.8%	266	−46.1%	875
11/9/03	30.88	1/19/06	75.45	144.3	802	−48.5	665
11/15/07	38.83	11/19/09	73.64	89.6	735	−27.4	675
9/25/11	53.43	9/30/12	68.97	29.1	371	−24.1	668
7/30/14	52.32	11/21/16	110.15	110.5	845	−40.1	393
12/19/17	65.95	11/3/19	119.62	81.4	684	−46.6	660
8/24/21	63.90	3/20/23	105.38	64.9	573	−18.6	221
10/27/23	85.76	9/3/29	381.17	344.5	2138	−47.9	71
11/13/29	198.69	4/17/30	294.07	48.0	155	−86.0	813
7/8/32	41.22	9/7/32	79.93	93.9	61	−37.2	173
2/27/33	50.16	2/5/34	110.74	120.8	343	−22.8	171
7/26/34	85.51	3/10/37	194.40	127.3	958	−49.1	386
3/31/38	98.95	11/12/38	158.41	60.1	226	−23.3	147
4/8/39	121.44	9/12/39	155.92	28.4	157	−40.4	959
4/28/42	92.92	5/29/46	212.50	128.7	1492	−23.2	353
5/17/47	163.21	6/15/48	193.16	18.4	395	−16.3	363
6/13/49	161.60	1/5/53	293.79	81.8	1302	−13.0	252
9/14/53	255.49	4/6/56	521.05	103.9	935	−19.4	564
10/22/57	419.79	1/5/60	685.47	63.3	805	−17.4	294
10/25/60	566.05	12/13/61	734.91	29.8	414	−27.1	195
6/26/62	535.76	2/9/66	995.15	85.7	1324	−25.2	240
10/7/66	744.32	12/3/68	985.21	32.4	788	−35.9	539
5/26/70	631.16	4/28/71	950.82	50.6	337	−16.1	209
11/23/71	797.97	1/11/73	1051.70	31.8	415	−45.1	694
12/6/74	577.60	9/21/76	1014.79	75.7	655	−26.9	525
2/28/78	742.12	9/8/78	907.74	22.3	192	−16.4	591
4/21/80	759.13	4/27/81	1024.05	34.9	371	−24.1	472
8/12/82	776.92	11/29/83	1287.20	65.7	474	−15.6	238
7/24/84	1086.57	8/25/87	2722.42	150.6	1127	−36.1	55
10/19/87	1738.74	7/17/90	2999.75	72.5	1002	−21.2	86
10/11/90	2365.10	7/17/98	9337.97	294.8	2836	−19.3	45
8/31/98	7539.07	1/14/00	11722.98	55.5	501	−29.7	616
9/21/01	8235.81	3/19/02	10635.25	29.1	179	−31.5	204
10/9/02	7286.27	10/9/07	14164.53	94.4	1826	−53.8	517
3/9/09	6547.05	4/29/11	12810.54	95.7	781	−16.8	157
10/3/11	10655.30	5/19/15	18312.39	71.9	1324	−14.5	268
2/11/16	15660.18	2/12/20	29551.42	88.7	1462	−37.1	40
3/23/20	18591.93	6/8/20	27572.44	48.3*	77*		

* As of June 8, 2020—not in averages

		Average		**85.6%**	**791**	**−30.8%**	**389**

Based on Dow Jones Industrial Average.
The NYSE was closed from 7/31/1914 to 12/11/1914 due to World War I.
DJIA figures were then adjusted back to reflect the composition change from 12 to 20 stocks in September 1916.

1900–2000 Data: Ned Davis Research

STANDARD & POOR'S 500 BULL AND BEAR MARKETS SINCE 1929
NASDAQ COMPOSITE SINCE 1971

A constant debate of the definition and timing of bull and bear markets permeates Wall Street like the bell that signals the open and close of every trading day. We have relied on the Ned Davis Research parameters for years to track bulls and bears on the Dow (see page 131). Standard & Poor's 500 index has been a stalwart indicator for decades and at times marched to a slightly different beat than the Dow. The moves of the S&P 500 and NASDAQ have been correlated to the bull and bear dates on page 131. Many dates line up for the three indices, but you will notice quite a lag or lead on several occasions, including NASDAQ's independent cadence from 1975 to 1980.

STANDARD & POOR'S 500 BULL AND BEAR MARKETS

— Beginning —		— Ending —		Bull		Bear	
Date	S&P 500	Date	S&P 500	% Gain	Days	% Change	Days
11/13/29	17.66	4/10/30	25.92	46.8%	148	−83.0%	783
6/1/32	4.40	9/7/32	9.31	111.6	98	−40.6	173
2/27/33	5.53	2/6/34	11.82	113.7	344	−31.8	401
3/14/35	8.06	3/6/37	18.68	131.8	723	−49.0	390
3/31/38	8.50	11/9/38	13.79	62.2	223	−26.2	150
4/8/39	10.18	10/25/39	13.21	29.8	200	−43.5	916
4/28/42	7.47	5/29/46	19.25	157.7	1492	−28.8	353
5/17/47	13.71	6/15/48	17.06	24.4	395	−20.6	363
6/13/49	13.55	1/5/53	26.66	96.8	1302	−14.8	252
9/14/53	22.71	8/2/56	49.74	119.0	1053	−21.6	446
10/22/57	38.98	8/3/59	60.71	55.7	650	−13.9	449
10/25/60	52.30	12/12/61	72.64	38.9	413	−28.0	196
6/26/62	52.32	2/9/66	94.06	79.8	1324	−22.2	240
10/7/66	73.20	11/29/68	108.37	48.0	784	−36.1	543
5/26/70	69.29	4/28/71	104.77	51.2	337	−13.9	209
11/23/71	90.16	1/11/73	120.24	33.4	415	−48.2	630
10/3/74	62.28	9/21/76	107.83	73.1	719	−19.4	531
3/6/78	86.90	9/12/78	106.99	23.1	190	−8.2	562
3/27/80	98.22	11/28/80	140.52	43.1	246	−27.1	622
8/12/82	102.42	10/10/83	172.65	68.6	424	−14.4	288
7/24/84	147.82	8/25/87	336.77	127.8	1127	−33.5	101
12/4/87	223.92	7/16/90	368.95	64.8	955	−19.9	87
10/11/90	295.46	7/17/98	1186.75	301.7	2836	−19.3	45
8/31/98	957.28	3/24/00	1527.46	59.6	571	−36.8	546
9/21/01	965.80	1/4/02	1172.51	21.4	105	−33.8	278
10/9/02	776.76	10/9/07	1565.15	101.5	1826	−56.8	517
3/9/09	676.53	4/29/11	1363.61	101.6	781	−19.4	157
10/3/11	1099.23	5/21/15	2130.82	93.8	1326	−14.2	266
2/11/16	1829.08	2/19/20	3386.15	85.1	1469	−33.9	33
3/23/20	2237.40	6/8/20	3232.39	44.5*	77*		
			Average	81.6%	775	−29.8%	363

*As of June 8, 2020 — not in averages

NASDAQ COMPOSITE BULL AND BEAR MARKETS

— Beginning —		— Ending —		Bull		Bear	
Date	NASDAQ	Date	NASDAQ	% Gain	Days	% Change	Days
11/23/71	100.31	1/11/73	136.84	36.4%	415	−59.9%	630
10/3/74	54.87	7/15/75	88.00	60.4	285	−16.2	63
9/16/75	73.78	9/13/78	139.25	88.7	1093	−20.4	62
11/14/78	110.88	2/8/80	165.25	49.0	451	−24.9	48
3/27/80	124.09	5/29/81	223.47	80.1	428	−28.8	441
8/13/82	159.14	6/24/83	328.91	106.7	315	−31.5	397
7/25/84	225.30	8/26/87	455.26	102.1	1127	−35.9	63
10/28/87	291.88	10/9/89	485.73	66.4	712	−33.0	372
10/16/90	325.44	7/20/98	2014.25	518.9	2834	−29.5	80
10/8/98	1419.12	3/10/00	5048.62	255.8	519	−71.8	560
9/21/01	1423.19	1/4/02	2059.38	44.7	105	−45.9	278
10/9/02	1114.11	10/31/07	2859.12	156.6	1848	−55.6	495
3/9/09	1268.64	4/29/11	2873.54	126.5	781	−18.7	157
10/3/11	2335.83	7/20/15	5218.86	123.4	1386	−18.2	206
2/11/16	4266.84	2/19/20	9817.18	130.1	1469	−30.1	33
3/23/20	6860.67	6/10/20	10020.35	46.1*	79*		
			Average	129.7%	918	−34.7%	259

*As of June 10, 2020 — not in averages

JANUARY DAILY POINT CHANGES DOW JONES INDUSTRIALS

	2011	2012	2013	2014	2015	2016	2017	2018	2019	2020
Previous Month Close	11577.51	12217.56	13104.14	16576.66	17823.07	17425.03	19762.60	24719.22	23327.46	28538.44
1	S	S	H	H	H	H	H	H	H	H
2	S	H	308.41	-135.31	9.92	S	H	104.79	18.78	330.36
3	93.24	179.82	-21.19	28.64	S	S	119.16	98.67	-660.02	-233.92
4	20.43	21.04	43.85	S	S	-276.09	60.40	152.45	746.94	S
5	31.71	-2.72	S	S	-331.34	9.72	-42.87	220.74	S	S
6	-25.58	-55.78	S	-44.89	-130.01	-252.15	64.51	S	S	68.50
7	-22.55	S	-50.92	105.84	212.88	-392.41	S	S	98.19	-119.70
8	S	S	-55.44	-68.20	323.35	-167.65	S	-12.87	256.10	161.41
9	S	32.77	61.66	-17.98	-170.50	S	-76.42	102.80	91.67	211.81
10	-37.31	69.78	80.71	-7.71	S	S	-31.85	-16.67	122.80	-133.13
11	34.43	-13.02	17.21	S	S	52.12	98.75	205.60	-5.97	S
12	83.56	21.57	S	S	-96.53	117.65	-63.28	228.46	S	S
13	-23.54	-48.96	S	-179.11	-27.16	-364.81	-5.27	S	S	83.28
14	55.48	S	18.89	115.92	-186.59	227.64	S	S	-86.11	32.62
15	S	S	27.57	108.08	-106.38	-390.97	S	H	155.75	90.55
16	S	H	-23.66	-64.93	190.86	S	H	-10.33	141.57	267.42
17	H	60.01	84.79	41.55	S	S	-58.96	322.79	162.94	50.46
18	50.55	96.88	53.68	S	S	H	-22.05	-97.84	336.25	S
19	-12.64	45.03	S	S	H	27.94	-72.32	53.91	S	S
20	-2.49	96.50	S	H	3.66	-249.28	94.85	S	S	H
21	49.04	S	H	-44.12	39.05	115.94	S	S	H	-152.06
22	S	S	62.51	-41.10	259.70	210.83	S	142.88	-301.87	-9.77
23	S	-11.66	67.12	-175.99	-141.38	S	-27.40	-3.79	171.14	-26.18
24	108.68	-33.07	46.00	-318.24	S	S	112.86	41.31	-22.38	-170.36
25	-3.33	81.21	70.65	S	S	-208.29	155.80	140.67	183.96	S
26	8.25	-22.33	S	S	6.10	282.01	32.40	223.92	S	S
27	4.39	-74.17	S	-41.23	-291.49	-222.77	-7.13	S	S	-453.93
28	-166.13	S	-14.05	90.68	-195.84	125.18	S	S	-208.98	187.05
29	S	S	72.49	-189.77	225.48	396.66	S	-177.23	51.74	11.60
30	S	-6.74	-44.00	109.82	-251.90	S	-122.65	-362.59	434.90	124.99
31	68.23	-20.81	-49.84	-149.76	S	S	-107.04	72.50	-15.19	-603.41
Close	11891.93	12632.91	13860.58	15698.85	17164.95	16466.30	19864.09	26149.39	24999.67	28256.03
Change	314.42	415.35	756.44	-877.81	-658.12	-958.73	101.49	1430.17	1672.21	-282.41

FEBRUARY DAILY POINT CHANGES DOW JONES INDUSTRIALS

	2011	2012	2013	2014	2015	2016	2017	2018	2019	2020
Previous Month Close	11891.93	12632.91	13860.58	15698.85	17164.95	16466.30	19864.09	26149.39	24999.67	28256.03
1	148.23	83.55	149.21	S	S	-17.12	26.85	37.32	64.22	S
2	1.81	-11.05	S	S	196.09	-295.64	-6.03	-665.75	S	S
3	20.29	156.82	S	-326.05	305.36	183.12	186.55	S	S	143.78
4	29.89	S	-129.71	72.44	6.62	79.92	S	S	175.48	407.82
5	S	S	99.22	-5.01	211.86	-211.61	S	-1175.21	172.15	483.22
6	S	-17.10	7.22	188.30	-60.59	S	-19.04	567.02	-21.22	88.92
7	69.48	33.07	-42.47	165.55	S	S	37.87	-19.42	-220.77	-277.26
8	71.52	5.75	48.92	S	S	-177.92	-35.95	-1032.89	-63.20	S
9	6.74	6.51	S	S	-95.08	-12.67	118.06	330.44	S	S
10	-10.60	-89.23	S	7.71	139.55	-99.64	96.97	S	S	174.31
11	43.97	S	-21.73	192.98	-6.62	-254.56	S	S	-53.22	-0.48
12	S	S	47.46	-30.83	110.24	313.66	S	410.37	372.65	275.08
13	S	72.81	-35.79	63.65	46.97	S	142.79	39.18	117.51	-128.11
14	-5.07	4.24	-9.52	126.80	S	S	92.25	253.04	-103.88	-25.23
15	-41.55	-97.33	8.37	S	S	H	107.45	306.88	443.86	S
16	61.53	123.13	S	S	H	222.57	7.91	19.01	S	S
17	29.97	45.79	S	H	28.23	257.42	4.28	S	S	H
18	73.11	S	H	-23.99	-17.73	-40.40	S	S	H	-165.89
19	S	S	53.91	-89.84	-44.08	-21.44	S	H	8.07	115.84
20	S	S	-108.13	92.67	154.67	S	H	-254.63	63.12	-128.05
21	H	15.82	-46.92	-29.93	S	S	118.95	-166.97	-103.81	-227.57
22	-178.46	-27.02	119.95	S	S	228.67	32.60	164.70	181.18	S
23	-107.01	46.02	S	S	-23.60	-188.88	34.72	347.51	S	S
24	-37.28	-1.74	S	103.84	92.35	53.21	11.44	S	S	-1031.61
25	61.95	S	-216.40	-27.48	15.38	212.30	S	S	60.14	-879.44
26	S	S	115.96	18.75	-10.15	-57.32	S	399.28	-33.97	-123.77
27	S	-1.44	175.24	74.24	-81.72	S	15.68	-299.24	-72.82	-1190.95
28	95.89	23.61	-20.88	49.06	S	S	-25.20	-380.83	-69.16	-357.28
29		-53.05				-123.47				
Close	12226.34	12952.07	14054.49	16321.71	18132.70	16516.50	20812.24	25029.20	25916.00	25409.36
Change	334.41	319.16	193.91	622.86	967.75	50.20	948.15	-1120.19	916.33	-2846.67

MARCH DAILY POINT CHANGES DOW JONES INDUSTRIALS

	2011	2012	2013	2014	2015	2016	2017	2018	2019	2020
Previous Month Close	12226.34	12952.07	14054.49	16321.71	18132.70	16516.50	20812.24	25029.20	25916.00	25409.36
1	−168.32	28.23	35.17	S	S	348.58	303.31	−420.22	110.32	S
2	8.78	−2.73	S	S	155.93	34.24	−112.58	−70.92	S	1293.96
3	191.40	S	S	−153.68	−85.26	44.58	2.74	S	S	−785.91
4	−88.32	S	38.16	227.85	−106.47	62.87	S	S	−206.67	1173.45
5	S	−14.76	125.95	−35.70	38.82	S	S	336.70	−13.02	−969.58
6	S	−203.66	42.47	61.71	−278.94	S	−51.37	9.36	−133.17	−256.50
7	−79.85	78.18	33.25	30.83	S	67.18	−29.58	−82.76	−200.23	S
8	124.35	70.61	67.58	S	S	−109.85	−69.03	93.85	−22.99	S
9	−1.29	14.08	S	S	138.94	36.26	2.46	440.53	S	−2013.76
10	−228.48	S	S	−34.04	−332.78	−5.23	44.79	S	S	1167.14
11	59.79	S	50.22	−67.43	−27.55	218.18	S	S	200.64	−1464.94
12	S	37.69	2.77	−11.17	259.83	S	S	−157.13	−96.22	−2352.60
13	S	217.97	5.22	−231.19	−145.91	S	−21.50	−171.58	148.23	1985.00
14	−51.24	16.42	83.86	−43.22	S	15.82	−44.11	−248.91	7.05	S
15	−137.74	58.66	−25.03	S	S	22.40	112.73	115.54	138.93	S
16	−242.12	−20.14	S	S	228.11	74.23	−15.55	72.85	S	−2997.10
17	161.29	S	S	181.55	−128.34	155.73	−19.93	S	S	1048.86
18	83.93	S	−62.05	88.97	227.11	120.81	S	S	65.23	−1338.46
19	S	6.51	3.76	−114.02	−117.16	S	S	−335.60	−26.72	188.27
20	S	−68.94	55.91	108.88	168.62	S	−8.76	116.36	−141.71	−913.21
21	178.01	−45.57	−90.24	−28.28	S	21.57	−237.85	−44.96	216.84	S
22	−17.90	−78.48	90.54	S	S	−41.30	−6.71	−724.42	−460.19	S
23	67.39	34.59	S	S	−11.61	−79.98	−4.72	−424.69	S	−582.05
24	84.54	S	S	−26.08	−104.90	13.14	−59.86	S	S	2112.98
25	50.03	S	−64.28	91.19	−292.60	H	S	S	14.51	495.64
26	S	160.90	111.90	−98.89	−40.31	S	S	669.40	140.90	1351.62
27	S	−43.90	−33.49	−4.76	34.43	S	−45.74	−344.89	−32.14	−915.39
28	−22.71	−71.52	52.38	58.83	S	19.66	150.52	−9.29	91.87	S
29	81.13	19.61	H	S	S	97.72	−42.18	254.69	211.22	S
30	71.60	66.22	S	S	263.65	83.55	69.17	H	S	690.70
31	−30.88	S	S	134.60	−200.19	−31.57	−65.27	S	S	−410.32
Close	12319.73	13212.04	14578.54	16457.66	17776.12	17685.09	20663.22	24103.11	25928.68	21917.16
Change	93.39	259.97	524.05	135.95	−356.58	1168.59	−149.02	−926.09	12.68	−3492.20

APRIL DAILY POINT CHANGES DOW JONES INDUSTRIALS

	2011	2012	2013	2014	2015	2016	2017	2018	2019	2020
Previous Month Close	12319.73	13212.04	14578.54	16457.66	17776.12	17685.09	20663.22	24103.11	25928.68	21917.16
1	56.99	S	−5.69	74.95	−77.94	107.66	S	S	329.74	−973.65
2	S	52.45	89.16	40.39	65.06	S	S	−458.92	−79.29	469.93
3	S	−64.94	−111.66	−0.45	H	S	−13.01	389.17	39.00	−360.91
4	23.31	−124.80	55.76	−159.84	S	−55.75	39.03	230.94	166.50	S
5	−6.13	−14.61	−40.86	S	S	−133.68	−41.09	240.92	40.36	S
6	32.85	H	S	S	117.61	112.73	14.80	−572.46	S	1627.46
7	−17.26	S	S	−166.84	−5.43	−174.09	−6.85	S	S	−26.13
8	−29.44	S	48.23	10.27	27.09	35.00	S	S	−83.97	779.71
9	S	−130.55	59.98	181.04	56.22	S	S	46.34	−190.44	285.80
10	S	−213.66	128.78	−266.96	98.92	S	1.92	428.90	6.58	H
11	1.06	89.46	62.90	−143.47	S	−20.55	−6.72	−218.55	−14.11	S
12	−117.53	181.19	−0.08	S	S	164.84	−59.44	293.60	269.25	S
13	7.41	−136.99	S	S	−80.61	187.03	−138.61	−122.91	S	−328.60
14	14.16	S	S	146.49	59.66	18.15	H	S	S	558.99
15	56.68	S	−265.86	89.32	75.91	−28.97	S	S	−27.53	−445.41
16	S	71.82	157.58	162.29	−6.84	S	S	212.90	67.89	33.33
17	S	194.13	−138.19	−16.31	−279.47	S	183.67	213.59	−3.12	704.81
18	−140.24	−82.79	−81.45	H	S	106.70	−113.64	−38.56	110.00	S
19	65.16	−68.65	10.37	S	S	49.44	−118.79	−83.18	H	S
20	186.79	65.16	S	S	208.63	42.67	174.22	−201.95	S	−592.05
21	52.45	S	S	40.71	−85.34	−113.75	−30.95	S	S	−631.56
22	H	S	19.66	65.12	88.68	21.23	S	S	−48.49	456.94
23	S	−102.09	152.29	−12.72	20.42	S	S	−14.25	145.34	39.44
24	S	74.39	−43.16	0.00	21.45	S	216.13	−424.56	−59.34	260.01
25	−26.11	89.16	24.50	−140.19	S	−26.51	232.23	59.70	−134.97	S
26	115.49	113.90	11.75	S	S	13.08	−21.03	238.51	81.25	S
27	95.59	23.69	S	S	−42.17	51.23	6.24	−11.15	S	358.51
28	72.35	S	S	87.28	72.17	−210.79	−40.82	S	S	−32.23
29	47.23	S	106.20	86.63	−74.61	−57.12	S	S	11.06	532.31
30	S	−14.68	21.05	45.47	−195.01	S	S	−148.04	38.52	−288.14
Close	12810.54	13213.63	14839.80	16580.84	17840.52	17773.64	20940.51	24163.15	26592.91	24345.72
Change	490.81	1.59	261.26	123.18	64.40	88.55	277.29	60.04	664.23	2428.56

MAY DAILY POINT CHANGES DOW JONES INDUSTRIALS

Previous Month Close	2011	2012	2013	2014	2015	2016	2017	2018	2019	2020
	12810.54	13213.63	14839.80	16580.84	17840.52	17773.64	20940.51	24163.15	26592.91	24345.72
1	S	65.69	-138.85	-21.97	183.54	S	-27.05	-64.10	-162.77	-622.03
2	-3.18	-10.75	130.63	-45.98	S	117.52	36.43	-174.07	-122.35	S
3	0.15	-61.98	142.38	S	S	-140.25	8.01	5.17	197.16	S
4	-83.93	-168.32	S	S	17.66	-99.65	-6.43	332.36	S	26.07
5	-139.41	S	S	46.34	-142.20	9.45	55.47	S	S	133.33
6	54.57	S	-5.07	-129.53	-86.22	79.92	S	S	-66.47	-218.45
7	S	-29.74	87.31	117.52	82.08	S	S	94.81	-473.39	211.25
8	S	-76.44	48.92	32.43	267.05	S	5.34	2.89	2.24	455.43
9	45.94	-97.03	-22.50	32.37	S	-34.72	-36.50	182.33	-138.97	S
10	75.68	19.98	35.87	S	S	222.44	-32.67	196.99	114.01	S
11	-130.33	-34.44	S	S	-85.94	-217.23	-23.69	91.64	S	-109.33
12	65.89	S	S	112.13	-36.94	9.38	-22.81	S	S	-457.21
13	-100.17	S	-26.81	19.97	-7.74	-185.18	S	S	-617.38	-516.81
14	S	-125.25	123.57	-101.47	191.75	S	S	68.24	207.06	377.37
15	S	-63.35	60.44	-167.16	20.32	S	85.33	-193.00	115.97	60.08
16	-47.38	-33.45	-42.47	44.50	S	175.39	-2.19	62.52	214.66	S
17	-68.79	-156.06	121.18	S	S	-180.73	-372.82	-54.95	-98.68	S
18	80.60	-73.11	S	S	26.32	-3.36	56.09	1.11	S	911.95
19	45.14	S	S	20.55	13.51	-91.22	141.82	S	S	-390.51
20	-93.28	S	-19.12	-137.55	-26.99	65.54	S	S	-84.10	369.04
21	S	135.10	52.30	158.75	0.34	S	S	298.20	197.43	-101.78
22	S	-1.67	-80.41	10.02	-53.72	S	89.99	-178.88	-100.72	-8.96
23	-130.78	-6.66	-12.67	63.19	S	-8.01	43.08	52.40	-286.14	S
24	-25.05	33.60	8.60	S	S	213.12	74.51	-75.05	95.22	S
25	38.45	-74.92	S	S	H	145.46	70.53	-58.67	S	H
26	8.10	S	S	H	-190.48	-23.22	-2.67	S	S	529.95
27	38.82	S	H	69.23	121.45	44.93	S	S	H	553.16
28	S	H	106.29	-42.32	-36.87	S	S	H	-237.92	-147.63
29	S	125.86	-106.59	65.56	-115.44	S	H	-391.64	-221.36	-17.53
30	H	-160.83	21.73	18.43	S	H	-50.81	306.33	43.47	S
31	128.21	-26.41	-208.96	S	S	-86.02	-20.82	-251.94	-354.84	S
Close	12569.79	12393.45	15115.57	16717.17	18010.68	17787.20	21008.65	24415.84	24815.04	25383.11
Change	-240.75	-820.18	275.77	136.33	170.16	13.56	68.14	252.69	-1777.87	1037.39

JUNE DAILY POINT CHANGES DOW JONES INDUSTRIALS

Previous Month Close	2010	2011	2012	2013	2014	2015	2016	2017	2018	2019
	10136.63	12569.79	12393.45	15115.57	16717.17	18010.68	17787.20	21008.65	24415.84	24815.04
1	-112.61	-279.65	-274.88	S	S	29.69	2.47	135.53	219.37	S
2	225.52	-41.59	S	S	26.46	-28.43	48.89	62.11	S	S
3	5.74	-97.29	S	138.46	-21.29	64.33	-31.50	S	S	4.74
4	-323.31	S	-17.11	-76.49	15.19	-170.69	S	S	178.48	512.40
5	S	S	26.49	-216.95	98.58	-56.12	S	-22.25	-13.71	207.39
6	S	-61.30	286.84	80.03	88.17	S	113.27	-47.81	346.41	181.09
7	-115.48	-19.15	46.17	207.50	S	S	17.95	37.46	95.02	263.28
8	123.49	-21.87	93.24	S	S	-82.91	66.77	8.84	75.12	S
9	-40.73	75.42	S	S	18.82	-2.51	-19.86	89.44	S	S
10	273.28	-172.45	S	-9.53	2.82	236.36	-119.85	S	S	78.74
11	38.54	S	-142.97	-116.57	-102.04	38.97	S	S	5.78	-14.17
12	S	S	162.57	-126.79	-109.69	-140.53	S	-36.30	-1.58	-43.68
13	S	1.06	-77.42	180.85	41.55	S	-132.86	92.80	-119.53	101.94
14	-20.18	123.14	155.53	-105.90	S	S	-57.66	46.09	-25.89	-17.16
15	213.88	-178.84	115.26	S	S	-107.67	-34.65	-14.66	-84.83	S
16	4.69	64.25	S	S	5.27	113.31	92.93	24.38	S	S
17	24.71	42.84	S	109.67	27.48	31.26	-57.94	S	S	22.92
18	16.47	S	-25.35	138.38	98.13	180.10	S	S	-103.01	353.01
19	S	S	95.51	-206.04	14.84	-99.89	S	144.71	-287.26	38.46
20	S	76.02	-12.94	-353.87	25.62	S	129.71	-61.85	-42.41	249.17
21	-8.23	109.63	-250.82	41.08	S	S	24.86	-57.11	-196.10	-34.04
22	-148.89	-80.34	67.21	S	S	103.83	-48.90	-12.74	119.19	S
23	4.92	-59.67	S	S	-9.82	24.29	230.24	-2.53	S	S
24	-145.64	-115.42	S	-139.84	-119.13	-178.00	-610.32	S	S	8.41
25	-8.99	S	-138.12	100.75	49.38	-75.71	S	S	-328.09	-179.32
26	S	S	32.01	149.83	-21.38	56.32	S	14.79	30.31	-11.40
27	S	108.98	92.34	114.35	5.71	S	-260.51	-98.89	-165.52	-10.24
28	-5.29	145.13	-24.75	-114.89	S	S	269.48	143.95	98.46	73.38
29	-268.22	72.73	277.83	S	S	-350.33	284.96	-167.58	55.36	S
30	-96.28	152.92	S	S	-25.24	23.16	235.31	62.60	S	S
Close	9774.02	12414.34	12880.09	14909.60	16826.60	17619.51	17929.99	21349.63	24271.41	26599.96
Change	-362.61	-155.45	486.64	-205.97	109.43	-391.17	142.79	340.98	-144.43	1784.92

JULY DAILY POINT CHANGES DOW JONES INDUSTRIALS

Previous Month Close	2010	2011	2012	2013	2014	2015	2016	2017	2018	2019
	9774.02	12414.34	12880.09	14909.60	16826.60	17619.51	17929.99	21349.63	24271.41	26599.96
1	−41.49	168.43	S	65.36	129.47	138.40	19.38	S	S	117.47
2	−46.05	S	−8.70	−42.55	20.17	−27.80	S	S	35.77	69.25
3	S	S	72.43*	56.14*	92.02	H	S	129.64*	−132.36*	179.32*
4	S	H	H	H	H	S	H	H	H	H
5	H	−12.90	−47.15	147.29	S	S	−108.75	−1.10	181.92	−43.88
6	57.14	56.15	−124.20	S	S	−46.53	78.00	−158.13	99.74	S
7	274.66	93.47	S	S	−44.05	93.33	−22.74	94.30	S	S
8	120.71	−62.29	S	88.85	−117.59	−261.49	250.86	S	S	−115.98
9	59.04	S	−36.18	75.65	78.99	33.20	S	S	320.11	−22.65
10	S	S	−83.17	−8.68	−70.54	211.79	S	−5.82	143.07	76.71
11	S	−151.44	−48.59	169.26	28.74	S	80.19	0.55	−219.21	227.88
12	18.24	−58.88	−31.26	3.38	S	S	120.74	123.07	224.44	243.95
13	146.75	44.73	203.82	S	S	217.27	24.45	20.95	94.52	S
14	3.70	−54.49	S	S	111.61	75.90	134.29	84.65	S	S
15	−7.41	42.61	S	19.96	5.26	−3.41	10.14	S	S	27.13
16	−261.41	S	−49.88	−32.41	77.52	70.08	S	S	44.95	−23.53
17	S	S	78.33	18.67	−161.39	−33.80	S	−8.02	55.53	−115.78
18	S	−94.57	103.16	78.02	123.37	S	16.50	−54.99	79.40	3.12
19	56.53	202.26	34.66	−4.80	S	S	25.96	66.02	−134.79	−68.77
20	75.53	−15.51	−120.79	S	S	13.96	36.02	−28.97	−6.38	S
21	−109.43	152.50	S	S	−48.45	−181.12	−77.80	−31.71	S	S
22	201.77	−43.25	S	1.81	61.81	−68.25	53.62	S	S	17.70
23	102.32	S	−101.11	22.19	−26.91	−119.12	S	S	−13.83	177.29
24	S	−88.36	−104.14	−25.50	−2.83	−163.39	S	−66.90	197.65	−79.22
25	S	−88.36	58.73	13.37	−123.23	S	−77.79	100.26	172.16	−128.99
26	100.81	−91.50	211.88	3.22	S	S	−19.31	97.58	112.97	51.47
27	12.26	−198.75	187.73	S	S	−127.94	−1.58	85.54	−76.01	S
28	−39.81	−62.44	S	S	22.02	189.68	−15.82	33.76	S	S
29	−30.72	−96.87	S	−36.86	−70.48	121.12	−24.11	S	S	28.90
30	−1.22	S	−2.65	−1.38	−31.75	−5.41	S	S	−144.23	−23.33
31			−64.33	−21.05	−317.06	−56.12	S	60.81	108.36	−333.75
Close	10465.94	12143.24	13008.68	15499.54	16563.30	17689.86	18432.24	21891.12	25415.19	26864.27
Change	691.92	−271.10	128.59	589.94	−263.30	70.35	502.25	541.49	1143.78	264.31

*Shortened trading day

AUGUST DAILY POINT CHANGES DOW JONES INDUSTRIALS

Previous Month Close	2010	2011	2012	2013	2014	2015	2016	2017	2018	2019
	10465.94	12143.24	13008.68	15499.54	16563.30	17689.86	18432.24	21891.12	25415.19	26864.27
1	S	−10.75	−37.62	128.48	−69.93	S	−27.73	72.80	−81.37	−280.85
2	208.44	−265.87	−92.18	30.34	S	S	−90.74	52.32	−7.66	−98.41
3	−38.00	29.82	217.29	S	S	−91.66	41.23	9.86	136.42	S
4	44.05	−512.76	S	S	75.91	−47.51	−2.95	66.71	S	S
5	−5.45	60.93	S	−46.23	−139.81	−10.22	191.48	S	S	−767.27
6	−21.42	S	21.34	−93.39	13.87	−120.72	S	S	39.60	311.78
7	S	S	51.09	−48.07	−75.07	−46.37	S	25.61	126.73	−22.45
8	S	−634.76	7.04	27.65	185.66	S	−14.24	−33.08	−45.16	371.12
9	45.19	429.92	−10.45	−72.81	S	S	3.76	−36.64	−74.52	−90.75
10	−54.50	−519.83	42.76	S	S	241.79	−37.39	−204.69	−196.09	S
11	−265.42	423.37	S	−5.83	16.05	−212.33	117.86	14.31	S	S
12	−58.88	125.71	S	−9.44	−0.33	−37.05	S	S	−380.07	
13	−16.80	S	−38.52	31.33	91.26	5.74	S	S	−125.44	372.54
14	S	213.88	2.71	−113.35	61.78	69.15	S	135.39	112.22	−800.49
15	S	213.88	−7.36	−225.47	−50.67	S	59.58	5.28	−137.51	99.97
16	−1.14	−76.97	85.33	−30.72	S	S	−84.03	25.88	396.32	306.62
17	103.84	4.28	25.09	S	S	67.78	21.92	−274.14	110.59	S
18	9.69	−419.63	S	S	175.83	−33.84	23.76	−76.22	S	S
19	−144.33	−172.93	S	−70.73	80.85	−162.61	−45.13	S	S	249.78
20	−57.59	S	−3.56	−7.75	59.54	−358.04	S	S	89.37	−173.35
21	S	S	−68.06	−105.44	60.36	−530.94	S	29.24	63.60	240.29
22	S	37.00	−30.82	66.19	−38.27	S	−23.15	196.14	−88.69	49.51
23	−39.21	322.11	−115.30	46.77	S	S	17.88	−87.80	−76.62	−623.34
24	−133.96	143.95	100.51	S	S	−588.40	−65.82	−28.69	133.37	S
25	19.61	−170.89	S	S	75.65	−204.91	−33.07	30.27	S	S
26	−74.25	134.72	S	−64.05	29.83	619.07	−53.01	S	S	269.93
27	164.84	S	−33.30	−170.33	15.31	369.26	S	S	259.29	−120.93
28	S	S	−21.68	48.38	−42.44	−11.76	S	−5.27	14.38	258.20
29	S	254.71	4.49	16.44	18.88	S	107.59	56.97	60.55	326.15
30	−140.92	20.70	−106.77	−30.64	S	S	−48.69	27.06	−137.65	41.03
31	4.99	53.58	90.13	S	S	−114.98	−53.42	55.67	−22.10	S
Close	10014.72	11613.53	13090.84	14810.31	17098.45	16528.03	18400.88	21948.10	25964.82	26403.28
Change	−451.22	−529.71	82.16	−689.23	535.15	−1161.83	−31.36	56.98	549.63	−460.99

SEPTEMBER DAILY POINT CHANGES DOW JONES INDUSTRIALS

Previous Month Close	2010	2011	2012	2013	2014	2015	2016	2017	2018	2019
	10014.72	11613.53	13090.84	14810.31	17098.45	16528.03	18400.88	21948.10	25964.82	26403.28
1	254.75	−119.96	S	S	H	−469.68	18.42	39.46	S	S
2	50.63	−253.31	S	H	−30.89	293.03	72.66	S	S	H
3	157.83	S	H	23.65	10.72	23.38	S	S	H	−285.26
4	S	S	−54.90	96.91	−8.70	−272.38	S	H	−12.34	237.45
5	S	H	11.54	6.61	67.78	S	H	−234.25	22.51	372.68
6	H	−100.96	244.52	−14.98	S	S	46.16	54.33	20.88	69.31
7	−137.24	275.56	14.64	S	S	H	−11.98	−22.86	−79.33	S
8	46.32	−119.05	S	S	−25.94	390.30	−46.23	13.01	S	S
9	28.23	−303.68	S	140.62	−97.55	−239.11	−394.46	S	S	38.05
10	47.53	S	−52.35	127.94	54.84	76.83	S	S	−59.47	73.92
11	S	S	69.07	135.54	−19.71	102.69	S	259.58	113.99	227.61
12	S	68.99	9.99	−25.96	−61.49	S	239.62	61.49	27.86	45.41
13	81.36	44.73	206.51	75.42	S	S	−258.32	39.32	147.07	37.07
14	−17.64	140.88	53.51	S	S	−62.13	−31.98	45.30	8.68	S
15	46.24	186.45	S	S	43.63	228.89	177.71	64.86	S	S
16	22.10	75.91	S	118.72	100.83	140.10	−88.68	S	S	−142.70
17	13.02	S	−40.27	34.95	24.88	−65.21	S	S	−92.55	33.98
18	S	S	11.54	147.21	109.14	−290.16	S	63.01	184.84	36.28
19	S	−108.08	13.32	−40.39	13.75	S	−3.63	39.45	158.80	−52.29
20	145.77	7.65	18.97	−185.46	S	S	9.79	41.79	251.22	−159.72
21	7.41	−283.82	−17.46	S	S	125.61	163.74	−53.36	86.52	S
22	−21.72	−391.01	S	S	−107.06	−179.72	98.76	−9.64	S	S
23	−76.89	37.65	S	−49.71	−116.81	−50.58	−131.01	S	S	14.92
24	197.84	S	−20.55	−66.79	154.19	−78.57	S	S	−181.45	−142.22
25	S	S	−101.37	−61.33	−264.26	113.35	S	−53.50	−69.84	162.94
26	S	272.38	−44.04	55.04	167.35	S	−166.62	−11.77	−106.93	−79.59
27	−48.22	146.83	72.46	−70.06	S	S	133.47	56.39	54.65	−70.87
28	46.10	−179.79	−48.84	S	S	−312.78	110.94	40.49	18.38	S
29	−22.86	143.08	S	S	−41.93	47.24	−195.79	23.89	S	S
30	−47.23	−240.60	S	−128.57	−28.32	234.87	164.70	S	S	96.58
Close	10788.05	10913.38	13437.13	15129.67	17042.90	16284.00	18308.15	22405.09	26458.31	26916.83
Change	773.33	−700.15	346.29	319.36	−55.55	−244.03	−92.73	456.99	493.49	513.55

OCTOBER DAILY POINT CHANGES DOW JONES INDUSTRIALS

Previous Month Close	2010	2011	2012	2013	2014	2015	2016	2017	2018	2019
	10788.05	10913.38	13437.13	15129.67	17042.90	16284.00	18308.15	22405.09	26458.31	26916.83
1	41.63	S	77.98	62.03	−238.19	−11.99	S	S	192.90	−343.79
2	S	S	−32.75	−58.56	−3.66	200.36	S	152.51	122.73	−494.42
3	S	−258.08	12.25	−136.66	208.64	S	−54.30	84.07	54.45	122.42
4	−78.41	153.41	80.75	76.10	S	S	−85.40	19.97	−200.91	372.68
5	193.45	131.24	34.79	S	S	304.06	112.58	113.75	−180.43	S
6	22.93	183.38	S	S	−17.78	13.76	−12.53	−1.72	S	S
7	−19.07	−20.21	S	−136.34	−272.52	122.10	−28.01	S	S	−95.70
8	57.90	S	−26.50	−159.71	274.83	138.46	S	S	39.73	−313.98
9	S	S	−110.12	26.45	−334.97	33.74	S	−12.60	−56.21	181.97
10	S	330.06	−128.56	323.09	−115.15	S	88.55	69.61	−831.83	150.66
11	3.86	−16.88	−18.58	111.04	S	S	−200.38	42.21	−545.91	319.92
12	10.06	102.55	2.46	S	S	47.37	15.54	−31.88	287.16	S
13	75.68	−40.72	S	S	−223.03	−49.97	−45.26	30.71	S	S
14	−1.51	166.36	S	64.15	−5.88	−157.14	39.44	S	S	−29.23
15	−31.79	S	95.38	−133.25	−173.45	217.00	S	S	−89.44	237.44
16	S	S	127.55	205.82	−24.50	74.22	S	85.24	547.87	−22.82
17	S	−247.49	5.22	−2.18	263.17	S	−51.98	40.48	−91.74	23.90
18	80.91	180.05	−8.06	28.00	S	S	75.54	160.16	−327.23	−255.68
19	−165.07	−72.43	−205.43	S	S	14.57	40.68	5.44	64.89	S
20	129.35	37.16	S	S	19.26	−13.43	−40.27	165.59	S	S
21	38.60	267.01	S	−7.45	215.14	−48.50	−16.64	S	S	57.44
22	−14.01	S	2.38	75.46	−153.49	320.55	S	S	−126.93	−39.54
23	S	S	−243.36	−54.33	216.58	157.54	S	−54.67	−125.98	45.85
24	S	104.83	−25.19	95.88	127.51	S	77.32	167.80	−608.01	−28.42
25	31.49	−207.00	26.34	61.07	S	S	−53.76	−112.30	401.13	152.53
26	5.41	162.42	3.53	S	S	−23.65	30.06	71.40	−296.24	S
27	−43.18	339.51	S	S	12.53	−41.62	−29.65	33.33	S	S
28	−12.33	22.56	S	−1.35	187.81	198.09	−8.49	S	S	132.66
29	4.54	S	H*	111.42	−31.44	−23.72	S	S	−245.39	−19.26
30	S	S	H*	−61.59	221.11	−92.26	S	−85.45	431.72	115.23
31	S	−276.10	−10.75	−73.01	195.10	S	−18.77	28.50	241.12	−140.46
Close	11118.49	11955.01	13096.46	15545.75	17390.52	17663.54	18142.42	23377.24	25115.76	27046.23
Change	330.44	1041.63	−340.67	416.08	347.62	1379.54	−165.73	972.15	−1342.55	129.40

*Hurricane Sandy

NOVEMBER DAILY POINT CHANGES DOW JONES INDUSTRIALS

Previous Month Close	2010	2011	2012	2013	2014	2015	2016	2017	2018	2019
	11118.49	11955.01	13096.46	15545.75	17390.52	17663.54	18142.42	23377.24	25115.76	27046.23
1	6.13	−297.05	136.16	69.80	S	S	−105.32	57.77	264.98	301.13
2	64.10	178.08	−139.46	S	S	165.22	−77.46	81.25	−109.91	S
3	26.41	208.43	S	S	−24.28	89.39	−28.97	22.93	S	S
4	219.71	−61.23	S	23.57	17.60	−50.57	−42.39	S	S	114.75
5	9.24	S	19.28	−20.90	100.69	−4.15	S	S	190.87	30.52
6	S	85.15	133.24	128.66	69.94	46.90	S	9.23	173.31	−0.07
7	S	101.79	−312.95	−152.90	19.46	S	371.32	8.81	545.29	182.24
8	−37.24	−389.24	−121.41	167.80	S	S	73.14	6.13	10.92	6.44
9	−60.09	112.85	4.07	S	S	−179.85	256.95	−101.42	−201.92	S
10	10.29	259.89	S	S	39.81	27.73	218.19	−39.73	S	S
11	−73.94	S	S	21.32	1.16	−55.99	39.78	S	S	10.25
12	−90.52	S	−0.31	−32.43	−2.70	−254.15	S	S	−602.12	0.00
13	S	−74.70	−58.90	70.96	40.59	−202.83	S	17.49	−100.69	92.10
14	S	17.18	−185.23	54.59	−18.05	S	21.03	−30.23	−205.99	−1.63
15	9.39	−190.57	−28.57	85.48	S	S	54.37	−138.19	208.77	222.93
16	−178.47	−134.86	45.93	S	S	237.77	−54.92	187.08	123.95	S
17	−15.62	25.43	S	S	13.01	6.49	35.68	−100.12	S	S
18	173.35	S	S	14.32	40.07	247.66	−35.89	S	S	31.33
19	22.32	S	207.65	−8.99	−2.09	−4.41	S	S	−395.78	−102.20
20	S	−248.85	−7.45	−66.21	33.27	91.06	S	72.09	−551.80	−112.93
21	S	−53.59	48.38	109.17	91.06	S	88.76	160.50	−0.95	−54.80
22	−24.97	−236.17	H	54.78	S	S	67.18	−64.65	H	109.33
23	−142.21	H	172.79*	S	S	−31.13	59.31	H	−178.74*	S
24	150.91	−25.77*	S	S	7.84	19.51	H	31.81*	S	S
25	H	S	S	7.77	−2.96	1.20	68.96*	S	S	190.85
26	−95.28*	S	−42.31	0.26	−2.69	H	S	S	354.29	55.21
27	S	S	−89.24	24.53	H	−14.90*	S	22.79	108.49	42.32
28	S	291.23	106.98	H	15.99*	S	−54.24	255.93	617.70	H
29	−39.51	32.62	36.71	−10.92*	S	S	23.70	103.97	−27.59	−112.59*
30	−46.47	490.05	3.76	S	S	−78.57	1.98	331.67	199.62	S
Close	11006.02	12045.68	13025.58	16086.41	17828.24	17719.92	19123.58	24272.35	25538.46	28051.41
Change	−112.47	90.67	−70.88	540.66	437.72	56.38	981.16	895.11	422.70	1005.18

*Shortened trading day

DECEMBER DAILY POINT CHANGES DOW JONES INDUSTRIALS

Previous Month Close	2010	2011	2012	2013	2014	2015	2016	2017	2018	2019
	11006.02	12045.68	13025.58	16086.41	17828.24	17719.92	19123.58	24272.35	25538.46	28051.41
1	249.76	−25.65	S	S	−51.44	168.43	68.35	−40.76	S	S
2	106.63	−0.61	S	−77.64	102.75	−158.67	−21.51	S	S	−268.37
3	19.68	S	−59.98	−94.15	33.07	−252.01	S	S	287.97	−280.23
4	S	S	−13.82	−24.85	−12.52	369.96	S	58.46	−799.36	146.97
5	S	78.41	82.71	−68.26	58.69	S	45.82	−109.41	H**	28.01
6	−19.90	52.30	39.55	198.69	S	S	35.54	−39.73	−79.40	337.27
7	−3.03	46.24	81.09	S	S	−117.12	297.84	70.57	−558.72	S
8	13.32	−198.67	S	S	−106.31	−162.51	65.19	117.68	S	S
9	−2.42	186.56	S	5.33	−51.28	−75.70	142.04	S	S	−105.46
10	40.26	S	14.75	−52.40	−268.05	82.45	S	S	34.31	−27.88
11	S	S	78.56	−129.60	63.19	−309.54	S	56.87	−53.02	29.58
12	S	−162.87	−2.99	−104.10	−315.51	S	39.58	118.77	157.03	220.75
13	18.24	−66.45	−74.73	15.93	S	S	114.78	80.63	70.11	3.33
14	47.98	−131.46	−35.71	S	S	103.29	−118.68	−76.77	−496.87	S
15	−19.07	45.33	S	S	−99.99	156.41	59.71	143.08	S	S
16	41.78	−2.42	S	129.21	−111.97	224.18	−8.83	S	S	100.51
17	−7.34	S	100.38	−9.31	288.00	−253.25	S	S	−507.53	31.27
18	S	S	115.57	292.71	421.28	−367.29	S	140.46	82.66	−27.88
19	S	−100.13	−98.99	11.11	26.65	S	39.65	−37.45	−351.98	137.68
20	−13.78	337.32	59.75	42.06	S	S	91.56	−28.10	−464.06	78.13
21	55.03	4.16	−120.88	S	S	123.07	−32.66	55.64	−414.23	S
22	26.33	61.91	S	S	154.64	165.65	−23.08	−28.23	S	S
23	14.00	124.35	S	73.47	64.73	185.34	14.93	S	S	96.44
24	H	S	−51.76*	62.94*	6.04*	−50.44*	S	S	−653.17*	−36.08*
25	S	S	H	H	H	H	S	H	H	H
26	S	H	−24.49	122.33	23.50	S	H	−7.85	1086.25	105.94
27	−18.46	−2.65	−18.28	−1.47	S	S	11.23	28.09	260.37	23.87
28	20.51	−139.94	−158.20	S	S	−23.90	−111.36	63.21	−76.42	S
29	9.84	135.63	S	S	−15.48	192.71	−13.90	−118.29	S	S
30	−15.67	−69.48	S	25.88	−55.16	−117.11	−57.18	S	S	−183.12
31	7.80	S	166.03	72.37	−160.00	−178.84	S	S	265.06	76.30
Close	11577.51	12217.56	13104.14	16576.66	17823.07	17425.03	19762.60	24719.22	23327.46	28538.44
Change	571.49	171.88	78.56	490.25	−5.17	−294.89	639.02	446.87	−2211.00	487.03

* Shortened trading day,   ** President H.W. Bush Funeral

A TYPICAL DAY IN THE MARKET

Half-hourly data became available for the Dow Jones Industrial Average starting in January 1987. The NYSE switched 10:00 a.m. openings to 9:30 a.m. in October 1985. Below is the comparison between half-hourly performance from January 1987 to June 5, 2020, and hourly performance from November 1963 to June 1985. Stronger closings in a more bullish climate are evident. Morning and afternoon weaknesses appear an hour earlier.

MARKET % PERFORMANCE EACH HALF-HOUR OF THE DAY
(January 1987–June 5, 2020)

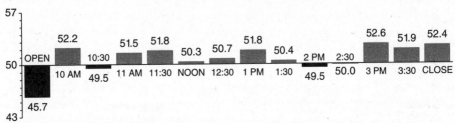

Based on the number of times the Dow Jones Industrial Average increased over the previous half-hour.

MARKET % PERFORMANCE EACH HOUR OF THE DAY
(November 1963–June 1985)

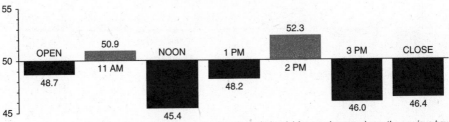

Based on the number of times the Dow Jones Industrial Average increased over the previous hour.

On the next page, half-hourly movements since January 1987 are separated by day of the week. From 1953 to 1989, Monday was the worst day of the week, especially during long bear markets, but times changed. Monday reversed positions and became the best day of the week and on the plus side eleven years in a row from 1990 to 2000.

During the last 19 years (2001–June 5, 2020) Monday is a net loser. Tuesday through Thursday are solid gainers, Tuesday the best (page 70). On all days, stocks do tend to firm up near the close with weakness in the early morning and from 1:30 to 2:30 frequently.

THROUGH THE WEEK ON A HALF-HOURLY BASIS

From the chart showing the percentage of times the Dow Jones Industrial Average rose over the preceding half-hour (January 1987 to June 5, 2020*), the typical week unfolds.

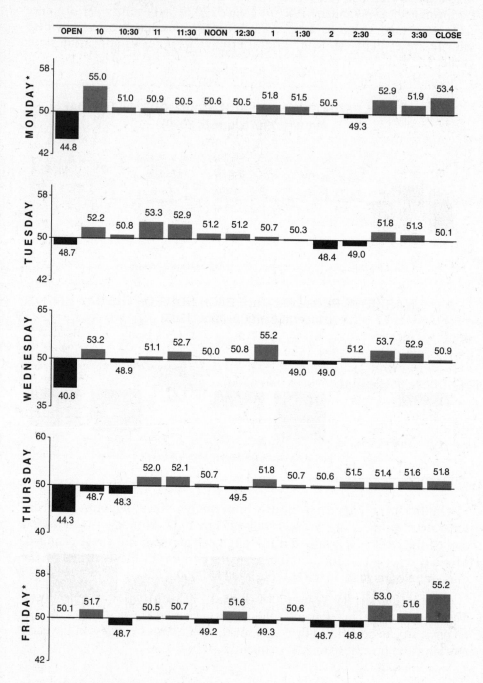

* Monday denotes first trading day of week, Friday denotes last trading day of week

TUESDAY MOST PROFITABLE DAY OF WEEK

Between 1952 and 1989, Monday was the worst trading day of the week. The first trading day of the week (including Tuesday when Monday is a holiday) rose only 44.3% of the time, while the other trading days closed higher 54.8% of the time. (NYSE Saturday trading was discontinued in June 1952.)

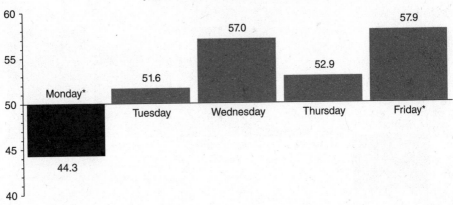

MARKET % PERFORMANCE EACH DAY OF THE WEEK
(June 1952–December 1989)

A dramatic reversal occurred in 1990—Monday became the most powerful day of the week. However, during the last 19 years, Tuesday has produced the most gains. Since the top in 2000, traders have not been inclined to stay long over the weekend nor buy up equities at the outset of the week. This is not uncommon during uncertain market times. Monday was the worst day during the 2007–2009 bear, and only Tuesday was a net gainer. Since the March 2009 bottom, Tuesday and Wednesday are best. See pages 70 and 143.

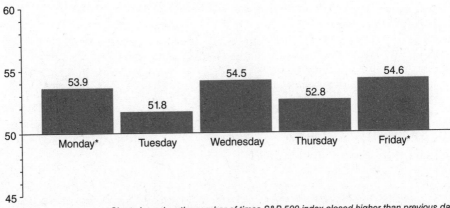

MARKET % PERFORMANCE EACH DAY OF THE WEEK
(January 1990–June 12, 2020)

Charts based on the number of times S&P 500 index closed higher than previous day.
*Monday denotes first trading day of the week, Friday denotes last trading day of the week.

NASDAQ STRONGEST LAST 3 DAYS OF WEEK

Despite 20 years less data, daily trading patterns on NASDAQ through 1989 appear to be fairly similar to the S&P on page 141, except for more bullishness on Thursdays. During the mostly flat markets of the 1970s and early 1980s, it would appear that apprehensive investors decided to throw in the towel over weekends and sell on Mondays and Tuesdays.

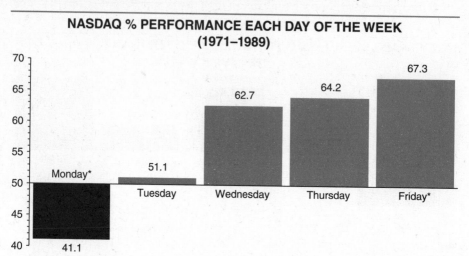

NASDAQ % PERFORMANCE EACH DAY OF THE WEEK
(1971–1989)

Notice the modest difference in the daily trading pattern between NASDAQ and S&P from January 1, 1990, to recent times. NASDAQ's weekly patterns are beginning to move in step with the rest of the market as technology continues to take an ever-increasing role throughout the economy. Notice the similarities to the S&P since 2001 on pages 143 and 144—Monday and Friday weakness, midweek strength during periods of uncertainty like 2015 to 2016.

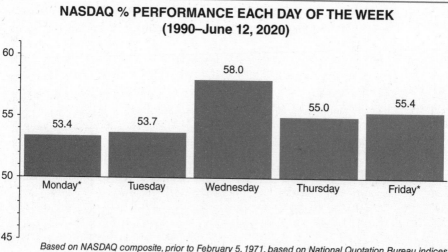

NASDAQ % PERFORMANCE EACH DAY OF THE WEEK
(1990–June 12, 2020)

Based on NASDAQ composite, prior to February 5, 1971, based on National Quotation Bureau indices.
*Monday denotes first trading day of the week, Friday denotes last trading day of the week.

S&P DAILY PERFORMANCE EACH YEAR SINCE 1952

To determine if market trend alters performance of different days of the week, we separated 23 bear years—1953, '56, '57, '60, '62, '66, '69, '70, '73, '74, '77, '78, '81, '84, '87, '90, '94, 2000, 2001, 2002, 2008, 2011 and 2015—from 45 bull market years. While Tuesdays and Thursdays did not vary much between bull and bear years, Mondays and Fridays were sharply affected. There was a swing of 10.2 percentage points in Monday's performance and 9.6 in Friday's. Tuesday is the best day of the week based on total points gained. See page 70.

PERCENTAGE OF TIMES MARKET CLOSED HIGHER THAN PREVIOUS DAY
(JUNE 1952 - JUNE 12, 2020)

	Monday*	Tuesday	Wednesday	Thursday	Friday**
1952	48.4%	55.6%	58.1%	51.9%	66.7%
1953	32.7	50.0	54.9	57.5	56.6
1954	50.0	57.5	63.5	59.2	73.1
1955	50.0	45.7	63.5	60.0	78.9
1956	36.5	39.6	46.9	50.0	59.6
1957	25.0	54.0	66.7	48.9	44.2
1958	59.6	52.0	59.6	68.1	72.6
1959	42.3	53.1	55.8	48.9	69.8
1960	34.6	50.0	44.2	54.0	59.6
1961	52.9	54.4	64.7	56.0	67.3
1962	28.3	52.1	54.0	51.0	50.0
1963	46.2	63.3	51.0	57.5	69.2
1964	40.4	48.0	61.5	58.7	77.4
1965	44.2	57.5	55.8	51.0	71.2
1966	36.5	47.8	53.9	42.0	57.7
1967	38.5	50.0	60.8	64.0	69.2
1968†	49.1	57.5	64.3	42.6	54.9
1969	30.8	45.8	50.0	67.4	50.0
1970	38.5	46.0	63.5	48.9	52.8
1971	44.2	64.6	57.7	55.1	51.9
1972	38.5	60.9	57.7	51.0	67.3
1973	32.1	51.1	52.9	44.9	44.2
1974	32.7	57.1	51.0	36.7	30.8
1975	53.9	38.8	61.5	56.3	55.8
1976	55.8	55.3	55.8	40.8	58.5
1977	40.4	40.4	46.2	53.1	53.9
1978	51.9	43.5	59.6	54.0	48.1
1979	54.7	53.2	58.8	66.0	44.2
1980	55.8	54.2	71.7	35.4	59.6
1981	44.2	38.8	55.8	53.2	47.2
1982	46.2	39.6	44.2	52.0	50.0
1983	55.8	46.8	61.5	46.0	55.8
1984	39.6	63.8	31.4	46.0	44.2
1985	44.2	61.2	54.9	56.3	53.9
1986	51.9	44.9	67.3	58.3	55.8
1987	51.9	57.1	63.5	61.7	49.1
1988	51.9	61.7	51.9	48.0	59.6
1989	51.9	47.8	69.2	58.0	69.2
1990	67.9	53.2	52.9	40.0	51.9
1991	44.2	46.9	52.9	49.0	51.9
1992	51.9	49.0	53.9	56.3	45.3
1993	65.4	41.7	55.8	44.9	48.1
1994	55.8	46.8	52.9	48.0	59.6
1995	63.5	56.5	63.5	62.0	63.5
1996	54.7	44.9	51.0	57.1	57.7
1997	67.3	67.4	42.3	41.7	60.4
1998	57.7	62.5	57.7	38.3	57.7
1999	46.2	29.8	67.3	53.1	46.2
2000	51.9	43.5	40.4	56.0	43.1
2001	45.3	51.1	44.0	59.2	48.1
2002	40.4	37.5	56.9	38.8	50.0
2003	59.6	62.5	42.3	58.3	52.8
2004	51.9	61.7	59.6	52.1	55.8
2005	59.6	47.8	59.6	56.0	48.1
2006	55.8	55.6	67.3	52.0	61.5
2007	47.2	50.0	64.0	50.0	55.8
2008	42.3	50.0	41.5	60.4	52.8
2009	53.9	50.0	57.7	63.8	57.7
2010	61.5	57.5	55.8	53.1	57.7
2011	48.1	56.5	55.8	56.0	53.9
2012	52.8	48.9	50.0	58.0	65.4
2013	51.9	60.4	54.9	59.2	61.5
2014	53.9	56.3	57.7	56.3	43.4
2015	51.9	43.8	44.2	53.2	46.2
2016	50.0	58.7	55.8	50.0	61.5
2017	55.8	55.6	61.5	50.0	53.9
2018	52.8	60.9	50.0	46.0	67.3
2019	50.0	54.2	60.8	65.3	50.0
2020‡	60.9	45.0	60.9	52.2	
Average	**48.4%**	**51.8%**	**55.8%**	**52.8%**	**56.5%**
45 Bull Years	**51.9%**	**53.4%**	**58.0%**	**53.6%**	**59.7%**
23 Bear Years	**41.7%**	**48.7%**	**51.4%**	**51.3%**	**50.2%**

Based on S&P 500

† Most Wednesdays closed last 7 months of 1968.   ‡ Through 6/12/2020 only, not included in averages.
*Monday denotes first trading day of week, Friday denotes last trading day of week.

NASDAQ DAILY PERFORMANCE EACH YEAR SINCE 1971

After dropping a hefty 77.9% from its 2000 high (versus −37.8% on the Dow and −49.1% on the S&P 500), NASDAQ tech stocks still outpace the blue chips and big caps—but not nearly by as much as they did. From January 1, 1971, through June 12, 2020, NASDAQ moved up an impressive 10601%. The Dow (up 2952%) and the S&P (up 3200%) gained less than half as much.

Monday's performance on NASDAQ was lackluster during the three-year bear market of 2000–2002. As NASDAQ rebounded (up 50% in 2003), strength returned to Monday during 2003–2006. During the bear market from late 2007 to early 2009, weakness was most consistent on Monday and Friday. At press time, Mondays, Thursdays and Fridays have been challenging.

PERCENTAGE OF TIMES NASDAQ CLOSED HIGHER THAN PREVIOUS DAY
(1971 - JUNE 12, 2020)

	Monday*	Tuesday	Wednesday	Thursday	Friday**
1971	51.9%	52.1%	59.6%	65.3%	71.2%
1972	30.8	60.9	63.5	57.1	78.9
1973	34.0	48.9	52.9	53.1	48.1
1974	30.8	44.9	52.9	51.0	42.3
1975	44.2	42.9	63.5	64.6	63.5
1976	50.0	63.8	67.3	59.2	58.5
1977	51.9	40.4	53.9	63.3	73.1
1978	48.1	47.8	73.1	72.0	84.6
1979	45.3	53.2	64.7	86.0	82.7
1980	46.2	64.6	84.9	52.1	73.1
1981	42.3	32.7	67.3	76.6	69.8
1982	34.6	47.9	59.6	51.0	63.5
1983	42.3	44.7	67.3	68.0	73.1
1984	22.6	53.2	35.3	52.0	51.9
1985	36.5	59.2	62.8	68.8	66.0
1986	38.5	55.1	65.4	72.9	75.0
1987	42.3	49.0	65.4	68.1	66.0
1988	50.0	55.3	61.5	66.0	63.5
1989	38.5	54.4	71.2	72.0	75.0
1990	54.7	42.6	60.8	46.0	55.8
1991	51.9	59.2	66.7	65.3	51.9
1992	44.2	53.1	59.6	60.4	45.3
1993	55.8	56.3	69.2	57.1	67.3
1994	51.9	46.8	54.9	52.0	55.8
1995	50.0	52.2	63.5	64.0	63.5
1996	50.9	57.1	64.7	61.2	63.5
1997	65.4	59.2	53.9	52.1	55.8
1998	59.6	58.3	65.4	44.7	58.5
1999	61.5	40.4	63.5	57.1	65.4
2000	40.4	41.3	42.3	60.0	57.7
2001	41.5	57.8	52.0	55.1	47.1
2002	44.2	37.5	56.9	46.9	46.2
2003	57.7	60.4	40.4	60.4	46.2
2004	57.7	59.6	53.9	50.0	50.9
2005	61.5	47.8	51.9	48.0	59.6
2006	55.8	51.1	65.4	50.0	44.2
2007	47.2	63.0	66.0	56.0	57.7
2008	34.6	52.1	49.1	54.2	42.3
2009	51.9	54.2	63.5	63.8	50.9
2010	61.5	53.2	61.5	55.1	61.5
2011	50.0	56.5	50.0	64.0	53.9
2012	49.1	53.3	50.0	54.0	51.9
2013	57.7	60.4	52.9	59.2	67.3
2014	57.7	58.3	57.7	52.1	59.6
2015	55.8	39.6	53.9	59.6	49.1
2016	51.9	52.2	55.8	50.0	57.7
2017	59.6	62.2	67.3	50.0	67.3
2018	54.7	69.6	50.0	46.0	50.0
2019	50.0	58.3	62.8	59.2	59.6
2020†	69.6	50.0	73.9	52.2	54.2
Average	**48.3%**	**52.7%**	**59.5%**	**58.6%**	**60.1%**
36 Bull Years	**50.6%**	**55.0%**	**61.8%**	**59.3%**	**62.7%**
13 Bear Years	**41.9%**	**46.4%**	**53.4%**	**59.3%**	**52.8%**

Based on NASDAQ composite; prior to Feb. 5, 1971 based on National Quotation Bureau indices
† Through 6/12/2020 only, not included in averages
*Monday denotes first trading day of week, Friday denotes last trading day of week

MONTHLY CASH INFLOWS INTO S&P STOCKS

For many years, the last trading day of the month, plus the first four of the following month, were the best market days of the month. This pattern is quite clear in the first chart, showing these five consecutive trading days towering above the other 16 trading days of the average month in the 1953–1981 period. The rationale was that individuals and institutions tended to operate similarly, causing a massive flow of cash into stocks near beginnings of months.

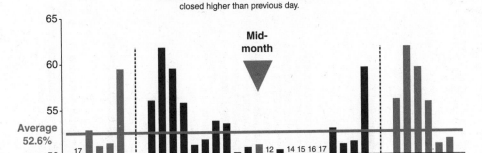

MARKET % PERFORMANCE EACH DAY OF THE MONTH
(January 1953 to December 1981)
Based on the number of times the S&P 500
closed higher than previous day.

Clearly, "front-running" traders took advantage of this phenomenon, drastically altering the previous pattern. The second chart from 1982 onward shows the trading shift caused by these "anticipators" to the last three trading days of the month, plus the first two. Another astonishing development shows the ninth, tenth and eleventh trading days rising strongly as well. Growth of 401(k) retirement plans, IRAs, and similar plans (participants' salaries are usually paid twice monthly) is responsible for this midmonth bulge. First trading days of the month have produced the greatest gains in recent years (see page 88).

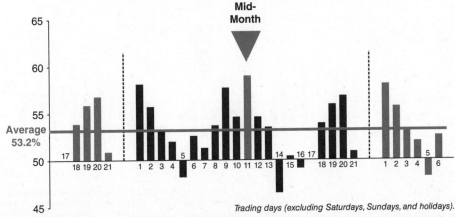

MARKET % PERFORMANCE EACH DAY OF THE MONTH
(January 1982 to December 2019)

Trading days (excluding Saturdays, Sundays, and holidays).

145

MONTHLY CASH INFLOWS INTO NASDAQ STOCKS

NASDAQ stocks moved up 58.1% of the time through 1981 compared to 52.6% for the S&P on page 145. Ends and beginnings of the month are fairly similar, specifically the last plus the first four trading days. But notice how investors piled into NASDAQ stocks until midmonth. NASDAQ rose 118.6% from January 1, 1971, to December 31, 1981, compared to 33.0% for the S&P.

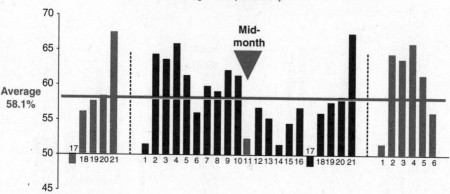

NASDAQ % PERFORMANCE EACH DAY OF THE MONTH
(January 1971 to December 1981)
Based on the number of times the NASDAQ composite closed higher than previous day.

After the air was let out of the tech market in 2000–2002, S&P's 2536% gain over the last 38 years is more evenly matched with NASDAQ's 4482% gain. Last three, first four, and middle ninth, tenth, eleventh and twelfth days rose the most. Where the S&P has three days of the month that go down more often than up, NASDAQ has one. NASDAQ exhibits the most strength on the first trading day of the month. Over the past 20 years, last days have weakened considerably, down more frequently than not.

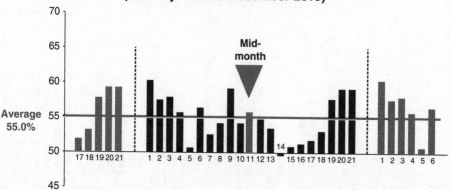

NASDAQ % PERFORMANCE EACH DAY OF THE MONTH
(January 1982 to December 2019)

Trading days (excluding Saturdays, Sundays, and holidays).
Based on NASDAQ composite, prior to February 5, 1971, based on National Quotation Bureau indices.

146

NOVEMBER, DECEMBER AND JANUARY: YEAR'S BEST THREE-MONTH SPAN

The most important observation to be made from a chart showing the average monthly percent change in market prices since 1950 is that institutions (mutual funds, pension funds, banks, etc.) determine the trading patterns in today's market.

The "investment calendar" reflects the annual, semiannual, and quarterly operations of institutions during January, April, and July. October, besides being the last campaign month before elections, is also the time when most bear markets seem to end, as in 1946, 1957, 1960, 1966, 1974, 1987, 1990, 1998 and 2002. (August and September tend to combine to make the worst consecutive two-month period.)

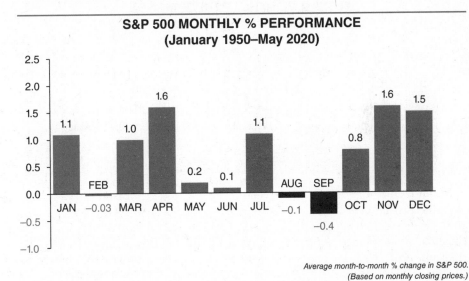

S&P 500 MONTHLY % PERFORMANCE
(January 1950–May 2020)

Average month-to-month % change in S&P 500.
(Based on monthly closing prices.)

Unusual year-end strength comes from corporate and private pension funds, producing a 4.2% gain on average between November 1 and January 31. In 2007–2008, these three months were all down for the fourth time since 1930; previously in 1931–1932, 1940–1941 and 1969–1970, also bear markets. September's dismal performance makes it the worst month of the year. However, in the last 16 years, it has been up 11 times after being down 5 in a row 1999–2003.

In post-election years since 1950, July is the best month +2.1% (11–6). November is second best with an average 1.8% gain. January, March, April, May, October and December are also positive. February is the worst month, –1.5. June, August and September are also net decliners.

See page 50 for monthly performance tables for the S&P 500 and the Dow Jones industrials. See pages 52, 54, 60 and 62 for unique switching strategies.

On page 66, you can see how the first month of the first three quarters far outperforms the second and third months since 1950, and note the improvement in May's and October's performance since 1991.

NOVEMBER THROUGH JUNE:
NASDAQ'S EIGHT-MONTH RUN

The two-and-a-half-year plunge of 77.9% in NASDAQ stocks, between March 10, 2000, and October 9, 2002, brought several horrendous monthly losses (the two greatest were November 2000, −22.9% and February 2001, −22.4%), which trimmed average monthly performance over the $48\frac{1}{3}$-year period. Ample Octobers in 15 of the last 22 years, including three huge turnarounds in 2001 (+12.8%), 2002 (+13.5%) and 2011 (+11.1%) have put bear-killing October in the number one spot since 1998. January's 2.8% average gain is still awesome, and more than twice S&P's 1.3% January average since 1971.

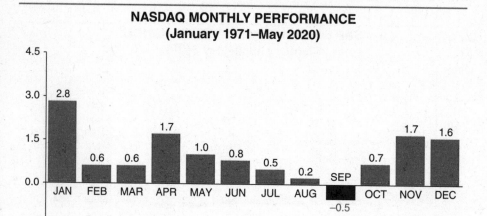

NASDAQ MONTHLY PERFORMANCE
(January 1971–May 2020)

Average month-to-month % change in NASDAQ composite, prior to February 5, 1971, based on National Quotation Bureau indices. (Based on monthly closing prices.)

Bear in mind, when comparing NASDAQ to the S&P on page 147, that there are 22 fewer years of data here. During this $49\frac{1}{3}$-year (1971–May 2020) period, NASDAQ gained 10490%, while the S&P and the Dow rose only 3024% and 2926%, respectively. On page 58, you can see a statistical monthly comparison between NASDAQ and the Dow.

Year-end strength is even more pronounced in NASDAQ, producing a 6.1% gain on average between November 1 and January 31—nearly 1.5 times greater than that of the S&P 500 on page 147. September is the worst month of the year for the over-the-counter index as well, posting an average loss of −0.5%. These extremes underscore NASDAQ's higher volatility—and moves of greater magnitude.

In post-election years since 1971, July is best with an average gain of 3.4% (10–2). January, April, May, June October, November and December are all also positive. March, August and September are all losers. February is the worst, −3.3% (4–8).

DOW JONES INDUSTRIALS ANNUAL HIGHS, LOWS & CLOSES SINCE 1901

YEAR	HIGH DATE	HIGH CLOSE	LOW DATE	LOW CLOSE	YEAR CLOSE	YEAR	HIGH DATE	HIGH CLOSE	LOW DATE	LOW CLOSE	YEAR CLOSE
1901	6/17	57.33	12/24	45.07	47.29	1958	12/31	583.65	2/25	436.89	583.65
1902	4/24	50.14	12/15	43.64	47.10	1959	12/31	679.36	2/9	574.46	679.36
1903	2/16	49.59	11/9	30.88	35.98	1960	1/5	685.47	10/25	566.05	615.89
1904	12/5	53.65	3/12	34.00	50.99	1961	12/13	734.91	1/3	610.25	731.14
1905	12/29	70.74	1/25	50.37	70.47	1962	1/3	726.01	6/26	535.76	652.10
1906	1/19	75.45	7/13	62.40	69.12	1963	12/18	767.21	1/2	646.79	762.95
1907	1/7	70.60	11/15	38.83	43.04	1964	11/18	891.71	1/2	766.08	874.13
1908	11/13	64.74	2/13	42.94	63.11	1965	12/31	969.26	6/28	840.59	969.26
1909	11/19	73.64	2/23	58.54	72.56	1966	2/9	995.15	10/7	744.32	785.69
1910	1/3	72.04	7/26	53.93	59.60	1967	9/25	943.08	1/3	786.41	905.11
1911	6/19	63.78	9/25	53.43	59.84	1968	12/3	985.21	3/21	825.13	943.75
1912	9/30	68.97	2/10	58.72	64.37	1969	5/14	968.85	12/17	769.93	800.36
1913	1/9	64.88	6/11	52.83	57.71	1970	12/29	842.00	5/26	631.16	838.92
1914	3/20	61.12	7/30	52.32	54.58	1971	4/28	950.82	11/23	797.97	890.20
1915	12/27	99.21	2/24	54.22	99.15	1972	12/11	1036.27	1/26	889.15	1020.02
1916	11/21	110.15	4/22	84.96	95.00	1973	1/11	1051.70	12/5	788.31	850.86
1917	1/3	99.18	12/19	65.95	74.38	1974	3/13	891.66	12/6	577.60	616.24
1918	10/18	89.07	1/15	73.38	82.20	1975	7/15	881.81	1/2	632.04	852.41
1919	11/3	119.62	2/8	79.15	107.23	1976	9/21	1014.79	1/2	858.71	1004.65
1920	1/3	109.88	12/21	66.75	71.95	1977	1/3	999.75	11/2	800.85	831.17
1921	12/15	81.50	8/24	63.90	81.10	1978	9/8	907.74	2/28	742.12	805.01
1922	10/14	103.43	1/10	78.59	98.73	1979	10/5	897.61	11/7	796.67	838.74
1923	3/20	105.38	10/27	85.76	95.52	1980	11/20	1000.17	4/21	759.13	963.99
1924	12/31	120.51	5/20	88.33	120.51	1981	4/27	1024.05	9/25	824.01	875.00
1925	11/6	159.39	3/30	115.00	156.66	1982	12/27	1070.55	8/12	776.92	1046.54
1926	8/14	166.64	3/30	135.20	157.20	1983	11/29	1287.20	1/3	1027.04	1258.64
1927	12/31	202.40	1/25	152.73	202.40	1984	1/6	1286.64	7/24	1086.57	1211.57
1928	12/31	300.00	2/20	191.33	300.00	1985	12/16	1553.10	1/4	1184.96	1546.67
1929	9/3	381.17	11/13	198.69	248.48	1986	12/2	1955.57	1/22	1502.29	1895.95
1930	4/17	294.07	12/16	157.51	164.58	1987	8/25	2722.42	10/19	1738.74	1938.83
1931	2/24	194.36	12/17	73.79	77.90	1988	10/21	2183.50	1/20	1879.14	2168.57
1932	3/8	88.78	7/8	41.22	59.93	1989	10/9	2791.41	1/3	2144.64	2753.20
1933	7/18	108.67	2/27	50.16	99.90	1990	7/17	2999.75	10/11	2365.10	2633.66
1934	2/5	110.74	7/26	85.51	104.04	1991	12/31	3168.83	1/9	2470.30	3168.83
1935	11/19	148.44	3/14	96.71	144.13	1992	6/1	3413.21	10/9	3136.58	3301.11
1936	11/17	184.90	1/6	143.11	179.90	1993	12/29	3794.33	1/20	3241.95	3754.09
1937	3/10	194.40	11/24	113.64	120.85	1994	1/31	3978.36	4/4	3593.35	3834.44
1938	11/12	158.41	3/31	98.95	154.76	1995	12/13	5216.47	1/30	3832.08	5117.12
1939	9/12	155.92	4/8	121.44	150.24	1996	12/27	6560.91	1/10	5032.94	6448.27
1940	1/3	152.80	6/10	111.84	131.13	1997	8/6	8259.31	4/11	6391.69	7908.25
1941	1/10	133.59	12/23	106.34	110.96	1998	11/23	9374.27	8/31	7539.07	9181.43
1942	12/26	119.71	4/28	92.92	119.40	1999	12/31	11497.12	1/22	9120.67	11497.12
1943	7/14	145.82	1/8	119.26	135.89	2000	1/14	11722.98	3/7	9796.03	10786.85
1944	12/16	152.53	2/7	134.22	152.32	2001	5/21	11337.92	9/21	8235.81	10021.50
1945	12/11	195.82	1/24	151.35	192.91	2002	3/19	10635.25	10/9	7286.27	8341.63
1946	5/29	212.50	10/9	163.12	177.20	2003	12/31	10453.92	3/11	7524.06	10453.92
1947	7/24	186.85	5/17	163.21	181.16	2004	12/28	10854.54	10/25	9749.99	10783.01
1948	6/15	193.16	3/16	165.39	177.30	2005	3/4	10940.55	4/20	10012.36	10717.50
1949	12/30	200.52	6/13	161.60	200.13	2006	12/27	12510.57	1/20	10667.39	12463.15
1950	11/24	235.47	1/13	196.81	235.41	2007	10/9	14164.53	3/5	12050.41	13264.82
1951	9/13	276.37	1/3	238.99	269.23	2008	5/2	13058.20	11/20	7552.29	8776.39
1952	12/30	292.00	5/1	256.35	291.90	2009	12/30	10548.51	3/9	6547.05	10428.05
1953	1/5	293.79	9/14	255.49	280.90	2010	12/29	11585.38	7/2	9686.48	11577.51
1954	12/31	404.39	1/11	279.87	404.39	2011	4/29	12810.54	10/3	10655.30	12217.56
1955	12/30	488.40	1/17	388.20	488.40	2012	10/5	13610.15	6/4	12101.46	13104.14
1956	4/6	521.05	1/23	462.35	499.47	2013	12/31	16576.66	1/8	13328.85	16576.66
1957	7/12	520.77	10/22	419.79	435.69	2014	12/26	18053.71	2/3	15372.80	17823.07

continued

DOW JONES INDUSTRIALS ANNUAL HIGHS, LOWS & CLOSES SINCE 1901 (continued)

YEAR	HIGH DATE	HIGH CLOSE	LOW DATE	LOW CLOSE	YEAR CLOSE	YEAR	HIGH DATE	HIGH CLOSE	LOW DATE	LOW CLOSE	YEAR CLOSE
2015	5/19	18312.39	8/25	15666.44	17425.03	2018	10/3	26828.39	12/24	21792.20	23327.46
2016	12/20	19974.62	2/11	15660.18	19762.60	2019	12/27	28645.26	1/3	22686.22	28538.44
2017	12/28	24837.51	1/19	19732.40	24719.22	2020	2/12	29551.4	3/23	18591.9	At press time

*Through June 12, 2020

S&P 500 ANNUAL HIGHS, LOWS & CLOSES SINCE 1930

YEAR	HIGH DATE	HIGH CLOSE	LOW DATE	LOW CLOSE	YEAR CLOSE	YEAR	HIGH DATE	HIGH CLOSE	LOW DATE	LOW CLOSE	YEAR CLOSE
1930	4/10	25.92	12/16	14.44	15.34	1976	9/21	107.83	1/2	90.90	107.46
1931	2/24	18.17	12/17	7.72	8.12	1977	1/3	107.00	11/2	90.71	95.10
1932	9/7	9.31	6/1	4.40	6.89	1978	9/12	106.99	3/6	86.90	96.11
1933	7/18	12.20	2/27	5.53	10.10	1979	10/5	111.27	2/27	96.13	107.94
1934	2/6	11.82	7/26	8.36	9.50	1980	11/28	140.52	3/27	98.22	135.76
1935	11/19	13.46	3/14	8.06	13.43	1981	1/6	138.12	9/25	112.77	122.55
1936	11/9	17.69	1/2	13.40	17.18	1982	11/9	143.02	8/12	102.42	140.64
1937	3/6	18.68	11/24	10.17	10.55	1983	10/10	172.65	1/3	138.34	164.93
1938	11/9	13.79	3/31	8.50	13.21	1984	11/6	170.41	7/24	147.82	167.24
1939	1/4	13.23	4/8	10.18	12.49	1985	12/16	212.02	1/4	163.68	211.28
1940	1/3	12.77	6/10	8.99	10.58	1986	12/2	254.00	1/22	203.49	242.17
1941	1/10	10.86	12/29	8.37	8.69	1987	8/25	336.77	12/4	223.92	247.08
1942	12/31	9.77	4/28	7.47	9.77	1988	10/21	283.66	1/20	242.63	277.72
1943	7/14	12.64	1/2	9.84	11.67	1989	10/9	359.80	1/3	275.31	353.40
1944	12/16	13.29	2/7	11.56	13.28	1990	7/16	368.95	10/11	295.46	330.22
1945	12/10	17.68	1/23	13.21	17.36	1991	12/31	417.09	1/9	311.49	417.09
1946	5/29	19.25	10/9	14.12	15.30	1992	12/18	441.28	4/8	394.50	435.71
1947	2/8	16.20	5/17	13.71	15.30	1993	12/28	470.94	1/8	429.05	466.45
1948	6/15	17.06	2/14	13.84	15.20	1994	2/2	482.00	4/4	438.92	459.27
1949	12/30	16.79	6/13	13.55	16.76	1995	12/13	621.69	1/3	459.11	615.93
1950	12/29	20.43	1/14	16.65	20.41	1996	11/25	757.03	1/10	598.48	740.74
1951	10/15	23.85	1/3	20.69	23.77	1997	12/5	983.79	1/2	737.01	970.43
1952	12/30	26.59	2/20	23.09	26.57	1998	12/29	1241.81	1/9	927.69	1229.23
1953	1/5	26.66	9/14	22.71	24.81	1999	12/31	1469.25	1/14	1212.19	1469.25
1954	12/31	35.98	1/11	24.80	35.98	2000	3/24	1527.46	12/20	1264.74	1320.28
1955	11/14	46.41	1/17	34.58	45.48	2001	2/1	1373.47	9/21	965.80	1148.08
1956	8/2	49.74	1/23	43.11	46.67	2002	1/4	1172.51	10/9	776.76	879.82
1957	7/15	49.13	10/22	38.98	39.99	2003	12/31	1111.92	3/11	800.73	1111.92
1958	12/31	55.21	1/2	40.33	55.21	2004	12/30	1213.55	8/12	1063.23	1211.92
1959	8/3	60.71	2/9	53.58	59.89	2005	12/14	1272.74	4/20	1137.50	1248.29
1960	1/5	60.39	10/25	52.30	58.11	2006	12/15	1427.09	6/13	1223.69	1418.30
1961	12/12	72.64	1/3	57.57	71.55	2007	10/9	1565.15	3/5	1374.12	1468.36
1962	1/3	71.13	6/26	52.32	63.10	2008	1/2	1447.16	11/20	752.44	903.25
1963	12/31	75.02	1/2	62.69	75.02	2009	12/28	1127.78	3/9	676.53	1115.10
1964	11/20	86.28	1/2	75.43	84.75	2010	12/29	1259.78	7/2	1022.58	1257.64
1965	11/15	92.63	6/28	81.60	92.43	2011	4/29	1363.61	10/3	1099.23	1257.60
1966	2/9	94.06	10/7	73.20	80.33	2012	9/14	1465.77	1/3	1277.06	1426.19
1967	9/25	97.59	1/3	80.38	96.47	2013	12/31	1848.36	1/8	1457.15	1848.36
1968	11/29	108.37	3/5	87.72	103.86	2014	12/29	2090.57	2/3	1741.89	2058.90
1969	5/14	106.16	12/17	89.20	92.06	2015	5/21	2130.82	8/25	1867.61	2043.94
1970	1/5	93.46	5/26	69.29	92.15	2016	12/13	2271.72	2/11	1829.08	2238.83
1971	4/28	104.77	11/23	90.16	102.09	2017	12/18	2690.16	1/3	2257.83	2673.61
1972	12/11	119.12	1/3	101.67	118.05	2018	9/20	2930.75	12/24	2351.10	2506.85
1973	1/11	120.24	12/5	92.16	97.55	2019	12/27	3240.02	1/3	2447.89	3230.78
1974	1/3	99.80	10/3	62.68	68.56	2020*	2/19	3386.15	3/23	2237.40	At press time
1975	7/15	95.61	1/8	70.04	90.19						

*Through June 12, 2020

150

NASDAQ ANNUAL HIGHS, LOWS & CLOSES SINCE 1971

YEAR	HIGH DATE	HIGH CLOSE	LOW DATE	LOW CLOSE	YEAR CLOSE	YEAR	HIGH DATE	HIGH CLOSE	LOW DATE	LOW CLOSE	YEAR CLOSE
1971	12/31	114.12	1/5	89.06	114.12	1996	12/9	1316.27	1/15	988.57	1291.03
1972	12/8	135.15	1/3	113.65	133.73	1997	10/9	1745.85	4/2	1201.00	1570.35
1973	1/11	136.84	12/24	88.67	92.19	1998	12/31	2192.69	10/8	1419.12	2192.69
1974	3/15	96.53	10/3	54.87	59.82	1999	12/31	4069.31	1/4	2208.05	4069.31
1975	7/15	88.00	1/2	60.70	77.62	2000	3/10	5048.62	12/20	2332.78	2470.52
1976	12/31	97.88	1/2	78.06	97.88	2001	1/24	2859.15	9/21	1423.19	1950.40
1977	12/30	105.05	4/5	93.66	105.05	2002	1/4	2059.38	10/9	1114.11	1335.51
1978	9/13	139.25	1/11	99.09	117.98	2003	12/30	2009.88	3/11	1271.47	2003.37
1979	10/5	152.29	1/2	117.84	151.14	2004	12/30	2178.34	8/12	1752.49	2175.44
1980	11/28	208.15	3/27	124.09	202.34	2005	12/2	2273.37	4/28	1904.18	2205.32
1981	5/29	223.47	9/28	175.03	195.84	2006	11/22	2465.98	7/21	2020.39	2415.29
1982	12/8	240.70	8/13	159.14	232.41	2007	10/31	2859.12	3/5	2340.68	2652.28
1983	6/24	328.91	1/3	230.59	278.60	2008	1/2	2609.63	11/20	1316.12	1577.03
1984	1/6	287.90	7/25	225.30	247.35	2009	12/30	2291.28	3/9	1268.64	2269.15
1985	12/16	325.16	1/2	245.91	324.93	2010	12/22	2671.48	7/2	2091.79	2652.87
1986	7/3	411.16	1/9	323.01	349.33	2011	4/29	2873.54	10/3	2335.83	2605.15
1987	8/26	455.26	10/28	291.88	330.47	2012	9/14	3183.95	1/4	2648.36	3019.51
1988	7/5	396.11	1/12	331.97	381.38	2013	12/31	4176.59	1/8	3091.81	4176.59
1989	10/9	485.73	1/3	378.56	454.82	2014	12/29	4806.91	2/3	3996.96	4736.05
1990	7/16	469.60	10/16	325.44	373.84	2015	7/20	5218.86	8/25	4506.49	5007.41
1991	12/31	586.34	1/14	355.75	586.34	2016	12/27	5487.44	2/11	4266.84	5383.12
1992	12/31	676.95	6/26	547.84	676.95	2017	12/18	6994.76	1/3	5429.08	6903.39
1993	10/15	787.42	4/26	645.87	776.80	2018	8/29	8109.69	12/24	6192.92	6635.28
1994	3/18	803.93	6/24	693.79	751.96	2019	12/26	9022.39	1/3	6463.50	8972.60
1995	12/4	1069.79	1/3	743.58	1052.13	2020*	6/10	10020.35	3/23	6860.67	At press time

RUSSELL 1000 ANNUAL HIGHS, LOWS & CLOSES SINCE 1979

YEAR	HIGH DATE	HIGH CLOSE	LOW DATE	LOW CLOSE	YEAR CLOSE	YEAR	HIGH DATE	HIGH CLOSE	LOW DATE	LOW CLOSE	YEAR CLOSE
1979	10/5	61.18	2/27	51.83	59.87	2000	9/1	813.71	12/20	668.75	700.09
1980	11/28	78.26	3/27	53.68	75.20	2001	1/30	727.35	9/21	507.98	604.94
1981	1/6	76.34	9/25	62.03	67.93	2002	3/19	618.74	10/9	410.52	466.18
1982	11/9	78.47	8/12	55.98	77.24	2003	12/31	594.56	3/11	425.31	594.56
1983	10/10	95.07	1/3	76.04	90.38	2004	12/30	651.76	8/13	566.06	650.99
1984	1/6	92.80	7/24	79.49	90.31	2005	12/14	692.09	4/20	613.37	679.42
1985	12/16	114.97	1/4	88.61	114.39	2006	12/15	775.08	6/13	665.81	770.08
1986	7/2	137.87	1/22	111.14	130.00	2007	10/9	852.32	3/5	749.85	799.82
1987	8/25	176.22	12/4	117.65	130.02	2008	1/2	788.62	11/20	402.91	487.77
1988	10/21	149.94	1/20	128.35	146.99	2009	12/28	619.22	3/9	367.55	612.01
1989	10/9	189.93	1/3	145.78	185.11	2010	12/29	698.11	7/2	562.58	696.90
1990	7/16	191.56	10/11	152.36	171.22	2011	4/29	758.45	10/3	604.42	693.36
1991	12/31	220.61	1/9	161.94	220.61	2012	9/14	809.01	1/4	703.72	789.90
1992	12/18	235.06	4/8	208.87	233.59	2013	12/31	1030.36	1/8	807.95	1030.36
1993	10/15	252.77	1/8	229.91	250.71	2014	12/29	1161.45	2/3	972.95	1144.37
1994	2/1	258.31	4/4	235.38	244.65	2015	5/21	1189.55	8/25	1042.77	1131.88
1995	12/13	331.18	1/3	244.41	328.89	2016	12/13	1260.06	2/11	1005.89	1241.66
1996	12/2	401.21	1/10	318.24	393.75	2017	12/18	1490.06	1/3	1252.11	1481.81
1997	12/5	519.72	4/11	389.03	513.79	2018	9/20	1624.28	12/24	1298.02	1384.26
1998	12/29	645.36	1/9	490.26	642.87	2019	12/26	1789.56	1/3	1351.87	1784.21
1999	12/31	767.97	2/9	632.53	767.97	2020*	2/19	1875.24	3/23	1224.45	At press time

RUSSELL 2000 ANNUAL HIGHS, LOWS & CLOSES SINCE 1979

YEAR	HIGH DATE	HIGH CLOSE	LOW DATE	LOW CLOSE	YEAR CLOSE	YEAR	HIGH DATE	HIGH CLOSE	LOW DATE	LOW CLOSE	YEAR CLOSE
1979	12/31	55.91	1/2	40.81	55.91	2000	3/9	606.05	12/20	443.80	483.53
1980	11/28	77.70	3/27	45.36	74.80	2001	5/22	517.23	9/21	378.89	488.50
1981	6/15	85.16	9/25	65.37	73.67	2002	4/16	522.95	10/9	327.04	383.09
1982	12/8	91.01	8/12	60.33	88.90	2003	12/30	565.47	3/12	345.94	556.91
1983	6/24	126.99	1/3	88.29	112.27	2004	12/28	654.57	8/12	517.10	651.57
1984	1/12	116.69	7/25	93.95	101.49	2005	12/2	690.57	4/28	575.02	673.22
1985	12/31	129.87	1/2	101.21	129.87	2006	12/27	797.73	7/21	671.94	787.66
1986	7/3	155.30	1/9	128.23	135.00	2007	7/13	855.77	11/26	735.07	766.03
1987	8/25	174.44	10/28	106.08	120.42	2008	6/5	763.27	11/20	385.31	499.45
1988	7/15	151.42	1/12	121.23	147.37	2009	12/24	634.07	3/9	343.26	625.39
1989	10/9	180.78	1/3	146.79	168.30	2010	12/27	792.35	2/8	586.49	783.65
1990	6/15	170.90	10/30	118.82	132.16	2011	4/29	865.29	10/3	609.49	740.92
1991	12/31	189.94	1/15	125.25	189.94	2012	9/14	864.70	6/4	737.24	849.35
1992	12/31	221.01	7/8	185.81	221.01	2013	12/31	1163.64	1/3	872.60	1163.64
1993	11/2	260.17	2/23	217.55	258.59	2014	12/29	1219.11	10/13	1049.30	1204.70
1994	3/18	271.08	12/9	235.16	250.36	2015	6/23	1295.80	9/29	1083.91	1135.89
1995	9/14	316.12	1/30	246.56	315.97	2016	12/9	1388.07	2/11	953.72	1357.13
1996	5/22	364.61	1/16	301.75	362.61	2017	12/28	1548.93	4/13	1345.24	1535.51
1997	10/13	465.21	4/25	335.85	437.02	2018	8/31	1740.75	12/24	1266.92	1348.56
1998	4/21	491.41	10/8	310.28	421.96	2019	12/24	1678.01	1/3	1330.83	1668.47
1999	12/31	504.75	3/23	383.37	504.75	2020*	1/16	1705.22	3/18	991.6	At press time

*Through June 12, 2020

DOW JONES INDUSTRIALS MONTHLY PERCENT CHANGES SINCE 1950

	Jan	Feb	Mar	Apr	May	Jun	Jul	Aug	Sep	Oct	Nov	Dec	Year's Change
1950	0.8	0.8	1.3	4.0	4.2	−6.4	0.1	3.6	4.4	−0.6	1.2	3.4	17.6
1951	5.7	1.3	−1.6	4.5	−3.7	−2.8	6.3	4.8	0.3	−3.2	−0.4	3.0	14.4
1952	0.5	−3.9	3.6	−4.4	2.1	4.3	1.9	−1.6	−1.6	−0.5	5.4	2.9	8.4
1953	−0.7	−1.9	−1.5	−1.8	−0.9	−1.5	2.7	−5.1	1.1	4.5	2.0	−0.2	−3.8
1954	4.1	0.7	3.0	5.2	2.6	1.8	4.3	−3.5	7.3	−2.3	9.8	4.6	44.0
1955	1.1	0.7	−0.5	3.9	−0.2	6.2	3.2	0.5	−0.3	−2.5	6.2	1.1	20.8
1956	−3.6	2.7	5.8	0.8	−7.4	3.1	5.1	−3.0	−5.3	1.0	−1.5	5.6	2.3
1957	−4.1	−3.0	2.2	4.1	2.1	−0.3	1.0	−4.8	−5.8	−3.3	2.0	−3.2	−12.8
1958	3.3	−2.2	1.6	2.0	1.5	3.3	5.2	1.1	4.6	2.1	2.6	4.7	34.0
1959	1.8	1.6	−0.3	3.7	3.2	−0.03	4.9	−1.6	−4.9	2.4	1.9	3.1	16.4
1960	−8.4	1.2	−2.1	−2.4	4.0	2.4	−3.7	1.5	−7.3	0.04	2.9	3.1	−9.3
1961	5.2	2.1	2.2	0.3	2.7	−1.8	3.1	2.1	−2.6	0.4	2.5	1.3	18.7
1962	−4.3	1.1	−0.2	−5.9	−7.8	−8.5	6.5	1.9	−5.0	1.9	10.1	0.4	−10.8
1963	4.7	−2.9	3.0	5.2	1.3	−2.8	−1.6	4.9	0.5	3.1	−0.6	1.7	17.0
1964	2.9	1.9	1.6	−0.3	1.2	1.3	1.2	−0.3	4.4	−0.3	0.3	−0.1	14.6
1965	3.3	0.1	−1.6	3.7	−0.5	−5.4	1.6	1.3	4.2	3.2	−1.5	2.4	10.9
1966	1.5	−3.2	−2.8	1.0	−5.3	−1.6	−2.6	−7.0	−1.8	4.2	−1.9	−0.7	−18.9
1967	8.2	−1.2	3.2	3.6	−5.0	0.9	5.1	−0.3	2.8	−5.1	−0.4	3.3	15.2
1968	−5.5	−1.7	0.02	8.5	−1.4	−0.1	−1.6	1.5	4.4	1.8	3.4	−4.2	4.3
1969	0.2	−4.3	3.3	1.6	−1.3	−6.9	−6.6	2.6	−2.8	5.3	−5.1	−1.5	−15.2
1970	−7.0	4.5	1.0	−6.3	−4.8	−2.4	7.4	4.1	−0.5	−0.7	5.1	5.6	4.8
1971	3.5	1.2	2.9	4.1	−3.6	−1.8	−3.7	4.6	−1.2	−5.4	−0.9	7.1	6.1
1972	1.3	2.9	1.4	1.4	0.7	−3.3	−0.5	4.2	−1.1	0.2	6.6	0.2	14.6
1973	−2.1	−4.4	−0.4	−3.1	−2.2	−1.1	3.9	−4.2	6.7	1.0	−14.0	3.5	−16.6
1974	0.6	0.6	−1.6	−1.2	−4.1	0.03	−5.6	−10.4	−10.4	9.5	−7.0	−0.4	−27.6
1975	14.2	5.0	3.9	6.9	1.3	5.6	−5.4	0.5	−5.0	5.3	2.9	−1.0	38.3
1976	14.4	−0.3	2.8	−0.3	−2.2	2.8	−1.8	−1.1	1.7	−2.6	−1.8	6.1	17.9
1977	−5.0	−1.9	−1.8	0.8	−3.0	2.0	−2.9	−3.2	−1.7	−3.4	1.4	0.2	−17.3
1978	−7.4	−3.6	2.1	10.6	0.4	−2.6	5.3	1.7	−1.3	−8.5	0.8	0.7	−3.1
1979	4.2	−3.6	6.6	−0.8	−3.8	2.4	0.5	4.9	−1.0	−7.2	0.8	2.0	4.2
1980	4.4	−1.5	−9.0	4.0	4.1	2.0	7.8	−0.3	−0.02	−0.9	7.4	−3.0	14.9
1981	−1.7	2.9	3.0	−0.6	−0.6	−1.5	−2.5	−7.4	−3.6	0.3	4.3	−1.6	−9.2
1982	−0.4	−5.4	−0.2	3.1	−3.4	−0.9	−0.4	11.5	−0.6	10.7	4.8	0.7	19.6
1983	2.8	3.4	1.6	8.5	−2.1	1.8	−1.9	1.4	1.4	−0.6	4.1	−1.4	20.3
1984	−3.0	−5.4	0.9	0.5	−5.6	2.5	−1.5	9.8	−1.4	0.1	−1.5	1.9	−3.7
1985	6.2	−0.2	−1.3	−0.7	4.6	1.5	0.9	−1.0	−0.4	3.4	7.1	5.1	27.7
1986	1.6	8.8	6.4	−1.9	5.2	0.9	−6.2	6.9	−6.9	6.2	1.9	−1.0	22.6
1987	13.8	3.1	3.6	−0.8	0.2	5.5	6.3	3.5	−2.5	−23.2	−8.0	5.7	2.3
1988	1.0	5.8	−4.0	2.2	−0.1	5.4	−0.6	−4.6	4.0	1.7	−1.6	2.6	11.8
1989	8.0	−3.6	1.6	5.5	2.5	−1.6	9.0	2.9	−1.6	−1.8	2.3	1.7	27.0
1990	−5.9	1.4	3.0	−1.9	8.3	0.1	0.9	−10.0	−6.2	−0.4	4.8	2.9	−4.3
1991	3.9	5.3	1.1	−0.9	4.8	−4.0	4.1	0.6	−0.9	1.7	−5.7	9.5	20.3
1992	1.7	1.4	−1.0	3.8	1.1	−2.3	2.3	−4.0	0.4	−1.4	2.4	−0.1	4.2
1993	0.3	1.8	1.9	−0.2	2.9	−0.3	0.7	3.2	−2.6	3.5	0.1	1.9	13.7
1994	6.0	−3.7	−5.1	1.3	2.1	−3.5	3.8	4.0	−1.8	1.7	−4.3	2.5	2.1
1995	0.2	4.3	3.7	3.9	3.3	2.0	3.3	−2.1	3.9	−0.7	6.7	0.8	33.5
1996	5.4	1.7	1.9	−0.3	1.3	0.2	−2.2	1.6	4.7	2.5	8.2	−1.1	26.0
1997	5.7	0.9	−4.3	6.5	4.6	4.7	7.2	−7.3	4.2	−6.3	5.1	1.1	22.6
1998	−0.02	8.1	3.0	3.0	−1.8	0.6	−0.8	−15.1	4.0	9.6	6.1	0.7	16.1
1999	1.9	−0.6	5.2	10.2	−2.1	3.9	−2.9	1.6	−4.5	3.8	1.4	5.7	25.2
2000	−4.8	−7.4	7.8	−1.7	−2.0	−0.7	0.7	6.6	−5.0	3.0	−5.1	3.6	−6.2
2001	0.9	−3.6	−5.9	8.7	1.6	−3.8	0.2	−5.4	−11.1	2.6	8.6	1.7	−7.1
2002	−1.0	1.9	2.9	−4.4	−0.2	−6.9	−5.5	−0.8	−12.4	10.6	5.9	−6.2	−16.8
2003	−3.5	−2.0	1.3	6.1	4.4	1.5	2.8	2.0	−1.5	5.7	−0.2	6.9	25.3
2004	0.3	0.9	−2.1	−1.3	−0.4	2.4	−2.8	0.3	−0.9	−0.5	4.0	3.4	3.1
2005	−2.7	2.6	−2.4	−3.0	2.7	−1.8	3.6	−1.5	0.8	−1.2	3.5	−0.8	−0.6
2006	1.4	1.2	1.1	2.3	−1.7	−0.2	0.3	1.7	2.6	3.4	1.2	2.0	16.3
2007	1.3	−2.8	0.7	5.7	4.3	−1.6	−1.5	1.1	4.0	0.2	−4.0	−0.8	6.4
2008	−4.6	−3.0	−0.03	4.5	−1.4	−10.2	0.2	1.5	−6.0	−14.1	−5.3	−0.6	−33.8
2009	−8.8	−11.7	7.7	7.3	4.1	−0.6	8.6	3.5	2.3	0.005	6.5	0.8	18.8
2010	−3.5	2.6	5.1	1.4	−7.9	−3.6	7.1	−4.3	7.7	3.1	−1.0	5.2	11.0
2011	2.7	2.8	0.8	4.0	−1.9	−1.2	−2.2	−4.4	−6.0	9.5	0.8	1.4	5.5
2012	3.4	2.5	2.0	0.01	−6.2	3.9	1.0	0.6	2.6	−2.5	−0.5	0.6	7.3

continued

152

DOW JONES INDUSTRIALS MONTHLY PERCENT CHANGES SINCE 1950 (continued)

	Jan	Feb	Mar	Apr	May	Jun	Jul	Aug	Sep	Oct	Nov	Dec	Year's Change
2013	5.8	1.4	3.7	1.8	1.9	−1.4	4.0	−4.4	2.2	2.8	3.5	3.0	26.5
2014	−5.3	4.0	0.8	0.7	0.8	0.7	−1.6	3.2	−0.3	2.0	2.5	−0.03	7.5
2015	−3.7	5.6	−2.0	0.4	1.0	−2.2	0.4	−6.6	−1.5	8.5	0.3	−1.7	−2.2
2016	−5.5	0.3	7.1	0.5	0.1	0.8	2.8	−0.2	−0.5	−0.9	5.4	3.3	13.4
2017	0.5	4.8	−0.7	1.3	0.3	1.6	2.5	0.3	2.1	4.3	3.8	1.8	25.1
2018	5.8	−4.3	−3.7	0.2	1.0	−0.6	4.7	2.2	1.9	−5.1	1.7	−8.7	−5.6
2019	7.2	3.7	0.1	2.6	−6.7	7.2	1.0	−1.7	1.9	0.5	3.7	1.7	22.3
2020	−1.0	−10.1	−13.7	11.1	4.3								
TOTALS	70.2	8.2	59.6	142.8	−2.5	−12.9	86.9	−11.4	−44.7	42.1	113.7	105.9	
AVG.	1.0	0.1	0.8	2.0	−0.04	−0.2	1.2	−0.2	−0.6	0.6	1.6	1.5	
# Up	45	42	45	49	38	33	45	39	29	42	48	49	
# Down	26	29	26	22	33	37	25	31	41	28	22	21	

DOW JONES INDUSTRIALS MONTHLY POINT CHANGES SINCE 1950

	Jan	Feb	Mar	Apr	May	Jun	Jul	Aug	Sep	Oct	Nov	Dec	Year's Close
1950	1.66	1.65	2.61	8.28	9.09	−14.31	0.29	7.47	9.49	−1.35	2.59	7.81	235.41
1951	13.42	3.22	−4.11	11.19	−9.48	−7.01	15.22	12.39	0.91	−8.81	−1.08	7.96	269.23
1952	1.46	−10.61	9.38	−11.83	5.31	11.32	5.30	−4.52	−4.43	−1.38	14.43	8.24	291.90
1953	−2.13	−5.50	−4.40	−5.12	−2.47	−4.02	7.12	−14.16	2.82	11.77	5.56	−0.47	280.90
1954	11.49	2.15	8.97	15.82	8.16	6.04	14.39	−12.12	24.66	−8.32	34.63	17.62	404.39
1955	4.44	3.04	−2.17	15.95	−0.79	26.52	14.47	2.33	−1.56	−11.75	28.39	5.14	488.40
1956	−17.66	12.91	28.14	4.33	−38.07	14.73	25.03	−15.77	−26.79	4.60	−7.07	26.69	499.47
1957	−20.31	−14.54	10.19	19.55	10.57	−1.64	5.23	−24.17	−28.05	−15.26	8.83	−14.18	435.69
1958	14.33	−10.10	6.84	9.10	6.84	15.48	24.81	5.64	23.46	11.13	14.24	26.19	583.65
1959	10.31	9.54	−1.79	22.04	20.04	−0.19	31.28	−10.47	−32.73	14.92	12.58	20.18	679.36
1960	−56.74	7.50	−13.53	−14.89	23.80	15.12	−23.89	9.26	−45.85	0.22	16.86	18.67	615.89
1961	32.31	13.88	14.55	2.08	18.01	−12.76	21.41	14.57	−18.73	2.71	17.68	9.54	731.14
1962	−31.14	8.05	−1.10	−41.62	−51.97	−52.08	36.65	11.25	−30.20	10.79	59.53	2.80	652.10
1963	30.75	−19.91	19.58	35.18	9.26	−20.08	−11.45	33.89	3.47	22.44	−4.71	12.43	762.95
1964	22.39	14.80	13.15	−2.52	9.79	10.94	9.60	−2.62	36.89	−2.29	2.35	−1.30	874.13
1965	28.73	0.62	−14.43	33.26	−4.27	−50.01	13.71	11.36	37.48	30.24	−14.11	22.55	969.26
1966	14.25	−31.62	−27.12	8.91	−49.61	−13.97	−22.72	−58.97	−14.19	32.85	−15.48	−5.90	785.69
1967	64.20	−10.52	26.61	31.07	−44.49	7.70	43.98	−2.95	25.37	−46.92	−3.93	29.30	905.11
1968	−49.64	−14.97	0.17	71.55	−13.22	−1.20	−14.80	13.01	39.78	16.60	32.69	−41.33	943.75
1969	2.30	−40.84	30.27	14.70	−12.62	−64.37	−57.72	21.25	−23.63	42.90	−43.69	−11.94	800.36
1970	−56.30	33.53	7.98	−49.50	−35.63	−16.91	50.59	30.46	−3.90	−5.07	38.48	44.83	838.92
1971	29.58	10.33	25.54	37.38	−33.94	−16.67	−32.71	39.64	−10.88	−48.19	−7.66	58.86	890.20
1972	11.97	25.96	12.57	13.47	6.55	−31.69	−4.29	38.99	−10.46	2.25	62.69	1.81	1020.02
1973	−21.00	−43.95	−4.06	−29.58	−20.02	−9.70	34.69	−38.83	59.53	9.48	−134.33	28.61	850.86
1974	4.69	4.98	−13.85	−9.93	−34.58	0.24	−44.98	−78.85	−70.71	57.65	−46.86	−2.42	616.24
1975	87.45	35.36	29.10	53.19	10.95	46.70	−47.48	3.83	−41.46	42.16	24.63	−8.26	852.41
1976	122.87	−2.67	26.84	−2.60	−21.62	27.55	−18.14	−10.90	16.45	−25.26	−17.71	57.43	1004.65
1977	−50.28	−17.95	−17.29	7.77	−28.24	17.64	−26.23	−28.58	−14.38	−28.76	11.35	1.47	831.17
1978	−61.25	−2780	15.24	79.96	3.29	−21.66	43.32	14.55	−11.00	−73.37	6.58	5.98	805.01
1979	34.21	−30.40	53.36	−7.28	−32.57	19.65	4.44	41.21	−9.05	−62.88	6.65	16.39	838.74
1980	37.11	−12.71	−77.39	31.31	33.79	17.07	67.40	−2.73	−0.17	−7.93	68.85	−29.35	963.99
1981	−16.72	27.31	29.29	−6.12	−6.00	−14.87	−24.54	−70.87	−31.49	2.57	36.43	−13.98	875.00
1982	−3.90	−46.71	−1.62	25.59	−28.82	−7.61	−3.33	92.71	−5.06	95.47	47.56	7.26	1046.54
1983	29.16	36.92	17.41	96.17	−26.22	21.98	−22.74	16.94	16.97	−7.93	50.82	−17.38	1258.64
1984	−38.06	−65.95	10.26	5.86	−65.90	27.55	−17.12	109.10	−17.67	0.67	−18.44	22.63	1211.57
1985	75.20	−2.76	−17.23	−8.72	57.35	20.05	11.99	−13.44	−5.38	45.68	97.82	74.54	1546.67
1986	24.32	138.07	109.55	−34.63	92.73	16.01	−117.41	123.03	−130.76	110.23	36.42	−18.28	1895.95
1987	262.09	65.95	80.70	−18.33	5.21	126.96	153.54	90.88	−66.67	−602.75	−159.98	105.28	1938.83
1988	19.39	113.40	−83.56	44.27	−1.21	110.59	−12.98	−97.08	81.26	35.74	−34.14	54.06	2168.57
1989	173.75	−83.93	35.23	125.18	61.35	−40.09	220.60	76.61	−44.45	−47.74	61.19	46.93	2753.20
1990	−162.66	36.71	79.96	−50.45	219.90	4.03	24.51	−290.84	−161.88	−10.15	117.32	74.01	2633.66
1991	102.73	145.79	31.68	−25.99	139.63	−120.75	118.07	18.78	−26.83	52.33	−174.42	274.15	3168.83
1992	54.56	44.28	−32.20	123.65	37.76	−78.36	75.26	−136.43	14.31	−45.38	78.88	−4.05	3301.11

continued

	Jan	Feb	Mar	Apr	May	Jun	Jul	Aug	Sep	Oct	Nov	Dec	Year's Close
1993	8.92	60.78	64.30	-7.56	99.88	-11.35	23.39	111.78	-96.13	125.47	3.36	70.14	3754.09
1994	224.27	-146.34	-196.06	45.73	76.68	-133.41	139.54	148.92	-70.23	64.93	-168.89	95.21	3834.44
1995	9.42	167.19	146.64	163.58	143.87	90.96	152.37	-97.91	178.52	-33.60	319.01	42.63	5117.12
1996	278.18	90.32	101.52	-18.06	74.10	11.45	-125.72	87.30	265.96	147.21	492.32	-73.43	6448.27
1997	364.82	64.65	-294.26	425.51	322.05	341.75	549.82	-600.19	322.84	-503.18	381.05	85.12	7908.25
1998	-1.75	639.22	254.09	263.56	-163.42	52.07	-68.73	-1344.22	303.55	749.48	524.45	64.88	9181.43
1999	177.40	-52.25	479.58	1002.88	-229.30	411.06	-315.65	174.13	-492.33	392.91	147.95	619.31	11497.12
2000	-556.59	-812.22	793.61	-188.01	-211.58	-74.44	74.09	693.12	-564.18	320.22	-556.65	372.36	10786.85
2001	100.51	-392.08	-616.50	856.19	176.97	-409.54	20.41	-573.06	-1102.19	227.58	776.42	169.94	10021.50
2002	-101.50	186.13	297.81	-457.72	-20.97	-681.99	-506.67	-73.09	-1071.57	805.10	499.06	-554.46	8341.63
2003	-287.82	-162.73	101.05	487.96	370.17	135.18	248.36	182.02	-140.76	526.06	-18.66	671.46	10453.92
2004	34.15	95.85	-226.22	-132.13	-37.12	247.03	-295.77	34.21	-93.65	-52.80	400.55	354.99	10783.01
2005	-293.07	276.29	-262.47	-311.25	274.97	-192.51	365.94	-159.31	87.10	-128.63	365.80	-88.37	10717.50
2006	147.36	128.55	115.91	257.82	-198.83	-18.09	35.46	195.47	297.92	401.66	141.20	241.22	12463.15
2007	158.54	-353.06	85.72	708.56	564.73	-219.02	-196.63	145.75	537.89	34.38	-558.29	-106.90	13264.82
2008	-614.46	-383.97	-3.50	557.24	-181.81	-1288.31	28.01	165.53	-692.89	-1525.65	-495.97	-52.65	8776.39
2009	-775.53	-937.93	545.99	559.20	332.21	-53.33	724.61	324.67	216.00	0.45	632.11	83.21	10428.05
2010	-360.72	257.93	531.37	151.98	-871.98	-362.61	691.92	-451.22	773.33	330.44	-112.47	571.49	11577.51
2011	314.42	334.41	93.39	490.81	-240.75	-155.45	-271.10	-529.71	-700.15	1041.63	90.67	171.88	12217.56
2012	415.35	319.16	259.97	1.59	-820.18	486.64	128.59	82.16	346.29	-340.67	-70.88	78.56	13104.14
2013	756.44	193.91	524.05	261.26	275.77	-205.97	589.94	-689.23	319.36	416.08	540.66	490.25	16576.66
2014	-877.81	622.86	135.95	123.18	136.33	109.43	-263.30	535.15	-55.55	347.62	437.72	-5.17	17823.07
2015	-658.12	967.75	-356.58	64.40	170.16	-391.17	70.35	-1161.83	-244.03	1379.54	56.38	-294.89	17425.03
2016	-958.73	50.20	1168.59	88.55	13.56	142.79	502.25	-31.36	-92.73	-165.73	981.16	639.02	19762.60
2017	101.49	948.15	-149.02	277.29	68.14	340.98	541.49	56.98	456.99	972.15	895.11	446.87	24719.22
2018	1430.17	-1120.19	-926.09	60.04	252.69	-144.43	1143.78	549.63	493.49	-1342.55	422.70	-2211.00	23327.46
2019	1672.21	916.33	12.68	664.23	-1777.87	1784.92	264.31	-460.99	513.55	129.40	1005.18	487.03	28538.44
2020	-282.41	-2846.67	-3492.20	2428.56	1037.39								
TOTALS	1158.47	-585.25	-391.36	9453.09	-136.50	-223.44	4821.43	-2760.45	-799.11	3913.41	7443.47	3289.22	
# Up	45	42	45	49	38	33	45	39	29	42	48	49	
# Down	26	29	26	22	33	37	25	31	41	28	22	21	

	Jan	Feb	Mar	Apr	May	Jun	Jul	Aug	Sep	Oct	Nov	Dec
1950	201.79	203.44	206.05	214.33	223.42	209.11	209.40	216.87	226.36	225.01	227.60	235.41
1951	248.83	252.05	247.94	259.13	249.65	242.64	257.86	270.25	271.16	262.35	261.27	269.23
1952	270.69	260.08	269.46	257.63	262.94	274.26	279.56	275.04	270.61	269.23	283.66	291.90
1953	289.77	284.27	279.87	274.75	272.28	268.26	275.38	261.22	264.04	275.81	281.37	280.90
1954	292.39	294.54	303.51	319.33	327.49	333.53	347.92	335.80	360.46	352.14	386.77	404.39
1955	408.83	411.87	409.70	425.65	424.86	451.38	465.85	468.18	466.62	454.87	483.26	488.40
1956	470.74	483.65	511.79	516.12	478.05	492.78	517.81	502.04	475.25	479.85	472.78	499.47
1957	479.16	464.62	474.81	494.36	504.93	503.29	508.52	484.35	456.30	441.04	449.87	435.69
1958	450.02	439.92	446.76	455.86	462.70	478.18	502.99	508.63	532.09	543.22	557.46	583.65
1959	593.96	603.50	601.71	623.75	643.79	643.60	674.88	664.41	631.68	646.60	659.18	679.36
1960	622.62	630.12	616.59	601.70	625.50	640.62	616.73	625.99	580.14	580.36	597.22	615.89
1961	648.20	662.08	676.63	678.71	696.72	683.96	705.37	719.94	701.21	703.92	721.60	731.14
1962	700.00	708.05	706.95	665.33	613.36	561.28	597.93	609.18	578.98	589.77	649.30	652.10
1963	682.85	662.94	682.52	717.70	726.96	706.88	695.43	729.32	732.79	755.23	750.52	762.95
1964	785.34	800.14	813.29	810.77	820.56	831.50	841.10	838.48	875.37	873.08	875.43	874.13
1965	902.86	903.48	889.05	922.31	918.04	868.03	881.74	893.10	930.58	960.82	946.71	969.26
1966	983.51	951.89	924.77	933.68	884.07	870.10	847.38	788.41	774.22	807.07	791.59	785.69
1967	849.89	839.37	865.98	897.05	852.56	860.26	904.24	901.29	926.66	879.74	875.81	905.11
1968	855.47	840.50	840.67	912.22	899.00	897.80	883.00	896.01	935.79	952.39	985.08	943.75
1969	946.05	905.21	935.48	950.18	937.56	873.19	815.47	836.72	813.09	855.99	812.30	800.36
1970	744.06	777.59	785.57	736.07	700.44	683.53	734.12	764.58	760.68	755.61	794.09	838.92
1971	868.50	878.83	904.37	941.75	907.81	891.14	858.43	898.07	887.19	839.00	831.34	890.20
1972	902.17	928.13	940.70	954.17	960.72	929.03	924.74	963.73	953.27	955.52	1018.21	1020.02
1973	999.02	955.07	951.01	921.43	901.41	891.71	926.40	887.57	947.10	956.58	822.25	850.86

154

continued

	Jan	Feb	Mar	Apr	May	Jun	Jul	Aug	Sep	Oct	Nov	Dec
1974	855.55	860.53	846.68	836.75	802.17	802.41	757.43	678.58	607.87	665.52	618.66	616.24
1975	703.69	739.05	768.15	821.34	832.29	878.99	831.51	835.34	793.88	836.04	860.67	852.41
1976	975.28	972.61	999.45	996.85	975.23	1002.78	984.64	973.74	990.19	964.93	947.22	1004.65
1977	954.37	936.42	919.13	926.90	898.66	916.30	890.07	861.49	847.11	818.35	829.70	831.17
1978	769.92	742.12	757.36	837.32	840.61	818.95	862.27	876.82	865.82	792.45	799.03	805.01
1979	839.22	808.82	862.18	854.90	822.33	841.98	846.42	887.63	878.58	815.70	822.35	838.74
1980	875.85	863.14	785.75	817.06	850.85	867.92	935.32	932.59	932.42	924.49	993.34	963.99
1981	947.27	974.58	1003.87	997.75	991.75	976.88	952.34	881.47	849.98	852.55	888.98	875.00
1982	871.10	824.39	822.77	848.36	819.54	811.93	808.60	901.31	896.25	991.72	1039.28	1046.54
1983	1075.70	1112.62	1130.03	1226.20	1199.98	1221.96	1199.22	1216.16	1233.13	1225.20	1276.02	1258.64
1984	1220.58	1154.63	1164.89	1170.75	1104.85	1132.40	1115.28	1224.38	1206.71	1207.38	1188.94	1211.57
1985	1286.77	1284.01	1266.78	1258.06	1315.41	1335.46	1347.45	1334.01	1328.63	1374.31	1472.13	1546.67
1986	1570.99	1709.06	1818.61	1783.98	1876.71	1892.72	1775.31	1898.34	1767.58	1877.81	1914.23	1895.95
1987	2158.04	2223.99	2304.69	2286.36	2291.57	2418.53	2572.07	2662.95	2596.28	1993.53	1833.55	1938.83
1988	1958.22	2071.62	1988.06	2032.33	2031.12	2141.71	2128.73	2031.65	2112.91	2148.65	2114.51	2168.57
1989	2342.32	2258.39	2293.62	2418.80	2480.15	2440.06	2660.66	2737.27	2692.82	2645.08	2706.27	2753.20
1990	2590.54	2627.25	2707.21	2656.76	2876.66	2880.69	2905.20	2614.36	2452.48	2442.33	2559.65	2633.66
1991	2736.39	2882.18	2913.86	2887.87	3027.50	2906.75	3024.82	3043.60	3016.77	3069.10	2894.68	3168.83
1992	3223.39	3267.67	3235.47	3359.12	3396.88	3318.52	3393.78	3257.35	3271.66	3226.28	3305.16	3301.11
1993	3310.03	3370.81	3435.11	3427.55	3527.43	3516.08	3539.47	3651.25	3555.12	3680.59	3683.95	3754.09
1994	3978.36	3832.02	3635.96	3681.69	3758.37	3624.96	3764.50	3913.42	3843.19	3908.12	3739.23	3834.44
1995	3843.86	4011.05	4157.69	4321.27	4465.14	4556.10	4708.47	4610.56	4789.08	4755.48	5074.49	5117.12
1996	5395.30	5485.62	5587.14	5569.08	5643.18	5654.63	5528.91	5616.21	5882.17	6029.38	6521.70	6448.27
1997	6813.09	6877.74	6583.48	7008.99	7331.04	7672.79	8222.61	7622.42	7945.26	7442.08	7823.13	7908.25
1998	7906.50	8545.72	8799.81	9063.37	8899.95	8952.02	8883.29	7539.07	7842.62	8592.10	9116.55	9181.43
1999	9358.83	9306.58	9786.16	10789.04	10559.74	10970.80	10655.15	10829.28	10336.95	10729.86	10877.81	11497.12
2000	10940.53	10128.31	10921.92	10733.91	10522.33	10447.89	10521.98	11215.10	10650.92	10971.14	10414.49	10786.85
2001	10887.36	10495.28	9878.78	10734.97	10911.94	10502.40	10522.81	9949.75	8847.56	9075.14	9851.56	10021.50
2002	9920.00	10106.13	10403.94	9946.22	9925.25	9243.26	8736.59	8663.50	7591.93	8397.03	8896.09	8341.63
2003	8053.81	7891.08	7992.13	8480.09	8850.26	8985.44	9233.80	9415.82	9275.06	9801.12	9782.46	10453.92
2004	10488.07	10583.92	10357.70	10225.57	10188.45	10435.48	10139.71	10173.92	10080.27	10027.47	10428.02	10783.01
2005	10489.94	10766.23	10503.76	10192.51	10467.48	10274.97	10640.91	10481.60	10568.70	10440.07	10805.87	10717.50
2006	10864.86	10993.41	11109.32	11367.14	11168.31	11150.22	11185.68	11381.15	11679.07	12080.73	12221.93	12463.15
2007	12621.69	12268.63	12354.35	13062.91	13627.64	13408.62	13211.99	13357.74	13895.63	13930.01	13371.72	13264.82
2008	12650.36	12266.39	12262.89	12820.13	12638.32	11350.01	11378.02	11543.55	10850.66	9325.01	8829.04	8776.39
2009	8000.86	7062.93	7608.92	8168.12	8500.33	8447.00	9171.61	9496.28	9712.28	9712.73	10344.84	10428.05
2010	10067.33	10325.26	10856.63	11008.61	10136.63	9774.02	10465.94	10014.72	10788.05	11118.49	11006.02	11577.51
2011	11891.93	12226.34	12319.73	12810.54	12569.79	12414.34	12143.24	11613.53	10913.38	11955.01	12045.68	12217.56
2012	12632.91	12952.07	13212.04	13213.63	12393.45	12880.09	13008.68	13090.84	13437.13	13096.46	13025.58	13104.14
2013	13860.58	14054.49	14578.54	14839.80	15115.57	14909.60	15499.54	14810.31	15129.67	15545.75	16086.41	16576.66
2014	15698.85	16321.71	16457.66	16580.84	16717.17	16826.60	16563.30	17098.45	17042.90	17390.52	17828.24	17823.07
2015	17164.95	18132.70	17776.12	17840.52	18010.68	17619.51	17689.86	16528.03	16284.00	17663.54	17719.92	17425.03
2016	16466.30	16516.50	17685.09	17773.64	17787.20	17929.99	18432.24	18400.88	18308.15	18142.42	19123.58	19762.60
2017	19864.09	20812.24	20663.22	20940.51	21008.65	21349.63	21891.12	21948.10	22405.09	23377.24	24272.35	24719.22
2018	26149.39	25029.20	24103.11	24163.15	24415.84	24271.41	25415.19	25964.82	26458.31	25115.76	25538.46	23327.46
2019	24999.67	25916.00	25928.68	26592.91	24815.04	26599.96	26864.27	26403.28	26916.83	27046.23	28051.41	28538.44
2020	28256.03	25409.36	21917.16	24345.72	25383.11							

STANDARD & POOR'S 500 MONTHLY PERCENT CHANGES SINCE 1950

	Jan	Feb	Mar	Apr	May	Jun	Jul	Aug	Sep	Oct	Nov	Dec	Year's Change
1950	1.7	1.0	0.4	4.5	3.9	−5.8	0.8	3.3	5.6	0.4	−0.1	4.6	21.8
1951	6.1	0.6	−1.8	4.8	−4.1	−2.6	6.9	3.9	−0.1	−1.4	−0.3	3.9	16.5
1952	1.6	−3.6	4.8	−4.3	2.3	4.6	1.8	−1.5	−2.0	−0.1	4.6	3.5	11.8
1953	−0.7	−1.8	−2.4	−2.6	−0.3	−1.6	2.5	−5.8	0.1	5.1	0.9	0.2	−6.6
1954	5.1	0.3	3.0	4.9	3.3	0.1	5.7	−3.4	8.3	−1.9	8.1	5.1	45.0
1955	1.8	0.4	−0.5	3.8	−0.1	8.2	6.1	−0.8	1.1	−3.0	7.5	−0.1	26.4
1956	−3.6	3.5	6.9	−0.2	−6.6	3.9	5.2	−3.8	−4.5	0.5	−1.1	3.5	2.6
1957	−4.2	−3.3	2.0	3.7	3.7	−0.1	1.1	−5.6	−6.2	−3.2	1.6	−4.1	−14.3
1958	4.3	−2.1	3.1	3.2	1.5	2.6	4.3	1.2	4.8	2.5	2.2	5.2	38.1

continued

	Jan	Feb	Mar	Apr	May	Jun	Jul	Aug	Sep	Oct	Nov	Dec	Year's Change
1959	0.4	−0.02	0.1	3.9	1.9	−0.4	3.5	−1.5	−4.6	1.1	1.3	2.8	8.5
1960	−7.1	0.9	−1.4	−1.8	2.7	2.0	−2.5	2.6	−6.0	−0.2	4.0	4.6	−3.0
1961	6.3	2.7	2.6	0.4	1.9	−2.9	3.3	2.0	−2.0	2.8	3.9	0.3	23.1
1962	−3.8	1.6	−0.6	−6.2	−8.6	−8.2	6.4	1.5	−4.8	0.4	10.2	1.3	−11.8
1963	4.9	−2.9	3.5	4.9	1.4	−2.0	−0.3	4.9	−1.1	3.2	−1.1	2.4	18.9
1964	2.7	1.0	1.5	0.6	1.1	1.6	1.8	−1.6	2.9	0.8	−0.5	0.4	13.0
1965	3.3	−0.1	−1.5	3.4	−0.8	−4.9	1.3	2.3	3.2	2.7	−0.9	0.9	9.1
1966	0.5	−1.8	−2.2	2.1	−5.4	−1.6	−1.3	−7.8	−0.7	4.8	0.3	−0.1	−13.1
1967	7.8	0.2	3.9	4.2	−5.2	1.8	4.5	−1.2	3.3	−2.9	0.1	2.6	20.1
1968	−4.4	−3.1	0.9	8.2	1.1	0.9	−1.8	1.1	3.9	0.7	4.8	−4.2	7.7
1969	−0.8	−4.7	3.4	2.1	−0.2	−5.6	−6.0	4.0	−2.5	4.4	−3.5	−1.9	−11.4
1970	−7.6	5.3	0.1	−9.0	−6.1	−5.0	7.3	4.4	3.3	−1.1	4.7	5.7	0.1
1971	4.0	0.9	3.7	3.6	−4.2	0.1	−4.1	3.6	−0.7	−4.2	−0.3	8.6	10.8
1972	1.8	2.5	0.6	0.4	1.7	−2.2	0.2	3.4	−0.5	0.9	4.6	1.2	15.6
1973	−1.7	−3.7	−0.1	−4.1	−1.9	−0.7	3.8	−3.7	4.0	−0.1	−11.4	1.7	−17.4
1974	−1.0	−0.4	−2.3	−3.9	−3.4	−1.5	−7.8	−9.0	−11.9	16.3	−5.3	−2.0	−29.7
1975	12.3	6.0	2.2	4.7	4.4	4.4	−6.8	−2.1	−3.5	6.2	2.5	−1.2	31.5
1976	11.8	−1.1	3.1	−1.1	−1.4	4.1	−0.8	−0.5	2.3	−2.2	−0.8	5.2	19.1
1977	−5.1	−2.2	−1.4	0.02	−2.4	4.5	−1.6	−2.1	−0.2	−4.3	2.7	0.3	−11.5
1978	−6.2	−2.5	2.5	8.5	0.4	−1.8	5.4	2.6	−0.7	−9.2	1.7	1.5	1.1
1979	4.0	−3.7	5.5	0.2	−2.6	3.9	0.9	5.3	N/C	−6.9	4.3	1.7	12.3
1980	5.8	−0.4	−10.2	4.1	4.7	2.7	6.5	0.6	2.5	1.6	10.2	−3.4	25.8
1981	−4.6	1.3	3.6	−2.3	−0.2	−1.0	−0.2	−6.2	−5.4	4.9	3.7	−3.0	−9.7
1982	−1.8	−6.1	−1.0	4.0	−3.9	−2.0	−2.3	11.6	0.8	11.0	3.6	1.5	14.8
1983	3.3	1.9	3.3	7.5	−1.2	3.5	−3.3	1.1	1.0	−1.5	1.7	−0.9	17.3
1984	−0.9	−3.9	1.3	0.5	−5.9	1.7	−1.6	10.6	−0.3	−0.01	−1.5	2.2	1.4
1985	7.4	0.9	−0.3	−0.5	5.4	1.2	−0.5	−1.2	−3.5	4.3	6.5	4.5	26.3
1986	0.2	7.1	5.3	−1.4	5.0	1.4	−5.9	7.1	−8.5	5.5	2.1	−2.8	14.6
1987	13.2	3.7	2.6	−1.1	0.6	4.8	4.8	3.5	−2.4	−21.8	−8.5	7.3	2.0
1988	4.0	4.2	−3.3	0.9	0.3	4.3	−0.5	−3.9	4.0	2.6	−1.9	1.5	12.4
1989	7.1	−2.9	2.1	5.0	3.5	−0.8	8.8	1.6	−0.7	−2.5	1.7	2.1	27.3
1990	−6.9	0.9	2.4	−2.7	9.2	−0.9	−0.5	−9.4	−5.1	−0.7	6.0	2.5	−6.6
1991	4.2	6.7	2.2	0.03	3.9	−4.8	4.5	2.0	−1.9	1.2	−4.4	11.2	26.3
1992	−2.0	1.0	−2.2	2.8	0.1	−1.7	3.9	−2.4	0.9	0.2	3.0	1.0	4.5
1993	0.7	1.0	1.9	−2.5	2.3	0.1	−0.5	3.4	−1.0	1.9	−1.3	1.0	7.1
1994	3.3	−3.0	−4.6	1.2	1.2	−2.7	3.1	3.8	−2.7	2.1	−4.0	1.2	−1.5
1995	2.4	3.6	2.7	2.8	3.6	2.1	3.2	−0.03	4.0	−0.5	4.1	1.7	34.1
1996	3.3	0.7	0.8	1.3	2.3	0.2	−4.6	1.9	5.4	2.6	7.3	−2.2	20.3
1997	6.1	0.6	−4.3	5.8	5.9	4.3	7.8	−5.7	5.3	−3.4	4.5	1.6	31.0
1998	1.0	7.0	5.0	0.9	−1.9	3.9	−1.2	−14.6	6.2	8.0	5.9	5.6	26.7
1999	4.1	−3.2	3.9	3.8	−2.5	5.4	−3.2	−0.6	−2.9	6.3	1.9	5.8	19.5
2000	−5.1	−2.0	9.7	−3.1	−2.2	2.4	−1.6	6.1	−5.3	−0.5	−8.0	0.4	−10.1
2001	3.5	−9.2	−6.4	7.7	0.5	−2.5	−1.1	−6.4	−8.2	1.8	7.5	0.8	−13.0
2002	−1.6	−2.1	3.7	−6.1	−0.9	−7.2	−7.9	0.5	−11.0	8.6	5.7	−6.0	−23.4
2003	−2.7	−1.7	1.0	8.0	5.1	1.1	1.6	1.8	−1.2	5.5	0.7	5.1	26.4
2004	1.7	1.2	−1.6	−1.7	1.2	1.8	−3.4	0.2	0.9	1.4	3.9	3.2	9.0
2005	−2.5	1.9	−1.9	−2.0	3.0	−0.01	3.6	−1.1	0.7	−1.8	3.5	−0.1	3.0
2006	2.5	0.05	1.1	1.2	−3.1	0.01	0.5	2.1	2.5	3.2	1.6	1.3	13.6
2007	1.4	−2.2	1.0	4.3	3.3	−1.8	−3.2	1.3	3.6	1.5	−4.4	−0.9	3.5
2008	−6.1	−3.5	−0.6	4.8	1.1	−8.6	−1.0	1.2	−9.1	−16.9	−7.5	0.8	−38.5
2009	−8.6	−11.0	8.5	9.4	5.3	0.02	7.4	3.4	3.6	−2.0	5.7	1.8	23.5
2010	−3.7	2.9	5.9	1.5	−8.2	−5.4	6.9	−4.7	8.8	3.7	−0.2	6.5	12.8
2011	2.3	3.2	−0.1	2.8	−1.4	−1.8	−2.1	−5.7	−7.2	10.8	−0.5	0.9	−0.003
2012	4.4	4.1	3.1	−0.7	−6.3	4.0	1.3	2.0	2.4	−2.0	0.3	0.7	13.4
2013	5.0	1.1	3.6	1.8	2.1	−1.5	4.9	−3.1	3.0	4.5	2.8	2.4	29.6
2014	−3.6	4.3	0.7	0.6	2.1	1.9	−1.5	3.8	−1.6	2.3	2.5	−0.4	11.4
2015	−3.1	5.5	−1.7	0.9	1.0	−2.1	2.0	−6.3	−2.6	8.3	0.1	−1.8	−0.7
2016	−5.1	−0.4	6.6	0.3	1.5	0.1	3.6	−0.1	−0.1	−1.9	3.4	1.8	9.5
2017	1.8	3.7	−0.04	0.9	1.2	0.5	1.9	0.1	1.9	2.2	2.8	1.0	19.4
2018	5.6	−3.9	−2.7	0.3	2.2	0.5	3.6	3.0	0.4	−6.9	1.8	−9.2	−6.2
2019	7.9	3.0	1.8	3.9	−6.6	6.9	1.3	−1.8	1.7	2.0	3.4	2.9	28.9
2020	−0.2	−8.4	−12.5	12.7	4.5								
TOTALS	77.9	−2.5	70.0	116.6	15.8	5.8	74.9	−4.8	−30.3	57.7	110.4	103.2	
AVG.	1.1	−0.03	1.0	1.6	0.2	0.1	1.1	−0.1	−0.4	0.8	1.6	1.5	
# Up	43	39	45	51	42	38	40	38	32	42	48	52	
# Down	28	32	26	20	29	32	30	32	37	28	22	18	

	Jan	Feb	Mar	Apr	May	Jun	Jul	Aug	Sep	Oct	Nov	Dec
1950	17.05	17.22	17.29	18.07	18.78	17.69	17.84	18.42	19.45	19.53	19.51	20.41
1951	21.66	21.80	21.40	22.43	21.52	20.96	22.40	23.28	23.26	22.94	22.88	23.77
1952	24.14	23.26	24.37	23.32	23.86	24.96	25.40	25.03	24.54	24.52	25.66	26.57
1953	26.38	25.90	25.29	24.62	24.54	24.14	24.75	23.32	23.35	24.54	24.76	24.81
1954	26.08	26.15	26.94	28.26	29.19	29.21	30.88	29.83	32.31	31.68	34.24	35.98
1955	36.63	36.76	36.58	37.96	37.91	41.03	43.52	43.18	43.67	42.34	45.51	45.48
1956	43.82	45.34	48.48	48.38	45.20	46.97	49.39	47.51	45.35	45.58	45.08	46.67
1957	44.72	43.26	44.11	45.74	47.43	47.37	47.91	45.22	42.42	41.06	41.72	39.99
1958	41.70	40.84	42.10	43.44	44.09	45.24	47.19	47.75	50.06	51.33	52.48	55.21
1959	55.42	55.41	55.44	57.59	58.68	58.47	60.51	59.60	56.88	57.52	58.28	59.89
1960	55.61	56.12	55.34	54.37	55.83	56.92	55.51	56.96	53.52	53.39	55.54	58.11
1961	61.78	63.44	65.06	65.31	66.56	64.64	66.76	68.07	66.73	68.62	71.32	71.55
1962	68.84	69.96	69.55	65.24	59.63	54.75	58.23	59.12	56.27	56.52	62.26	63.10
1963	66.20	64.29	66.57	69.80	70.80	69.37	69.13	72.50	71.70	74.01	73.23	75.02
1964	77.04	77.80	78.98	79.46	80.37	81.69	83.18	81.83	84.18	84.86	84.42	84.75
1965	87.56	87.43	86.16	89.11	88.42	84.12	85.25	87.17	89.96	92.42	91.61	92.43
1966	92.88	91.22	89.23	91.06	86.13	84.74	83.60	77.10	76.56	80.20	80.45	80.33
1967	86.61	86.78	90.20	94.01	89.08	90.64	94.75	93.64	96.71	93.90	94.00	96.47
1968	92.24	89.36	90.20	97.59	98.68	99.58	97.74	98.86	102.67	103.41	108.37	103.86
1969	103.01	98.13	101.51	103.69	103.46	97.71	91.83	95.51	93.12	97.24	93.81	92.06
1970	85.02	89.50	89.63	81.52	76.55	72.72	78.05	81.52	84.21	83.25	87.20	92.15
1971	95.88	96.75	100.31	103.95	99.63	99.70	95.58	99.03	98.34	94.23	93.99	102.09
1972	103.94	106.57	107.20	107.67	109.53	107.14	107.39	111.09	110.55	111.58	116.67	118.05
1973	116.03	111.68	111.52	106.97	104.95	104.26	108.22	104.25	108.43	108.29	95.96	97.55
1974	96.57	96.22	93.98	90.31	87.28	86.00	79.31	72.15	63.54	73.90	69.97	68.56
1975	76.98	81.59	83.36	87.30	91.15	95.19	88.75	86.88	83.87	89.04	91.24	90.19
1976	100.86	99.71	102.77	101.64	100.18	104.28	103.44	102.91	105.24	102.90	102.10	107.46
1977	102.03	99.82	98.42	98.44	96.12	100.48	98.85	96.77	96.53	92.34	94.83	95.10
1978	89.25	87.04	89.21	96.83	97.24	95.53	100.68	103.29	102.54	93.15	94.70	96.11
1979	99.93	96.28	101.59	101.76	99.08	102.91	103.81	109.32	109.32	101.82	106.16	107.94
1980	114.16	113.66	102.09	106.29	111.24	114.24	121.67	122.38	125.46	127.47	140.52	135.76
1981	129.55	131.27	136.00	132.81	132.59	131.21	130.92	122.79	116.18	121.89	126.35	122.55
1982	120.40	113.11	111.96	116.44	111.88	109.61	107.09	119.51	120.42	133.71	138.54	140.64
1983	145.30	148.06	152.96	164.42	162.39	168.11	162.56	164.40	166.07	163.55	166.40	164.93
1984	163.41	157.06	159.18	160.05	150.55	153.18	150.66	166.68	166.10	166.09	163.58	167.24
1985	179.63	181.18	180.66	179.83	189.55	191.85	190.92	188.63	182.08	189.82	202.17	211.28
1986	211.78	226.92	238.90	235.52	247.35	250.84	236.12	252.93	231.32	243.98	249.22	242.17
1987	274.08	284.20	291.70	288.36	290.10	304.00	318.66	329.80	321.83	251.79	230.30	247.08
1988	257.07	267.82	258.89	261.33	262.16	273.50	272.02	261.52	271.91	278.97	273.70	277.72
1989	297.47	288.86	294.87	309.64	320.52	317.98	346.08	351.45	349.15	340.36	345.99	353.40
1990	329.08	331.89	339.94	330.80	361.23	358.02	356.15	322.56	306.05	304.00	322.22	330.22
1991	343.93	367.07	375.22	375.35	389.83	371.16	387.81	395.43	387.86	392.46	375.22	417.09
1992	408.79	412.70	403.69	414.95	415.35	408.14	424.21	414.03	417.80	418.68	431.35	435.71
1993	438.78	443.38	451.67	440.19	450.19	450.53	448.13	463.56	458.93	467.83	461.79	466.45
1994	481.61	467.14	445.77	450.91	456.50	444.27	458.26	475.49	462.69	472.35	453.69	459.27
1995	470.42	487.39	500.71	514.71	533.40	544.75	562.06	561.88	584.41	581.50	605.37	615.93
1996	636.02	640.43	645.50	654.17	669.12	670.63	639.95	651.99	687.31	705.27	757.02	740.74
1997	786.16	790.82	757.12	801.34	848.28	885.14	954.29	899.47	947.28	914.62	955.40	970.43
1998	980.28	1049.34	1101.75	1111.75	1090.82	1133.84	1120.67	957.28	1017.01	1098.67	1163.63	1229.23
1999	1279.64	1238.33	1286.37	1335.18	1301.84	1372.71	1328.72	1320.41	1282.71	1362.93	1388.91	1469.25
2000	1394.46	1366.42	1498.58	1452.43	1420.60	1454.60	1430.83	1517.68	1436.51	1429.40	1314.95	1320.28
2001	1366.01	1239.94	1160.33	1249.46	1255.82	1224.42	1211.23	1133.58	1040.94	1059.78	1139.45	1148.08
2002	1130.20	1106.73	1147.39	1076.92	1067.14	989.82	911.62	916.07	815.28	885.76	936.31	879.82
2003	855.70	841.15	849.18	916.92	963.59	974.50	990.31	1008.01	995.97	1050.71	1058.20	1111.92
2004	1131.13	1144.94	1126.21	1107.30	1120.68	1140.84	1101.72	1104.24	1114.58	1130.20	1173.82	1211.92
2005	1181.27	1203.60	1180.59	1156.85	1191.50	1191.33	1234.18	1220.33	1228.81	1207.01	1249.48	1248.29
2006	1280.08	1280.66	1294.83	1310.61	1270.09	1270.20	1276.66	1303.82	1335.85	1377.94	1400.63	1418.30
2007	1438.24	1406.82	1420.86	1482.37	1530.62	1503.35	1455.27	1473.99	1526.75	1549.38	1481.14	1468.36
2008	1378.55	1330.63	1322.70	1385.59	1400.38	1280.00	1267.38	1282.83	1166.36	968.75	896.24	903.25
2009	825.88	735.09	797.87	872.81	919.14	919.32	987.48	1020.62	1057.08	1036.19	1095.63	1115.10
2010	1073.87	1104.49	1169.43	1186.69	1089.41	1030.71	1101.60	1049.33	1141.20	1183.26	1180.55	1257.64
2011	1286.12	1327.22	1325.83	1363.61	1345.20	1320.64	1292.28	1218.89	1131.42	1253.30	1246.96	1257.60
2012	1312.41	1365.68	1408.47	1397.91	1310.33	1362.16	1379.32	1406.58	1440.67	1412.16	1416.18	1426.19

continued

	Jan	Feb	Mar	Apr	May	Jun	Jul	Aug	Sep	Oct	Nov	Dec
2013	1498.11	1514.68	1569.19	1597.57	1630.74	1606.28	1685.73	1632.97	1681.55	1756.54	1805.81	1848.36
2014	1782.59	1859.45	1872.34	1883.95	1923.57	1960.23	1930.67	2003.37	1972.29	2018.05	2067.56	2058.90
2015	1994.99	2104.50	2067.89	2085.51	2107.39	2063.11	2103.84	1972.18	1920.03	2079.36	2080.41	2043.94
2016	1940.24	1932.23	2059.74	2065.30	2096.96	2098.86	2173.60	2170.95	2168.27	2126.15	2198.81	2238.83
2017	2278.87	2363.64	2362.72	2384.20	2411.80	2423.41	2470.30	2471.65	2519.36	2575.26	2647.58	2673.61
2018	2823.81	2713.83	2640.87	2648.05	2705.27	2718.37	2816.29	2901.52	2913.98	2711.74	2760.16	2506.85
2019	2704.10	2784.49	2834.40	2945.83	2752.06	2941.76	2980.38	2926.46	2976.74	3037.56	3140.98	3230.78
2020	3225.52	2954.22	2584.59	2912.43	3044.31							

NASDAQ COMPOSITE MONTHLY PERCENT CHANGES SINCE 1971

	Jan	Feb	Mar	Apr	May	Jun	Jul	Aug	Sep	Oct	Nov	Dec	Year's Change
1971	10.2	2.6	4.6	6.0	−3.6	−0.4	−2.3	3.0	0.6	−3.6	−1.1	9.8	27.4
1972	4.2	5.5	2.2	2.5	0.9	−1.8	−1.8	1.7	−0.3	0.5	2.1	0.6	17.2
1973	−4.0	−6.2	−2.4	−8.2	−4.8	−1.6	7.6	−3.5	6.0	−0.9	−15.1	−1.4	−31.1
1974	3.0	−0.6	−2.2	−5.9	−7.7	−5.3	−7.9	−10.9	−10.7	17.2	−3.5	−5.0	−35.1
1975	16.6	4.6	3.6	3.8	5.8	4.7	−4.4	−5.0	−5.9	3.6	2.4	−1.5	29.8
1976	12.1	3.7	0.4	−0.6	−2.3	2.6	1.1	−1.7	1.7	−1.0	0.9	7.4	26.1
1977	−2.4	−1.0	−0.5	1.4	0.1	4.3	0.9	−0.5	0.7	−3.3	5.8	1.8	7.3
1978	−4.0	0.6	4.7	8.5	4.4	0.05	5.0	6.9	−1.6	−16.4	3.2	2.9	12.3
1979	6.6	−2.6	7.5	1.6	−1.8	5.1	2.3	6.4	−0.3	−9.6	6.4	4.8	28.1
1980	7.0	−2.3	−17.1	6.9	7.5	4.9	8.9	5.7	3.4	2.7	8.0	−2.8	33.9
1981	−2.2	0.1	6.1	3.1	3.1	−3.5	−1.9	−7.5	−8.0	8.4	3.1	−2.7	−3.2
1982	−3.8	−4.8	−2.1	5.2	−3.3	−4.1	−2.3	6.2	5.6	13.3	9.3	0.04	18.7
1983	6.9	5.0	3.9	8.2	5.3	3.2	−4.6	−3.8	1.4	−7.4	4.1	−2.5	19.9
1984	−3.7	−5.9	−0.7	−1.3	−5.9	2.9	−4.2	10.9	−1.8	−1.2	−1.8	2.0	−11.2
1985	12.7	2.0	−1.7	0.5	3.6	1.9	1.7	−1.2	−5.8	4.4	7.3	3.5	31.4
1986	3.3	7.1	4.2	2.3	4.4	1.3	−8.4	3.1	−8.4	2.9	−0.3	−2.8	7.5
1987	12.2	8.4	1.2	−2.8	−0.3	2.0	2.4	4.6	−2.3	−27.2	−5.6	8.3	−5.4
1988	4.3	6.5	2.1	1.2	−2.3	6.6	−1.9	−2.8	3.0	−1.4	−2.9	2.7	15.4
1989	5.2	−0.4	1.8	5.1	4.4	−2.4	4.3	3.4	0.8	−3.7	0.1	−0.3	19.3
1990	−8.6	2.4	2.3	−3.6	9.3	0.7	−5.2	−13.0	−9.6	−4.3	8.9	4.1	−17.8
1991	10.8	9.4	6.5	0.5	4.4	−6.0	5.5	4.7	0.2	3.1	−3.5	11.9	56.8
1992	5.8	2.1	−4.7	−4.2	1.1	−3.7	3.1	−3.0	3.6	3.8	7.9	3.7	15.5
1993	2.9	−3.7	2.9	−4.2	5.9	0.5	0.1	5.4	2.7	2.2	−3.2	3.0	14.7
1994	3.0	−1.0	−6.2	−1.3	0.2	−4.0	2.3	6.0	−0.2	1.7	−3.5	0.2	−3.2
1995	0.4	5.1	3.0	3.3	2.4	8.0	7.3	1.9	2.3	−0.7	2.2	−0.7	39.9
1996	0.7	3.8	0.1	8.1	4.4	−4.7	−8.8	5.6	7.5	−0.4	5.8	−0.1	22.7
1997	6.9	−5.1	−6.7	3.2	11.1	3.0	10.5	−0.4	6.2	−5.5	0.4	−1.9	21.6
1998	3.1	9.3	3.7	1.8	−4.8	6.5	−1.2	−19.9	13.0	4.6	10.1	12.5	39.6
1999	14.3	−8.7	7.6	3.3	−2.8	8.7	−1.8	3.8	0.2	8.0	12.5	22.0	85.6
2000	−3.2	19.2	−2.6	−15.6	−11.9	16.6	−5.0	11.7	−12.7	−8.3	−22.9	−4.9	−39.3
2001	12.2	−22.4	−14.5	15.0	−0.3	2.4	−6.2	−10.9	−17.0	12.8	14.2	1.0	−21.1
2002	−0.8	−10.5	6.6	−8.5	−4.3	−9.4	−9.2	−1.0	−10.9	13.5	11.2	−9.7	−31.5
2003	−1.1	1.3	0.3	9.2	9.0	1.7	6.9	4.3	−1.3	8.1	1.5	2.2	50.0
2004	3.1	−1.8	−1.8	−3.7	3.5	3.1	−7.8	−2.6	3.2	4.1	6.2	3.7	8.6
2005	−5.2	−0.5	−2.6	−3.9	7.6	−0.5	6.2	−1.5	−0.02	−1.5	5.3	−1.2	1.4
2006	4.6	−1.1	2.6	−0.7	−6.2	−0.3	−3.7	4.4	3.4	4.8	2.7	−0.7	9.5
2007	2.0	−1.9	0.2	4.3	3.1	−0.05	−2.2	2.0	4.0	5.8	−6.9	−0.3	9.8
2008	−9.9	−5.0	0.3	5.9	4.6	−9.1	1.4	1.8	−11.6	−17.7	−10.8	2.7	−40.5
2009	−6.4	−6.7	10.9	12.3	3.3	3.4	7.8	1.5	5.6	−3.6	4.9	5.8	43.9
2010	−5.4	4.2	7.1	2.6	−8.3	−6.5	6.9	−6.2	12.0	5.9	−0.4	6.2	16.9
2011	1.8	3.0	−0.04	3.3	−1.3	−2.2	−0.6	−6.4	−6.4	11.1	−2.4	−0.6	−1.8
2012	8.0	5.4	4.2	−1.5	−7.2	3.8	0.2	4.3	1.6	−4.5	1.1	0.3	15.9
2013	4.1	0.6	3.4	1.9	3.8	−1.5	6.6	−1.0	5.1	3.9	3.6	2.9	38.3
2014	−1.7	5.0	−2.5	−2.0	3.1	3.9	−0.9	4.8	−1.9	3.1	3.5	−1.2	13.4
2015	−2.1	7.1	−1.3	0.8	2.6	−1.6	2.8	−6.9	−3.3	9.4	1.1	−2.0	5.7
2016	−7.9	−1.2	6.8	−1.9	3.6	−2.1	6.6	1.0	1.9	−2.3	2.6	1.1	7.5
2017	4.3	3.8	1.5	2.3	2.5	−0.9	3.4	1.3	1.0	3.6	2.2	0.4	28.2
2018	7.4	−1.9	−2.9	0.04	5.3	0.9	2.2	5.7	−0.8	−9.2	0.3	−9.5	−3.9
2019	9.7	3.4	2.6	4.7	−7.9	7.4	2.1	−2.6	0.5	3.7	4.5	3.5	35.2
2020	2.0	−6.4	−10.1	15.4	6.8								
TOTALS	139.0	29.5	32.3	84.3	50.1	38.5	23.8	9.8	−23.6	32.5	81.5	79.2	
AVG.	2.8	0.6	0.6	1.7	1.0	0.8	0.5	0.2	−0.5	0.7	1.7	1.6	
# Up	33	27	31	33	31	27	27	27	27	27	34	29	
# Down	17	23	19	17	19	22	22	22	22	22	15	20	

Based on NASDAQ composite; prior to February 5, 1971, based on National Quotation Bureau indices.

NASDAQ COMPOSITE MONTHLY CLOSING PRICES SINCE 1971

	Jan	Feb	Mar	Apr	May	Jun	Jul	Aug	Sep	Oct	Nov	Dec
1971	98.77	101.34	105.97	112.30	108.25	107.80	105.27	108.42	109.03	105.10	103.97	114.12
1972	118.87	125.38	128.14	131.33	132.53	130.08	127.75	129.95	129.61	130.24	132.96	133.73
1973	128.40	120.41	117.46	107.85	102.64	100.98	108.64	104.87	111.20	110.17	93.51	92.19
1974	94.93	94.35	92.27	86.86	80.20	75.96	69.99	62.37	55.67	65.23	62.95	59.82
1975	69.78	73.00	75.66	78.54	83.10	87.02	83.19	79.01	74.33	76.99	78.80	77.62
1976	87.05	90.26	90.62	90.08	88.04	90.32	91.29	89.70	91.26	90.35	91.12	97.88
1977	95.54	94.57	94.13	95.48	95.59	99.73	100.65	100.10	100.85	97.52	103.15	105.05
1978	100.84	101.47	106.20	115.18	120.24	120.30	126.32	135.01	132.89	111.12	114.69	117.98
1979	125.82	122.56	131.76	133.82	131.42	138.13	141.33	150.44	149.98	135.53	144.26	151.14
1980	161.75	158.03	131.00	139.99	150.45	157.78	171.81	181.52	187.76	192.78	208.15	202.34
1981	197.81	198.01	210.18	216.74	223.47	215.75	211.63	195.75	180.03	195.24	201.37	195.84
1982	188.39	179.43	175.65	184.70	178.54	171.30	167.35	177.71	187.65	212.63	232.31	232.41
1983	248.35	260.67	270.80	293.06	308.73	318.70	303.96	292.42	296.65	274.55	285.67	278.60
1984	268.43	252.57	250.78	247.44	232.82	239.65	229.70	254.64	249.94	247.03	242.53	247.35
1985	278.70	284.17	279.20	280.56	290.80	296.20	301.29	297.71	280.33	292.54	313.95	324.93
1986	335.77	359.53	374.72	383.24	400.16	405.51	371.37	382.86	350.67	360.77	359.57	349.33
1987	392.06	424.97	430.05	417.81	416.54	424.67	434.93	454.97	444.29	323.30	305.16	330.47
1988	344.66	366.95	374.64	379.23	370.34	394.66	387.33	376.55	387.71	382.46	371.45	381.38
1989	401.30	399.71	406.73	427.55	446.17	435.29	453.84	469.33	472.92	455.63	456.09	454.82
1990	415.81	425.83	435.54	420.07	458.97	462.29	438.24	381.21	344.51	329.84	359.06	373.84
1991	414.20	453.05	482.30	484.72	506.11	475.92	502.04	525.68	526.88	542.98	523.90	586.34
1992	620.21	633.47	603.77	578.68	585.31	563.60	580.83	563.12	583.27	605.17	652.73	676.95
1993	696.34	670.77	690.13	661.42	700.53	703.95	704.70	742.84	762.78	779.26	754.39	776.80
1994	800.47	792.50	743.46	733.84	735.19	705.96	722.16	765.62	764.29	777.49	750.32	751.96
1995	755.20	793.73	817.21	843.98	864.58	933.45	1001.21	1020.11	1043.54	1036.06	1059.20	1052.13
1996	1059.79	1100.05	1101.40	1190.52	1243.43	1185.02	1080.59	1141.50	1226.92	1221.51	1292.61	1291.03
1997	1379.85	1309.00	1221.70	1260.76	1400.32	1442.07	1593.81	1587.32	1685.69	1593.61	1600.55	1570.35
1998	1619.36	1770.51	1835.68	1868.41	1778.87	1894.74	1872.39	1499.25	1693.84	1771.39	1949.54	2192.69
1999	2505.89	2288.03	2461.40	2542.85	2470.52	2686.12	2638.49	2739.35	2746.16	2966.43	3336.16	4069.31
2000	3940.35	4696.69	4572.83	3860.66	3400.91	3966.11	3766.99	4206.35	3672.82	3369.63	2597.93	2470.52
2001	2772.73	2151.83	1840.26	2116.24	2110.49	2160.54	2027.13	1805.43	1498.80	1690.20	1930.58	1950.40
2002	1934.03	1731.49	1845.35	1688.23	1615.73	1463.21	1328.26	1314.85	1172.06	1329.75	1478.78	1335.51
2003	1320.91	1337.52	1341.17	1464.31	1595.91	1622.80	1735.02	1810.45	1786.94	1932.21	1960.26	2003.37
2004	2066.15	2029.82	1994.22	1920.15	1986.74	2047.79	1887.36	1838.10	1896.84	1974.99	2096.81	2175.44
2005	2062.41	2051.72	1999.23	1921.65	2068.22	2056.96	2184.83	2152.09	2151.69	2120.30	2232.82	2205.32
2006	2305.82	2281.39	2339.79	2322.57	2178.88	2172.09	2091.47	2183.75	2258.43	2366.71	2431.77	2415.29
2007	2463.93	2416.15	2421.64	2525.09	2604.52	2603.23	2545.57	2596.36	2701.50	2859.12	2660.96	2652.28
2008	2389.86	2271.48	2279.10	2412.80	2522.66	2292.98	2325.55	2367.52	2091.88	1720.95	1535.57	1577.03
2009	1476.42	1377.84	1528.59	1717.30	1774.33	1835.04	1978.50	2009.06	2122.42	2045.11	2144.60	2269.15
2010	2147.35	2238.26	2397.96	2461.19	2257.04	2109.24	2254.70	2114.03	2368.62	2507.41	2498.23	2652.87
2011	2700.08	2782.27	2781.07	2873.54	2835.30	2773.52	2756.38	2579.46	2415.40	2684.41	2620.34	2605.15
2012	2813.84	2966.89	3091.57	3046.36	2827.34	2935.05	2939.52	3066.96	3116.23	2977.23	3010.24	3019.51
2013	3142.13	3160.19	3267.52	3328.79	3455.91	3403.25	3626.37	3589.87	3771.48	3919.71	4059.89	4176.59
2014	4103.88	4308.12	4198.99	4114.56	4242.62	4408.18	4369.77	4580.27	4493.39	4630.74	4791.63	4736.05
2015	4635.24	4963.53	4900.88	4941.42	5070.03	4986.87	5128.28	4776.51	4620.16	5053.75	5108.67	5007.41
2016	4613.95	4557.95	4869.85	4775.36	4948.05	4842.67	5162.13	5213.22	5312.00	5189.13	5323.68	5383.12
2017	5614.79	5825.44	5911.74	6047.61	6198.52	6140.42	6348.12	6428.66	6495.96	6727.67	6873.97	6903.39
2018	7411.48	7273.01	7063.44	7066.27	7442.12	7510.30	7671.79	8109.54	8046.35	7305.90	7330.54	6635.28
2019	7281.74	7532.53	7729.32	8095.39	7453.15	8006.24	8175.42	7962.88	7999.34	8292.36	8665.47	8972.60
2020	9150.94	8567.37	7700.10	8889.55	9489.87							

Based on NASDAQ composite; prior to February 5, 1971, based on National Quotation Bureau indices.

159

RUSSELL 1000 INDEX MONTHLY PERCENT CHANGES SINCE 1979

	Jan	Feb	Mar	Apr	May	Jun	Jul	Aug	Sep	Oct	Nov	Dec	Year's Change
1979	4.2	−3.5	6.0	0.3	−2.2	4.3	1.1	5.6	0.02	−7.1	5.1	2.1	16.1
1980	5.9	−0.5	−11.5	4.6	5.0	3.2	6.4	1.1	2.6	1.8	10.1	−3.9	25.6
1981	−4.6	1.0	3.8	−1.9	0.2	−1.2	−0.1	−6.2	−6.4	5.4	4.0	−3.3	−9.7
1982	−2.7	−5.9	−1.3	3.9	−3.6	−2.6	−2.3	11.3	1.2	11.3	4.0	1.3	13.7
1983	3.2	2.1	3.2	7.1	−0.2	3.7	−3.2	0.5	1.3	−2.4	2.0	−1.2	17.0
1984	−1.9	−4.4	1.1	0.3	−5.9	2.1	−1.8	10.8	−0.2	−0.1	−1.4	2.2	−0.1
1985	7.8	1.1	−0.4	−0.3	5.4	1.6	−0.8	−1.0	−3.9	4.5	6.5	4.1	26.7
1986	0.9	7.2	5.1	−1.3	5.0	1.4	−5.9	6.8	−8.5	5.1	1.4	−3.0	13.6
1987	12.7	4.0	1.9	−1.8	0.4	4.5	4.2	3.8	−2.4	−21.9	−8.0	7.2	0.02
1988	4.3	4.4	−2.9	0.7	0.2	4.8	−0.9	−3.3	3.9	2.0	−2.0	1.7	13.1
1989	6.8	−2.5	2.0	4.9	3.8	−0.8	8.2	1.7	−0.5	−2.8	1.5	1.8	25.9
1990	−7.4	1.2	2.2	−2.8	8.9	−0.7	−1.1	−9.6	−5.3	−0.8	6.4	2.7	−7.5
1991	4.5	6.9	2.5	−0.1	3.8	−4.7	4.6	2.2	−1.5	1.4	−4.1	11.2	28.8
1992	−1.4	0.9	−2.4	2.3	0.3	−1.9	4.1	−2.5	1.0	0.7	3.5	1.4	5.9
1993	0.7	0.6	2.2	−2.8	2.4	0.4	−0.4	3.5	−0.5	1.2	−1.7	1.6	7.3
1994	2.9	−2.9	−4.5	1.1	1.0	−2.9	3.1	3.9	−2.6	1.7	−3.9	1.2	−2.4
1995	2.4	3.8	2.3	2.5	3.5	2.4	3.7	0.5	3.9	−0.6	4.2	1.4	34.4
1996	3.1	1.1	0.7	1.4	2.1	−0.1	−4.9	2.5	5.5	2.1	7.1	−1.8	19.7
1997	5.8	0.2	−4.6	5.3	6.2	4.0	8.0	−4.9	5.4	−3.4	4.2	1.9	30.5
1998	0.6	7.0	4.9	0.9	−2.3	3.6	−1.3	−15.1	6.5	7.8	6.1	6.2	25.1
1999	3.5	−3.3	3.7	4.2	−2.3	5.1	−3.2	−1.0	−2.8	6.5	2.5	6.0	19.5
2000	−4.2	−0.4	8.9	−3.3	−2.7	2.5	−1.8	7.4	−4.8	−1.2	−9.3	1.1	−8.8
2001	3.2	−9.5	−6.7	8.0	0.5	−2.4	−1.4	−6.2	−8.6	2.0	7.5	0.9	−13.6
2002	−1.4	−2.1	4.0	−5.8	−1.0	−7.5	−7.5	0.3	−10.9	8.1	5.7	−5.8	−22.9
2003	−2.5	−1.7	0.9	7.9	5.5	1.2	1.8	1.9	−1.2	5.7	1.0	4.6	27.5
2004	1.8	1.2	−1.5	−1.9	1.3	1.7	−3.6	0.3	1.1	1.5	4.1	3.5	9.5
2005	−2.6	2.0	−1.7	−2.0	3.4	0.3	3.8	−1.1	0.8	−1.9	3.5	0.01	4.4
2006	2.7	0.01	1.3	1.1	−3.2	0.003	0.1	2.2	2.3	3.3	1.9	1.1	13.3
2007	1.8	−1.9	0.9	4.1	3.4	−2.0	−3.2	1.2	3.7	1.6	−4.5	−0.8	3.9
2008	−6.1	−3.3	−0.8	5.0	1.6	−8.5	−1.3	1.2	−9.7	−17.6	−7.9	1.3	−39.0
2009	−8.3	−10.7	8.5	10.0	5.3	0.1	7.5	3.4	3.9	−2.3	5.6	2.3	25.5
2010	−3.7	3.1	6.0	1.8	−8.1	−5.7	6.8	−4.7	9.0	3.8	0.1	6.5	13.9
2011	2.3	3.3	0.1	2.9	−1.3	−1.9	−2.3	−6.0	−7.6	11.1	−0.5	0.7	−0.5
2012	4.8	4.1	3.0	−0.7	−6.4	3.7	1.1	2.2	2.4	−1.8	0.5	0.8	13.9
2013	5.3	1.1	3.7	1.7	2.0	−1.5	5.2	−3.0	3.3	4.3	2.6	2.5	30.4
2014	−3.3	4.5	0.5	0.4	2.1	2.1	−1.7	3.9	−1.9	2.3	2.4	−0.4	11.1
2015	−2.8	5.5	−1.4	0.6	1.1	−2.0	1.8	−6.2	−2.9	8.0	0.1	−2.0	−1.1
2016	−5.5	−0.3	6.8	0.4	1.5	0.1	3.7	−0.1	−0.1	−2.1	3.7	1.7	9.7
2017	1.9	3.6	−0.1	0.9	1.0	0.5	1.9	0.1	2.0	2.2	2.8	1.0	19.3
2018	5.4	−3.9	−2.4	0.2	2.3	0.5	3.3	3.2	0.2	−7.2	1.8	−9.3	−6.6
2019	8.2	3.2	1.6	3.9	−6.6	6.9	1.4	−2.0	1.6	2.0	3.6	2.7	28.9
2020	−0.01	−8.3	−13.4	13.1	5.1								
TOTALS	48.3	8.0	32.2	76.8	38.5	14.3	33.1	8.6	−20.7	34.2	72.2	53.2	
AVG.	1.1	0.2	0.8	1.8	0.9	0.3	0.8	0.2	−0.5	0.8	1.8	1.3	
# Up	26	25	27	30	29	25	21	25	21	26	31	31	
# Down	16	17	15	12	13	16	20	16	20	15	10	10	

RUSSELL 1000 INDEX MONTHLY CLOSING PRICES SINCE 1979

	Jan	Feb	Mar	Apr	May	Jun	Jul	Aug	Sep	Oct	Nov	Dec
1979	53.76	51.88	54.97	55.15	53.92	56.25	56.86	60.04	60.05	55.78	58.65	59.87
1980	63.40	63.07	55.79	58.38	61.31	63.27	67.30	68.05	69.84	71.08	78.26	75.20
1981	71.75	72.49	75.21	73.77	73.90	73.01	72.92	68.42	64.06	67.54	70.23	67.93
1982	66.12	62.21	61.43	63.85	61.53	59.92	58.54	65.14	65.89	73.34	76.28	77.24
1983	79.75	81.45	84.06	90.04	89.89	93.18	90.18	90.65	91.85	89.69	91.50	90.38
1984	88.69	84.76	85.73	86.00	80.94	82.61	81.13	89.87	89.67	89.62	88.36	90.31
1985	97.31	98.38	98.03	97.72	103.02	104.65	103.78	102.76	98.75	103.16	109.91	114.39
1986	115.39	123.71	130.07	128.44	134.82	136.75	128.74	137.43	125.70	132.11	133.97	130.00
1987	146.48	152.29	155.20	152.39	152.94	159.84	166.57	172.95	168.83	131.89	121.28	130.02
1988	135.55	141.54	137.45	138.37	138.66	145.31	143.99	139.26	144.68	147.55	144.59	146.99
1989	156.93	152.98	155.99	163.63	169.85	168.49	182.27	185.33	184.40	179.17	181.85	185.11
1990	171.44	173.43	177.28	172.32	187.66	186.29	184.32	166.69	157.83	156.62	166.69	171.22
1991	179.00	191.34	196.15	195.94	203.32	193.78	202.67	207.18	204.02	206.96	198.46	220.61
1992	217.52	219.50	214.29	219.13	219.71	215.60	224.37	218.86	221.15	222.65	230.44	233.59
1993	235.25	236.67	241.80	235.13	240.80	241.78	240.78	249.20	247.95	250.97	246.70	250.71
1994	258.08	250.52	239.19	241.71	244.13	237.11	244.44	254.04	247.49	251.62	241.82	244.65
1995	250.52	260.08	266.11	272.81	282.48	289.29	299.98	301.40	313.28	311.37	324.36	328.89
1996	338.97	342.56	345.01	349.84	357.35	357.10	339.44	347.79	366.77	374.38	401.05	393.75
1997	416.77	417.46	398.19	419.15	445.06	462.95	499.89	475.33	500.78	483.86	504.25	513.79
1998	517.02	553.14	580.31	585.46	572.16	592.57	584.97	496.66	529.11	570.63	605.31	642.87
1999	665.64	643.67	667.49	695.25	679.10	713.61	690.51	683.27	663.83	707.19	724.66	767.97
2000	736.08	733.04	797.99	771.58	750.98	769.68	755.57	811.17	772.60	763.06	692.40	700.09
2001	722.55	654.25	610.36	658.90	662.39	646.64	637.43	597.67	546.46	557.29	599.32	604.94
2002	596.66	583.88	607.35	572.04	566.18	523.72	484.39	486.08	433.22	468.51	495.00	466.18
2003	454.30	446.37	450.35	486.09	512.92	518.94	528.53	538.40	532.15	562.51	568.32	594.56
2004	605.21	612.58	603.42	591.83	599.40	609.31	587.21	589.09	595.66	604.51	629.26	650.99
2005	633.99	646.93	635.78	623.32	644.28	645.92	670.26	663.13	668.53	656.09	679.35	679.42
2006	697.79	697.83	706.74	714.37	691.78	691.80	692.59	707.55	723.48	747.30	761.43	770.08
2007	784.11	768.92	775.97	807.82	835.14	818.17	792.11	801.22	830.59	844.20	806.44	799.82
2008	750.97	726.42	720.32	756.03	768.28	703.22	694.07	702.17	634.08	522.47	481.43	487.77
2009	447.32	399.61	433.67	476.84	501.95	502.27	539.88	558.21	579.97	566.50	598.41	612.01
2010	589.41	607.45	643.79	655.06	601.79	567.37	606.09	577.68	629.78	653.57	654.24	696.90
2011	712.97	736.24	737.07	758.45	748.75	734.48	717.77	674.79	623.45	692.41	688.77	693.36
2012	726.33	756.42	778.92	773.50	724.12	750.61	758.60	775.07	793.74	779.35	783.37	789.90
2013	831.74	840.97	872.11	886.89	904.44	890.67	937.16	909.28	939.50	979.68	1004.97	1030.36
2014	996.48	1041.36	1046.42	1050.20	1071.96	1094.59	1075.60	1117.71	1096.43	1121.98	1148.90	1144.37
2015	1111.85	1173.46	1156.95	1164.03	1176.67	1152.64	1173.55	1100.51	1068.46	1153.55	1154.66	1131.88
2016	1069.78	1066.58	1138.84	1143.76	1160.95	1161.57	1204.43	1203.05	1202.25	1177.22	1220.68	1241.66
2017	1265.35	1311.34	1310.06	1322.44	1336.18	1343.52	1368.57	1369.61	1396.90	1427.43	1467.42	1481.81
2018	1561.66	1501.23	1464.87	1468.28	1502.31	1509.96	1560.36	1610.70	1614.54	1498.65	1525.56	1384.26
2019	1498.36	1545.73	1570.23	1631.87	1524.42	1629.02	1652.40	1618.61	1644.18	1677.08	1736.85	1784.21
2020	1784.03	1635.21	1416.49	1601.82	1682.75							

RUSSELL 2000 INDEX MONTHLY PERCENT CHANGES SINCE 1979

	Jan	Feb	Mar	Apr	May	Jun	Jul	Aug	Sep	Oct	Nov	Dec	Year's Change
1979	9.0	−3.2	9.7	2.3	−1.8	5.3	2.9	7.8	−0.7	−11.3	8.1	6.6	38.0
1980	8.2	−2.1	−18.5	6.0	8.0	4.0	11.0	6.5	2.9	3.9	7.0	−3.7	33.8
1981	−0.6	0.3	7.7	2.5	3.0	−2.5	−2.6	−8.0	−8.6	8.2	2.8	−2.0	−1.5
1982	−3.7	−5.3	−1.5	5.1	−3.2	−4.0	−1.7	7.5	3.6	14.1	8.8	1.1	20.7
1983	7.5	6.0	2.5	7.2	7.0	4.4	−3.0	−4.0	1.6	−7.0	5.0	−2.1	26.3
1984	−1.8	−5.9	0.4	−0.7	−5.4	2.6	−5.0	11.5	−1.0	−2.0	−2.9	1.4	−9.6
1985	13.1	2.4	−2.2	−1.4	3.4	1.0	2.7	−1.2	−6.2	3.6	6.8	4.2	28.0
1986	1.5	7.0	4.7	1.4	3.3	−0.2	−9.5	3.0	−6.3	3.9	−0.5	−3.1	4.0
1987	11.5	8.2	2.4	−3.0	−0.5	2.3	2.8	2.9	−2.0	−30.8	−5.5	7.8	−10.8
1988	4.0	8.7	4.4	2.0	−2.5	7.0	−0.9	−2.8	2.3	−1.2	−3.6	3.8	22.4
1989	4.4	0.5	2.2	4.3	4.2	−2.4	4.2	2.1	0.01	−6.0	0.4	0.1	14.2
1990	−8.9	2.9	3.7	−3.4	6.8	0.1	−4.5	−13.6	−9.2	−6.2	7.3	3.7	−21.5
1991	9.1	11.0	6.9	−0.2	4.5	−6.0	3.1	3.7	0.6	2.7	−4.7	7.7	43.7
1992	8.0	2.9	−3.5	−3.7	1.2	−5.0	3.2	−3.1	2.2	3.1	7.5	3.4	16.4
1993	3.2	−2.5	3.1	−2.8	4.3	0.5	1.3	4.1	2.7	2.5	−3.4	3.3	17.0
1994	3.1	−0.4	−5.4	0.6	−1.3	−3.6	1.6	5.4	−0.5	−0.4	−4.2	2.5	−3.2
1995	−1.4	3.9	1.6	2.1	1.5	5.0	5.7	1.9	1.7	−4.6	4.2	2.4	26.2
1996	−0.2	3.0	1.8	5.3	3.9	−4.2	−8.8	5.7	3.7	−1.7	4.0	2.4	14.8
1997	1.9	−2.5	−4.9	0.1	11.0	4.1	4.6	2.2	7.2	−4.5	−0.8	1.7	20.5
1998	−1.6	7.4	4.1	0.5	−5.4	0.2	−8.2	−19.5	7.6	4.0	5.2	6.1	−3.4
1999	1.2	−8.2	1.4	8.8	1.4	4.3	−2.8	−3.8	−0.1	0.3	5.9	11.2	19.6
2000	−1.7	16.4	−6.7	−6.1	−5.9	8.6	−3.2	7.4	−3.1	−4.5	−10.4	8.4	−4.2
2001	5.1	−6.7	−5.0	7.7	2.3	3.3	−5.4	−3.3	−13.6	5.8	7.6	6.0	1.0
2002	−1.1	−2.8	7.9	0.8	−4.5	−5.1	−15.2	−0.4	−7.3	3.1	8.8	−5.7	−21.6
2003	−2.9	−3.1	1.1	9.4	10.6	1.7	6.2	4.5	−2.0	8.3	3.5	1.9	45.4
2004	4.3	0.8	0.8	−5.2	1.5	4.1	−6.8	−0.6	4.6	1.9	8.6	2.8	17.0
2005	−4.2	1.6	−3.0	−5.8	6.4	3.7	6.3	−1.9	0.2	−3.2	4.7	−0.6	3.3
2006	8.9	−0.3	4.7	−0.1	−5.7	0.5	−3.3	2.9	0.7	5.7	2.5	0.2	17.0
2007	1.6	−0.9	0.9	1.7	4.0	−1.6	−6.9	2.2	1.6	2.8	−7.3	−0.2	−2.7
2008	−6.9	−3.8	0.3	4.1	4.5	−7.8	3.6	3.5	−8.1	−20.9	−12.0	5.6	−34.8
2009	−11.2	−12.3	8.7	15.3	2.9	1.3	9.5	2.8	5.6	−6.9	3.0	7.9	25.2
2010	−3.7	4.4	8.0	5.6	−7.7	−7.9	6.8	−7.5	12.3	4.0	3.4	7.8	25.3
2011	−0.3	5.4	2.4	2.6	−2.0	−2.5	−3.7	−8.8	−11.4	15.0	−0.5	0.5	−5.5
2012	7.0	2.3	2.4	−1.6	−6.7	4.8	−1.4	3.2	3.1	−2.2	0.4	3.3	14.6
2013	6.2	1.0	4.4	−0.4	3.9	−0.7	6.9	−3.3	6.2	2.5	3.9	1.8	37.0
2014	−2.8	4.6	−0.8	−3.9	0.7	5.2	−6.1	4.8	−6.2	6.5	−0.02	2.7	3.5
2015	−3.3	5.8	1.6	−2.6	2.2	0.6	−1.2	−6.4	−5.1	5.6	3.1	−5.2	−5.7
2016	−8.8	−0.1	7.8	1.5	2.1	−0.2	5.9	1.6	0.9	−4.8	11.0	2.6	19.5
2017	0.3	1.8	−0.1	1.0	−2.2	3.3	0.7	−1.4	6.1	0.8	2.8	−0.6	13.1
2018	2.6	−4.0	1.1	0.8	5.9	0.6	1.7	4.2	−2.5	−10.9	1.4	−12.0	−12.2
2019	11.2	5.1	−2.3	3.3	−7.9	6.9	0.5	−5.1	1.9	2.6	4.0	2.7	23.7
2020	−3.3	−8.5	−21.9	13.7	6.4								
TOTALS	64.5	40.8	32.9	74.8	54.2	31.7	−9.0	6.7	−14.6	−18.2	85.9	88.4	
AVG.	1.5	1.0	0.8	1.8	1.3	0.8	−0.2	0.2	−0.4	−0.4	2.1	2.2	
# Up	23	24	29	27	27	26	21	23	23	23	28	31	
# Down	19	18	13	15	15	15	20	18	18	18	13	10	

	Jan	Feb	Mar	Apr	May	Jun	Jul	Aug	Sep	Oct	Nov	Dec
1979	44.18	42.78	46.94	48.00	47.13	49.62	51.08	55.05	54.68	48.51	52.43	55.91
1980	60.50	59.22	48.27	51.18	55.26	57.47	63.81	67.97	69.94	72.64	77.70	74.80
1981	74.33	74.52	80.25	82.25	84.72	82.56	80.41	73.94	67.55	73.06	75.14	73.67
1982	70.96	67.21	66.21	69.59	67.39	64.67	63.59	68.38	70.84	80.86	87.96	88.90
1983	95.53	101.23	103.77	111.20	118.94	124.17	120.43	115.60	117.43	109.17	114.66	112.27
1984	110.21	103.72	104.10	103.34	97.75	100.30	95.25	106.21	105.17	103.07	100.11	101.49
1985	114.77	117.54	114.92	113.35	117.26	118.38	121.56	120.10	112.65	116.73	124.62	129.87
1986	131.78	141.00	147.63	149.66	154.61	154.23	139.65	143.83	134.73	139.95	139.26	135.00
1987	150.48	162.84	166.79	161.82	161.02	164.75	169.42	174.25	170.81	118.26	111.70	120.42
1988	125.24	136.10	142.15	145.01	141.37	151.30	149.89	145.74	149.08	147.25	142.01	147.37
1989	153.84	154.56	157.89	164.68	171.53	167.42	174.50	178.20	178.21	167.47	168.17	168.30
1990	153.27	157.72	163.63	158.09	168.91	169.04	161.51	139.52	126.70	118.83	127.50	132.16
1991	144.17	160.00	171.01	170.61	178.34	167.61	172.76	179.11	180.16	185.00	176.37	189.94
1992	205.16	211.15	203.69	196.25	198.52	188.64	194.74	188.79	192.92	198.90	213.81	221.01
1993	228.10	222.41	229.21	222.68	232.19	233.35	236.46	246.19	252.95	259.18	250.41	258.59
1994	266.52	265.53	251.06	252.55	249.28	240.29	244.06	257.32	256.12	255.02	244.25	250.36
1995	246.85	256.57	260.77	266.17	270.25	283.63	299.72	305.31	310.38	296.25	308.58	315.97
1996	315.38	324.93	330.77	348.28	361.85	346.61	316.00	333.88	346.39	340.57	354.11	362.61
1997	369.45	360.05	342.56	343.00	380.76	396.37	414.48	423.43	453.82	433.26	429.92	437.02
1998	430.05	461.83	480.68	482.89	456.62	457.39	419.75	337.95	363.59	378.16	397.75	421.96
1999	427.22	392.26	397.63	432.81	438.68	457.68	444.77	427.83	427.30	428.64	454.08	504.75
2000	496.23	577.71	539.09	506.25	476.18	517.23	500.64	537.89	521.37	497.68	445.94	483.53
2001	508.34	474.37	450.53	485.32	496.50	512.64	484.78	468.56	404.87	428.17	460.78	488.50
2002	483.10	469.36	506.46	510.67	487.47	462.64	392.42	390.96	362.27	373.50	406.35	383.09
2003	372.17	360.52	364.54	398.68	441.00	448.37	476.02	497.42	487.68	528.22	546.51	556.91
2004	580.76	585.56	590.31	559.80	568.28	591.52	551.29	547.93	572.94	583.79	633.77	651.57
2005	624.02	634.06	615.07	579.38	616.71	639.66	679.75	666.51	667.80	646.61	677.29	673.22
2006	733.20	730.64	765.14	764.54	721.01	724.67	700.56	720.53	725.59	766.84	786.12	787.66
2007	800.34	793.30	800.71	814.57	847.19	833.69	776.13	792.86	805.45	828.02	767.77	766.03
2008	713.30	686.18	687.97	716.18	748.28	689.66	714.52	739.50	679.58	537.52	473.14	499.45
2009	443.53	389.02	422.75	487.56	501.58	508.28	556.71	572.07	604.28	562.77	579.73	625.39
2010	602.04	628.56	678.64	716.60	661.61	609.49	650.89	602.06	676.14	703.35	727.01	783.65
2011	781.25	823.45	843.55	865.29	848.30	827.43	797.03	726.81	644.16	741.06	737.42	740.92
2012	792.82	810.94	830.30	816.88	761.82	798.49	786.94	812.09	837.45	818.73	821.92	849.35
2013	902.09	911.11	951.54	947.46	984.14	977.48	1045.26	1010.90	1073.79	1100.15	1142.89	1163.64
2014	1130.88	1183.03	1173.04	1126.86	1134.50	1192.96	1120.07	1174.35	1101.68	1173.51	1173.23	1204.70
2015	1165.39	1233.37	1252.77	1220.13	1246.53	1253.95	1238.68	1159.45	1100.69	1161.86	1198.11	1135.89
2016	1035.38	1033.90	1114.03	1130.84	1154.79	1151.92	1219.94	1239.91	1251.65	1191.39	1322.34	1357.13
2017	1361.82	1386.68	1385.92	1400.43	1370.21	1415.36	1425.14	1405.28	1490.86	1502.77	1544.14	1535.51
2018	1574.98	1512.45	1529.43	1541.88	1633.61	1643.07	1670.80	1740.75	1696.57	1511.41	1533.27	1348.56
2019	1499.42	1575.55	1539.74	1591.21	1465.49	1566.57	1574.61	1494.84	1523.37	1562.45	1624.50	1668.47
2020	1614.06	1476.43	1153.10	1310.66	1394.04							

10 BEST DAYS BY PERCENT AND POINT

	BY PERCENT CHANGE				BY POINT CHANGE		
DAY	CLOSE	PNT CHANGE	% CHANGE	DAY	CLOSE	PNT CHANGE	% CHANGE
			DJIA 1901 to 1949				
3/15/33	62.10	8.26	15.3	10/30/29	258.47	28.40	12.3
10/6/31	99.34	12.86	14.9	11/14/29	217.28	18.59	9.4
10/30/29	258.47	28.40	12.3	10/5/29	341.36	16.19	5.0
9/21/32	75.16	7.67	11.4	10/31/29	273.51	15.04	5.8
8/3/32	58.22	5.06	9.5	10/6/31	99.34	12.86	14.9
2/11/32	78.60	6.80	9.5	11/15/29	228.73	11.45	5.3
11/14/29	217.28	18.59	9.4	6/19/30	228.97	10.13	4.6
12/18/31	80.69	6.90	9.4	9/5/39	148.12	10.03	7.3
2/13/32	85.82	7.22	9.2	11/22/28	290.34	9.81	3.5
5/6/32	59.01	4.91	9.1	10/1/30	214.14	9.24	4.5
			DJIA 1950 to JUNE 12, 2020				
3/24/2020	20704.91	2112.98	11.4	3/24/2020	20704.91	2112.98	11.4
10/13/2008	9387.61	936.42	11.1	3/13/2020	23185.62	1985.00	9.4
10/28/2008	9065.12	889.35	10.9	4/6/2020	22679.99	1627.46	7.7
10/21/1987	2027.85	186.84	10.2	3/26/2020	22552.17	1351.62	6.4
3/13/2020	23185.62	1985.00	9.4	3/2/2020	26703.32	1293.96	5.1
4/6/2020	22679.99	1627.46	7.7	3/4/2020	27090.86	1173.45	4.5
3/23/2009	7775.86	497.48	6.8	3/10/2020	25018.16	1167.14	4.9
11/13/2008	8835.25	552.59	6.7	12/26/2018	22878.45	1086.25	5.0
11/21/2008	8046.42	494.13	6.5	3/17/2020	21237.38	1048.86	5.2
3/26/2020	22552.17	1351.62	6.4	10/13/2008	9387.61	936.42	11.1
			S&P 500 1930 to JUNE 12, 2020				
3/15/1933	6.81	0.97	16.6	3/13/2020	2711.02	230.38	9.3
10/6/1931	9.91	1.09	12.4	3/24/2020	2447.33	209.93	9.4
9/21/1932	8.52	0.90	11.8	4/6/2020	2663.68	175.03	7.0
10/13/2008	1003.35	104.13	11.6	3/26/2020	2630.07	154.51	6.2
10/28/2008	940.51	91.59	10.8	3/17/2020	2529.19	143.06	6.0
2/16/1935	10.00	0.94	10.4	3/2/2020	3090.23	136.01	4.6
8/17/1935	11.70	1.08	10.2	3/10/2020	2882.23	135.67	4.9
3/16/1935	9.05	0.82	10.0	3/4/2020	3130.12	126.75	4.2
9/12/1938	12.06	1.06	9.6	12/26/2018	2467.70	116.60	5.0
9/5/1939	12.64	1.11	9.6	10/13/2008	1003.35	104.13	11.6
			NASDAQ 1971 to JUNE 12, 2020				
1/3/2001	2616.69	324.83	14.2	3/13/2020	7874.88	673.08	9.4
10/13/2008	1844.25	194.74	11.8	3/24/2020	7417.86	557.19	8.1
12/5/2000	2889.80	274.05	10.5	4/6/2020	7913.24	540.16	7.3
10/28/2008	1649.47	143.57	9.5	3/17/2020	7334.78	430.19	6.2
3/13/2020	7874.88	673.08	9.4	3/26/2020	7797.54	413.24	5.6
4/5/2001	1785.00	146.20	8.9	3/10/2020	8344.25	393.57	5.0
3/24/2020	7417.86	557.19	8.1	3/2/2020	8952.17	384.80	4.5
4/18/2001	2079.44	156.22	8.1	12/26/2018	6554.36	361.44	5.8
5/30/2020	3459.48	254.37	7.9	3/4/2020	9018.09	334.00	3.9
10/13/2000	3316.77	242.09	7.9	1/3/2001	2616.69	324.83	14.2
			RUSSELL 1000 1979 to JUNE 12, 2020				
10/13/2008	542.98	56.75	11.7	3/13/2020	1488.04	123.38	9.0
10/28/2008	503.74	47.68	10.5	3/24/2020	1340.32	115.87	9.5
3/24/2020	1340.32	115.87	9.5	4/6/2020	1455.56	96.55	7.1
3/13/2020	1488.04	123.38	9.0	3/26/2020	1442.70	83.87	6.2
10/21/1987	135.85	11.15	8.9	3/17/2020	1381.49	74.98	5.7
4/6/2020	1455.56	96.55	7.1	3/10/2020	1588.36	73.59	4.9
3/23/2009	446.90	29.36	7.0	3/2/2020	1708.13	72.92	4.5
11/13/2008	489.83	31.99	7.0	3/4/2020	1729.80	68.44	4.1
11/24/2008	456.14	28.26	6.6	12/26/2018	1362.48	64.46	5.0
3/10/2009	391.01	23.46	6.4	10/13/2008	542.98	56.75	11.7
			RUSSELL 2000 1979 to JUNE 12, 2020				
3/24/2020	1096.54	94.14	9.4	3/24/2020	1096.54	94.14	9.4
10/13/2008	570.89	48.41	9.3	3/13/2020	1210.13	87.20	7.8
11/13/2008	491.23	38.43	8.5	4/6/2020	1138.78	86.73	8.2
3/23/2009	433.72	33.61	8.4	5/18/2020	1333.69	76.70	6.1
4/6/2020	1138.78	86.73	8.2	3/26/2020	1180.32	69.95	6.3
3/13/2020	1210.13	87.20	7.8	3/17/2020	1106.51	69.09	6.7
10/21/1987	130.65	9.26	7.6	3/19/2020	1058.75	67.59	6.8
10/28/2008	482.55	34.15	7.6	12/26/2018	1329.81	62.89	5.0
11/24/2008	436.80	30.26	7.4	4/29/2020	1360.76	62.68	4.8
3/10/2009	367.75	24.49	7.1	6/5/2020	1507.15	55.09	3.8

10 <u>WORST</u> DAYS BY PERCENT AND POINT

BY PERCENT CHANGE				BY POINT CHANGE			
DAY	CLOSE	PNT CHANGE	% CHANGE	DAY	CLOSE	PNT CHANGE	% CHANGE
DJIA 1901 to 1949							
10/28/1929	260.64	−38.33	−12.8	10/28/1929	260.64	−38.33	−12.8
10/29/1929	230.07	−30.57	−11.7	10/29/1929	230.07	−30.57	−11.7
11/6/1929	232.13	−25.55	−9.9	11/6/1929	232.13	−25.55	−9.9
8/12/1932	63.11	−5.79	−8.4	10/23/1929	305.85	−20.66	−6.3
3/14/1907	55.84	−5.05	−8.3	11/11/1929	220.39	−16.14	−6.8
7/21/1933	88.71	−7.55	−7.8	11/4/1929	257.68	−15.83	−5.8
10/18/1937	125.73	−10.57	−7.8	12/12/1929	243.14	−15.30	−5.9
2/1/1917	88.52	−6.91	−7.2	10/3/1929	329.95	−14.55	−4.2
10/5/1932	66.07	−5.09	−7.2	6/16/1930	230.05	−14.20	−5.8
9/24/1931	107.79	−8.20	−7.1	8/9/1929	337.99	−14.11	−4.0
DJIA 1950 to JUNE 12, 2020							
10/19/1987	1738.74	−508.00	−22.6	3/16/2020	20188.52	−2997.10	−12.9
3/16/2020	20188.52	−2997.10	−12.9	3/12/2020	21200.62	−2352.60	−10.0
3/12/2020	21200.62	−2352.60	−10.0	3/9/2020	23851.02	−2013.76	−7.8
10/26/1987	1793.93	−156.83	−8.0	6/11/2020	25128.17	−1861.82	−6.9
10/15/2008	8577.91	−733.08	−7.9	3/11/2020	23553.22	−1464.94	−5.9
3/9/2020	23851.02	−2013.76	−7.8	3/18/2020	19898.92	−1338.46	−6.3
12/1/2008	8149.09	−679.95	−7.7	2/27/2020	25766.64	−1190.95	−4.4
10/9/2008	8579.19	−678.91	−7.3	2/5/2018	24345.75	−1175.21	−4.6
10/27/1997	7161.15	−554.26	−7.2	2/8/2018	23860.46	−1032.89	−4.2
9/17/2001	8920.70	−684.81	−7.1	2/24/2020	27960.80	−1031.61	−3.6
S&P 500 1930 to JUNE 12, 2020							
10/19/1987	224.84	−57.86	−20.5	3/16/2020	2386.13	−324.89	−12.0
3/16/2020	2386.13	−324.89	−12.0	3/12/2020	2480.64	−260.74	−9.5
3/18/1935	8.14	−0.91	−10.1	3/9/2020	2746.56	−225.81	−7.6
4/16/1935	8.22	−0.91	−10.0	6/11/2020	3002.10	−188.04	−5.9
9/3/1946	15.00	−1.65	−9.9	3/11/2020	2741.38	−140.85	−4.9
3/12/2020	2480.64	−260.74	−9.5	2/27/2020	2978.76	−137.63	−4.4
10/18/1937	10.76	−1.10	−9.3	3/18/2020	2398.10	−131.09	−5.2
10/15/2008	907.84	−90.17	−9.0	4/1/2020	2470.50	−114.09	−4.4
12/1/2008	816.21	−80.03	−8.9	2/5/2018	2648.94	−113.19	−4.1
7/20/1933	10.57	−1.03	−8.9	2/24/2020	3225.89	−111.86	−3.4
NASDAQ 1971 to JUNE 12, 2020							
3/16/2020	6904.59	−970.29	−12.3	3/16/2020	6904.59	−970.29	−12.3
10/19/1987	360.21	−46.12	−11.4	3/12/2020	7201.80	−750.25	−9.4
4/14/2000	3321.29	−355.49	−9.7	3/9/2020	7950.68	−624.94	−7.3
3/12/2020	7201.80	−750.25	−9.4	6/11/2020	9492.73	−527.62	−5.3
9/29/2008	1983.73	−199.61	−9.1	2/27/2020	8566.48	−414.29	−4.6
10/26/1987	298.90	−29.55	−9.0	3/11/2020	7952.05	−392.20	−4.7
10/20/1987	327.79	−32.42	−9.0	4/14/2000	3321.29	−355.49	−9.7
12/1/2008	1398.07	−137.50	−9.0	2/24/2020	9221.28	−355.31	−3.7
8/31/1998	1499.25	−140.43	−8.6	4/3/2000	4223.68	−349.15	−7.6
10/15/2008	1628.33	−150.68	−8.5	3/18/2020	6989.84	−344.94	−4.7
RUSSELL 1000 1979 to JUNE 12, 2020							
10/19/1987	121.04	−28.40	−19.0	3/16/2020	1306.51	−181.53	−12.2
3/16/2020	1306.51	−181.53	−12.2	3/12/2020	1364.66	−144.34	−9.6
3/12/2020	1364.66	−144.34	−9.6	3/9/2020	1514.77	−127.21	−7.8
10/15/2008	489.71	−49.11	−9.1	6/11/2020	1660.70	−104.50	−5.9
12/1/2008	437.75	−43.68	−9.1	3/11/2020	1509.00	−79.36	−5.0
9/29/2008	602.34	−57.35	−8.7	3/18/2020	1304.56	−76.93	−5.6
10/26/1987	119.45	−10.74	−8.3	2/27/2020	1649.14	−75.62	−4.4
3/9/2020	1514.77	−127.21	−7.8	4/1/2020	1352.66	−63.83	−4.5
10/9/2008	492.13	−40.05	−7.5	2/24/2020	1787.99	−61.44	−3.3
8/8/2011	617.28	−45.56	−6.9	2/5/2018	1466.98	−61.29	−4.0
RUSSELL 2000 1979 to JUNE 12, 2020							
3/16/2020	1037.42	−172.71	−14.3	3/16/2020	1037.42	−172.71	−14.3
10/19/1987	133.60	−19.14	−12.5	3/12/2020	1122.93	−141.37	−11.2
12/1/2008	417.07	−56.07	−11.9	3/9/2020	1313.44	−135.78	−9.4
3/12/2020	1122.93	−141.37	−11.2	3/18/2020	991.16	−115.35	−10.4
3/18/2020	991.16	−115.35	−10.4	6/11/2020	1356.22	−111.17	−7.6
10/15/2008	502.11	−52.54	−9.5	3/11/2020	1264.30	−86.60	−6.4
3/9/2020	1313.44	−135.78	−9.4	4/1/2020	1071.99	−81.11	−7.0
10/26/1987	110.33	−11.26	−9.3	12/4/2018	1480.75	−68.21	−4.4
10/20/1987	121.39	−12.21	−9.1	8/8/2011	650.96	−63.67	−8.9
8/8/2011	650.96	−63.67	−8.9	10/24/2018	1468.70	−57.89	−3.8

10 BEST WEEKS BY PERCENT AND POINT

	BY PERCENT CHANGE				BY POINT CHANGE		
WEEK ENDS	CLOSE	PNT CHANGE	% CHANGE	WEEK ENDS	CLOSE	PNT CHANGE	% CHANGE
DJIA 1901 to 1949							
8/6/1932	66.56	12.30	22.7	12/7/1929	263.46	24.51	10.3
6/25/1938	131.94	18.71	16.5	6/25/1938	131.94	18.71	16.5
2/13/1932	85.82	11.37	15.3	6/27/1931	156.93	17.97	12.9
4/22/1933	72.24	9.36	14.9	11/22/1929	245.74	17.01	7.4
10/10/1931	105.61	12.84	13.8	8/17/1929	360.70	15.86	4.6
7/30/1932	54.26	6.42	13.4	12/22/1928	285.94	15.22	5.6
6/27/1931	156.93	17.97	12.9	8/24/1929	375.44	14.74	4.1
9/24/1932	74.83	8.39	12.6	2/21/1929	310.06	14.21	4.8
8/27/1932	75.61	8.43	12.6	5/10/1930	272.01	13.70	5.3
3/18/1933	60.56	6.72	12.5	11/15/1930	186.68	13.54	7.8
DJIA 1950 to JUNE 12, 2020							
3/27/2020	21636.78	2462.80	12.8	4/9/2020	23719.37	2666.84	12.7
4/9/2020	23719.37	2666.84	12.7	3/27/2020	21636.78	2462.80	12.8
10/11/1974	658.17	73.61	12.6	6/5/2020	27110.98	1727.87	6.8
10/31/2008	9325.01	946.06	11.3	11/30/2018	25538.46	1252.51	5.2
8/20/1982	869.29	81.24	10.3	6/7/2019	25983.94	1168.90	4.7
11/28/2008	8829.04	782.62	9.7	2/16/2018	25219.38	1028.48	4.3
3/13/2009	7223.98	597.04	9.0	11/11/2016	18847.66	959.38	5.4
10/8/1982	986.85	79.11	8.7	10/31/2008	9325.01	946.06	11.3
3/21/2003	8521.97	662.26	8.4	5/29/2020	25383.11	917.95	3.8
8/3/1984	1202.08	87.46	7.9	2/7/2020	29102.51	846.48	3.0
S&P 500 1930 to JUNE 12, 2020							
8/6/1932	7.22	1.12	18.4	4/9/2020	2789.82	301.17	12.1
6/25/1938	11.39	1.72	17.8	3/27/2020	2541.47	236.55	10.3
7/30/1932	6.10	0.89	17.1	6/5/2020	3193.93	149.62	4.9
4/22/1933	7.75	1.09	16.4	11/30/2018	2760.16	127.60	4.9
10/11/1974	71.14	8.80	14.1	6/7/2019	2873.34	121.28	4.4
2/13/1932	8.80	1.08	14.0	2/16/2018	2732.22	112.67	4.3
9/24/1932	8.52	1.02	13.6	2/7/2020	3327.71	102.19	3.2
10/10/1931	10.64	1.27	13.6	5/8/2020	2929.80	99.63	3.5
8/27/1932	8.57	1.01	13.4	6/2/2000	1477.26	99.24	7.2
3/18/1933	6.61	0.77	13.2	11/28/2008	896.24	96.21	12.0
NASDAQ 1971 to JUNE 12, 2020							
6/2/2000	3813.38	608.27	19.0	4/9/2020	8153.58	780.50	10.6
4/12/2001	1961.43	241.07	14.0	3/27/2020	7502.38	622.86	9.1
11/28/2008	1535.57	151.22	10.9	6/2/2000	3813.38	608.27	19.0
10/31/2008	1720.95	168.92	10.9	5/8/2020	9121.32	516.37	6.0
3/13/2009	1431.50	137.65	10.6	4/17/2020	8650.14	496.56	6.1
4/9/2020	8153.58	780.50	10.6	11/30/2018	7330.54	391.56	5.6
4/20/2001	2163.41	201.98	10.3	2/7/2020	9520.51	369.57	4.0
12/8/2000	2917.43	272.14	10.3	2/16/2018	7239.47	364.98	5.3
4/20/2000	3643.88	322.59	9.7	2/4/2000	4244.14	357.07	9.2
10/11/1974	60.42	5.26	9.5	3/3/2000	4914.79	324.29	7.1
RUSSELL 1000 1979 to JUNE 12, 2020							
4/9/2020	1530.05	171.04	12.6	4/9/2020	1530.05	171.04	12.6
11/28/2008	481.43	53.55	12.5	3/27/2020	1394.65	133.96	10.6
10/31/2008	522.47	50.94	10.8	6/5/2020	1767.94	85.19	5.1
3/13/2009	411.10	39.88	10.7	11/30/2018	1525.56	69.33	4.8
3/27/2020	1394.65	133.96	10.6	6/7/2019	1591.13	66.71	4.4
8/20/1982	61.51	4.83	8.5	2/16/2018	1512.36	62.68	4.3
6/2/2000	785.02	57.93	8.0	5/8/2020	1616.10	60.32	3.9
9/28/2001	546.46	38.48	7.6	6/2/2000	785.02	57.93	8.0
10/16/1998	546.09	38.45	7.6	2/7/2020	1839.68	55.65	3.1
8/3/1984	87.43	6.13	7.5	5/22/2020	1632.46	55.00	3.5
RUSSELL 2000 1979 to JUNE 12, 2020							
4/9/2020	1246.73	194.68	18.5	4/9/2020	1246.73	194.68	18.5
11/28/2008	473.14	66.60	16.4	11/11/2016	1282.38	118.94	10.2
10/31/2008	537.52	66.40	14.1	3/27/2020	1131.99	118.10	11.7
6/2/2000	513.03	55.66	12.2	6/5/2020	1507.15	113.11	8.1
3/13/2009	393.09	42.04	12.0	5/22/2020	1355.53	98.54	7.8
3/27/2020	1131.99	118.10	11.7	12/9/2016	1388.07	73.82	5.6
12/2/2011	735.02	68.86	10.3	9/13/2019	1578.14	72.97	4.9
11/11/2016	1282.38	118.94	10.2	5/8/2020	1329.64	69.16	5.5
10/14/2011	712.46	56.25	8.6	12/2/2011	735.02	68.86	10.3
6/5/2020	1507.15	113.11	8.1	1/11/2019	1447.38	66.63	4.8

166

10 WORST WEEKS BY PERCENT AND POINT

	BY PERCENT CHANGE				BY POINT CHANGE		
WEEK ENDS	CLOSE	PNT CHANGE	% CHANGE	WEEK ENDS	CLOSE	PNT CHANGE	% CHANGE
DJIA 1901 to 1949							
7/22/1933	88.42	−17.68	−16.7	11/8/1929	236.53	−36.98	−13.5
5/18/1940	122.43	−22.42	−15.5	12/8/1928	257.33	−33.47	−11.5
10/8/1932	61.17	−10.92	−15.2	6/21/1930	215.30	−28.95	−11.9
10/3/1931	92.77	−14.59	−13.6	10/19/1929	323.87	−28.82	−8.2
11/8/1929	236.53	−36.98	−13.5	5/3/1930	258.31	−27.15	−9.5
9/17/1932	66.44	−10.10	−13.2	10/31/1929	273.51	−25.46	−8.5
10/21/1933	83.64	−11.95	−12.5	10/26/1929	298.97	−24.90	−7.7
12/12/1931	78.93	−11.21	−12.4	5/18/1940	122.43	−22.42	−15.5
5/8/1915	62.77	−8.74	−12.2	2/8/1929	301.53	−18.23	−5.7
6/21/1930	215.30	−28.95	−11.9	10/11/1930	193.05	−18.05	−8.6
DJIA 1950 to JUNE 12, 2020							
10/10/2008	8451.19	−1874.19	−18.2	3/20/2020	19173.98	−4011.64	−17.3
3/20/2020	19173.98	−4011.64	−17.3	2/28/2020	25409.36	−3583.05	−12.4
9/21/2001	8235.81	−1369.70	−14.3	3/13/2020	23185.62	−2679.16	−10.4
10/23/1987	1950.76	−295.98	−13.2	10/10/2008	8451.19	−1874.19	−18.2
2/28/2020	25409.36	−3583.05	−12.4	12/21/2018	22445.37	−1655.14	−6.9
3/13/2020	23185.62	−2679.16	−10.4	6/12/2020	25605.54	−1505.44	−5.6
10/16/1987	2246.74	−235.47	−9.5	3/23/2018	23533.20	−1413.31	−5.7
10/13/1989	2569.26	−216.26	−7.8	9/21/2001	8235.81	−1369.70	−14.3
3/16/2001	9823.41	−821.21	−7.7	2/9/2018	24190.90	−1330.06	−5.2
7/19/2002	8019.26	−665.27	−7.7	12/7/2018	24388.95	−1149.51	−4.5
S&P 500 1930 to JUNE 12, 2020							
7/22/1933	9.71	−2.20	−18.5	3/20/2020	2304.92	−406.10	−15.0
10/10/2008	899.22	−200.01	−18.2	2/28/2020	2954.22	−383.53	−11.5
5/18/1940	9.75	−2.05	−17.4	3/13/2020	2711.02	−261.35	−8.8
10/8/1932	6.77	−1.38	−16.9	10/10/2008	899.22	−200.01	−18.2
3/20/2020	2304.92	−406.10	−15.0	12/21/2018	2416.62	−183.33	−7.1
9/17/1932	7.50	−1.28	−14.6	3/23/2018	2588.26	−163.75	−6.0
10/21/1933	8.57	−1.31	−13.3	4/14/2000	1356.56	−159.79	−10.5
10/3/1931	9.37	−1.36	−12.7	6/12/2020	3041.31	−152.62	−4.8
10/23/1987	248.22	−34.48	−12.2	2/9/2018	2619.55	−142.58	−5.2
12/12/1931	8.20	−1.13	−12.1	12/7/2018	2633.08	−127.08	−4.6
NASDAQ 1971 to JUNE 12, 2020							
4/14/2000	3321.29	−1125.16	−25.3	4/14/2000	3321.29	−1125.16	−25.3
10/23/1987	328.45	−77.88	−19.2	2/28/2020	8567.37	−1009.22	−10.5
9/21/2001	1423.19	−272.19	−16.1	3/20/2020	6879.52	−995.36	−12.6
10/10/2008	1649.51	−297.88	−15.3	3/13/2020	7874.88	−700.74	−8.2
3/20/2020	6879.52	−995.36	−12.6	12/21/2018	6332.99	−577.67	−8.4
11/10/2000	3028.99	−422.59	−12.2	3/23/2018	6992.67	−489.32	−6.5
10/3/2008	1947.39	−235.95	−10.8	7/28/2000	3663.00	−431.45	−10.5
7/28/2000	3663.00	−431.45	−10.5	11/10/2000	3028.99	−422.59	−12.2
2/28/2020	8567.37	−1009.22	−10.5	3/31/2000	4572.83	−390.20	−7.9
10/24/2008	1552.03	−159.26	−9.3	2/9/2018	6874.49	−366.46	−5.1
RUSSELL 1000 1979 to JUNE 12, 2020							
10/10/2008	486.23	−108.31	−18.2	3/20/2020	1260.69	−227.35	−15.3
3/20/2020	1260.69	−227.35	−15.3	2/28/2020	1635.21	−214.22	−11.6
10/23/1987	130.19	−19.25	−12.9	3/13/2020	1488.04	−153.94	−9.4
9/21/2001	507.98	−67.59	−11.7	10/10/2008	486.23	−108.31	−18.2
2/28/2020	1635.21	−214.22	−11.6	12/21/2018	1333.95	−102.36	−7.1
4/14/2000	715.20	−90.39	−11.2	4/14/2000	715.20	−90.39	−11.2
10/3/2008	594.54	−65.15	−9.9	3/23/2018	1436.72	−88.62	−5.8
3/13/2020	1488.04	−153.94	−9.4	6/12/2020	1682.92	−85.02	−4.8
10/16/1987	149.44	−14.42	−8.8	2/9/2018	1449.68	−78.59	−5.1
11/21/2008	427.88	−41.15	−8.8	12/7/2018	1455.80	−69.76	−4.6
RUSSELL 2000 1979 to JUNE 12, 2020							
10/23/1987	121.59	−31.15	−20.4	3/13/2020	1210.13	−239.09	−16.5
3/13/2020	1210.13	−239.09	−16.5	2/28/2020	1476.43	−202.18	−12.0
4/14/2000	453.72	−89.27	−16.4	3/20/2020	1013.89	−196.24	−16.2
3/20/2020	1013.89	−196.24	−16.2	6/12/2020	1387.68	−119.47	−7.9
10/10/2008	522.48	−96.92	−15.7	12/21/2018	1292.09	−118.72	−8.4
9/21/2001	378.89	−61.84	−14.0	10/10/2008	522.48	−96.92	−15.7
10/3/2008	619.40	−85.39	−12.1	1/8/2016	1046.20	−89.69	−7.9
2/28/2020	1476.43	−202.18	−12.0	4/14/2000	453.72	−89.27	−16.4
11/21/2008	406.54	−49.98	−11.0	10/12/2018	1546.68	−85.43	−5.2
10/24/2008	471.12	−55.31	−10.5	10/3/2008	619.40	−85.39	−12.1

10 BEST MONTHS BY PERCENT AND POINT

	BY PERCENT CHANGE				BY POINT CHANGE		
MONTH	CLOSE	PNT CHANGE	% CHANGE	MONTH	CLOSE	PNT CHANGE	% CHANGE
DJIA 1901 to 1949							
Apr-1933	77.66	22.26	40.2	Nov-1928	293.38	41.22	16.3
Aug-1932	73.16	18.90	34.8	Jun-1929	333.79	36.38	12.2
Jul-1932	54.26	11.42	26.7	Aug-1929	380.33	32.63	9.4
Jun-1938	133.88	26.14	24.3	Jun-1938	133.88	26.14	24.3
Apr-1915	71.78	10.95	18.0	Aug-1928	240.41	24.41	11.3
Jun-1931	150.18	21.72	16.9	Apr-1933	77.66	22.26	40.2
Nov-1928	293.38	41.22	16.3	Feb-1931	189.66	22.11	13.2
Nov-1904	52.76	6.59	14.3	Jun-1931	150.18	21.72	16.9
May-1919	105.50	12.62	13.6	Aug-1932	73.16	18.90	34.8
Sep-1939	152.54	18.13	13.5	Jan-1930	267.14	18.66	7.5
DJIA 1950 to May 2020							
Jan-1976	975.28	122.87	14.4	Apr-2020	24345.72	2428.56	11.1
Jan-1975	703.69	87.45	14.2	Jun-2019	26599.96	1784.92	7.2
Jan-1987	2158.04	262.09	13.8	Jan-2019	24999.67	1672.21	7.2
Aug-1982	901.31	92.71	11.5	Jan-2018	26149.39	1430.17	5.8
Apr-2020	24345.72	2428.56	11.1	Oct-2015	17663.54	1379.54	8.5
Oct-1982	991.72	95.47	10.7	Mar-2016	17685.09	1168.59	7.1
Oct-2002	8397.03	805.10	10.6	Jul-2018	25415.19	1143.78	4.7
Apr-1978	837.32	79.96	10.6	Oct-2011	11955.01	1041.63	9.5
Apr-1999	10789.04	1002.88	10.3	May-2020	25383.11	1037.39	4.3
Nov-1962	649.30	59.53	10.1	Nov-2019	28051.41	1005.18	3.7
S&P 500 1930 to May 2020							
Apr-1933	8.32	2.47	42.2	Apr-2020	2912.43	327.84	12.7
Jul-1932	6.10	1.67	37.7	Jan-2019	2704.10	197.25	7.9
Aug-1932	8.39	2.29	37.5	Jun-2019	2941.76	189.70	6.9
Jun-1938	11.56	2.29	24.7	Oct-2015	2079.36	159.33	8.3
Sep-1939	13.02	1.84	16.5	Jan-2018	2823.81	150.20	5.6
Oct-1974	73.90	10.36	16.3	Mar-2000	1498.58	132.16	9.7
May-1933	9.64	1.32	15.9	May-2020	3044.31	131.88	4.5
Apr-1938	9.70	1.20	14.1	Mar-2016	2059.74	127.51	6.6
Jun-1931	14.83	1.81	13.9	Oct-2011	1253.30	121.88	10.8
Jan-1987	274.08	31.91	13.2	Apr-2019	2945.83	111.43	3.9
NASDAQ 1971 to May 2020							
Dec-1999	4069.31	733.15	22.0	Apr-2020	8889.55	1189.45	15.5
Feb-2000	4696.69	756.34	19.2	Feb-2000	4696.69	756.34	19.2
Oct-1974	65.23	9.56	17.2	Dec-1999	4069.31	733.15	22.0
Jan-1975	69.78	9.96	16.7	Jan-2019	7281.74	646.46	9.7
Jun-2000	3966.11	565.20	16.6	May-2020	9489.87	600.32	6.8
Apr-2020	8889.55	1189.45	15.5	Jun-2000	3966.11	565.20	16.6
Apr-2001	2116.24	275.98	15.0	Jun-2019	8006.24	553.09	7.4
Jan-1999	2505.89	313.20	14.3	Jan-2018	7411.48	508.09	7.4
Nov-2001	1930.58	240.38	14.2	Aug-2000	4206.35	439.36	11.7
Oct-2002	1329.75	157.69	13.5	Aug-2018	8109.54	437.75	5.7
RUSSELL 1000 1979 to May 2020							
Apr-2020	1601.82	185.33	13.1	Apr-2020	1601.82	185.33	13.1
Jan-1987	146.48	16.48	12.7	Jan-2019	1498.36	114.10	8.2
Oct-1982	73.34	7.45	11.3	Jun-2019	1629.02	104.60	6.9
Aug-1982	65.14	6.60	11.3	Oct-2015	1153.55	85.09	8.0
Dec-1991	220.61	22.15	11.2	May-2020	1682.75	80.93	5.1
Oct-2011	692.41	68.96	11.1	Jan-2018	1561.66	79.85	5.4
Aug-1984	89.87	8.74	10.8	Mar-2016	1138.84	72.26	6.8
Nov-1980	78.26	7.18	10.1	Oct-2011	692.41	68.96	11.1
Apr-2009	476.84	43.17	10.0	Mar-2000	797.99	64.95	8.9
Sep-2010	629.78	52.10	9.0	Apr-2019	1631.87	61.64	3.9
RUSSELL 2000 1979 to May 2020							
Feb-2000	577.71	81.48	16.4	Apr-2020	1310.66	157.56	13.7
Apr-2009	487.56	64.81	15.3	Jan-2019	1499.42	150.86	11.2
Oct-2011	741.06	96.90	15.0	Nov-2016	1322.34	130.95	11.0
Oct-1982	80.86	10.02	14.1	Jun-2019	1566.57	101.08	6.9
Apr-2020	1310.66	157.56	13.7	Oct-2011	741.06	96.90	15.0
Jan-1985	114.77	13.28	13.1	May-2018	1633.61	91.73	6.0
Sep-2010	676.14	74.08	12.3	Sep-2017	1490.86	85.58	6.1
Aug-1984	106.21	10.96	11.5	May-2020	1394.04	83.38	6.4
Jan-1987	150.48	15.48	11.5	Feb-2000	577.71	81.48	16.4
Jan-2019	1499.42	150.86	11.2	Mar-2016	1114.03	80.13	7.8

10 <u>WORST</u> MONTHS BY PERCENT AND POINT

	BY PERCENT CHANGE				BY POINT CHANGE		
MONTH	CLOSE	PNT CHANGE	% CHANGE	MONTH	CLOSE	PNT CHANGE	% CHANGE
DJIA 1901 to 1949							
Sep-1931	96.61	−42.80	−30.7	Oct-1929	273.51	−69.94	−20.4
Mar-1938	98.95	−30.69	−23.7	Jun-1930	226.34	−48.73	−17.7
Apr-1932	56.11	−17.17	−23.4	Sep-1931	96.61	−42.80	−30.7
May-1940	116.22	−32.21	−21.7	Sep-1929	343.45	−36.88	−9.7
Oct-1929	273.51	−69.94	−20.4	Sep-1930	204.90	−35.52	−14.8
May-1932	44.74	−11.37	−20.3	Nov-1929	238.95	−34.56	−12.6
Jun-1930	226.34	−48.73	−17.7	May-1940	116.22	−32.21	−21.7
Dec-1931	77.90	−15.97	−17.0	Mar-1938	98.95	−30.69	−23.7
Feb-1933	51.39	−9.51	−15.6	Sep-1937	154.57	−22.84	−12.9
May-1931	128.46	−22.73	−15.0	May-1931	128.46	−22.73	−15.0
DJIA 1950 to May 2020							
Oct-1987	1993.53	−602.75	−23.2	Mar-2020	21917.16	−3492.20	−13.7
Aug-1998	7539.07	−1344.22	−15.1	Feb-2020	25409.36	−2846.67	−10.1
Oct-2008	9325.01	−1525.65	−14.1	Dec-2018	23327.46	−2211.00	−8.7
Nov-1973	822.25	−134.33	−14.0	May-2019	24815.04	−1777.87	−6.7
Mar-2020	21917.16	−3492.20	−13.7	Oct-2008	9325.01	−1525.65	−14.1
Sep-2002	7591.93	−1071.57	−12.4	Aug-1998	7539.07	−1344.22	−15.1
Feb-2009	7062.93	−937.93	−11.7	Oct-2018	25115.76	−1342.55	−5.1
Sep-2001	8847.56	−1102.19	−11.1	Jun-2008	11350.01	−1288.31	−10.2
Sep-1974	607.87	−70.71	−10.4	Aug-2015	16528.03	−1161.83	−6.6
Aug-1974	678.58	−78.85	−10.4	Feb-2018	25029.20	−1120.19	−4.3
S&P 500 1930 to May 2020							
Sep-1931	9.71	−4.15	−29.9	Mar-2020	2584.59	−369.63	−12.5
Mar-1938	8.50	−2.84	−25.0	Feb-2020	2954.22	−271.30	−8.4
May-1940	9.27	−2.92	−24.0	Dec-2018	2506.85	−253.31	−9.2
May-1932	4.47	−1.36	−23.3	Oct-2018	2711.74	−202.24	−6.9
Oct-1987	251.79	−70.04	−21.8	Oct-2008	968.75	−197.61	−16.9
Apr-1932	5.83	−1.48	−20.2	May-2019	2752.06	−193.77	−6.6
Feb-1933	5.66	−1.28	−18.4	Aug-1998	957.28	−163.39	−14.6
Oct-2008	968.75	−197.61	−16.9	Aug-2015	1972.18	−131.66	−6.3
Jun-1930	20.46	−4.03	−16.5	Feb-2001	1239.94	−126.07	−9.2
Aug-1998	957.28	−163.39	−14.6	Jun-2008	1280.00	−120.38	−8.6
NASDAQ 1971 to May 2020							
Oct-1987	323.30	−120.99	−27.2	Mar-2020	7700.10	−867.27	−10.1
Nov-2000	2597.93	−771.70	−22.9	Nov-2000	2597.93	−771.70	−22.9
Feb-2001	2151.83	−620.90	−22.4	Oct-2018	7305.90	−740.45	−9.2
Aug-1998	1499.25	−373.14	−19.9	Apr-2000	3860.66	−712.17	−15.6
Oct-2008	1720.95	−370.93	−17.7	Dec-2018	6635.28	−695.26	−9.5
Mar-1980	131.00	−27.03	−17.1	May-2019	7453.15	−642.24	−7.9
Sep-2001	1498.80	−306.63	−17.0	Feb-2001	2151.83	−620.90	−22.4
Oct-1978	111.12	−21.77	−16.4	Feb-2020	8567.37	−583.57	−6.4
Apr-2000	3860.66	−712.17	−15.6	Sep-2000	3672.82	−533.53	−12.7
Nov-1973	93.51	−16.66	−15.1	May-2010	3400.91	−459.75	−11.9
RUSSELL 1000 1979 to May 2020							
Oct-1987	131.89	−36.94	−21.9	Mar-2020	1416.49	−218.72	−13.4
Oct-2008	522.47	−111.61	−17.6	Feb-2020	1635.21	−148.82	−8.3
Aug-1998	496.66	−88.31	−15.1	Dec-2018	1384.26	−141.30	−9.3
Mar-2020	1416.49	−218.72	−13.4	Oct-2018	1498.65	−115.89	−7.2
Mar-1980	55.79	−7.28	−11.5	Oct-2008	522.47	−111.61	−17.6
Sep-2002	433.22	−52.86	−10.9	May-2019	1524.42	−107.45	−6.6
Feb-2009	399.61	−47.71	−10.7	Aug-1998	496.66	−88.31	−15.1
Sep-2008	634.08	−68.09	−9.7	Aug-2015	1100.51	−73.04	−6.2
Aug-1990	166.69	−17.63	−9.6	Nov-2000	692.40	−70.66	−9.3
Feb-2001	654.25	−68.30	−9.5	Feb-2001	654.25	−68.30	−9.5
RUSSELL 2000 1979 to May 2020							
Oct-1987	118.26	−52.55	−30.8	Mar-2020	1153.10	−323.33	−21.9
Mar-2020	1153.10	−323.33	−21.9	Oct-2018	1511.41	−185.16	−10.9
Oct-2008	537.52	−142.06	−20.9	Dec-2018	1348.56	−184.71	−12.0
Aug-1998	337.95	−81.80	−19.5	Oct-2008	537.52	−142.06	−20.9
Mar-1980	48.27	−10.95	−18.5	Feb-2020	1476.43	−137.63	−8.5
Jul-2002	392.42	−70.22	−15.2	May-2019	1465.49	−125.72	−7.9
Aug-1990	139.52	−21.99	−13.6	Jan-2016	1035.38	−100.51	−8.8
Sep-2001	404.87	−63.69	−13.6	Sep-2011	644.16	−82.65	−11.4
Feb-2009	389.02	−54.51	−12.3	Aug-1998	337.95	−81.80	−19.5
Dec-2018	1348.56	−184.71	−12.0	Aug-2019	1494.84	−79.77	−5.1

10 BEST QUARTERS BY PERCENT AND POINT

	BY PERCENT CHANGE				BY POINT CHANGE		
QUARTER	CLOSE	PNT CHANGE	% CHANGE	QUARTER	CLOSE	PNT CHANGE	% CHANGE
DJIA 1901 to 1949							
Jun-1933	98.14	42.74	77.1	Dec-1928	300.00	60.57	25.3
Sep-1932	71.56	28.72	67.0	Jun-1933	98.14	42.74	77.1
Jun-1938	133.88	34.93	35.3	Mar-1930	286.10	37.62	15.1
Sep-1915	90.58	20.52	29.3	Jun-1938	133.88	34.93	35.3
Dec-1928	300.00	60.57	25.3	Sep-1927	197.59	31.36	18.9
Dec-1904	50.99	8.80	20.9	Sep-1928	239.43	28.88	13.7
Jun-1919	106.98	18.13	20.4	Sep-1932	71.56	28.72	67.0
Sep-1927	197.59	31.36	18.9	Jun-1929	333.79	24.94	8.1
Dec-1905	70.47	10.47	17.4	Sep-1939	152.54	21.91	16.8
Jun-1935	118.21	17.40	17.3	Sep-1915	90.58	20.52	29.3
DJIA 1950 to MARCH 2020							
Mar-1975	768.15	151.91	24.7	Mar-2019	25928.68	2601.22	11.2
Mar-1987	2304.69	408.74	21.6	Dec-2017	24719.22	2314.13	10.3
Mar-1986	1818.61	271.94	17.6	Sep-2018	26458.31	2186.90	9.0
Mar-1976	999.45	147.04	17.2	Dec-2019	28538.44	1621.61	6.0
Dec-1998	9181.43	1338.81	17.1	Mar-2013	14578.54	1474.40	11.3
Dec-1982	1046.54	150.29	16.8	Dec-2016	19762.60	1454.45	7.9
Jun-1997	7672.79	1089.31	16.5	Dec-2013	16576.66	1446.99	9.6
Dec-1985	1546.67	218.04	16.4	Dec-1998	9181.43	1338.81	17.1
Sep-2009	9712.28	1265.28	15.0	Dec-2011	12217.56	1304.18	12.0
Jun-1975	878.99	110.84	14.4	Sep-2009	9712.28	1265.28	15.0
S&P 500 1930 to MARCH 2020							
Jun-1933	10.91	5.06	86.5	Mar-2019	2834.40	327.55	13.1
Sep-1932	8.08	3.65	82.4	Dec-2019	3230.78	254.04	8.5
Jun-1938	11.56	3.06	36.0	Dec-1998	1229.23	212.22	20.9
Mar-1975	83.36	14.80	21.6	Sep-2018	2913.98	195.61	7.2
Dec-1998	1229.23	212.22	20.9	Dec-1999	1469.25	186.54	14.5
Jun-1935	10.23	1.76	20.8	Dec-2013	1848.36	166.81	9.9
Mar-1987	291.70	49.53	20.5	Dec-2017	2673.61	154.25	6.1
Sep-1939	13.02	2.16	19.9	Mar-2012	1408.47	150.87	12.0
Mar-1943	11.58	1.81	18.5	Mar-2013	1569.19	143.00	10.0
Mar-1930	25.14	3.69	17.2	Sep-2009	1057.08	137.76	15.0
NASDAQ 1971 to MARCH 2020							
Dec-1999	4069.31	1323.15	48.2	Dec-1999	4069.31	1323.15	48.2
Dec-2001	1950.40	451.60	30.1	Mar-2019	7729.32	1094.04	16.5
Dec-1998	2192.69	498.85	29.5	Dec-2019	8972.60	973.26	12.2
Mar-1991	482.30	108.46	29.0	Sep-2018	8046.35	536.05	7.1
Mar-1975	75.66	15.84	26.5	Mar-2017	5911.74	528.62	9.8
Dec-1982	232.41	44.76	23.9	Mar-2000	4572.83	503.52	12.4
Mar-1987	430.05	80.72	23.1	Dec-1998	2192.69	498.85	29.5
Jun-2003	1622.80	281.63	21.0	Mar-2012	3091.57	486.42	18.7
Jun-1980	157.78	26.78	20.4	Sep-2016	5312.00	469.33	9.7
Jun-2009	1835.04	306.45	20.0	Dec-2001	1950.40	451.60	30.1
RUSSELL 1000 1979 to MARCH 2020							
Dec-1998	642.87	113.76	21.5	Mar-2019	1570.23	185.97	13.4
Mar-1987	155.20	25.20	19.4	Dec-2019	1784.21	140.03	8.5
Dec-1982	77.24	11.35	17.2	Dec-1998	642.87	113.76	21.5
Jun-1997	462.95	64.76	16.3	Sep-2018	1614.54	104.58	6.9
Dec-1985	114.39	15.64	15.8	Dec-1999	767.97	104.14	15.7
Jun-2009	502.27	68.60	15.8	Dec-2013	1030.36	90.86	9.7
Dec-1999	767.97	104.14	15.7	Mar-2012	778.92	85.56	12.3
Sep-2009	579.97	77.70	15.5	Dec-2017	1481.81	84.91	6.1
Jun-2003	518.94	68.59	15.2	Mar-2013	872.11	82.21	10.4
Mar-1991	196.15	24.93	14.6	Sep-2009	579.97	77.70	15.5
RUSSELL 2000 1979 to MARCH 2020							
Mar-1991	171.01	38.85	29.4	Mar-2019	1539.74	191.18	14.2
Dec-1982	88.90	18.06	25.5	Dec-2019	1668.47	145.10	9.5
Mar-1987	166.79	31.79	23.5	Jun-2018	1643.07	113.64	7.4
Jun-2003	448.37	83.83	23.0	Dec-2010	783.65	107.51	15.9
Sep-1980	69.94	12.47	21.7	Dec-2016	1357.13	105.48	8.4
Dec-2001	488.50	83.63	20.7	Dec-2014	1204.70	103.02	9.4
Jun-1983	124.17	20.40	19.7	Mar-2013	951.54	102.19	12.0
Jun-1980	57.47	9.20	19.1	Sep-2016	1251.65	99.73	8.7
Dec-1999	504.75	77.45	18.1	Dec-2011	740.92	96.76	15.0
Sep-2009	604.28	96.00	18.9	Sep-2013	1073.79	96.31	9.9

10 <u>WORST</u> QUARTERS BY PERCENT AND POINT

	BY PERCENT CHANGE				BY POINT CHANGE		
QUARTER	CLOSE	PNT CHANGE	% CHANGE	QUARTER	CLOSE	PNT CHANGE	% CHANGE
DJIA 1901 to 1949							
Jun-1932	42.84	−30.44	−41.5	Dec-1929	248.48	−94.97	−27.7
Sep-1931	96.61	−53.57	−35.7	Jun-1930	226.34	−59.76	−20.9
Dec-1929	248.48	−94.97	−27.7	Sep-1931	96.61	−53.57	−35.7
Sep-1903	33.55	−9.73	−22.5	Dec-1930	164.58	−40.32	−19.7
Dec-1937	120.85	−33.72	−21.8	Dec-1937	120.85	−33.72	−21.8
Jun-1930	226.34	−59.76	−20.9	Sep-1946	172.42	−33.20	−16.1
Dec-1930	164.58	−40.32	−19.7	Jun-1932	42.84	−30.44	−41.5
Dec-1931	77.90	−18.71	−19.4	Jun-1940	121.87	−26.08	−17.6
Mar-1938	98.95	−21.90	−18.1	Mar-1939	131.84	−22.92	−14.8
Jun-1940	121.87	−26.08	−17.6	Jun-1931	150.18	−22.18	−12.9
DJIA 1950 to MARCH 2020							
Dec-1987	1938.83	−657.45	−25.3	Mar-2020	21917.16	−6621.28	−23.2
Sep-1974	607.87	−194.54	−24.2	Dec-2018	23327.46	−3130.85	−11.8
Mar-2020	21917.16	−6621.28	−23.2	Dec-2008	8776.39	−2074.27	−19.1
Jun-1962	561.28	−145.67	−20.6	Sep-2001	8847.56	−1654.84	−15.8
Dec-2008	8776.39	−2074.27	−19.1	Sep-2002	7591.93	−1651.33	−17.9
Sep-2002	7591.93	−1651.33	−17.9	Sep-2011	10913.38	−1500.96	−12.1
Sep-2001	8847.56	−1654.84	−15.8	Sep-2015	16284.00	−1335.51	−7.6
Sep-1990	2452.48	−428.21	−14.9	Mar-2009	7608.92	−1167.47	−13.3
Mar-2009	7608.92	−1167.47	−13.3	Jun-2002	9243.26	−1160.68	−11.2
Sep-1981	849.98	−126.90	−13.0	Sep-1998	7842.62	−1109.40	−12.4
S&P 500 1930 to MARCH 2020							
Jun-1932	4.43	−2.88	−39.4	Mar-2020	2584.59	−646.19	−20.0
Sep-1931	9.71	−5.12	−34.5	Dec-2018	2506.85	−407.13	−14.0
Sep-1974	63.54	−22.46	−26.1	Dec-2008	903.25	−263.11	−22.6
Dec-1937	10.55	−3.21	−23.3	Sep-2011	1131.42	−189.22	−14.3
Dec-1987	247.08	−74.75	−23.2	Sep-2001	1040.94	−183.48	−15.0
Dec-2008	903.25	−263.11	−22.6	Sep-2002	815.28	−174.54	−17.6
Jun-1962	54.75	−14.80	−21.3	Mar-2001	1160.33	−159.95	−12.1
Mar-2020	2584.59	−646.19	−20.0	Jun-2002	989.82	−157.57	−13.7
Mar-1938	8.50	−2.05	−19.4	Mar-2008	1322.70	−145.66	−9.9
Jun-1970	72.72	−16.91	−18.9	Sep-2015	1920.03	−143.08	−6.9
NASDAQ 1971 to MARCH 2020							
Dec-2000	2470.52	−1202.30	−32.7	Dec-2018	6635.28	−1411.07	−17.5
Sep-2001	1498.80	−661.74	−30.6	Mar-2020	7700.10	−1272.50	−14.2
Sep-1974	55.67	−20.29	−26.7	Dec-2000	2470.52	−1202.30	−32.7
Dec-1987	330.47	−113.82	−25.6	Sep-2001	1498.80	−661.74	−30.6
Mar-2001	1840.26	−630.26	−25.5	Mar-2001	1840.26	−630.26	−25.5
Sep-1990	344.51	−117.78	−25.5	Jun-2000	3966.11	−606.72	−13.3
Dec-2008	1577.03	−514.85	−24.6	Dec-2008	1577.03	−514.85	−24.6
Jun-2002	1463.21	−382.14	−20.7	Jun-2002	1463.21	−382.14	−20.7
Sep-2002	1172.06	−291.15	−19.9	Mar-2008	2279.10	−373.18	−14.1
Jun-1974	75.96	−16.31	−17.7	Sep-2015	4620.16	−366.71	−7.4
RUSSELL 1000 1979 to MARCH 2020							
Dec-2008	487.77	−146.31	−23.1	Mar-2020	1416.49	−367.72	−20.6
Dec-1987	130.02	−38.81	−23.0	Dec-2018	1384.26	−230.28	−14.3
Mar-2020	1416.49	−367.72	−20.6	Dec-2008	487.77	−146.31	−23.1
Sep-2002	433.22	−90.50	−17.3	Sep-2011	623.45	−111.03	−15.1
Sep-2001	546.46	−100.18	−15.5	Sep-2001	546.46	−100.18	−15.5
Sep-1990	157.83	−28.46	−15.3	Sep-2002	433.22	−90.50	−17.3
Sep-2011	623.45	−111.03	−15.1	Mar-2001	610.36	−89.73	−12.8
Dec-2018	1384.26	−230.28	−14.3	Sep-2015	1068.46	−84.18	−7.3
Jun-2002	523.72	−83.63	−13.8	Jun-2002	523.72	−83.63	−13.8
Mar-2001	610.36	−89.73	−12.8	Mar-2008	720.32	−79.50	−9.9
RUSSELL 2000 1979 to MARCH 2020							
Mar-2020	1153.10	−515.37	−30.9	Mar-2020	1153.10	−515.37	−30.9
Dec-1987	120.42	−50.39	−29.5	Dec-2018	1348.56	−348.01	−20.5
Dec-2008	499.45	−180.13	−26.5	Sep-2011	644.16	−183.27	−22.1
Sep-1990	126.70	−42.34	−25.0	Dec-2008	499.45	−180.13	−26.5
Sep-2011	644.16	−183.27	−22.1	Sep-2015	1100.69	−153.26	−12.2
Sep-2002	362.27	−100.37	−21.7	Sep-2001	404.87	−107.77	−21.0
Sep-2001	404.87	−107.77	−21.0	Sep-2002	362.27	−100.37	−21.7
Dec-2018	1348.56	−348.01	−20.5	Sep-1998	363.59	−93.80	−20.5
Sep-1998	363.59	−93.80	−20.5	Sep-2014	1101.68	−91.28	−7.7
Sep-1981	67.55	−15.01	−18.2	Mar-2008	687.97	−78.06	−10.2

10 <u>BEST</u> YEARS BY PERCENT AND POINT

	BY PERCENT CHANGE				BY POINT CHANGE		
YEAR	CLOSE	PNT CHANGE	% CHANGE	YEAR	CLOSE	PNT CHANGE	% CHANGE
DJIA 1901 to 1949							
1915	99.15	44.57	81.7	1928	300.00	97.60	48.2
1933	99.90	39.97	66.7	1927	202.40	45.20	28.8
1928	300.00	97.60	48.2	1915	99.15	44.57	81.7
1908	63.11	20.07	46.6	1945	192.91	40.59	26.6
1904	50.99	15.01	41.7	1935	144.13	40.09	38.5
1935	144.13	40.09	38.5	1933	99.90	39.97	66.7
1905	70.47	19.48	38.2	1925	156.66	36.15	30.0
1919	107.23	25.03	30.5	1936	179.90	35.77	24.8
1925	156.66	36.15	30.0	1938	154.76	33.91	28.1
1927	202.40	45.20	28.8	1919	107.23	25.03	30.5
DJIA 1950 to 2019							
1954	404.39	123.49	44.0	2019	28538.44	5210.98	22.3
1975	852.41	236.17	38.3	2017	24719.22	4956.62	25.1
1958	583.65	147.96	34.0	2013	16576.66	3472.52	26.5
1995	5117.12	1282.68	33.5	2016	19762.60	2337.57	13.4
1985	1546.67	335.10	27.7	1999	11497.12	2315.69	25.2
1989	2753.20	584.63	27.0	2003	10453.92	2112.29	25.3
2013	16576.66	3472.52	26.5	2006	12463.15	1745.65	16.3
1996	6448.27	1331.15	26.0	2009	10428.05	1651.66	18.8
2003	10453.92	2112.29	25.3	1997	7908.25	1459.98	22.6
1999	11497.12	2315.69	25.2	1996	6448.27	1331.15	26.0
S&P 500 1930 to 2019							
1933	10.10	3.21	46.6	2019	3230.78	723.93	28.9
1954	35.98	11.17	45.0	2017	2673.61	434.78	19.4
1935	13.43	3.93	41.4	2013	1848.36	422.17	29.6
1958	55.21	15.22	38.1	1998	1229.23	258.80	26.7
1995	615.93	156.66	34.1	1999	1469.25	240.02	19.5
1975	90.19	21.63	31.5	2003	1111.92	232.10	26.4
1997	970.43	229.69	31.0	1997	970.43	229.69	31.0
1945	17.36	4.08	30.7	2009	1115.10	211.85	23.5
2013	1848.36	422.17	29.6	2014	2058.90	210.54	11.4
2019	3230.78	723.93	28.9	2016	2238.83	194.89	9.5
NASDAQ 1971 to 2019							
1999	4069.31	1876.62	85.6	2019	8972.60	2337.32	35.2
1991	586.34	212.50	56.8	1999	4069.31	1876.62	85.6
2003	2003.37	667.86	50.0	2017	6903.39	1520.27	28.2
2009	2269.15	692.12	43.9	2013	4176.59	1157.08	38.3
1995	1052.13	300.17	39.9	2009	2269.15	692.12	43.9
1998	2192.69	622.34	39.6	2003	2003.37	667.86	50.0
2013	4176.59	1157.08	38.3	1998	2192.69	622.34	39.6
2019	8972.60	2337.32	35.2	2014	4736.05	559.46	13.4
1980	202.34	51.20	33.9	2012	3019.51	414.36	15.9
1985	324.93	77.58	31.4	2010	2652.87	383.72	16.9
RUSSELL 1000 1979 to 2019							
1995	328.89	84.24	34.4	2019	1784.21	399.95	28.9
1997	513.79	120.04	30.5	2013	1030.36	240.46	30.4
2013	1030.36	240.46	30.4	2017	1481.81	240.15	19.3
2019	1784.21	399.95	28.9	1998	642.87	129.08	25.1
1991	220.61	49.39	28.9	2003	594.56	128.38	27.5
2003	594.56	128.38	27.5	1999	767.97	125.10	19.5
1985	114.39	24.08	26.7	2009	612.01	124.24	25.5
1989	185.11	38.12	25.9	1997	513.79	120.04	30.5
1980	75.20	15.33	25.6	2014	1144.37	114.01	11.1
2009	612.01	124.24	25.5	2016	1241.66	109.78	9.7
RUSSELL 2000 1979 to 2019							
2003	556.91	173.82	45.4	2019	1668.47	319.91	23.7
1991	189.94	57.78	43.7	2013	1163.64	314.29	37.0
1979	55.91	15.39	38.0	2016	1357.13	221.24	19.5
2013	1163.64	314.29	37.0	2017	1535.51	178.38	13.1
1980	74.80	18.89	33.8	2003	556.91	173.82	45.4
1985	129.87	28.38	28.0	2010	783.65	158.26	25.3
1983	112.27	23.37	26.3	2009	625.39	125.94	25.2
1995	315.97	65.61	26.2	2006	787.66	114.44	17.0
2010	783.65	158.26	25.3	2012	849.35	108.43	14.6
2009	625.39	125.94	25.2	2004	651.57	94.66	17.0

10 <u>WORST</u> YEARS BY PERCENT AND POINT

BY PERCENT CHANGE				BY POINT CHANGE			
YEAR	CLOSE	PNT CHANGE	% CHANGE	YEAR	CLOSE	PNT CHANGE	% CHANGE
DJIA 1901 to 1949							
1931	77.90	−86.68	−52.7	1931	77.90	−86.68	−52.7
1907	43.04	−26.08	−37.7	1930	164.58	−83.90	−33.8
1930	164.58	−83.90	−33.8	1937	120.85	−59.05	−32.8
1920	71.95	−35.28	−32.9	1929	248.48	−51.52	−17.2
1937	120.85	−59.05	−32.8	1920	71.95	−35.28	−32.9
1903	35.98	−11.12	−23.6	1907	43.04	−26.08	−37.7
1932	59.93	−17.97	−23.1	1917	74.38	−20.62	−21.7
1917	74.38	−20.62	−21.7	1941	110.96	−20.17	−15.4
1910	59.60	−12.96	−17.9	1940	131.13	−19.11	−12.7
1929	248.48	−51.52	−17.2	1932	59.93	−17.97	−23.1
DJIA 1950 to 2019							
2008	8776.39	−4488.43	−33.8	2008	8776.39	−4488.43	−33.8
1974	616.24	−234.62	−27.6	2002	8341.63	−1679.87	−16.8
1966	785.69	−183.57	−18.9	2018	23327.46	−1391.76	−5.6
1977	831.17	−173.48	−17.3	2001	10021.50	−765.35	−7.1
2002	8341.63	−1679.87	−16.8	2000	10786.85	−710.27.	−6.2
1973	850.86	−169.16	−16.6	2015	17425.03	−398.04	−2.2
1969	800.36	−143.39	−15.2	1974	616.24	−234.62	−27.6
1957	435.69	−63.78	−12.8	1966	785.69	−183.57	−18.9
1962	652.10	−79.04	−10.8	1977	831.17	−173.48	−17.3
1960	615.89	−63.47	−9.3	1973	850.86	−169.16	−16.6
S&P 500 1930 to 2019							
1931	8.12	−7.22	−47.1	2008	903.25	−565.11	−38.5
1937	10.55	−6.63	−38.6	2002	879.82	−268.26	−23.4
2008	903.25	−565.11	−38.5	2001	1148.08	−172.20	−13.0
1974	68.56	−28.99	−29.7	2018	2506.85	−166.76	−6.2
1930	15.34	−6.11	−28.5	2000	1320.28	−148.97	−10.1
2002	879.82	−268.26	−23.4	1974	68.56	−28.99	−29.7
1941	8.69	−1.89	−17.9	1990	330.22	−23.18	−6.6
1973	97.55	−20.50	−17.4	1973	97.55	−20.50	−17.4
1940	10.58	−1.91	−15.3	2015	2043.94	−14.96	−0.7
1932	6.89	−1.23	−15.1	1981	122.55	−13.21	−9.7
NASDAQ 1971 to 2019							
2008	1577.03	−1075.25	−40.5	2000	2470.52	−1598.79	−39.3
2000	2470.52	−1598.79	−39.3	2008	1577.03	−1075.25	−40.5
1974	59.82	−32.37	−35.1	2002	1335.51	−614.89	−31.5
2002	1335.51	−614.89	−31.5	2001	1950.40	−520.12	−21.1
1973	92.19	−41.54	−31.1	2018	6635.28	−268.11	−3.9
2001	1950.40	−520.12	−21.1	1990	373.84	−80.98	−17.8
1990	373.84	−80.98	−17.8	2011	2605.15	−47.72	−1.8
1984	247.35	−31.25	−11.2	1973	92.19	−41.54	−31.1
1987	330.47	−18.86	−5.4	1974	59.82	−32.37	−35.1
2018	6635.28	−268.11	−3.9	1984	247.35	−31.25	−11.2
RUSSELL 1000 1979 to 2019							
2008	487.77	−312.05	−39.0	2008	487.77	−312.05	−39.0
2002	466.18	−138.76	−22.9	2002	466.18	−138.76	−22.9
2001	604.94	−95.15	−13.6	2018	1384.26	−97.55	−6.6
1981	67.93	−7.27	−9.7	2001	604.94	−95.15	−13.6
2000	700.09	−67.88	−8.8	2000	700.09	−67.88	−8.8
1990	171.22	−13.89	−7.5	1990	171.22	−13.89	−7.5
2018	1384.26	−97.55	−6.6	2015	1131.88	−12.49	−1.1
1994	244.65	−6.06	−2.4	1981	67.93	−7.27	−9.7
2015	1131.88	−12.49	−1.1	1994	244.65	−6.06	−2.4
2011	693.36	−3.54	−0.5	2011	693.36	−3.54	−0.5
RUSSELL 2000 1979 to 2019							
2008	499.45	−266.58	−34.8	2008	499.45	−266.58	−34.8
2002	383.09	−105.41	−21.6	2018	1348.56	−186.95	−12.2
1990	132.16	−36.14	−21.5	2002	383.09	−105.41	−21.6
2018	1348.56	−186.95	−12.2	2015	1135.89	−68.81	−5.7
1987	120.42	−14.58	−10.8	2011	740.92	−42.73	−5.5
1984	101.49	−10.78	−9.6	1990	132.16	−36.14	−21.5
2015	1135.89	−68.81	−5.7	2007	766.03	−21.63	−2.7
2011	740.92	−42.73	−5.5	2000	483.53	−21.22	−4.2
2000	483.53	−21.22	−4.2	1998	421.96	−15.06	−3.4
1998	421.96	−15.06	−3.4	1987	120.42	−14.58	−10.8

STRATEGY PLANNING AND RECORD SECTION

CONTENTS

These forms are available at our website, www.stocktradersalmanac.com.

PORTFOLIO AT START OF 2021

DATE ACQUIRED	NO. OF SHARES	SECURITY	PRICE	TOTAL COST	PAPER PROFITS	PAPER LOSSES

ADDITIONAL PURCHASES

DATE ACQUIRED	NO. OF SHARES	SECURITY	PRICE	TOTAL COST	REASON FOR PURCHASE PRIME OBJECTIVE, ETC.

ADDITIONAL PURCHASES

DATE ACQUIRED	NO. OF SHARES	SECURITY	PRICE	TOTAL COST	REASON FOR PURCHASE PRIME OBJECTIVE, ETC.

SHORT-TERM TRANSACTIONS

Pages 178–181 can accompany next year's income tax return (Schedule D). Enter transactions as completed to avoid last-minute pressures.

NO. OF SHARES	SECURITY	DATE ACQUIRED	DATE SOLD	SALE PRICE	COST	LOSS	GAIN

TOTALS:

Carry over to next page

SHORT-TERM TRANSACTIONS (continued)

NO. OF SHARES	SECURITY	DATE ACQUIRED	DATE SOLD	SALE PRICE	COST	LOSS	GAIN

TOTALS:

LONG-TERM TRANSACTIONS

Pages 178–181 can accompany next year's income tax return (Schedule D). Enter transactions as completed to avoid last-minute pressures.

NO. OF SHARES	SECURITY	DATE ACQUIRED	DATE SOLD	SALE PRICE	COST	LOSS	GAIN

TOTALS: Carry over to next page

180

NO. OF SHARES	SECURITY	DATE ACQUIRED	DATE SOLD	SALE PRICE	COST	LOSS	GAIN

TOTALS:

INTEREST/DIVIDENDS RECEIVED DURING 2021

SHARES	STOCK/BOND	FIRST QUARTER		SECOND QUARTER		THIRD QUARTER		FOURTH QUARTER	
		$		$		$		$	

BROKERAGE ACCOUNT DATA 2021

	MARGIN INTEREST	TRANSFER TAXES	CAPITAL ADDED	CAPITAL WITHDRAWN
JAN				
FEB				
MAR				
APR				
MAY				
JUN				
JUL				
AUG				
SEP				
OCT				
NOV				
DEC				

WEEKLY PORTFOLIO PRICE RECORD 2021 (FIRST HALF)

Place purchase price above stock name and weekly closes below.

STOCKS / Week Ending	1	2	3	4	5	6	7	8	9	10
JANUARY 1										
8										
15										
22										
29										
FEBRUARY 5										
12										
19										
26										
MARCH 5										
12										
19										
26										
APRIL 2										
9										
16										
23										
30										
MAY 7										
14										
21										
28										
JUNE 4										
11										
18										
25										

WEEKLY PORTFOLIO PRICE RECORD 2021 (SECOND HALF)

Place purchase price above stock name and weekly closes below.

STOCKS Week Ending	1	2	3	4	5	6	7	8	9	10
JULY 2										
9										
16										
23										
30										
AUGUST 6										
13										
20										
27										
SEPTEMBER 3										
10										
17										
24										
OCTOBER 1										
8										
15										
22										
29										
NOVEMBER 5										
12										
19										
26										
DECEMBER 3										
10										
17										
24										
31										

184

WEEKLY INDICATOR DATA 2021 (FIRST HALF)

	Week Ending	Dow Jones Industrial Average	Net Change for Week	Net Change on Friday	Net Change Next Monday	S&P or NASDAQ	NYSE Advances	NYSE Declines	New Highs	New Lows	CBOE Put/Call Ratio	90-Day Treas. Rate	Moody's AAA Rate
JANUARY	1												
	8												
	15												
	22												
	29												
FEBRUARY	5												
	12												
	19												
	26												
MARCH	5												
	12												
	19												
	26												
APRIL	2												
	9												
	16												
	23												
	30												
MAY	7												
	14												
	21												
	28												
JUNE	4												
	11												
	18												
	25												

WEEKLY INDICATOR DATA 2021 (SECOND HALF)

	Week Ending	Dow Jones Industrial Average	Net Change for Week	Net Change on Friday	Net Change Next Monday	S&P or NASDAQ	NYSE Advances	NYSE Declines	New Highs	New Lows	CBOE Put/Call Ratio	90-Day Treas. Rate	Moody's AAA Rate
JULY	2												
	9												
	16												
	23												
	30												
AUGUST	6												
	13												
	20												
	27												
SEPTEMBER	3												
	10												
	17												
	24												
OCTOBER	1												
	8												
	15												
	22												
	29												
NOVEMBER	5												
	12												
	19												
	26												
DECEMBER	3												
	10												
	17												
	24												
	31												

MONTHLY INDICATOR DATA 2021

	DJIA% Last 3 + 1st 2 Days	DJIA% 9th to 11th Trading Days	DJIA% Change Rest of Month	DJIA% Change Whole Month	% Change Your Stocks	Gross Domestic Product	Prime Rate	Trade Deficit $ Billion	CPI % Change	% Unemployment Rate
JAN										
FEB										
MAR										
APR										
MAY										
JUN										
JUL										
AUG										
SEP										
OCT										
NOV										
DEC										

INSTRUCTIONS:

Weekly Indicator Data (pages 185–186). Keeping data on several indicators may give you a better feel of the market. In addition to the closing DJIA and its net change for the week, post the net change for Friday's Dow and also the following Monday's. A series of "down Fridays" followed by "down Mondays" often precedes a downswing (see page 76). Tracking either the S&P or NASDAQ composite, and advances and declines, will help prevent the Dow from misleading you. New highs and lows and put/call ratios (www.cboe.com) are also useful indicators. All these weekly figures appear in weekend papers or *Barron's* (https://www.barrons.com/market-data/market-lab). Data for the 90-day Treasury Rate and Moody's AAA Bond Rate are quite important for tracking short- and long-term interest rates. These figures are available from:

> Weekly U.S. Financial Data
> Federal Reserve Bank of St. Louis
> P.O. Box 442
> St. Louis, MO 63166
> **https://fred.stlouisfed.org/**

Monthly Indicator Data. The purpose of the first three columns is to enable you to track the market's bullish bias near the end, beginning and middle of the month, which has been shifting lately (see pages 84, 145 and 146). Market direction, performance of your stocks, gross domestic product, prime rate, trade deficit, Consumer Price Index, and unemployment rate are worthwhile indicators to follow. Or, readers may wish to gauge other data.

187

PORTFOLIO AT END OF 2021

DATE ACQUIRED	NO. OF SHARES	SECURITY	PRICE	TOTAL COST	PAPER PROFITS	PAPER LOSSES

IF YOU DON'T PROFIT FROM YOUR
INVESTMENT MISTAKES, SOMEONE ELSE WILL

No matter how much we may deny it, almost every successful person on Wall Street pays a great deal of attention to trading suggestions—especially when they come from "the right sources."

One of the hardest things to learn is to distinguish between good tips and bad ones. Usually, the best tips have a logical reason behind them, which accompanies the tip. Poor tips usually have no reason to support them.

The important thing to remember is that the market discounts. It does not review, it does not reflect. The Street's real interest in "tips," inside information, buying and selling suggestions and everything else of this kind emanates from a desire to find out just what the market has on hand to discount. The process of finding out involves separating the wheat from the chaff—and there is plenty of chaff.

HOW TO MAKE USE OF STOCK "TIPS"

- The source should be **reliable**. (By listing all "tips" and suggestions on a Performance Record of Recommendations, such as the form below, and then periodically evaluating the outcomes, you will soon know the "batting average" of your sources.)

- The story should make sense. Would the merger violate antitrust laws? Are there too many computers on the market already? How many years will it take to become profitable?

- The stock should not have had a recent sharp run-up. Otherwise, the story may already be discounted, and confirmation or denial in the press would most likely be accompanied by a sell-off in the stock.

PERFORMANCE RECORD OF RECOMMENDATIONS

STOCK RECOMMENDED	BY WHOM	DATE	PRICE	REASON FOR RECOMMENDATION	SUBSEQUENT ACTION OF STOCK

INDIVIDUAL RETIREMENT ACCOUNT (IRA): MOST AWESOME MASS INVESTMENT INCENTIVE EVER DEVISED

MAX IRA INVESTMENTS OF $6,000* A YEAR COMPOUNDED AT VARIOUS INTEREST RATES OF RETURN FOR DIFFERENT PERIODS

Annual Rate	5 Yrs	10 Yrs	15 Yrs	20 Yrs	25 Yrs	30 Yrs	35 Yrs	40 Yrs	45 Yrs	50 Yrs
1%	$30,912	$63,401	$97,547	$133,435	$171,154	$210,796	$252,461	$296,251	$342,275	$390,647
2%	31,849	67,012	105,836	148,700	196,025	248,277	305,966	369,660	439,983	517,626
3%	32,810	70,847	114,941	166,059	225,318	294,016	373,656	465,980	573,009	697,085
4%	33,798	74,918	124,947	185,815	259,870	349,970	459,590	592,959	755,223	952,643
5%	34,811	79,241	135,945	208,316	300,681	418,565	569,018	761,039	1,006,111	1,318,892
6%	35,852	83,830	148,035	233,956	348,938	502,810	708,725	984,286	1,353,049	1,846,536
7%	36,920	88,702	161,328	263,191	406,059	606,438	887,481	1,281,657	1,834,511	2,609,916
8%	38,016	93,873	175,946	296,538	473,726	734,075	1,116,613	1,678,686	2,504,556	3,718,031
9%	39,140	99,362	192,020	334,587	553,944	891,451	1,410,748	2,209,751	3,439,116	5,330,646
10%	40,294	105,187	209,698	378,015	649,091	1,085,661	1,788,761	2,921,111	4,744,772	7,681,796
11%	41,477	111,369	229,140	427,591	761,993	1,325,479	2,274,986	3,874,962	6,571,013	11,114,016
12%	42,691	117,927	250,520	484,192	896,004	1,621,756	2,900,779	5,154,854	9,127,306	16,128,123
13%	43,936	124,886	274,030	548,820	1,055,101	1,987,891	3,706,496	6,872,915	12,706,836	23,455,458
14%	45,213	132,267	299,882	622,611	1,243,996	2,440,422	4,744,037	9,179,452	17,719,463	34,162,526
15%	46,522	140,096	328,305	706,861	1,468,272	2,999,742	6,080,074	12,275,723	24,737,386	49,802,242
16%	47,865	148,397	359,550	803,043	1,734,530	3,690,970	7,800,162	16,430,870	34,558,306	72,632,115
17%	49,241	157,200	393,893	912,831	2,050,576	4,545,023	10,013,967	22,004,343	48,292,620	105,928,302
18%	50,652	166,531	431,634	1,038,126	2,425,633	5,599,912	12,861,893	29,475,548	67,483,566	154,436,703
19%	52,098	176,421	473,101	1,181,085	2,870,583	6,902,325	16,523,486	39,482,979	94,272,449	225,019,501
20%	53,580	186,903	518,653	1,344,154	3,398,264	8,509,547	21,228,056	52,875,776	131,625,432	327,579,773

* At press time—2021 Contribution Limit will be indexed to inflation.

G. M. LOEB'S "BATTLE PLAN" FOR INVESTMENT SURVIVAL

LIFE IS CHANGE: Nothing can ever be the same a minute from now as it was a minute ago. Everything you own is changing in price and value. You can find that last price of an active security on the stock ticker, but you cannot find the next price anywhere. The value of your money is changing. Even the value of your home is changing, though no one walks in front of it with a sandwich board consistently posting the changes.

RECOGNIZE CHANGE: Your basic objective should be to profit from change. The art of investing is being able to recognize change and to adjust investment goals accordingly.

WRITE THINGS DOWN: You will score more investment success and avoid more investment failures if you write things down. Very few investors have the drive and inclination to do this.

KEEP A CHECKLIST: If you aim to improve your investment results, get into the habit of keeping a checklist on every issue you consider buying. Before making a commitment, it will pay you to write down the answers to at least some of the basic questions—How much am I investing in this company? How much do I think I can make? How much do I have to risk? How long do I expect to take to reach my goal?

HAVE A SINGLE RULING REASON: Above all, writing things down is the best way to find "the ruling reason." When all is said and done, there is invariably a single reason that stands out above all others, why a particular security transaction can be expected to show a profit. All too often, many relatively unimportant statistics are allowed to obscure this single important point.

Any one of a dozen factors may be the point of a particular purchase or sale. It could be a technical reason—an increase in earnings or dividend not yet discounted in the market price—a change of management—a promising new product—an expected improvement in the market's valuation of earnings—or many others. But, in any given case, one of these factors will almost certainly be more important than all the rest put together.

CLOSING OUT A COMMITMENT: If you have a loss, the solution is automatic, provided you decide what to do at the time you buy. Otherwise, the question divides itself into two parts. Are we in a bull or bear market? Few of us really know until it is too late. For the sake of the record, if you think it is a bear market, just put that consideration first and sell as much as your conviction suggests and your nature allows.

If you think it is a bull market, or at least a market where some stocks move up, some mark time and only a few decline, do not sell unless:

- ✓ You see a bear market ahead.
- ✓ You see trouble for a particular company in which you own shares.
- ✓ Time and circumstances have turned up a new and seemingly far better buy than the issue you like least in your list.
- ✓ Your shares stop going up and start going down.

A subsidiary question is, which stock to sell first? Two further observations may help:

- ✓ Do not sell solely because you think a stock is "overvalued."
- ✓ If you want to sell some of your stocks and not all, in most cases it is better to go against your emotional inclinations and sell first the issues with losses, small profits or none at all, the weakest, the most disappointing and so on.

Mr. Loeb is the author of *The Battle for Investment Survival*, John Wiley & Sons.

G. M. LOEB'S INVESTMENT SURVIVAL CHECKLIST

OBJECTIVES AND RISKS

Security		Price	Shares	Date

"Ruling reason" for commitment

Amount of commitment

$_____

% of my investment capital

_____%

Price objective	Est. time to achieve it	I will risk _____ points	Which would be $_____

TECHNICAL POSITION

Price action of stock:

❏ Hitting new highs   ❏ In a trading range

❏ Pausing in an uptrend   ❏ Moving up from low ground

❏ Acting stronger than market   ❏ _____

Dow Jones Industrial Average

Trend of market

SELECTED YARDSTICKS

	Price Range		Earnings Per Share Actual or Projected	Price/Earnings Ratio Actual or Projected
	High	Low		
Current year				
Previous year				
Merger possibilities				Years for earnings to double in past
Comment on future				Years for market price to double in past

PERIODIC RECHECKS

Date	Stock Price	DJIA	Comment	Action taken, if any

COMPLETED TRANSACTIONS

Date closed	Period of time held	Profit or loss

Reason for profit or loss